At the Water's Edge

with Martin James

First
Nature

First published in the United Kingdom in 2010 by
First Nature Bwlchgwyn, Rhydlewis, Llandysul SA44 5RE, Wales, UK
email: enquiries@first-nature.com
website: www.first-nature.com

At The Water's Edge ISBN13: 978-0-9560544-5-6

By the same author, published by Crowood Press
Up Against It, 1994 ISBN 1-85223-792-9

Jacket Design by Andy Bleasdale and Bruce Carter

Jacket Photograph, River Teifi by Pat O'Reilly MBE
End Paper Photograph, The Avon at Britford, by Martin James
End Paper Photograph, Sunset by Ian Chapman, Anglers' Mail

Where possible, all photographs not supplied directly by Martin James have been credited to the photographer.

Any photographs inadvertantly not credited, please accept our apologies and contact us so we can correct this on a future reprint.

Design and Layout by Raydon Typesetters, raydon@btconnect.com
Typeset in Bembo

Print Production by Andy Bleasdale, bleasers@hotmail.com

FIRST
NATURE
www.first-nature.com

I count myself fortunate to have had Martin James as a friend for more years than either of us would admit to. It goes without saying that Martin is a very good angler – but then, there are lots of very good anglers around these days – what sets Martin apart from all the others is his amazing enthusiasm for, and dedication to the sport, also the gift he has of communicating his passion for fishing and inspiring all who meet him.

From the earliest days, when I first got to know Martin, he was actively 'spreading the word'. First in local newspapers, then the national press, radio, television and video – all the time promoting and, where necessary, defending field sports in general and angling in particular. He would address Public Meetings, lead protest marches and lobby MPs. Fearless with a microphone, whether the audience was a thousand or a dozen, he would speak with a passion which endeared him to all but the Anti-Angling-Brigade!

For as long as I have known him, Martin has had two heroes, Winston Churchill and Richard Walker. The former for his utter determination and the latter for his generosity of spirit and Martin does all he can to live up to these high standards.

Shortly after moving from Kent to Lancashire disaster struck and Martin was laid low by multiple sclerosis. In those dark days he and I would go fishing and it would take him half-an-hour of painful struggling with a walking- frame to cross a hundred yards of field to the river-bank. Any offers of help would be met with 'No thanks mate, I've got to do it myself' – nothing was going to stop him going fishing!

This determination carried him through to achieve the most amazing feats, travelling world-wide and fishing for exotic species in the most trying conditions, culminating in fishing the mighty River Amazon!

And he continues today in this seemingly unstoppable active life. His long-running Angling programme for Radio Five and Radio Lancashire requires him to travel extensively, he is on the pro-staff and acts as consultant to leading tackle-makers at home and in America, he goes on lecture tours and even flies regularly to the Arab Emirates to teach saltwater fly-fishing. If I had the talent, I would write a book about Martin James entitled 'The Most Extraordinary Person I Have Ever Met' but instead, I commend to you, within these pages, the man himself who, though having lived to see angling develop into almost to a science, still feels the magic and the mystery that was 'fishing' when we first met.

Rod Builder Mike Harris, working on another bamboo rod

I am indebted to Andy Bleasdale for controlling the project, managing the print and ensuring that everything ran on time. Bruce Carter of Raydon Typesetters for his valuable advice and design work on this tome. My publishers Pat O'Reilly MBE, Sue Parker and the staff at First Nature. I must thank the following for their unstinting support, help and encouragement – also their words of wisdom:

David Jones, one of my fishing companions for his friendship and advice when needed and for writing the introduction to this book.

Mike Harris, that fine rod builder from Kent, who is also a great roach-fisher; one of the nicest men one could wish to meet and have as a friend. When I was diagnosed with multiple sclerosis, it was Mike who made the long trek north to bring me home from hospital for a weekend. His advice over many years has been invaluable.

Will Carter, for his enormous help and encouragement in keeping my attention on getting this book completed and for all his help with photographs. I hope you get your wish to fish at Redmire in the summer time, and catch that 15lb barbel. To Len Arbery, Mick Holgate, Phil Chun, Martin Salisbury, Will Carter, Trevor Bross, Gary Newman and Scott Richmond I thank you for your valuable contributions. Colour Sgt Tam Miller of the Scots Guards and your fellow servicemen. PC Mark Hyde and the Lancashire Constabulary, on behalf of the Pendle Buddies I thank you all for giving these youngsters the chance of enjoying our great sport, also for your valued friendship.

My thanks go to the editors of: Countryman's Weekly, Angler's Mail, Angling Star, Coarse Angling Today, Coarse Fisherman and various newspapers both in the UK and the USA, too numerous to mention, for publishing my various features over the past fifty or more years. I wish to thank those who have allowed me access to fisheries on the Loddon, Kennet, Ribble, Wharfe, Ure, Swale, Thames, Ouse, Medway, Beult, Stour, Hampshire Avon and the many other rivers and still waters the length and breadth of the UK. Phil Chun for his professional advice on baits and how to use them, and others too numerous to mention. I thank you all.

To the best of my knowledge, the content of the following pages is truthful. However, the author reserves the right not to let facts get in the way of a good story! If errors exist herein, they are mine and mine alone.

Martin James
Lancashire
October 2010

I first met Martin on a wild, wet day in June back in the early nineties, on the banks of the River Ribble at Edisford Hall. The river had risen about two feet and Martin said, "This is a waste of time, let's go and have a brew."

We sat in the hut and started talking about the season, agreeing that the late, cold snap had kept the trout down. As we sat watching the rain coming down like stair rods, we started comparing other places we had fished: it was a no contest; he had fished everywhere.

I asked him if he had ever been bone-fishing. He said he had, and two hours later, through his description of a bone-fishing trip, I was totally hooked into a fishing expedition with him to the Bahamas. It was an outstanding success; I felt as if I had fished in a totally new world. This trip led to others and together we have fished: the Caribbean, North America, Scandinavia – as well as having various angling experiences in Britain.

I hope that as you read this book you will enjoy Martin's exploits as much as I, who has had the privilege of being with him on some of them. As you read on I am sure you will be inspired to try new challenges and experiences in our marvellous piscatorial world.

David Jones

Martin James and Hugh Miles, both passionate about their sport, in an interview

This book is dedicated to two old masters:

Richard Stuart Walker (1918-1985) who taught me I could catch big fish by design and not by luck. Richard taught me to be a better and more caring person. His book Still Water Angling was the biggest influence on anglers of any book on the sport published in the twentieth century. I first met Richard Walker in the fifties at a show in London. Many other anglers were queuing to meet the great man.

With autograph book in hand, I asked for his signature. I addressed him as Sir. 'Call me Dick,' he said charmingly. 'Yes sir,' I replied. I admired and loved the man like a father – in fact he really was the father of modern angling, and he gave us so much. One saying of his that I will never forget is, 'A fish will eat anything unless taught not to'.

Dick Walker Credit Tony Meers

Bernard Percival Venables MBE (1907-2001) created Mr. Crabtree. The Crabtree influence came to me through a comic strip in the Daily Mirror. Mr. Crabtree, the angler who was always catching big fish. I was enthralled by his writing and drawings on perch-fishing. In my last year at Temple School I won the school Book Prize.

The school secretary told me to choose a book, I opted for Mr. Crabtree Goes Fishing by Bernard Venables. It sold two million copies. Thank you, Bernard, for Mr. Crabtree and for all the other books which have flowed from your pen, the pictures from your brush and the time spent in your company.

Bernard Venables and the Author, with the famous 'Crabtree Net'

I 've had the pleasure of angling for the past sixty-eight years, having caught my first fish on 16 June 1941, when I had seven, small rudd on bits of worm.

Today, I'm still as passionately in love with this great pastime of angling as I was on that first day. In the beginning our fishing was the means of escaping the horrors of war: the loss of my favourite uncle Len who represented his Regiment, The Royal West Kent in competitions at Bisley before the war. He trained as a sniper, dying in the sands of North Africa fighting Rommel's Afrika Korps in the battle for El Alamein. Today, angling is an escape from the ravages of modern life.

At home, I am surrounded by 2000 or so fishing books, plus many others on wildlife, travel and art – fishing titles going back to the 1700s on big-game fishing, coarse, sea, trout and salmon angling. In my study are many awards I have been presented with for my work in angling, conservation, charity fund raising and helping youngsters to learn about this great sport, hobby, pastime or passion I reckon it's a bit of all four. As a youngster I read all the fishing, shooting and travel books from my local library, often reading some titles from cover to cover then starting all over again. Many of these books were about fishing in foreign lands.

I've been to Zane Grey's cabin on the Rogue River, fished at Winkle Bar, visited his old house on Catalina Island for dinner, fished the same pools on the Umpqua River in Oregon. I've visited other places where Zane Grey lived and fished. I have been a guest at Charles Holder's Avalon Tuna Club headquarters on Catalina Island during its Centenary celebrations. It was here in 1929 that the late Sir Winston Churchill, on the second day of his visit, went out

and caught the first fish of the season. This, after the regulars had been waiting many weeks to get a fish, I have also been lucky to meet many great angling writers for dinner or fishing. This great sport has been very kind to me.

Today we don't have to dream about catching tarpon in Florida, marlin in New Zealand, bluefin tuna off Nova Scotia, salmon in Alaska, the stripers of Chesapeake Bay or bonefish in the Bahamas. With the ease of modern air travel, lightweight clothing, excellent tackle designed specifically for the travelling angler in mind, more and more of us now fish foreign waters.

At The Water's Edge is a book containing some of my fishing adventures, of the fish caught, people I have met and much more.

I was four years of age when I caught my first fish from an old clay pit on Cliff Marshes in Kent. Before this important day in my life I would go to Rochester Pier with my granddad and fish for crabs, I would see him catching eels and flounders, and ask if I could catch a proper fish.

The answer was, "When you get older". I contented myself catching crabs from the pier, with small rudd from the clay pit. I was about nine or ten when I caught that first flounder. While in my last year at junior school I started catching little carp from a small village pond – to me and my friends these were giant fish but they were probably about about a pound, though later on we did catch them of two and three pounds. In between boxing, rugby, athletics and shooting, carp played a big part in my life through senior school and beyond.

I make no excuse for starting this book with some experiences of carp fishing, most boys and girls probably caught small perch or roach, my small pond didn't have these fish, just small carp. I used free lined bread paste as bait, in fact, last season I was catching carp in the same way as my very first carp on a free lined bread bait. The book starts with Len Arbery writing about his formative years of carp fishing some twenty years after I started. Then Will Carter writes of his dream of fishing Redmire. Let's go carp fishing.

I have great pleasure in presenting, over the next few pages, contributions from some very dear friends I have made over the years.

Engineer Len Arbery was the man who fitted rollers to the bale arms of Mitchell 300s back in the 1960s. He is married to June, a very friendly lady and they have two grown-up children, Karen and Tony. June even went out to work to cover Len's Redmire Pool expenses – bless her! Len catches lots of big fish. In the 1989/90 season he won the prestigious Drennan Cup, a trophy best described as the angler's equivalent of the British Open or Wimbledon. He is the author of several books including Catching Big Tench, In Pursuit of Big Tench, The Complete Book of River Fishing and Redmire Pool with Kevin Clifford

This story really starts long, long years ago, before I actually trod Redmire Pool's hallowed banks. In fact, the first time I heard the name Redmire, and therefore my introduction to it, was in 1952. As I write this, almost six decades have slipped from time's reel, but I can recall the scene as though it was yesterday, and my tale begins right back then.

I grew up in Barnes, southwest London, and as there was no fishing tackle shop adjacent at the time, a cycle ride was necessary to reach the nearest. On the day in question I'd pedalled the three-or-four miles to Hammersmith. Here, toward the Chiswick end of Kings Street, a red-painted shop had been divided into two separate businesses, both owned and run by a Mr. Cooper: to the left, pet stores, to the right, fishing tackle. Mr. Cooper (I was thirteen-years-old at the time and, as was generally the case in those days, had been brought up to be very respectful and deferential to my elders) was always to be found behind the fishing-tackle counter, while a lady of similar age, probably his wife, looked after the pet shop clientele.

When I close my eyes I can still see the interior of Cooper's quaint, little, tackle shop. First on the left as you went in, was the high, glass-fronted and glass-topped counter, under which lay a myriad of floats. Behind the counter were several shelves holding reels and books, the coloured backs of the "How to Catch Them" series being particularly memorable. There were also many beautiful examples of cased fish: roach, perch, chub, bream, pike, etc dotted around the shop. (Years later Fred J. Taylor, who knew all the retailers through his job as a sales executive for the tackle supplier, Efgeeco, told me that Mr. Cooper was the last member of the famous fish-taxidermists, John Cooper & Sons, to be involved with fishing.)

Anyway, back to the day in question. Whilst waiting to be served with six-pennyworth of gentles (2½p of gentles), Mr. Cooper and some of his (grown-up) customers were discussing the merits of the recently-reported new record carp, this fish, of course, being Richard Walker's 44lb common from Redmire Pool. Before being party to this conversation I'd certainly not heard of Redmire Pool nor, do I think, carp. But a fire within me had been ignited which seared into my very soul, and an ambition born: I now really wanted to catch a carp. Not that I coveted a monster such as Dick Walker's carp, no, any carp, of any size, would satisfy my craving, so long as it was of the species cyprinus carpio!

As it turned out I had very long time to wait before that particular ambition was realised. Carp weren't anything like as widespread as they are today, and neither I nor any of my friends were aware of a water which actually held them. In fact, I didn't actually see one with my own eyes until about ten years later . . .

It was lying virtually motionless in a culvert in one of the Barn Elms reservoirs, and the only way I could present a bait to it was through an inspection hatch. Of course, I tried that approach with the only bait I had with me, gentles, but the carp disdainfully ignored my, admittedly crude, attempts. Which is probably just as well, for my monofilament line was probably about 6lb breaking strain, and the carp, to my naive eyes, looked an absolute monster; thinking back now, I reckon it would have been about eighteen pounds, so there could only have been one possible outcome, and that would have been disaster – both for me and that beautiful and longed-for carp!

On holiday with my wife and young family a couple of years later, I met a fellow angler by chance and asked him my inveterate and inevitable question, "And do you know any carp waters?" After so many negatives replies previously, it was to my utter astonishment that he not only provided the name of a local water containing lots of carp (the Chichester canal), he also advised from where the necessary permit might be obtained.

Due to the previously mentioned family commitments, I couldn't find the time to fish the water until the very last morning of our holiday. I was up, out of the caravan and on the road before dawn, trying to allow myself just enough time to get set up and cast out prior to first light. The surface of the canal was covered in floating weed but eventually I found a clear hole just over halfway across. My whole being trembling with excitement and expectation – my fingers had trouble threading the already tied-on hook through the rod rings. Eventually however, the job was done and a large lump of crust impaled thereon. After being dunked, to provide some added weight, this was cast to land right in the centre of the little clearing, thankfully at the first attempt. Then I sat down behind a convenient screen of reeds to watch and wait.

Like so many summer dawns, that particular morning was quiet and without wind, enabling me to hear the wing beats of reed warblers as they flitted, to-and-fro in the rushes. When the light improved sufficiently for me to see my floating crust clearly, I could make out that it remained undisturbed, free even from the attentions of little fish, but now nestling up against a weedbed. Some little time passed, maybe as much as an hour, when without prior warning, and with a sound similar to water going down the plughole, my crust thankfully disappeared. With remarkable self-control and restraint in the circumstances, I allowed the line to tighten prior to setting the hook. This, the first carp I'd hooked, didn't disappoint: fighting with at least as much tenacity as my local Thames barbel. All went well though, and the 'wildie' shaped common carp – my carp, soon folded into the landing net. This was long before the advent of unhooking mats and carp sacks of course; therefore my prize was tenderly unhooked on the grass before being placed in my capacious keepnet which was sited in the shade of an adjacent, overhanging bush.

Whilst taking time to regain my composure, allowing my hands to become steady enough to pour a cup of tea from the flask, without scalding myself in the process, I was able to reflect on the last few minutes, and to plan my next move. The little clearing in the water was now gone, filled with drifting weed uprooted during the recent tussle. But there was another, perhaps a tad smaller than the first, and further to the right; it would necessitate a longer cast. This time it took three or four attempts to get the floating crust spot-on. Almost exactly one hour later, a repeat performance was enacted, identical down to all but one detail – a slightly smaller carp was landed. (Not that the first one was a giant!)

By late morning, with the sun near its zenith, I knew that the action was over for the time being and it was the right moment for a picture or two, only to discover I'd forgotten the camera! Fortunately, a fellow angler kept an eye on my gear, whilst I rushed off to get it – plus June and the kids! After June reeled-off a couple of shots, the carp weighed-in at 7lb and 5lb. Certainly not monsters, not even way back then, but you only catch your first carp once, and that morning has proved to be one of the most enduring memories of my long angling-career.

On returning home I lost no time informing friends of my success and we all returned repeatedly to the Chichester canal. In fact, with my closest fishing buddy at the time, Dave Short, I continued fishing for and catching those superb little 'wildie' type commons right

Len Arbury with his first two carp from the Chichester Canal
Picture by June Arbury

through the following winter, and – let me remind you, there were precious few anglers deliberately targeting winter carp in those days. But we never, ever beat, nor even equalled, that very first seven-pounder!

In springtime of the very next year, 1968, Dave and I had the massive stroke of good fortune that was to change our lives forever. A close workmate, Peter Bagg, asked if I'd like to meet his son-in-law's brother, Bill Quinlan. Initially, because there was a lot of good-natured mickey-taking, wind-ups, etc, in the toolroom, I took this invitation with a pinch of salt because Bill, together with his friends and fellow members of the Herts-Chiltern Anglers, Jack Hilton, Bob Buteux, Roger Smith, Bill Keal, Alec Lewis, etc, were right up at the very top of the big-fish tree even then. Perhaps like me, you too, dear reader, might have been a tad suspicious that 'Baggy' could provide an introduction to these exalted circles. Anyway, sooner or later, 'Baggy' convinced me of his sincerity and the date was fixed – and wonder of wonders, Bill actually turned up! I say this because, and I was to learn this pretty damn quick, that Bill was more than a tad unreliable. No! – Hollyhocks to political correctness – Bill could be the most unreliable git God ever put breath into!

One of the first trips Bill took me on was a work's party at Ashlea Pool, and this proved the occasion on which I met Roger Smith and Tom Mintram for the first time. Over tea and biscuits in the Ashlea Pool fishing hut, Bill, Roger and Tom discussed prospects for the coming season, not only here at Ashlea but – would you believe it – at Redmire Pool too! Evidently, Jack, who'd fished Redmire under the John Nixon scheme, had managed to acquire the fishing rights for the coming season, and three of the brand-new syndicate (of ten) were discussing their Redmire aspirations in front of a complete non-entity: ME! What must also be remembered is that this was confidential information, and perhaps a subtle ruse by Bill, Tom and Roger to check whether or not I was trustworthy and knew how to keep a confidence. If it was such a test I passed with flying colours: not for nothing is my nickname 'Secret Len'!

From that moment on, Bill kept me abreast of all the developments at Redmire: carp caught, syndicate issues, bait and tackle developments, etc. Sometime in 1971 Bill informed me that Jack had empowered him to ask me if I'd like to join the syndicate as replacement for another member who intended to resign at the end of the season. Here was the chance I had dreamt of for more than twenty years, and although I had no idea from where the syndicate fees could be scraped-up, I jumped at the chance and accepted. Even then though, my hopes were to be dashed. In September of that year I was involved in a horrific car-crash, an accident that could

easily have wiped out the whole family. For three months I couldn't walk, without the aid of crutches initially and sticks latterly. Unable to walk, also meant unable to work, unable to work meant money was even tighter than ever and reluctantly I telephoned Jack to cry-off. Bad news for me proved good news for someone else, and that someone else proved to be none other than: Chris Yates!

On the season's eve of 1973 I was first at the Longfield (Fox Pool) gate (actually witnessing Chris Yates drive past, Redmire bound – talk about rubbing salt into the wound!) in preparation for the season's opening when Tom Mintram surprisingly turned up. I say 'surprisingly', for Tom had already informed me of his plans, and they didn't include fishing Longfield!

Tom began by saying, "Hello, Len, June told me I'd find you here." "No, she didn't!" I countered. "She's far better trained than that!"

A young looking Chris Yates with a Common Carp from a Surrey water

"Of course you're right, but once I'd given her the password she relented and told me where I'd find you." Tom added. "Password, what password?" I knew Tom wouldn't be rushed until he'd had his bit of fun teasing me.

Tom then made me sweat for a few moments more before saying, "The password is "Redmire". Jack (Hilton) has phoned me today to say his brother-in-law, Kenny Ewington, has decided not to renew his Redmire syndicate place, and has empowered me to offer you Kenny's position. What do you say?

Despite having no idea from where I might get the £50 syndicate fees my immediate reply was, "Yes, yes, YES!" With that, Tom laughingly added, "Well, I'd better let Jack know, as I'm sure it will be a great load off his mind." And with that he disappeared, retracing his wheel tracks, back up the lane toward the outside world. (To try and put that £50 into perspective, let me tell you my take-home pay at the time, was about £12 a week, from which I had to provide for my wife and two young kids, and pay the mortgage, etc!)

Although the original intention had been to spend a few days fishing Longfield, my mind was in such turmoil, I just couldn't settle or concentrate on the job in hand so returned home early the next morning. Once bathed and changed I set off to find Bill Quinlan, eventually locating him in one of his usual watering holes. On hearing my news and knowing of my tight

Jack Hilton setting-up at Redmire Pool, 'no bivvies in those days!'
Credit Tony Meers

financial constraints – great mate that he was – Bill offered to loan me any funds I might require. (Bill, being a bachelor and still living at his parents' home, consequently had more disposable income.) Of course, this generous offer eased the pressure immediately, for I knew very well Bill's word was his bond in such situations, and I could pay Jack immediately. But in the long term a more permanent solution to the lack of money to fund my Redmire adventure was provided by June, my wife. For, believe it or not, in addition to looking after our two kids, she went out to work to cover my Redmire expenses: bless her!

Jack Hilton's syndicate consisted of him plus nine other anglers; these nine split into three rotas, with three individuals in each. The reason behind this arrangement was that the rules of the estate demanded only four anglers were allowed to fish at any one time; therefore, each rota would fish one week in three, with Jack, as reward for all the time and effort organising and running the syndicate, fishing any time.

The rota I would be part of was a carp-angler's dream as Tom Mintram and Bill Quinlan were the anglers I'd share the banks with. As these two were the closest of Jack's friends actually in the syndicate, it also meant that Jack would choose to spend most of his Redmire time with us too. As my entry into the syndicate was only confirmed at the very last minute, it left me with no time to arrange a whole week off work, therefore the earliest I could meet Bill at Redmire for the first time, was at dawn on Thursday, 28 June 1973.

It was raining, not heavy, but fine rain, you know, the type that penetrates the slightest chink in your waterproofs. Bill was set up in Pitchfords and, I assumed, still asleep. I didn't disturb him as I wanted my first-ever glimpses of Redmire to be a solitary introduction. My twenty-one year love affair with this magic pool was about to be consummated and I didn't want any prying eyes looking on – not even Bill's!

The surface of the pool was unruffled, not by even the slightest ripple, and the fine rain gave it a uniform grey appearance, except where weedbeds reached or nearly reached the surface; here the surface colour appeared darker, almost browny/black. The only sound which could be heard, apart from the distinct patter of rain drops from the overhanging trees and the clucking of a solitary moorhen, was the chuckling of trickling water as it exited the pool, and ran away under the corner of the dam, over countless pieces of red sandstone, so typical of the area and, of course, the inspiration for 'BB' (Denys Watkins-Pitchford MBE) christening the lake, 'Redmire Pool.'

I leaned on the dam rail, lost in the magic of my surroundings for an indeterminate length of time, just the same, no doubt, as Bob Richards, Dick Walker, Pete Thomas, 'BB', Fred J. Taylor, Maurice Ingham, Eddie Price, Dick Kefford, plus a host of others had done previously. I wished for that moment to last forever and, strangely enough, in a way it has. Then, framed by Redmire's majestic weeping willow, a large, common carp head-and-shouldered in a flurry of spray, as if to say, "You're here, in the right place at last, Arbery," and the spell was broken. I then went to wake Bill.

Over a couple of cups of tea, Bill told me that, although conditions appeared perfect, the Redmire carp hadn't played ball. I was then given a guided tour of the lake. We climbed several trees whose branches close to their trunks were gnarled and worn, betraying the countless times they been climbed previously. From these high vantage points Bill pointed out the extent of the deep central channel and where he knew snags were situated. He told me of the large carp he'd recently observed colouring the edge of the channel, and that this suspected feeding area changed from day-to-day, although every day at least some colour emanated from an area straight out in front of Pitchfords. Plainly, that was the reason Bill was fishing there.

The feeding areas pointed out to me were easier to reach from the opposite (west) bank from Bill's pitch, but a dense belt of weed extended almost the whole length of this side. Because of this weed, and from Bill's information, I chose to set-up next to Bill, in the Evening Pitch, for my first ever try for the Redmire carp.

Bill spent the great majority of the remainder of my first day stalking 'bubblers' in various areas of the pool with no success whilst I first baited my chosen area, then leisurely and carefully set up my brolly (no bivvies in those days!), bed-chair, tackle, etc. I'd had very little sleep in the previous forty-eight hours, in fact none at all since I'd got up for the Tuesday nightshift! After preparing and eating a hasty meal and casting out, I retired for the night. My chosen bait was tares, pre-cooked prior to leaving home.

I slept undisturbed until 6 a.m. when the buzzer on my right-hand rod roused me. Out of the bed-chair in a flash, the fresh, morning air immediately bringing me to my senses. Line was pouring from the spool and the silver-paper indicator jammed in the butt ring. I struck into a heavy and satisfying resistance. I hadn't had the chance to think, "these Redmire carp are easy," before the rod sprang back and the line fell limp!

Bill, who'd also heard my buzzer, silently appeared and, obviously noting my forlorn demeanour, did not resort to the usual banter and mickey-taking that such a disaster might normally elicit. Instead, he just remarked – perhaps by way of some scant consolation – that he had had a similar experience earlier. Until the Sunday morning that was the end of the action, it was then that Bill sneaked out the only fish of the week, just an hour or so before it was time to leave. This was a leather carp weighing in at exactly 25lb. Leathers are the ones with an abbreviated dorsal fin and long barbules.

I had to work Monday, Tuesday and Wednesday night of my next Redmire rota week, consequently did not arrive at a deserted pool until 3.45 p.m. on Thursday afternoon. During a quick recce it became obvious that the weed was much thicker, and surface scum (filamentous algae) much more in evidence than on my first visit. The clearest area looked to be in front of the Evening Pitch so I set up here again, but didn't cast out, instead, taking a pair of rods round to fish the shallows until nightfall from the opposite (west) bank, where there were quite a few carp bubbling and colouring the shallows a dark red. Not long after casting here, the fish moved away and I returned to the car to prepare my evening meal.

Tom arrived with Chris Yates; because the latter had experienced a broken-down car and Bill wasn't coming this week, Chris had been permitted to swap rotas. Tom fished Pitchfords, and Chris, Greenbanks.No action for any of us during darkness, so as soon as it got light enough I had a look round. Bubbling and colouring again close in to the west bank shallows so crept in there with just one rod at about 8 a.m.

At 10.15 a.m. I had a steaming run to a combination bait of sweetcorn and tares: line broke just above the hook. Don't like this: hooking and losing fish I mean, especially Redmire carp! Returned to the other bank to have some breakfast, and give the fish on the shallows time to regain their confidence. Kept an eye on the shallows periodically, and by 3.15 p.m. the bubbling and colouring in the pitch where I'd lost the fish earlier was just as intense. Almost immediately after I cast out, the silver-paper indicator slipped toward the butt ring. It didn't get there however – my strike saw to that. This wasn't the hoped-for leviathan, but I still got a boot full before netting a scamp of a common weighing all of nine pounds. But, you only catch your first Redmire carp once, and it wasn't my fault it weighed so little!

These first two visits set the pattern for the remainder of the summer's fishing for me at

Redmire: I could catch the lesser fish but something always seemed to go wrong when the more substantial ones were hooked. Here – let me now recount a tale I've never previously put down in print. A tale told exactly as it happened in my first season at Redmire. It is perfectly true and nothing even remotely similar has happened to me again, neither at Redmire nor elsewhere, in all the subsequent years:

Yet again the scene was the Evening Pitch, and yet again Tom was my companion, he was fishing next door to me in Pitchfords. The night was muggy, overcast, and calm. I had three rods in action: right bait cast to near side of central channel; centre bait cast to far side of channel; left bait placed in the margin, right in under an overhanging bush. No sign of any activity until 1.15 a.m. when the buzzer of the margin rod started screaming. Close the pick-up; wait for the line to tighten, and then strike. Result: Nothing! Never saw or felt a thing. Accurately replace the bait and return to bed. Within minutes the same buzzer was screeching again. Close the pick-up; wait for the line to tighten, and then strike. Result: a large swirl on the surface about ten feet out, then nothing.

To cut a long story short, this continued over and over again until daybreak, with similar results every single time; that is: not one solitary carp was hooked. Shortly after daybreak Tom came around, asking me what was wrong with my buzzers. Over a cup of tea I related my admittedly bizarre story. Then, believe it or not, the same buzzer cried out again. As I went for the rod, rattling in the rests with the power of the run, Tom exclaimed, "Well this one will be there!" Pick up the rod, close the pick-up, wait for the rod to be almost pulled from my hand, strike. Result: Absolutely bugger-all!

Tom was almost dumbfounded but managed to blurt out, "If I hadn't seen that with my own eyes, I'd never have believed it!" After breakfast some bubblers, just beyond the fringe of the weeping willow's trailing fronds, encouraged me to try for them. Slipped in with just a single rod and fished without an indication until 9 a.m. which left just sufficient time to pack up before returning to the hurly-burly of the outside world.

At 1 p.m. on Sunday, 16 September 1973, I met Chris Yates at Redmire's entrance, he on his way home, me about to start fishing. Chris reported that he'd caught the 'Thirty-Eight' from the dam, and that Rod Hutchinson had caught two carp of twenty pounds-plus from the Willow Pitch. Plus, Chris had caught another 'twenty' from the Fence Pitch. Furthermore, Jack Hilton had caught two 'twenties' from the Evening Pitch, where he remained, at the pool, fishing this very swim.

After discussing prospects with Jack, I chose to fish Keffords Pitch. Whilst setting-up I noticed some big fish moving onto the shallows, so, after reporting this to Jack, we both moved there, fishing adjacent pitches with a pair of rods each. In very short order indeed, Jack hooked and landed a common of about ten pounds, the resulting commotion scared every other carp off the shallows. Next day, at dawn, Bill (Quinlan) arrived, and at midday 'Hilty' left.

Bill set up in the Willow Pitch, whilst I decided to stay put in Keffords. Fish moved back onto the shallows mid-morning and I tried for them with just one rod. Within minutes hooked a 'biggie' only for it to shed the hook after scaring every other carp in the vicinity! Not long after recasting, back in Keffords for the night, hooked and landed a little scamp of a common weighing less than ten pounds. No further action during darkness. Not long after dawn, crept up to see how Bill was doing, and he amazed me by reporting he'd had no less than seven screaming runs since midnight. Now let me try and put that in perspective: seven runs in a week at Redmire would have been something to crow about in those days, seven runs in a morning being unheard of. Bill went on to inform me these seven runs had resulted in three fish landed, two under and one over twenty pounds. Plus, two other big fish had been lost when he'd 'clamped-up' on them, in failed attempts to prevent them making it to the jungle of weeds and snags in the far corner of the dam near the outfall. All runs had come to Bill's latest secret bait: luncheon meat!

Bill, in his usual generous fashion, then presented me with some of his precious stock of luncheon meat and, after first dicing it up into half-inch cubes, I pre-baited where some bubblers had been seen, directly in front of the Evening Pitch. Then, after lunch, moved my gear round from the opposite side of the lake. I got set up in the Evening Pitch just in time to save getting a soaking, for there was now a complete change in the weather: the previous night had been clear, calm and cold; now there were tearing winds from seemingly all directions, together with pouring and incessant rain; a really horrible night! At 3.45 a.m. a run resulted in a hard-scrapping common of about twelve pounds; I didn't weigh it due to the inclement conditions. Just got myself dry and comfortable when, of course, the same rod was 'away' again; didn't connect. Both these runs came not on Bill's luncheon meat, but my old favourite Redmire bait, tares. Bill also had one run in the night that he didn't connect with.

At this juncture, I'd now like to provide some idea of the lengths to which we resorted to keep things secret at Redmire. It had been known in the past for some rota members to surreptitiously search other members' vehicles for clues to their successful baits, etc. Bill had been a victim of this sort of scandalous behaviour on more than one occasion. Therefore, we kept baits in our vans that we had absolutely no intention of using at Redmire, by way of a 'blind alley'. Furthermore, as one of Bill's diaries had also been purloined in the past, we also wrote down our bait details in code! Our code for Bill's latest wonder bait being 'AJ': and how did we arrive at this seemingly unconnected code? The brand Bill had already discovered more successful than other luncheon meats was Jaka; so we decided that, by reversing the first and last letters of this brand name, it was unlikely any prying eyes would connect it with luncheon meat.

Of course, I readily acknowledge some might consider these tactics of ours to be quite out of context within the brotherhood of angling in general, and within a ten-member syndicate – quite scandalous and, perhaps, paranoid even – but whatever the jury's verdict over time decides, this is the truth of the matter; and Bill and I were far from the only ones playing this particular game within the Redmire syndicate. And no apologies either!

Another memorable event of this same week came after a completely action-less night. On Thursday morning at 7.45. I was sitting close by my three rods, fanned out in the Evening Pitch when, without any pre-warning, the centre buzzer cried out. I hooked a big, powerful, but slow-moving fish, which irresistibly just kept taking more and more line. So prolonged was this fight that Bill had time to amble round from the Willow Pitch on the opposite bank, to provide any assistance that might be required. On-and-on the battle raged, swinging one way and then the other: I'd gain a few yards before the hooked carp would take a bit back. At one stage Bill even suggested that the fish might be foul-hooked, which would explain the dogged and remorseless fight.

Eventually, however, as it inevitably does, the strength of sound and well-balanced tackle prevailed, and the hooked fish was drawn toward the waiting landing net held by Bill. It was a big common and both Bill and I could make out that it was not, after all, foul-hooked, for we both could clearly see my line disappearing into the cavernous depths of its wide-open mouth. Slowly, oh so slowly, the distance between me and my prize became less and less. The fish lay well-beaten on its side, with part of its head out of the water as I towed it toward the net. Only six inches from the thong the dratted hook lost its hold and whistled past my ear. Bill made a desperate lunge with the net in a last-ditch attempt to save the situation, but it was not to be. The fish slid silently, seemingly in slow motion, from our view, and back to its secret domain.

The Redmire carp that made Bill Quinlan the second man in history, (Jack Hilton being the first), to catch three thirty-pounders. Caught from the Willow Pitch on luncheon meat in October 1973 it weighed 38lb 2oz. This same fish became Chris Yates' 51lb 8oz record carp in 1980. Credit Tony Meers

At the time, Bill said he estimated the lost common at around twenty five pounds, but years later confessed he'd deliberately under- estimated the weight, trying to ease my pain and disappointment.

Bill reckoned the actual weight of that particular lost carp would have been closer to thirty five pounds! I could have cried at the time, and now, while penning the full account for the first time almost forty years on, the loss remains painful!

Couldn't get away from work until late Thursday of my next week's rota, so consequently didn't arrive until 8.45 p.m. and well after dark. Found Bill set up in the Willow Pitch, from where he'd hooked just one good carp earlier in the week, on 'AJ,' only to lose it in a snag. Decided to postpone setting-up until the following morning when I might see some feeding fish.

Over dinner Bill told me he'd recently dreamed of catching a monster carp, this was a rare event: Bill dreaming of catching a big fish, I mean. Afterwards, Bill returned to the Willow Pitch, whilst I got my head down in readiness for an early start.

At 2.30 a.m. Bill awoke me to tell me his dream had come true, as he'd just caught the '38' at 38lb 2oz precisely. This made Bill only the second man in this country, behind only Jack Hilton of course, to catch three carp weighing in excess of thirty pounds!

Shortly after dawn I was to be found circumnavigating the whole pool looking for signs of feeding fish, but finding very little evidence. The exception was some spasmodic bubbling in the Evening Pitch and Pitchfords area, so I set up in the former but also baited the latter, somewhat sparingly, with tares as well as luncheon meat. As the day progressed the bubbling seemed just that little more concentrated in Pitchfords, so slipped in there with a couple of rods. Forty-five minutes later the silver-paper indicator on the 'AJ' baited rod first twitched before steadily climbing toward the butt ring. Hooked the carp okay but it soon found a snag and regretfully had no option but to eventually 'pull for a break'. I wrote in my diary at the time, "This hooking and losing good fish is really getting me down!" After an uneventful night, at 8.15 a.m. on Saturday, 13 October my luck was about to change. A run came to my right-hand rod, cast about 110 feet out, directly in line with a telegraph pole on the opposite bank, and baited with 'AJ'. During the ensuing fight Bill materialised at my side and picked up the landing net.

"If you miss this one Bill, you'll never watch Popeye again!" I joked. But I really didn't feel like joking – I don't think I could stand losing yet another decent Redmire carp. As it turned out, there were no unexpected anxious moments, and as Bill raised the net around it, even though it was obviously a 'scraper', I knew instinctively that another ambition had at long last been achieved: that of landing my first Redmire 'twenty'. It was close run thing though, for the mirror weighed just 20lb 6oz.

I still look forward to visiting Redmire Pool about once a year, sometimes fishing, other times just for a walk round in the close season. Either way, it doesn't really matter, for at Redmire I always find a measure of inner peace: solace even.

Perhaps the reason for this tranquillity of the soul is that, while at Redmire I feel the close presence of so very many, lost friends. Friends who I feel privileged to have shared all those gloriously happy hours with: Bill Quinlan, Jack Hilton, Tom Mintram, Fred J. Taylor, Maurice Ingham, Peter Stone, Gerry Berth-Jones, Len Head, to name but a few.

Len Arbery's first 20 pounder at Redmire. Credit Tony Meers

In June 2008 I was once again at Redmire Pool. This time, son Tony and I were the guests of Les Bamford, helping him celebrate his 20th anniversary running Redmire. During this trip I was lucky enough to catch a pristine and photogenic common carp weighing within two ounces of that very first Redmire 'twenty'. When reporting the capture to Chris Ball he said, "Let's see, the years between those two captures, 1973 to 2008, being no less than thirty five years, provides you, Len, with the longest Redmire 'Twenties' pedigree!' " Chris is full of statistics!

Len Arbery about to return his first ever Redmire 20 pounder, caught from the Evening Pitch on luncheon meat in October 1973 it weighed 20lb 6oz. Credit Tony Meers

Will Carter, born just a few yards from the Hampshire Avon in Ringwood, now resides in the delightful county of Berkshire with Sonia and their three children: Harley, Becky and Liam. If he wasn't such a good angler, I reckon he could have been a great comedian. His lifelong dream is to fish Redmire Pool in the summer time.

It must have been sometime in the mid 1970s that I first became aware of this, the most secret of venues, known as Redmire Pool, and even then, conversations were conducted in hushed tones.

I was born and bred in Ringwood on the banks of the famous Hampshire Avon, and it was on these banks that I would overhear anglers talking about the latest monster carp to come to the banks of this mysterious place called Redmire. It seemed that, although many anglers could be heard talking about Redmire, hardly any could tell you exactly where it was, a lot would guess but very few were right. Today of course it would be easy, as there is not much you cannot find on the internet, but thirty-odd years ago all we had was the fishing grapevine, and a bit like Chinese whispers, you were never quite sure what to believe.

It was another five years before the fire was well and truly lit when on 16 June 1980 a certain Mr Chris Yates broke the previous carp record with a fish of 51lb 6oz, a truly magical moment. Once the pictures started to appear in the angling press over the next few weeks, it was there, in colour; every angler could see what beautiful fish Redmire held, and it probably became the number one venue on any carp-fisher's hit list. It would be another twenty-five years though before I would have the chance to set foot on its fabled banks.

It was in the autumn of 2005 when I spoke to Les Bamford who runs the booking for Redmire, and was lucky enough to secure a weekend's fishing at the pool for the following January. It didn't matter what time of year or what the weather would be like, I would finally be taking my first steps into a dream I've had since I was a young boy. After putting the phone down to Les I had a sudden feeling of panic; would actually going to Redmire live up to my heightened expectations?

After reading about the pool in many publications, including probably the best angling book ever written, Casting at the Sun by Chris Yates, my mind's eye had a picture that I didn't want to be shattered. Would it be like meeting a famous film star or pop star and finding out they are not all they are cracked up to be, or would it be just as I imagined it? Only time would tell, and until I got there I would just have to look forward to my trip and try not to think about it.

I arrived at the entrance to Bernithan Court Farm (the real name of Redmire) about 1 p.m. and would not be allowed in until 2 p.m. as that was hand-over time. As I drove along the drive at about quarter-to-two, the road split. Left would take you to the old manor house and right took you past two cottages to a gate.

Once through the gate I drove along a narrow road across the top of a field. All of a sudden I caught a glimpse of something reflecting below me through a tree line. As I looked closer I could make out water and there she was – through the trees as I got closer – I caught my first real glimpse of Redmire Pool. I drove down the hill to the gate of the car park which is situated by the Evening Pitch, the supposedly most haunted swim on the pool, and just sat for a few minutes not quite believing I was actually there. I guess the next thing I did has been done by every angler to have ever visited Redmire: I went and stood on the Dam. The dam; where so many famous anglers have stood. The dam; where pictures of monster Carp have been taken. The dam; where you can view the entire length of the pool in all its glory.

Next, it was a visit to the shed where the Redmire log is kept. This is an account of all the fish that have been caught throughout the season, and even if you don't catch a fish, you are supposed to fill it in with details of the weather, baits, swims fished, etc. It makes interesting reading. The next thing to do was to take a slow walk around the pool and try to decide where I was going to fish – not a job to be rushed.

I have to explain that Redmire is no bigger than a medium size farm-pond, probably less than three acres in size with a dam at one end tapering off to the shallows at the other. When you see the size of the place and remember the many tremendous captures that have happened there, it seems even more unbelievable – especially when, as on this day, the water was so clear you could see nearly three-quarters of the lake bed, yet no sign of a fish. Then all of a sudden, a bow wave came straight down the centre of the pool towards me; about thirty feet away it veered off left and disappeared, just like a ghost. Welcome to Redmire I thought to myself.

As I walked around the pool I felt as if I was walking through the pages of a history book. Each swim I came to had a story to tell: the Willow Pitch where Richard Walker battled and landed his record 44lb record carp in 1952, Greenbanks where Chris Yates caught his 51lb record in 1980, the Evening Pitch where many an angler past and present has reported strange happenings, and so on, history in every step.

That first trip produced no bites, but that didn't matter. There is so much more to fishing Redmire than actually catching fish – an old cliché but never more apt. The place is electric, and whilst you are there, it would be very easy to get lost in time. Even in the depths of winter it is still a beautiful place. You can never take away that special feeling when you are there on the bank. I had spent only two nights on that first visit but it was enough to etch Redmire in my mind as one the most special and memorable

DAY	PITCH FISHED	BAIT AND QUANTITY	FISH CAUGHT AND HOOKBAIT	CARP ACTIVITY AREAS	WEATHER	COMMENTS
SUNDAY	Stumps (Steve) / Willow (Lyndon)	Boilie + hemp / Boilie + Grains + hemp	1 fish lost 3.3 / NIL	NIL	mild	What a fantastic weeks weather, very mild and sunny spells. Fish begining to move around – mainly after dark.
MONDAY	Stumps (Steve) / Willow (Lyndon) / Greenbanks (Will)	Boilie + hemp / Spodded 3kg / Boilie + hemp pellet / Boilie	NIL / NIL / NIL	NIL	mild	We couldn't have asked for a better week given the time of year.
TUESDAY	—"—	—"—	23lb 4oz Common to Lyndon in Willows	Small carp seen laying against reeds Kaffords	mild	Redmire is in great condition and is a truely magical place to spend time.
WEDS	—"—	—"—	fish lost in Willow to Lyndon	Carp Surring opposite willow below common	mild	
THURS	Stumps (Steve) / Willow (Lyndon) / evening Pitch (Will)	—"—	5lb mirror Willow to Lyndon	Carp seen between evening Pitch + Comb near old oak	mild/wet	A credit to Les and the guys running it, We will be back!
FRIDAY	—"—	—"—	NIL	NIL	mild/Sunny	
SAT						
SUNDAY						

ANGLERS NAME Steve, Will, Lyndon   START OF SESSION DATE 15/02/09 – 20/02/09

23lb 4oz Yes!!!

✗ 23lb Common off of fallen tree in Willow margins 7.15am.
✗ lost + 5lb fish same spot 8.50am.

The Redmire Log. Credit Will Carter

places that I have ever had the privilege to visit.

The following year I was back, but again, only for a short two-night winter session. This time the weather was against us with a very cold northeasterly putting the fish down, but as I've said before; not catching fish doesn't matter, it's just being there that excites me. If I never caught a fish from Redmire it wouldn't matter as long as I could spend many more nights just being there. The following May I had arranged with Les to go down to the pool in the close season to take some pictures of Redmire in all its summer glory. The place looked even more magnificent, the sun was shining and it seemed that most of the pool's occupants were sunbathing; everywhere carp where just basking in the sun. I was at the pool for two hours but didn't take one picture, I spent the whole time sitting on top of the boathouse just watching. A picture would not have done it justice anyway: an amazing experience.

Soon it was time to leave. I went via Ross-on-Wye, making a promise to myself that I would definitely be back. Saying goodbye to the pool was like saying goodbye to an old friend, knowing that it wouldn't be long before you saw them again.

I had a unique opportunity in October 2007 to meet an angling legend. To make it even more special, the meeting would take place at Redmire Pool. My good friend Martin James had arranged an interview with Eddie Price, for his new book. Eddie Price was the second person to catch a 40lb carp, which he did in September 1959, and is also probably more famous for taking the picture of 'The Monster in the Weeds' in 1958 which showed one of Redmire's monster carp.

I was there to shoot some photographs for the interview but also, hopefully, to have the opportunity to talk with Eddie about his time at Redmire. When Eddie arrived he did so with his son and wife. This was the first time that Eddie had been back to the pool since he last fished it in the early 1960s. His wife had come along to see where her husband had spent many a night away from home during the late 1950s early 1960s.

Martin recorded his interview with Eddie and then went off around the pool to get some more interviews. This left me with the opportunity to speak with Eddie. I sat on the bench on the dam, and had a good half-an-hour with a true angling legend to just talk about fishing. Eddie was near his eighty-fourth birthday and was quite hard of hearing, and so all conversation had to be very deliberate and slow so he could hear clearly.

I asked him about his time at Redmire, and about the picture of the monster – it was fascinating listening to him first-hand. Bearing in mind Eddies' poor hearing, what happened next was amazing. All of a sudden he turned his head towards the far end of the Pool and said, "A fish jumped there," and as I turned I could just make out the ripples from a fish right down the far end of the pool. When you fish Redmire for any length of time it seems you develop a sixth sense; Chris Yates used to talk about it, as have others who have spent time there. Soon it was time for Eddie to leave and I felt truly honoured to have spent time in the company of this giant of angling history.

For various reasons, mostly work-related, it wasn't until 2008 that I would visit again. This time I had a five-day session booked in November which, looking back through the history books, can sometimes be a very productive month, dependent on the weather being favourable.

Unfortunately it wasn't – again, a very cold northerly wind killed the fishing. On the plus side I was able to spend five glorious nights at the pool. Also, I was lucky enough to have booked a five-night session for the following February so I knew I would be back soon.

Christmas arrived and went, and as the New Year approached, the weather became much colder: throughout January we had snow. The pool was unfishable for much of the time due to ice. The week prior to my going back for my booked session, the pool was still frozen but the weather forecast had predicted warmer weather, and with just a few days to go the weather changed. The ice had gone and the temperatures were unseasonably warm, in fact the mildest all winter. Weather-wise I couldn't have picked a better week if I'd tried.

For this visit I was to be joined by three other anglers who had never fished at Redmire before: David Miller, an artist who was hoping to join us at some time during the week, depending on the seminar he was attending in Gloucester, Lyndon Barrett, a police officer from Hampshire, and Steve Morgan, an angler local to me (who has an impressive list of big fish captures). Sunday was to be the start day of our session but I would not be able to make it until the Monday morning. I suggested that Lyndon and Steve go ahead and I would join them the next day. David would not be able to make it to fish at all but would be popping down mid-week to at least experience the atmosphere. One of the main reasons I wouldn't be going until the Monday morning was that I wanted Lyndon and Steve to experience Redmire for the first time on their own – to get a feeling for the place without me pointing out everything to them, it's something that will live with them in there own way for ever. I spoke to Lyndon on the Sunday morning and wished him and Steve good luck, I then made sure I had everything for the week ahead.

I arrived at the pool about 10 a.m. on the Monday and saw that Steve was in the Stumps. Lyndon was in the Willow Pitch – mainly due to the influence of Richard Walker and the history of the swim. I think Steve had chosen his swim for convenience as it is right by the car park. During their first night Steve had a run about three-thirty in the morning but lost the fish after a short fight. Although this was a shame, at least we knew that the fish were feeding – or at least one was, so confidence was high. I set up down near the shallows hoping that the warmer weather would see the fish entering the shallows more and more throughout the week ahead. After a chat and a few drinks it was time to retire to our bivvies and drift off to sleep listening to the sounds of Redmire, always hoping to be rudely awoken by the sound of the buzzer.

It was about seven when I woke and I decided to go for a walk around the pool to see if there were any signs of movement. I walked around to Lyndon's swim but he was still fast asleep so I continued my walk until I was back at mine. It couldn't have been more than ten minutes later when Lyndon came up and said that he had just had a fish, it must have taken his bait right after I had been to his swim. What is it I asked, a common he said, so I asked if he had weighed it yet. He said he had and told me the weight, 23lb 4oz. If I could catch any fish anywhere in the world, the one at the top of the list would be a twenty pound Redmire common, and here I had the chance to see one of these glorious creatures in the flesh. It didn't matter that I hadn't caught it, I couldn't have been happier for Lyndon, a good angler and a nice guy as well. I went and got my camera and we went round to his swim where the fish was safely sacked. We decided the best place to take the pictures would be on the dam so preparations were made and the fish was gently taken round for the portrait session. When the sack was unzipped I was greeted by the most stunning carp you could wish to see, a dark bronze colour with an orange belly and the classic Redmire Leney common shape: truly a magnificent creature. I took lots of photographs; then it was time to release her back to the depths where she lived.

We decided to release her by the outflow of the dam, as Lyndon could get into the water, wearing his waders, and release the fish safely. Whilst he was in the water I took some more pictures – this was a photo opportunity not to be missed. After a few moments she swam off as strong as ever to fight another day, and disappeared into the deeper centre channel. What a result: a Redmire twenty-pounder from Walker's Pitch.

Congratulations were exchanged and a glass of wine was taken, then myself and Lyndon went into Ross for a well-deserved breakfast, and to talk about the fight and the fish that he had just landed. After breakfast we got some supplies and went back to the pool.

Lyndon was to have a good week, with another run on the Wednesday evening; unfortunately he lost it in a snag, and another fish, this time a small mirror, about five pounds, caught on the Thursday evening – a good result for anybody fishing this fabulous place, especially for the first time. All the carp waters that Lyndon has fished in the past now pale into insignificance as none will ever be Redmire.

I will be back there as soon as I can get a booking, and maybe it will be my time to catch a fish – if not, then there is always next year and the year after that and the year after that, at least now, I have seen in the flesh the rewards that this place has to offer. Maybe someday, maybe soon!

Lyndon Barrett, pictured with a 23lbs 4oz Redmire Common. Credit Will Carter

Martin Salisbury, a solicitor, is married to Michelle, a senior maths teacher. Martin's book Where to Fish: Lancashire's Coarse Fisheries I reckon was a winner especially with those new to the sport or area. Though Martin is a keen supporter of Preston North End, he can still catch some good fish!

This is a tale of fishing frustration that charts my river-fishing education before successfully ending up on the banks of the beautiful river Wye.

As a youngster I learnt the art of fishing on the towpath of the Lancaster Canal. I spent many an hour trying to tempt roach, perch, bream, and the odd ruffe or two, to succumb to the charms of my clumsily-presented gentle or worm hook-bait.

Slowly, over time, I refined my tackle and tactics and learnt that pole-fishing, and the fine presentation it allowed, was the secret to success. I became skilled in presenting squatts or bloodworm on gossamer-fine hook lengths of less than 1lb to size 24 hooks or smaller! Rarely did I fish any heavier to capture the inhabitants of the canal and even when fishing the ponds, pits and lakes of Lancashire did I rarely move far away from my delicate canal presentations.

I had served my fishing apprenticeship well; it was time for the obligatory move into carp fishing! With it came the buzzers, boilies and bivvy. After several years of chasing carp and capturing fish to 24lb in the frozen north-west, I started to look for new fishing challenges. This led me to fish for a variety of species including: pike, chub, barbel, tench and rudd . It gave me a renewed interest in the sport and my rod, tackle and bait store rapidly increased in size in direct proportion to my bank account shrinking as I bought rods and bait for every occasion.

I had several flirtations with fishing the rivers, but in all honesty, struggled on my own to make sense of their moody ways. I read about what tactics to use on rivers and studied what areas I should be fishing, but I just couldn't translate this into any real success on the bank. I had some good days, trotting a stick float on the Ribble or down one of the smaller rivers near my Lancashire home but I never captured any specimen-sized fish. As I struggled to catch, my confidence dropped – and without any confidence you'll never catch much at all. I regularly retreated back to the safety of the local ponds and lakes to focus on the fish I knew how to catch.

The slacks, creases, glides, back eddies and the constantly changing face of the rising and falling rivers had me confused and I vowed to defeat them and unearth their treasures. A Barbel Society meeting where Martin James was the guest speaker was the event that started to unlock the door to those river secrets.

A few years previously I had appeared on Martin's radio show to promote a book that I had written. I spent a lot of my time carp fishing on one particular water, and when the ownership and stock changed, I needed to find somewhere new to fish and so Where to Fish: Lancashire Coarse Fisheries was written as I searched for new waters. It detailed over 100 fisheries in the area. After recording the radio show, Martin had suggested I should contact him to arrange some fishing but I thought it was just a polite offer and never took him up on the invite.

Years later, when I introduced myself again to Martin at the Barbel Society meeting, he reiterated his invite to fish with him anytime. I realised he was serious and I arranged a day's chub fishing on the River Aire with him. My river-fishing education had begun. Over a couple of years I had several sessions on the Aire with Martin and I started to learn how to capture those finicky chub. Martin introduced me to the simple methods of fishing breadcrust on a large size 4 hook and explained when to vary the tail depending on weather conditions and water temperature. From those early days I've added a thermometer to my tackle box and it is now an essential part of my river-fishing kit. When the breadcrust was failing to produce or the water was coloured and required a smelly bait, he would encourage me to switch over to cheese, luncheon meat or even one of his more exotic baits – meatballs in gravy!

In the clear and shallow waters of the upper Aire you would see the chub cruise into the swim and pick the bait up in their lips, and then trundle away again. Seeing the chub inspect the baits enhanced my understanding and river watercraft. Anyone who is struggling to come to terms with river fishing should try a small and intimate river and not worry about the size of the quarry but focus on how to present a bait and catch those fish.

One of my favourite, shared angling moments came on the Aire. Martin was downriver, no doubt doing what he does best by catching plenty of chub, and I had my own fishing apprentice with me in the figure of nine-year old, Jan Detko.

As evening started to descend, Jan's meatball hook-bait was picked up by an Aire chub of 3lb and he held on for dear life before I was able to put the net under a new personal best. The picture of his proud capture will forever remain in my fishing memories as this monster chub hung out either side of his small hands and an even broader smile beamed back at the camera.

With some experience of successful river-fishing under my belt, and a new found confidence, I started fishing the Ribble again; I changed methods a little. I stayed with bread as bait, but this time it was liquidised bread in a feeder with a bread flake hook-bait fished mid-river.

I had regularly kept up-to-date with the Ribble via the internet and picked up some hints and tips from behind my keyboard. I also went on a fishingmagic.com/Ribble fish-in and met, for real, some of those cyber-anglers! I sat behind Ribble regular John Conway, who many will know from the riverbank or maybe just his postings on the internet, including some excellent records of the chub capture-patterns on the Ribble.

Jan Detko with a River Aire chub

As I sat with John and observed and talked about his methods, I moved closer to my first Ribble five pound chub. Back on the river, on a bitterly cold winter evening, I replicated his methods and started to catch a few chub. Soon, a new personal best chub of 5lb 2oz was landed on the liquidised bread/bread flake combination. Not for the last time a good chub had been landed in cold temperatures when the landing net had frozen solid to the ground.

I've not ventured to those chub swims for a few seasons now and I don't miss fishing them as I never enjoyed sitting in the woods on my own. I'm normally quite comfortable with night fishing, but the woods and darkness would play havoc with my imagination, and I would sit in the swim for hours rigid with fear, never daring to look around. At one stage, I took to listening to the radio through headphones to block out the sounds.

Nor did I relish the long walk back to the car in darkness. Often I wouldn't be able to see more than one footstep ahead of me as my glasses steamed up with my warm breath in the cold mid-winter air.

You might find that, as my tale progresses, copying other anglers' tactics becomes a common theme. My motto, and one that I proudly share with others, is: 'imitation not innovation'. There are many great anglers out there and there are hours, months even years of experience that can be tapped into if you are polite enough. There are loads of ways to glean this knowledge such as: books, magazines, internet, TV and local fishing clubs. As a member of region 31 PAC, my knowledge of pike fishing is much better, through the talks and slideshows of experienced anglers and by joining club members on the bank. There is no better way of learning than being out fishing, and sharing experiences with other anglers. I'm always keen to introduce newcomers and feel that I accelerate their learning by sharing my skills and experience, and I would urge you to do the same to help preserve and protect our sport.

Back on the river it was time to start catching some barbel; Martin suggested we start on Berkshire's River Kennet. It was February and the weather had been cold. For the first couple of days I managed to land a few chub by using breadcrust on a size 4 hook and a 3in tail pinned down by 2 LG shot – a very simple method and a mobile one that rarely saw me staying in a swim more than fifteen minutes. If no bites were forthcoming in that short time span, I would deliver some free offerings to the swim and move on, perhaps to return later.

I can clearly remember catching a four pound-plus chub, just below a Kennet weir pool, within seconds of casting in. I dropped the breadcrust under the outer branches of an overhanging tree. Immediately, I saw the distinctive white lips of a big chub appear and engulf the bait and then turn to return under the canopy of the tree, dragging the rod with it.

A rise in temperature on the final day opened a window of opportunity for a barbel. The trusty breadcrust was cast mid-river, and by holding the rod high and using the faster current, the bait scooted across the surface, until it hit the inside slack and sank into the depths under a bush. The tip soon sharply pulled round and a powerful fish shot out from under the bush and across the flow to the far side of the river.

The current was fast and strong and the fish used all its strength and guile, utilising the flow to help it strip line, and power off downstream. The hook hold held firm and eventually my first barbel of 6lb 6oz was coaxed upstream and into the net. (Dare I mention it was the same weight as my first daughter Ellie? And yes, they were both handled with equal care and attention!)

Of course, that first barbel of mine was caught on bread! I would be amazed that if within the pages of this book Martin hasn't pointed out and preached many times to you: use bread for barbel. I can confirm on his behalf that bread's a great bait for barbel and that it works, time-and-again.I returned to the Kennet several times and caught plenty of chub and barbel on bread and luncheon meat, the meat being most effective when several large pieces were roughly torn from a chunk of meat and threaded onto the hook like a necklace. Bites would be several plucks followed by a slamming round of the rod tip, fish on!

On one occasion, and going against Martin's traditional river methods, I sneaked on a single halibut pellet and hooked and landed a short fat pig of a barbel of just under eight pounds. It looked significantly bigger, and even now, looking back at the picture, it still looks much larger. It was nice to get one over Martin for once with the change of hook bait.

The Kennet has also kindly provided me with some great memories of other species and lazy days. My personal best perch of two-and-a-half pounds was caught from the Kennet. I was fishing a large lobworm in a far-bank slack when it started trundling off downstream. Now please don't forget, I wasn't an expert on the intricacies of the river flow at that time, and forgive me, as I'm not sure to this day whether the bait was intercepted mid-river as it was washed out of the slack and downstream, or if the striped warrior had already picked up the bait in the slack. I have often replayed the incident in my mind but can't come to a satisfactory conclusion. Wherever it sucked in the large lobworm, the perch was still lip-hooked and produced a very lively scrap, using its spiky dorsal to create as much resistance as possible in the swift current. And although the confusion over how I hooked the bristling perch may take the shine off my story, it will never dull the pride in capturing my personal-best perch!

I was fortunate enough to fish the famous Kennet weed rack swim, which many of you will have seen featured in A Passion for Angling when Bob James captured two monster pike whilst Chris Yates was sleeping in. However, I wasn't successful in that well known swim but captured a six pound-plus bream on trotted gentle in the weir pool of one of the tiny tributaries that flowed into the Kennet, just upstream of one of its most recognised swims. What made the capture remarkable was that, the night before I had slept in a fishing hut with temperatures as low as -6°F, and the bream was caught in sub zero temperatures. It was the species we least expected in the tributary especially in those weather conditions.

Having a good day on the riverbank doesn't always need to include the capture of fish: I can still recall a blazing hot day on the Kennet. The sun was high in the clear blue sky, the bankside vegetation was at its summer peak and the river was lazily flowing by. I fished a halibut pellet between the slowly, rhythmically-swaying banks of weed. An angler just upstream had a couple of barbel to 8lb. It was a day when even Martin failed to catch much (if anything!) but I didn't care that I hadn't even had a rattle on the rod top. I could have sat there in that deep grass with the sun shining down forever. I often dream of returning to that small secret swim bathed in sunshine.

Back on home territory, I had also started capturing barbel on the Ribble. Tactics involved a heavy 2oz running lead on a 10lb mainline to a 12in mono hook length of normally about 12in.

The hook bait was a 14mm halibut pellet, drilled and hair rigged on a size 6 Drennan specimen hook. An imitation pop-up pellet was the hair stop and I frequently moulded a trout pellet paste around hook bait. I had many enjoyable barbel sessions on the upstream limit of the stretch I was fishing. I'd often start fishing late afternoon and try and drag out my Sunday evenings as long as possible. Not only to enjoy the fishing but to delay the inevitable arrival of Monday morning and the start of the working week. The swims weren't as spooky as my earlier chub swims and I'd happily fish into darkness, often with an owl sitting on the fence post behind me for company. The long walk back to the car was always entertaining, and, on several occasions, I'd take a wrong turn in the darkness and end up passing through far more fields than necessary. On one occasion, the twenty minute walk took over an hour as I totally lost my bearings. Heaven knows what the farmer thought if he saw a head torch zigzagging across his fields, and over fences and hedges on his land.

The long walk was always worth the effort; I learnt plenty and caught plenty. I experimented with baiting patterns and also started to understand when the river would fish well. My chosen swim was normally free but I do recall turning up one evening to learn from an angler that he had caught barbel all day when it was hot and bright, and that he was totally out of bait!

The halibut pellet hook-bait and upstream swim accounted for my personal-best barbel that was just short of double figures. It took me another four years to top that fish. I rarely fished the more convenient downstream swims but one warm summer's evening I joined my friend and bankside chef extraordinaire Mick Cottam, who had taken the easy option of fishing near the car park. He had arrived mid-afternoon and first baited his swim with hemp and corn, selecting to fish a spot where the river narrowed and the pace was much quicker.

When tackling-up, he discovered he'd forgotten his reels and had to pack up and return home. It was over an hour before he was back at his swim and the baiting-up and resting of the swim had obviously worked well. He'd already had a few barbel by the time I arrived.

In the next few hours, as the day started to cool, I witnessed some frenetic barbel action as Mick took one fish after another – he couldn't keep both rods in the water at once. I was assisting him with the landing of fish and rebaiting of the rods but even that wasn't enough. Even one of his rods couldn't keep up with the pace and the top section snapped after one bold barbel bite. He still landed that fish of about six pounds after an entertaining struggle.

The non-stop action was topped by a fish of 9lb 15oz. Mick could have felt cheated by that slightly cruel weight but, despite the broken rod, there were no complaints from him after the action he had just experienced. Throughout this unbelievable session my two rods, stationed only metres upstream but perhaps crucially out of the faster flowing water, remained untouched. Obviously, fish location and bait placement were important but that day clearly illustrated to me the advantage of baiting a swim and then retreating a safe distance for a short while. The fish had clearly confidently started feeding on the bait and couldn't get enough of it after that. It's also something I've observed Martin do frequently with success, and a tactic that has brought me front-cover success – but more of that later.

Martin has taught me so much about river fishing, and this tale would be incomplete without including much of what he has taught me or, perhaps more precisely, what I have observed and imitated! After I'd just about started mastering those Ribble barbel, the stretch I favoured was lost to many including me. I started fishing more with Martin on stretches further upstream that were predominantly chub water. Many a day was spent fishing a spot for 15–30 minutes with bread or meat on a size 4 hook with 2 to 4 LG shot, depending on flow, on a 6lb mainline. Each swim would often yield a chub or two before it was time to drop in a few free offerings and move to a new area.

I always felt that the rambling around in the day time was really just passing time, until the real action started as darkness descended and the chub felt safe from the cormorants, et al, and went hunting in the safety of the inky-blackness of night.

I always liked to make my way to my favourite swim for the last hour of light and then fish for an hour into darkness. It had been a cold, bright day and nobody had caught anything. I had two chub of about four pounds on bread flake, in quick succession after dark, and then it went quiet; it was a cold night. My hands and feet had gone numb, my nose was freezing, my breathe fogged my glasses, and it was so chilly that my ears were now not cold but burning up. When I returned to the car an hour later, the thermometer confirmed what I already knew: it was -3°F. After those two chub, I packed up and peeled my frozen landing net from the ground. Martin was fishing just downstream in a swim that he didn't normally fish, which in itself I had thought was unusual. I called in on him on my way back to the car and sat down for what was meant to be for only a brief moment.

He'd already had a few fish and within moments of my arrival landed another. Using just simple tactics of legered breadcrust, in the next hour he landed nine chub. It was amazing, and an education to watch. Martin isn't just a fantastic broadcaster and storyteller but he is genuinely a top-class angler. At times he reacted to little plucks and pulls that I barely saw register on the rod top, and had fish hooked before I'd even see the bite!

Martin combines simple methods, knowledge and experience, with amazing watercraft, and rarely fails to catch fish. I've seen it happen far too often for him to be just a lucky angler. I think, half the time nobody believes he uses such simple tactics, and, as far as Martin seems concerned, that's even better for him because he can exploit the situation even more! He always uses finely-balanced presentation, and although a size 4 hook and 6lb line might seem heavy for chub, it never seems to put them off when Martin is presenting the bait.

He lifts and manipulates the bait down the flow with his rod and line and is constantly on the move. He has an honest belief that there is a fish out there somewhere always ready to be caught and he's just got to be on that spot presenting the bait perfectly to catch. He also hovers over the rod like a heron. Martin uses the softest rod top possible as this registers more plucks and pick-ups. As soon as there is any unnatural movement on the rod top, he moves it forward just slightly to give the bait less resistance and provide the quarry with enough line to hang itself!

That magical night on the Ribble was also testament to Martin's watercraft. He just knew instinctively to fish that particular swim that I'd never seen him fish before. The swim had a near-bank tree, providing daytime cover from the bright sunshine, and was the only cover for several hundred metres. The flow was high enough to create a back eddy under the branches and the chub had obviously congregated in this area that was ordinarily uninhabitable.

Despite his many hours on the bank, Martin is always alert to situations to be exploited, and that evening he did so to the maximum. That cold evening, when Martin masterfully landed those chub in sub zero temperatures, will stay in the memory forever and the amount I learnt in that hour, watching him in action, was worth 100 plus hours of my own fishing time.

I've also done plenty of tench fishing with Martin. Despite this chapter primarily being a tale of my river-fishing, a detour into our tenching exploits reveals another similar story of being outclassed but learning so much by sitting alongside Martin. On a return from one of our summer Kennet trips, we decided to stop off at a mature gravel pit in the Cotswolds. Martin and I decided to fish more socially and chose a double swim on an island that involved us rafting our gear across to the swim in Swallows and Amazons fashion.

Baits were float-fished a rod length out in a pre-raked swim. The gentle, caster or corn hook-bait was fished just touching bottom in around 9ft of water. Martin had the right-hand of the swim and I was to the left. In an afternoon/evening session I was completely outfished, as Martin landed seven tench and a perch. For hours on end, the swim had been bubbling like a jacuzzi as the fish grubbed around the bottom, sucking in our groundbait and free offerings. We were fishing almost identical rigs and baits and our floats were approximately six feet apart. By evening those floats had moved to within inches of each other! However, he still continued to get bites and land fish whilst I remained fishless. It was terribly frustrating but a clear illustration of his skills and experience. We were both fishing 4lb line straight through and Martin was using even bigger hooks of size 12 with 5 casters, whereas, I tried a number of variations of larger and smaller hooks and still couldn't buy a bite.

Martin was carefully selecting the casters he was using as hook bait, choosing the darkest and, therefore, most buoyant. It was a secret he kindly shared with me the day after, just before we were leaving for home! I also discovered that he was fishing in a slight depression of about six inches deeper, whilst my bait, although very close, sat on the edge of the area. It shows that the tiniest of margins in presentation and depth can make a huge difference. Late in the evening my betalight float disappeared into the inky blackness and I finally managed to hook a fish. Moments later it slipped the hook as it angrily buried its head in the surrounding weed. We decided to call it a night and Martin happily strolled back to the summerhouse we were sleeping in. I skulked along behind, thoroughly frustrated and annoyed by my incompetence: I hatched a plan!

I decided that I needed to prove to myself (I know I can't compete with Martin!) that I could catch a tench from that swim and I felt I needed Martin's right-hand side of the swim to succeed. I decided to set my mobile-phone alarm for 3.30 a.m. first light. I deviously put it on vibrate, not ringtone, so as not to wake Martin. When the alarm went off I was up like a flash, dressed as quiet as a mouse, and left the summerhouse for the island tench-swim – I even had to climb out of the window as the door was metal and very rusty, and the window was the quietest escape route! I was free, and I gave Martin a triumphant but cheeky little wave goodbye as he lazily slept on.

Back on the island, I settled into the swim and baited-up. It wasn't long before the tell-tale tench bubbles started and my confidence rose accordingly. The hours soon rolled by and at six a.m, I was again becoming frustrated as the master plan was falling to pieces. I should have had a bite by now? I opted for a smaller size 16 hook and a small grain of corn; soon after, I missed a bite – I cursed Surely, Martin would be up soon, and start unintentionally rubbing my face in it again by catching tench! Another bite: fish on!

At last I had hooked a tench. It fought hard but I kept it under control. The rod top of my Drennan tench float-rod cushioned the lunges at short range and the clutch of the reel occasionally gave a little line but I was winning the battle as a golden-green flank turned on the surface. It was a good tench – certainly five pounds plus; one last lunge and, you've guessed, it was gone! The knot of the hook had given way, how I cursed myself.

It was soon 7 a.m. and Martin appeared. I felt my chances of a tench were rapidly slipping away. Martin asked how long I'd been up and I muttered only an hour or so and something about waking early and not wanting to disturb him. Only on reading this will he have learnt the truth about my very early morning disappearance and reason behind it that summer's day! The tench bubbles started to subside as the morning feeding session started to wane, Martin had no doubt bagged a couple more tench and I remained fishless. The sun was now high in the sky and, as the clock ticked towards 10 a.m. I knew time was rapidly running out; I could feel that Martin genuinely wanted me to catch a tench. He knew the journey home would be much more unpleasant if I hadn't caught! After a few dips of the float, I finally had another positive bite, to a bunch of casters on a size 12 hook, and struck into a good tench. I held on for dear life and bullied the fish into the net. No mistakes this time. I had my prize. It was a tench of 5lb 1oz and turned out to be the fish I had hooked only a few hours earlier. I found and removed my earlier size 16 hook, which was firmly in its top lip. I was relieved to have it in my net. I had my prized tench and Martin could keep his nine fish – I was delighted, and the relief was evident from my smile of belated success.

I learnt over those two days, that tench can be unbelievably timid, and counterbalancing the hook is crucial. Alongside my hook bait, I now always use very buoyant casters, pop-up imitation gentles, casters or corn, or even a small piece of coloured foam on the hook when fishing for tench. Neutralising the weight of the hook for timid tench can be the fine line between success and failure. I love just being out fishing and am normally very happy for anyone I'm with to catch. I can share in the capture almost as if it's my own, for the majority of the time. However, as the next tale unfolds, it seems that Martin's superior skills were beginning to test the joy of my sharing in the success of others.

We made a trip down to the river Wye and joined up with Will Carter for a few days. First up was a pleasurable detour to Redmire Pool. It was an honour to stand on the famous dam wall and soak up the atmosphere. It was a greater honour to meet Eddie Price who witnessed 'the monster carp in the weeds' at Redmire Pool in 1958. That Saturday afternoon, we fished the Ross-on-Wye town stretch; it was very busy and with steep banking in places. Martin decided not to fish. Will and I selected our swims and then Martin set up base camp behind my swim and listened to the football on his radio. I remember him asking what rods I was setting up and I can clearly remember silently thinking: "Please don't ask me that Martin. Just tell me what method you would use and where you'd fish in this swim and then let me catch all the fish for a change " I don't often listen to the radio whilst fishing, but was just getting into the football commentary when he wandered off, taking his radio with him, and found a swim that had been vacated. Will and I had a fishless afternoon; within an hour or so of Martin, depriving me of the radio, he had bagged two barbel to 9lb and a chub. The packed stretch had been dead for almost everyone, which made his captures even more phenomenal. Will had the pleasure of photographing the fish. My angling frustration was building.

The next morning, we sped off to a Wye & Usk Foundation stretch of the river Wye at Holme Lacy. The river was in perfect condition and tactics were straightforward. Two rods both on 6lb line straight through to a size 4 hook with either breadcrust or sausage meat for hook bait. 2–4 LG shot were used as leger weights. We had the stretch to ourselves and spread out along the bank. I was in the swim furthest downstream, with Martin above me on a wide bend in the river. I soon had two baits in the water, one mid-river and the other fishing the inside slack. Five minutes in and I'd had a small chub. I recall thinking I'd mastered this river-fishing: I'd turned up at a new venue, selected a swim and the creases to fish, and was away in minutes. Over the next few hours, things started to turn sour.

I could just see Martin upstream on the bend. From the corner of my eye I'd seen him catch a few, and I wandered up the bank to investigate. Within a few moments, Martin hooked and landed chub number five. I went back to my swim and fished on for another couple of hours. In that time, Martin doubled his chub tally – it was now ten chub to one! Every time I looked upstream he was into another fish; for the second time in two days, Martin was leading the way. It was no consolation that Will Carter, and our host Martin Mumby, had caught little. The many fishing sessions where I had been completely outclassed were now beginning to play on my mind. I stomped back up the bank to Martin's swim – in fact, by now, I was becoming a bit annoyed by the constant batterings, and the red mist had descended.

I had barely stepped into Martin's swim when he landed chub number eleven, and soon after, number twelve. This was now becoming ridiculous. My cool exterior hid my bubbling anger. Not for the first time my pride was dented, and I was questioning my own angling ability. Martin told me the water temperature was warm and that he had been feeding the swim aggressively as he expected the chub to be on the move and feeding well. He was obviously proving his assumption was correct too; he always seems to get it spot on. Once all the fine detail is identified, Martin hones his tactics to the required method. It just all added to the anger!

I really enjoy my fishing and just revel in being out in the country and relaxing by a lake or river, but that morning I really was wound up. I went back to my swim and mixed up some big balls of bread mash. I fed the swim, concentrating most of the feed down the inside crease. In desperation, and in a bid to at least compete with Martin, I decided to leave my rods out and rest the swim for an hour or so. I lay on the grass path that offered the only flat surface, curled up in a ball, counted to ten to calm down, and then went to sleep on the floor.

An hour or so later I woke up in a far more relaxed state. I had no idea how many more Martin had caught but I was determined to at least have something to show for the weekend. As the red mist seemed to have lifted, I recast the rods. I fished them both downstream on the inside crease using breadcrust on one rod and sausage meat on the other. I immediately started getting little plucks and indications on the rod tops, and missed a possible bite. I recast the sausage meat rod and within seconds the top slammed round and a fish was on. Because of the violence of the bite, I expected it to be one of the Wye's plentiful barbel but it held its position in the current rather than shooting off downstream. It certainly was a heavyweight and the resistance it offered, as it manoeuvred itself into the faster current of mid-river, was immense. The rod took an alarming curve as the fish was drawn upstream, resisting with all its might. As the fish came level with me, it surfaced a couple of rod lengths out. I could see it was a massive chub and a certain personal best. It just hung itself in the fast current and I went all jittery as I tried to grab my landing net and scoop up the beast. I was praying over and over that it

wouldn't throw the hook. I drew it upstream and then used the current to sweep it into the waiting net. I felt immense relief once I knew it was safely in the net, and, within seconds, was filled with elation – I did one of those silly dances reserved for a big-fish capture. Martin was quickly down to weigh-in my new personal best at 5lb 10oz, and the others came down and marvelled at its size.

Photographs were duly taken and the fish was carefully returned to fight another day. The blank of the day before and Martin's bag of chub were forgotten; I was on cloud-nine for days. The joy was topped off when the personal best chub and I graced the front cover of the Angler's Mail the following week!

Despite fishing the Wye only a few times, it has certainly been kind to me. Months after landing my personal best chub I returned to the Wye in early March. Martin had been due to travel with me but had to cancel due to a hospital appointment. I took along my wife Michelle and our three-month old daughter, Ellie. After a blank first day on the town stretch, when the sun was high in the sky, I returned the day after to have a fantastic day on the river topped off by personal best number two from the Wye. I had initially elected to fish the members' bank, but when I wandered along the river to select a swim it didn't feel right. The sun was again out and the members' bank was bathed in sunshine. The day-ticket side was more shaded, with trees casting a comforting shadow for the fish. Following a maxim taught to me by others: "If you think it, do it", the idea being that your thoughts and intuition are normally right, I carried all my gear back to where I had been dropped off and decided to set up on one of the first swims available on the day-ticket stretch.

I fished one rod for barbel and the other for pike. The barbel rod was a feeder packed with pellets (that could barely escape through the feeder holes) that had a very healthy dose of molasses poured over them. Hook bait was a 14mm halibut pellet hair rigged to a 12in braided hook-length. The rod was only cast infrequently to allow the molasses and pellet scent trail to be detected by the barbel. The pike rod kept me entertained for most of the day as I hooked and landed six pike on trotted baits. Despite only being fish into low double figures, all the pike scrapped hard in the current. I almost ran out of bait as I frequently fed chopped fish and gentles into the swim to keep the attraction level high. Several times I saw pike striking at the bleak shoals I had formed by feeding the gentles.

The best pike of the day was caught as Michelle arrived, with Ellie in her pram. I have a fantastic picture of Ellie, who weighed just into double figures, with a pike that was within ounces of her weight looking over the pram, as Ellie slept on, oblivious to all the commotion!

The barbel rod only sprang into life in late afternoon and a 7lb fish was duly landed. As evening drew in, the rain began to fall and the steep, clay bank became dangerous. I was about to pack up when I had a slamming bite on the halibut pellet and molasses feeder set-up. After slipping and sliding through the mud, I landed a big barbel. I weighed and photographed a personal best at 10lb 2oz at the water's edge before returning it. The banks were too dangerous to risk anything other than a quick snap of the fish lying in the net. I'm disappointed I don't have a better picture, but safety first dictated. I returned it and I won't forget personal best number two from the Wye.

Just before writing this chapter I made my third trip to the Wye in the hope of a third personal best after deciding on an all-out attack on the Wye pike, but it wasn't to be. I stayed in a cottage in Ross-on-Wye and was on the riverbank after the shortest of walks. Armed with several metres of rope and a dog spike that opened up many more swims on the slippery and steep banks, I wandered up and down the town stretch, trotting with smelt as I went. On the first morning I only fished for a few hours and had three pike. All of similar size, they fought hard in the strong current and would have weighed in at about eight pounds each. Incidentally, all of the fish came as I slowly retrieved the bait upstream after trotting as far downstream as possible.

I had great expectations for the remaining days but the February weather turned bitterly cold. I lost a small jack early on day two, again on the retrieve, and that was the end of the action. It snowed later that day and the fish seemed to turn off despite my best efforts. I should have switched over to the chubbing gear, but persevered for a big pike.

Martin Salisbury with Wye pike and daughter Ellie in pram

I've just bought a new boat and have still have my eye on a personal best pike, but I imagine it will come from a lake I have identified, rather than from the Wye and its fast-flowing depths.

The River Wye is a magical river stuffed with fish, and I very much imagine, I will still have an annual trip or two to fish for its chub, barbel and pike. I'm looking forward to the Wye being kind to me once again. I'm sure it'll deliver plenty of barbel and a six pound-plus chub would be a very nice treat. My personal best chub was of huge proportions and made a lasting memory – anything bigger will be a true monster chub of the Wye!

Mick Holgate is married to Carole; they have two children that they are both immensely proud of. Much of his working life is involved in football at a professional level with Macclesfield Town. An avid angler from being a young schoolboy his ambition is to catch a seven pound chub. Hopefully, one day, he will get his wish of joining me on the River Kennet for a few days.

I've been a coarse angler for some forty-plus years, fishing canals, lakes and rivers. Some years ago I joined a fishing club that had the rights to a nice stretch of the River Ribble; I wanted to improve my fishing on running water. The club held regular, roving matches on Sundays, and when work permitted, I would fish the match to look, listen and learn, and hopefully, catch more fish. I failed miserably. I observed some of the better anglers who made trotting or feeder-fishing look easy but I did improve when I got the right tackle for the job.

It was an enjoyable learning curve; running water became my favourite choice when planning a fishing trip. It was one Sunday, after a roving match, that I met Martin James on the River Ribble. I was so fed up catching small eels that I decided to call it a day. Making my way back to the car-park, I informed the lads I was going and I would see them the following Thursday at the club meeting. As I was putting my tackle in the car, another car rolled into the car-park, a man and his wife started to unload a rod, a landing net and a bag of bread. I looked across and shouted, "I hope you have more luck than me."

"Have you not caught anything then?" enquired the new arrival. "I've been plagued by eels, and decided to leave early." I said

"Oh dear." said the angler as he walked towards me. "Tell me," he asked, "What's the weight of your biggest chub?"

I looked at him and said, "I've had two chub that weighed 4lb 6oz each and they're the best chub I've had."

The angler pulled a small card from his wallet and said, "Give me a ring and have a day's fishing with me, I'll help you catch a 5lb chub."

I took the card and thanked him for his offer; before saying goodbye I wished him good luck as he and his wife walked towards the river with just rod, net and bread. As I got into my car I glanced at the card the angler had given to me. It read Martin James, Angling Author, broadcaster and consultant.

As I was talking to him in the car-park I thought I recognised his distinctive voice from hearing it on the radio. I was undecided as to whether or not to ring him. After about three days I decided I would ring Martin and see if he would let me have a day's fishing with him. "Oh," said Martin when I rang him, "I remember you. We met in the car-park didn't we?" "That's right." I said.

"When can you go fishing?" enquired Martin. "Friday is my day off." I told him. "That's it then," said Martin. "Meet me on Friday and I'll take you to the River Aire." After fixing the time and getting directions from Martin, I duly waited in great anticipation for Friday afternoon to arrive.

If I am being honest, I was quite nervous when I knocked at Martin's front door. I needn't have worried as he welcomed me in, then outlined where we were going and what our chances would be. Things didn't look good, with the day being very cold, an easterly wind and a cloudless sky. Martin said despite the weather we would probably find the odd fish later in the day.

On the drive over to the River Aire near Keighley, Martin explained that, due to the lack of rainfall, he expected a very low, clear river; we needed stealth in order to succeed. Once on the river bank Martin surprised me with the simplicity of the tackle, passing me an 11'6" Avon action rod to which was attached an old Mitchell 300 reel loaded with 6lb line. We had a landing net, a rod rest and a small bag containing some extra-thick bread. At the business end of the 6lb line Martin got me to attach a Partridge barbless hook size 4. Pinched on the line 3–4in above the hook were 2 LG shot.

Martin handed me a small square of sponge saying, "That's your seat for the day." Martin had me bait with crust then chuck it under a bush overhanging the water. A minute later the rod pulled round savagely: I lost the fish. During the afternoon as we walked from swim to swim, I listened and learned all the time as Martin passed on many tips regarding tackle, swims, feeding, casting and clothing. Despite fishing for a couple of hours without any more sign of a bite, Martin advised me to be patient, the chub would show as the sun began to set and light values decreased.

In fairness, the river was exceptionally clear and very low and the easterly wind did not help matters. After a fresh brew, courtesy of Martin's small stove, we fished on into dusk, warm and refreshed. Throughout the fishing session Martin did not fish; he guided and advised me, telling me that he needed to concentrate on what I was doing rather than fishing himself. As the daylight slowly started to fade we sat side-by-side watching the soft top of the Avon rod. Suddenly, the tip moved slightly then pulled steadily round. Martin shouted, "Strike!" I did, but missed the bite. I must admit, given how difficult the day had been, I might have blown my chance of a fish. Martin looked at me then said, "You missed that one, but what does that bite tell you?" Before I had chance to think Martin said, "It means you have one or more fish in your swim, re-bait and cast." Within five minutes of my large piece of crust settling on the bottom, my rod tip pulled round.

This time I was more alert, my timing was better. The rod hooped over a little, line was taken by the fish. "Good boy!" said Martin. "Keep the pressure on; don't give him any slack line." As I turned the fish, and eventually got it to the surface in front of me, Martin quickly had it in the net. He then produced a set of scales and weighed the fish: 4lb 10oz – a new personal best, I was elated. The fish was scale-perfect. "Well done", said Martin, "re-bait and cast again, I'll release the fish further along the river." Baiting with trembling hands, I dropped a piece of crust tight to the bank. Martin returned, sitting next to me in the semi-darkness. Ten minutes elapsed then the rod top came to life for a fraction of a second. I was on 'red alert.' Sure enough, as the tip pulled round, I was 'on the case' with a swift strike meeting with solid resistance. The fish stayed low and felt like a good one. The soft action rod did its work, and with steady pressure I started to gain line. The fish eventually surfaced, another large chub glinting back at me as it was illuminated by my head torch. Martin netted the fish then weighed it. He turned the scales towards me, the needle settled on 5lb exactly. I was ecstatic, a new personal best for the second time during the evening. We both laughed out loud, I thanked Martin for his help and advice. With the fish resting in the landing net Martin produced a small digital camera from his jacket pocket then said, "I'll take a couple of pictures before we release the chub."

Martin told me how to hold the fish safely – keeping many of my fingers out of the way so the fish would be the star of the picture. Martin then tilted my fishing hat upwards to avoid shadows being cast on my face. Pictures completed, the chub returned, we called an end to the session and walked back to the car.

As we drove back to Martin's house I told him how much I enjoyed the day, having learnt so much in just a few hours. Arriving back at Martin's he asked if I would like to go fishing the following week. I instantly said "Yes." That first fishing session took place several years ago. Since then, we have fished together once a week throughout the season whenever my work has allowed and Martin has not been abroad, fishing.

Over the past few years, whilst fishing with Martin, we have had many enjoyable sessions particularly on the River Ribble in Lancashire and the River Aire in Yorkshire. One productive year for big fish was 2003–2004 season; one session in particular stands out. It was February 2004 and I rang Martin to see if we were going fishing on the River Ribble.

Martin laughed and said fishing would be a waste of time. The temperature of the water was very low, there was a cold easterly wind, little cloud cover and the river was low and clear.

Martin thought it would be better to forget fishing until conditions changed. I wanted to go as it was my only day off work that week. I couldn't fish again until the next week. I suggested that we go and give it a couple of hours and see what happens. Martin reluctantly agreed. I set off in the afternoon to pick him up. We went to a private stretch of the Ribble, not surprisingly the car-park was empty. Only fools would fish with such grim prospects. Our quarry at that time of year would be chub, they will oblige with a bite or two when no other fish will.

Making our way up river, we selected two swims some thirty yards apart, close to an overhanging oak tree and two large alder trees. We then proceeded to fish. Try as I might, my bread crust hook-bait remained untouched, but Martin fared better, missing the first bite then getting a nice chub of 5lb 3oz. Half-an-hour before dark I made two mugs of tea; after a short break with a couple of sandwiches we fished on. Owls hooting in the far-bank trees provided the only noise apart from the sound of the river as it ran over some big boulders further downstream. The peaceful and pleasant scene was shattered as Martin shouted, "Mick I've got one, can you come down?" I wound my rod in and made my way briskly down to Martin's swim.

When I got there the swim was empty apart from Martin's chair, rod rest and tackle bag. Martin was some fifteen yards downstream with an alarming bend in his Chevin rod – a fish was stripping his 6lb breaking strain line from the reel at an alarming rate! I grabbed the landing net then watched the rest of the tussle between angler and fish. Eventually, after several forceful runs, I could make out the shape of a large barbel beginning to tire under the pressure Martin was applying. I carefully went downstream of Martin with the landing net ready. This allowed

Martin to drift the fish into the net. The barbel, obviously a double, was confirmed, pulling the scales round to 10lb 10oz. I did the honours with camera, Martin then released the fish. I shook his hand to say well done. Returning to my swim, I continued fishing. Fifteen minutes later Martin bellowed through the darkness, "Give us a lift Mick, this is a good'un!"

Once more I wound in, swiftly returning to Martin's swim. As I got closer I could see the soft-action rod bent into the sort of curve all anglers love. The clutch on his old Mitchell 300 reel was working overtime; Martin was up out of his seat continually adjusting the angle of his rod as he fought to subdue the fish. Eventually, he had the fish under control on the surface in front of him. It was the biggest chub I had ever seen. Martin was smiling like a Cheshire cat as the huge fish slid over the landing net. It was weighed on two sets of scales and they confirmed a weight of 7lb 10oz. "I've done it!" said Martin. "I've done a seven-pounder at last!" This fish was not only a personal best for Martin, it was also his first chub over the seven pound mark. For any angler it was a huge fish, coming from a North West river made it even more special. I did the honours with the camera – also reminding Martin that fishing in these conditions was a "waste of time!' What a brace of fish to catch in such poor conditions. Both had found Martin's bread hook-bait to their liking, although my own efforts that evening did not produce a bite.

When we packed up that night we talked all the way back to the car park about how that session might never have even taken place had I not persuaded him to fish for a couple of hours. We still laugh about Martin saying that we were wasting our time going fishing. On reflection,

Martin with 10lb 10oz Ribble Barbel

that session was probably the best few hours of 'wasted time' we ever spent together. Although I fished hard and caught nothing, I was pleased to witness such fish and to share in their capture. Some weeks later we would return to those very same swims and it would be my turn to have my stick bent and my string pulled.

It was the last day of the coarse-fishing season, 14 March 2004. I picked up Martin at his home to make a return trip to the River Ribble, fishing the same stretch where Martin caught his personal best chub along with a double figure barbel in February. We decided to fish the same swims fished previously. The river was low and clear but it was a bit warmer. We started about four o'clock in the afternoon, deciding we would fish for an hour or so into darkness.

In fairness, the daylight hours produced nothing, but I was confident that when the evening closed in, one or two chub might show, and dine on the mashed bread I had introduced into the swim. Martin was using similar tactics in his swim but he was using sausage meat paste. Just before darkness we had a fresh brew with a sandwich before continuing our quest for chub. Into darkness, my first bite brought me a chub of around three-and-a-half pounds, lower downstream Martin was catching one or two chub as well.

About an hour into darkness I noticed a small pluck on my rod tip. I was instantly ready for any further indication when ever so slowly and steadily the rod tip started to pull round. I lifted into the fish with a sweeping strike and felt a solid resistance from what was obviously a good fish. Although it took some line, it stayed down on the bottom of the river; the bend in my rod

7lb 10oz chub from River Ribble

6lbs 7oz Chub

caused me to smile as I played the chub firmly but carefully. Eventually, by the light of my head torch I could see the big white lips of a large Ribble chub coming towards me. With the fish safely landed, I could see it was obviously a personal best chub. I put the net back into the water to rest the fish, then hurriedly made my way downstream to inform Martin. "I've done it!" I exclaimed as I arrived at Martin's swim. "I've got a big chub. Can you bring the camera and scales up for me?"

Martin quickly wound his rod in. After carefully weighing the fish we settled on 6lb 7oz. I was delighted with my new personal best chub. Martin took a couple of trophy shots for my photo album. Our decision to return to the same swims we fished in the February had once again produced a big Ribble chub, only this time I was the lucky recipient. Since that particular season we have noticed a decline in the weights of big chub caught from the river. Five and six pound fish are still caught, but not so frequently. Although some anglers still insist on estimating weights of fish caught, this cannot be relied on. An example of this happened a couple of seasons ago. As I fished a cattle-drink swim on the River Ribble one evening, a game-angler was making his way past me just as my rod pulled round; I struck into a nice chub.

I netted the fish; the angler came down the river bank to take a closer look at what I had caught. The fish was over four pounds, a good shape but quite hollow. The game-angler said, "That's the biggest chub I've seen along this stretch, it must weigh about six pounds." I laughed saying it wouldn't make five pounds. He told me I was talking nonsense. I took out the weigh scales then let him see the dial of the scales as my 'six' pound chub pulled the needle round to just short of 4lb 8oz. He shook his head in disbelief, he was convinced the fish was bigger. I told him that looks can be very deceptive. Later in the season that same fish might weigh five pounds. This example illustrates how anglers get the weight wrong without scales; they're the only way to be sure of what your catch weighs. Over the years that I have fished with Martin, I have managed to glean lots of useful tips and knowledge from him, in fact, about three years ago, he taught me how to cast a fly, now each season I do a little bit of fly fishing; I have found this to be very enjoyable; it also helped my coarse fishing: by entering the water and wading, I now take note of fish-holding areas like underwater obstructions or depressions in the river bed.

I then return to these areas during the coarse season with a good understanding of the underwater topography. Fly fishing also lets you see the massive changes to the fish-holding areas caused by the winter floods and how last season's 'banker' swim can suddenly fail to produce, due to such changes.

We have also had lots of fun while out fishing and I have been the butt of Martin's humour several times due to my dislike of fishing near cows and bulls. Fishing on the River Aire one afternoon, we arrived at an area of the river that Martin said would be better fished from the other bank. I looked across, seeing a rather large brown bull in the field; I declined Martin's invitation to cross the river lower down and fish the swims he fancied. I said, "You go, I'll stay and fish from this bank." Off he went and sure enough the bull paid him no attention: he caught chub I didn't. With a bend in his rod Martin shouted across to me, "Fortune favours the brave!" I sat and watched Martin land three decent chub in quick succession whilst I remained biteless.

Mick Holgate with a nice Chub

As we walked back to the car that night, Martin said that he would return the next day to fish again. Sadly, I had to go to work. I said I would give him a call to see how the fishing was going. The next afternoon I rang Martin and said "How's the river fishing?"

Martin said, "I'm not fishing, I've just been charged by a bull. To escape I had to wade out into the river and get across to the other side!" Martin explained that if he walked upstream or downstream the bull would walk up or down to stay level with him, still snorting and pawing the ground. Martin decided to back off and take a detour around the field to make his way back to his car. I laughed along with Martin at his plight that day and reminded him of his message to me the previous day that "fortune favours the brave". Martin's escapade with the bull that day reminded me of a sign I had seen earlier that season whilst fishing for barbel on the River Teme in Worcestershire. In very large letters the farmer's sign stated: "Walkers and ramblers go free but the bulls charge". Needless to say I have never adopted Martin's policy of fortune favouring the brave and that's the way I plan to keep it!

I was delighted when Martin asked me to contribute to this book and I would like to take this opportunity to thank him for all the help and advice he has given me with over the years. We've had some real red-letter days, also days when the fish completely ignored our attempts to catch them, which are what makes fishing so enjoyable: no two days are the same. Even those days when we fail to catch, we enjoyed being at the water's edge, sharing a joke or putting the world to rights over a mug of tea. I think I should mention that over many years now, Martin has helped to raise many thousands of pounds for various charities.

He has guided and assisted many anglers, for which he makes no charges, to become better anglers. He has always welcomed the opportunity to help youngsters into this great sport or hobby of ours, and literally thousands of new converts have passed through his hands over the years. I feel that Martin has put more back into angling than he has taken out. These days that's something quite unique.

Despite Martin having a bus pass for some years, he has entered the twilight years of a lifetime's fishing still burning with enthusiasm and drive for all things angling. I, for one, hope he remains that way for many years to come. I also look forward to hearing his opening line when we speak on the telephone most weeks. "Hello my boy, are we fishing today?" Yes Martin we'll be fishing.

Phil Chun, the general manager of Tackle Discounts based in Swindon, is without doubt one of the finest anglers I have had the pleasure to share time with and gain knowledge from through being in his company. Married to Nina, who is not only a great lady but also a very good angler. They have a beautiful young daughter, Lauren, who no doubt will follow in Mum and Dad's footsteps. Watching Phil in action, I marvel at his casting and fishing skills.

Over the last twenty-seven years I have fished for most coarse fish species and had an odd venture into sea fishing. I have been lucky enough to fish some truly great waters, some that were un-fished, some busy day-ticket fisheries and some with no fish! But that's a story for another day.

During my fishing career I have spent a lot of time fishing with and talking to anglers from all over the world. One of the things that crops up in conversation time and time again is luck and skill. I have in the past had people say I am lucky, while on the flip side, others say I am a good angler and that I could catch fish in a muddy puddle when it rains. I have thought long and hard about these discussions and thought I would write about some captures I have had over the years, to decide if it was luck or skill that helped me catch the fish.

I'll start at the beginning as that's always a good place to start! I first went fishing with my parents and my uncle whilst on holiday in Swanage in Dorset. It was just crab-fishing with lines, but, to say I enjoyed it would be a massive understatement. I had the bug from day one and could not wait to go again. Each morning I would be up before everyone else in the house where we were staying and have all the gear ready to go as soon as I could get an adult willing to come with me. I started catching crabs relatively easily, which, to be honest, was down to luck more than judgement, however, even then, What I quickly started to work out was: there were some areas better than others, better times of the tide, and which baits caught the most crabs.

After a few sessions, I spotted some small wrasse and weavers and wanted to catch these – to be honest my first fish capture was a fluke. One day, the small tackle shop in Swanage did not have any frozen mackerel and so I bought some ragworm. Initially, I did not think this had been such a good idea when I got them out and realised the little blighters had nasty fangs which tried to bite me. By putting a small section of rag on the hook and fishing my rig off the bottom, instead of on the bottom where I was catching crabs, I soon caught what I later found out was a weaver fish. These little fish were great, I could catch quite a few and then, every now and again, I would catch a blenny or a small wrasse. I did not know that the weaver's spine had poison and so just used to grab hold of them to unhook them. One day a lady was chatting to my Dad when I caught one and she said, "You should use a rag for holding them as someone here last week had to go to hospital as the spine is poisonous." That was lucky!

From those early days onwards I could think of nothing else but going fishing. I found a stream in the local village and taught myself to catch minnows, then an odd dace and, the highlight of any day, a tiny chub. During this time I had some luck, but I worked at my fishing. I read every book I could find at local jumble sales, or ones bought for me as presents.

I walked up and down the stream and tried different swims. I have always been competitive and always played lots of sport. I do not see the point of doing anything in life unless you give it your all and do the best you can. This led to my early interest in bait to help give me an edge over two of lads in the village I had managed to convince that fishing was a good idea. I started raiding my Mum's cupboards for anything I could crush, mash up or turn into bait.

I bought an old hand-wind meat mincer from somewhere and started crushing Weetabix, Shreddies and all manner of cereals to create groundbaits. I did not think my Mum was missing the food from the cupboards until a few years ago when I started my specialist bait business and she told me how she knew her food supply kept disappearing. Anyway, back to the luck and skill debate. I believe this hard work and commitment helped me catch more and bigger fish than my friends could and this is when my angling passion really took hold.

I joined a local club that had four or five gravel pits and started on one called 'The Large Lake'. As the name suggests this was a big fifty acre-plus pit with most species of coarse fish present, but not easy fishing. First day out, I went with a friend from the village. Not knowing the lake, we went into a swim near the gate and started setting up. My friend was very meticulous about setting his gear up and so, by the time he was ready, I had been fishing with a basic float-rod set-up for a while and had already managed to catch around fifteen small roach.

We did not have a clue about fishing gravel pits and so just balled some groundbait made from mashed bread and curry powder and fed a few gentles over the top. We got off to a great start catching roach, almost one a chuck – and then I hooked something bigger than I had ever felt in my small village stream. A dogged fight ensued until I finally netted a perch of around one-and-a-half pounds. Lucky? Yes! But this is where the learning curve really began.

Over the coming weeks we continued to fish 'the large lake' and gradually learnt what we could by reading books, but things where only getting slightly better, until one day a chap started fishing the swim next door. He had two feeder rods out, fishing swim feeders for tench, a tactic I had read about but never actually seen. When he caught his first tench I had to go and have a look. I was amazed at how beautiful it was in the flesh rather than on the page of a book or in the Angler's Mail. I probably annoyed the angler with my onslaught of questions but have to say I owe him a big 'thank-you'.

He told me about fishing bread flake, showed me his tactics and generally gave me all the advice he could. If I ever see him on the bank I will let him know how that day changed my angling, from then on I wanted to catch the biggest fish I could; it sent me in the direction I followed for many years – specimen angling.

At school around this time, my friends used to say I was the luckiest angler they knew. But my very waking hour was spent thinking about my fishing. I got in trouble numerous times from drawing maps of swims and designing new rigs in the back of my school books. Just a few weeks ago my wife discovered my old history exercise book in the loft and found there was nothing in it apart from fishing diagrams! I persuaded my Dad to take me and drop me off at the lake as often as possible; then I began catching tench. The club had one junior match each year on the lake and so my fishing buddies and I entered. We were rubbish! I caught two roach and my mates blanked, but luck was on my side this day. I went to the far side to join my friend for the afternoon after the match. I was fishing the quiver tip for the first time and we sat there for around three hours without a bite. I was chatting to him when I thought I had knocked my rod with my basket (yes, basket not box!). I picked the rod up and put it back on my rod rest.

A few minutes later I thought I had carelessly knocked it off again and decided that I would have to move the feeder from the spot I was fishing; I started to wind in. The rig was stuck solid, presumably stuck in weed! No – it just pulled back! There was a nod, nod, nod on the end, but the fish was not fighting like the tench I had been catching. I knew I had a fish, but it felt so odd! When it got close I could not believe my eyes as a big dustbin lid-shaped bream came across my net. We weighed the fish and were so excited; I was the first person I had ever seen catch a bream – and not a small bream: it weighed in at 11lb 8oz. I sent the pictures to the Angler's Mail and won the weekly, junior prize: now, in my eyes, I was a proper angler.

Over the following couple of years I read more and more, and spoke to every angler possible to try and gain more information on targeting big fish, in particular the bream in the lake. In time I managed to catch forty-two bream including nine doubles. At that time I convinced my parents I had to night-fish and eventually they let me, as long as I was with a couple of friends. We used to cycle around eight miles to the lake and pre-bait a spot the evening before, when our parents thought we were at each other's houses! Then, we would night-fish under our umbrellas. We did not have all the luxuries that today's anglers enjoy and slept on mats on the floor – if we slept at all. My friends would generally stay up until about 1 a.m. but most nights I would sit up all night-long, watching a float or, with my now advanced tactics of feeder rods, my washing-up liquid bottle tops for indicators.

Without wanting to sound as if I am blowing my own trumpet, I normally caught more than my friends, and in fact, started to get known to the other anglers on the lake as 'the lad who catches all the fish!' I did hold the lake record for tench and bream at the time and also had the largest recorded catch of tench in a single session from the lake: in one afternoon I caught 192lb of tench and 72lb of bream.

Over the next few years I fished all of the lakes on the club ticket and caught the biggest tench, bream, roach and perch each season on all the lakes! Was I a lucky angler at this stage? Yes, sometimes, but I worked hard at my fishing, I experimented with various baits and tried to do things differently to other anglers. I had read everything possible about how different species would feed in various conditions and I spent hour upon hour walking around the lakes finding fish, baiting spots and learning all I could about my prey.

I am now going to jump around eight years to a time when I started carp-fishing. I had taught my (now wife) Nina to fish and am lucky to this day that she loves it and is now very good at it. We used to tench-fish two or three evenings every week and we would camp out three nights before the start of the fishing season to get the spot we wanted to fish for the first week. I had achieved a lot with my tench and bream, and by this time chub and perch-fishing too, but was always looking for more. Carp fishing was becoming more popular, and I had read articles about them, so decided that was my next target. I started on waters I knew had lots of them and caught numerous fish, even dabbling with match-fishing for them for while, but found I was always trying to catch as big a fish as possible and so match fishing was not really for me.

By this time, I was making virtually all my own baits, including the groundbaits, glugs, flavoured corn, and then eventually on to boilies. I joined a new water where I wanted to try a new bait I had been working on and to test it fairly against others that had a good reputation and following in the market. I hoped to see if I was lucky with my baits or were they in fact, good!

Before fishing the lake I went for a walk around and spoke to the anglers who were fishing. They all gave me the same information: that there were quite a few carp of double figures, but you would be doing well to catch one or two '20s' a year.

First session, I decided to go with minimal tackle and try to just get some bites. I turned up and walked right the way around the lake to see if I could see any fish and what other anglers were catching. Most of them were in the main part of the lake and had only caught a few; I asked why no one fished the narrow end of the lake and was told, nothing ever gets caught from there. Yes, you know where I was going – into the narrow end! I fished in the margins near an overhanging bush, baiting with some chopped worms and home-made groundbait. First cast: a bream of around four pounds – a great start. That evening I went on to catch eleven bream up to 9lb, three tench and six carp, the biggest going 21lb 6oz. I don't think this was luck: I walked the whole lake and spoke to everyone, but something had drawn me to the narrow end. I always like to look for places no one else fishes as often you catch better fish in these areas which are away from those more heavily fished.

Second session on the lake, I arrived to find the wind pushing into the far corner and was amazed. The six other anglers present were all on the back of the wind. I went to the far end and fished across to a large reed bed into where the wind was pushing. It was not going to plan; I could see fish stirring up the bottom by the reeds, but I was not getting a bite. After a bit of thought I decided to fish PVA bags as close to the reed line as I possible and stand close to my rods ready for a take. Fishing little bright home-made pop-ups, I went on to catch six twenty pounds-plus carp that afternoon before I ran out of bait! I had a new lake record of 29lb 13oz, and at one point, a brace of twenty-four-pounders. I fished the lake for the next three months to test my new baits and went on to catch thirteen different twenty-pound carp when, as far as I know, only three others were caught by other anglers. This success was not easy though and was not just down to the bait. I found the lake easy to catch numbers of carp, but catching the bigger ones was hard work. After lots and lots of trying different methods and fishing all areas, I finally sussed out how to catch them.

Most people would fish near to the point swim as carp seemed to always be present there and most people would bait with one, maybe two, kilos of bait. I had worked out that the narrow end, which was still being ignored by other anglers, held the better fish at night. The small carp moved in there as well but I tailored my tactics to target the twenty-pounders. I would only ever fish from 6 p.m. until 6 a.m. as I would then have to go to work. I would put in around 15kg of groundbait as soon as I arrived. This sounds a lot but there where a lot of bream and smaller carp. I fished one rod onto the bait with an 18mm boillie to catch what I could, and one rod off the edge of the baited spot. I could target the better fish by fishing double 24mm boilies (to avoid the bream).

I only fished the lake for around three months – to be honest, I was catching so many fish each night that I was no use at work the next day! During my time on that lake I started my bait company, as firstly all my friends, then everyone on the lake, kept asking for my special boilies. I worked full time during the day and then spent most evenings making baits and sourcing new ingredients. Around twelve months later I took the plunge and went full time into the bait business which had really taken off. This had its downside though: my fishing time was seriously limited.

I went through a real purple patch with my fishing even though my time was limited to quick overnight sessions. One weekend my intention was to go catfish fishing, as I had only ever caught one whilst on holiday a few years earlier, however, the lake was fully booked and so me and Nina my wife went back home! I said to Nina, "We have to go somewhere as I just have a feeling things are right today!" I cannot explain this feeling but I do get it from time to time – for some reason I just know I am going to catch. I made a call to my friend's brother to see if I could fish the lake that they used for water-skiing and kindly got permission, as long as I only fished from one swim which was away from the boats. I had carp gear with me but thought I would probably catch some of the tench present. At around seventy acres and with access to just one swim, options were limited and so I made up a spod mix containing hemp, a mixture of different sized pellets, sweet corn, bloodworm and my own boilies, which I deposited just off the marginal shelf to one side of me.

Phil Chun with a carp of 29lb 13 ounces

One rod went onto this spot and two rods I fished with just PVA bags of pellets and pop-up baits to areas I could find less weed! We settled down for the evening and had a nice bottle of wine in the hope of maybe getting a tench or two. Half-an-hour later I had a stuttery take and soon landed a nice tench of around six pounds. Nothing else occurred before we went to bed except a few tench rolling in the area. At around four in the morning I was awoken by my bite alarm on the nearside rod absolutely screaming and an angry fish taking line of the reel. I struck into what was obviously a good carp – and not a happy one! A terrific fight ensued, with the fish finding every weedbed possible on the way in. I had no idea how big it really was at this point as the biggest carp I know of that had ever been caught in the lake was 34lb.

Nina netted it first time and looked around to me and said, "It's a good carp." On the unhooking mat I unfolded the net and was amazed to see the most stunning carp I have ever seen: big, apple slice-like scales along its flank and then little pin prick scales around its shoulders. Onto the scales, they pulled round and settled on 37lb 8oz. What a result: first time on the lake and with no previous knowledge. I have to admit, there was certainly an element of luck.

I continued to fish the lake for the rest of that summer but it was very difficult, with a few blank sessions and getting pestered by signal crayfish – I could not even catch tench, so I had to work out a plan. I tried fishing almost every area of the swim and eventually found spots where there seemed to be less crayfish and I could catch tench. If I could catch tench from the spots I was sure I could catch the carp and so I went out every other evening and pre-baited the spots. I have to admit to being a bit of a bait monster often using more bait than other people. I would pre-bait with around twenty kilos of bait on a Sunday and Wednesday and then fish it on a Friday. I often get asked how much bait to put in and how can people afford it. The first question is a whole chapter in its own right, but I will say you should always take into account the stock of all species in the lake and the birdlife.

On a lake with a good head of tench, twenty kilos of bait can easily be cleared in a night, add to this the ducks diving down and eating some, and, hopefully, the carp. On some lakes it would be difficult to overdo it. How to afford it? Well, with a little thought it does not have to break the bank. I was baiting to attract all the species and keep the spots clear and so mixed ten kilos of sheep feed pellets into a bucket and added a good splash of salmon oil to help their attraction, then just mixed in pigeon condition bird-food and some sweet corn plus a scattering of my chosen boilies. All of this costs less than £10 twice a week, and so, for less than an evening in the pub, you can do it.

Right, back to the fish! The baiting was working and I steadily started to catch tench of a good average size with most fish over seven pounds. I would catch two or three tench most evenings just before dark and then I started getting carp – only one a session but that was excellent for the lake. I ended up doing eleven nights and a similar number of evening-only sessions and caught nine carp up to 32lb 8oz.

The week after I had the thirty seven-pounder on my first visit, Martin James called and asked if I would like to go and fish a lake with him for the bream. I happily accepted and so, a few days later, off we went. At the lake, Martin chose his swim and so I went into a little spot just to his right. I did not know what tactics would work best on the lake but I knew that Martin had recently caught some good bream at night in the margins. I used a marker float set-up to have a good plumb around the swim and finally settled on the near side of a plateau around thirty yards out. I spodded around eight kilos of mixed pellets, hemp and corn to the spot and fished two rods with balanced, plastic-corn hook-baits. Martin caught a couple of tench early in the evening but I had not seen anything on my spot. I was confident, with a gentle breeze blowing towards me, that I had found a good pitch. At around 10.30 p.m. my confidence was rewarded when I had a typically slow, stuttery take of a bream. As with most bream there was not much of a fight and I soon had it in my net; I lifted it out and called to Martin that I had one. He quickly arrived behind me where I was unravelling the net on my unhooking mat. It was a big, dark old bream and on the scales weighed 14lb 8oz, a new lake record. I managed two more in the night both around the eight pound mark, and lost a real big one the second night. I put some more bait onto the spot and put the rods out hoping they would return.

It was much quieter with not many fish rolling but just after dark I hooked into another bream. Martin had heard my bite alarm and was already by my side waiting with the net. The fish rolled close in and with one swoop, Martin netted what looked like another good bream. Yes, it was another personal best and another lake record weighing in at 15lb 6oz. I decided as

I had caught two personal best fish in a few days that I would try to catch personal bests of other species.

I called Martin a few days later and said I was going out for the evening to try and catch a PB barbel on a local stretch of the Bristol Avon. Martin advised me to look for some deep water near to an overhanging bush or other similar feature. Having never been to the stretch before, I went for a good walk along until I found a nice, overhanging willow with a deep hole under it. As it was just a short evening session, one rod with small PVA mesh bags of pellets and crushed boilies was going to be my plan of attack. First cast: the rod had hardly settled when the tip wrapped around and I caught a chub of around four pounds. Re-cast and the same again the rod hardly settled and I quickly landed a rainbow trout of 3lb 6oz a new personal best.

Phil Chun with a 15lbs 6oz bream from Wasings Shalford Lake which set a new lake record when caught

Phil with a nice Barbel from the Bristol Avon

Things then went quiet but as darkness crept in I got another bite and hit it! The rod hooped over and I was into what had to be a barbel. On scales she went 11lb 2oz, excellent – another personal best!

One last cast before dark and the rod settled, I had a few twitches then again the tip wrapped around and I was into another barble. She came much easier and I was surprised to see one at least as big, if not bigger than the last. I weighed her and was pleasantly shocked when the scales read 12lb 6oz! My first real attempt at catching barbel had been a success with two doubles, both personal bests, and a personal best trout. This session was lucky angling; sometimes, I think, we all have spells when things just go right. I felt that I should capitalise on my luck and so I went back to the seventy acre pit to target the tench and see if I could catch another personal best. Fishing as many evening as I could that week, for just a few hours at a time, I managed to catch eight over eight pounds, three over nine pounds and one, the personal best I was after, of 10lb 2oz. This was, and still is, my best period of catching, which I believe was largely down to luck and being in the right place at the right time. However, I would not have caught any of these fish if I had not picked the right area or baited to suit the conditions. When things are going well I get into 'the zone' and fish better, I work harder, concentrate more and really think about every little detail of my fishing from bait, to location and rig choice, and will even sit up all night watching the water for any sign of fish that will help me catch.

My bait business was rapidly growing and my time available to go fishing was seriously reduced, but I had been invited to enter a team into the British army carp-championships held at a lake in Kent. I made some phone calls and was told it was a lake that held lots of small carp that moved around in big shoals. At the event there were teams from the army as well as invited teams from the top, bait and tackle companies.

Lucky? Yes, we were that day as we came out first in the draw for swims. Once the draw was over, a few friends on other teams came and asked why I had chosen to fish the swim I had? My thought was that, with lots of anglers on the water, the fish would be looking for a quiet area. I had chosen a small channel swim away from the main area. The competition was for forty-eight hours, fishing in pairs and with six people per team.

We went to our swim and started to set up and could see all the other teams setting up bivvies and laying out all their kit; we decided that, as you were allowed to bait-up before the start, we would spend all this time finding the most likely spots and baiting them up. The whistle sounded for the start of the match and I had one rod ready to go. I cast it the ninety yards to a far-bank set of reeds that I had already baited with boilies. Whilst getting my other rods set up I had a take! This could not be right, we had only just started and it felt like a decent fish too! On the scales it went twenty-six pounds, a big carp for the water and just the start we needed.

Trophies won by Phil in the Army Carp Contests

We caught steadily throughout the day but people in the main lake where catching loads of smaller carp; we were catching slower but better fish. I know from experience a lot of carp anglers can be pretty lazy and hoped the other teams would all bait-up for the night, just sling their rods out and go to bed – and I was right! If we wanted to win (I always want to) we would have stay up continually for the match and bait-up on regular intervals and hope that during the nights we could catch up with the anglers in the main area. Well, it was hard work but well worth it as I won the competition with just over 200 pounds as well as catching the biggest-fish prize with my first fish. We won the pairs title and our team won the team title! All the guys on my team fished hard and worked at it, that's what got us the result.

The following year we were invited to defend our title. I hatched a plan based on what I had learned the previous year. I would take as much bait as I could afford and could fit into my van and if any of our team drew a swim in the main area of the lake they would bait heavily at regular intervals and try to hold one of the large shoals of fish. I knew other teams would have a similar idea but again, I know how hard work this would be and knew that my team and I would work harder.

Lucky? No! For some strange reason we came out last in the draw and got the swims that nobody else wanted, but we were in the main part of the lake. It was no surprise that other

Spodding

teams had opted for the swims from where we had won the previous year. There where lots of fish rolling around 300 yards to the left of us, in front of two other pairs, so Gary, my fishing partner for the event and I, decided we would find a feature as far out in the lake as we could possibly cast accurately (about 130 yards) and then bait it with thirty kilos of particles to start! Then we would spod particles out to the spot for a whole hour every third hour for the whole match and just pray that the carp would move past and we could hold them long enough to give us a chance in this un-favoured swim! Four hours of us both spodding at the start of the match, saw us get loads of bait out to the spot and some glares from other teams. By the following morning we were fishless and were getting stick from other teams who were saying that we had put too much bait out. My other team members were doing well though, with one of our other pairs leading the field. We had decisions to make, had we put too much bait in or not?

A long discussion, two cans of Red Bull to keep us awake and we decided to carry on with our plan and pray that at some point the fish would move in and we would fish our hearts out and capitalise if they did. Through the day we could see fish gradually moving up the lake closer and closer to us: Come on! As it got dark I had our first take then, whilst I was playing it, Gary had a take: here we go! Throughout the night we worked flat out with one of us spodding to the mark at 130 yards for a whole hour, and then the other one would take over.

We spodded bait out for the whole night and managed to hold the fish. I lost count of how many we caught but at the final whistle our tally was added up and yes, we had done it! We managed four hundred and five pounds of carp in the last twenty-four hours. Totally shattered but over the moon, I won the individual title, we won the pairs and the team event once again!

There was luck involved, the fish may not have moved in, but this really was all about work, commitment and a belief in what we were doing. We both had blisters all over our hands from continually spodding as far as we possibly could, we had bad backs and we had an empty van – apart from the trophies!

The final relevant story is from last year. I run a syndicate lake that is a stunning fishery but is very, very tricky. For a start, there are not many fish and there is a lot of natural food. The lake had not been fished for fifty years prior to me getting the lease and it was therefore a real mystery what would be in there. I would walk around the lake most evenings looking for fish and trying to work out their feeding patterns and habits. It is only a twelve-man syndicate with some good anglers but during the first three months I was the only one who caught any carp. I had four but none massive. I was also tench and bream–fishing the lake with some success. One day in July I was planning to go out tench fishing but it was raining hard and windy all morning, so I decided to get some of the jobs out of the way that I had promised my wife I would do.

By mid afternoon I just had to go fishing; I had that feeling again that things were right and I was sure I would catch. I realised I did not have much in the way of bait and then I thought of Martin! Not because he never has bait but because he is always singing the praises of good-old bread. To be honest, from those early days on 'the large lake' when I met that tench angler who inspired me, I had used bread for tench, but over the last few years and owning a bait company, I had been using more modern tactics. I stopped at the village shop and bought two loafs of thick sliced, white bread and headed for the lake. Upon arrival I had a walk around in the rain and opted to fish from one of the islands in a sheltered bay, as I thought the fish may be in there taking shelter from the driving wind and rain (and it would be more comfortable for me). I took minimal tackle: a float rod and a bucket with my bread in.

I put one loaf of bread into the bucket, tipped in enough water to cover it and then mashed it all up the best I could with my hands. I put all of this just two feet off the end of my rod in around eight feet of water, on the edge of a weed bed. I cast out my waggler, baited with a piece of bread flake, and sat back to see what may or may not occur. About an hour passed with no bites but there were a few bubbles in the swim so I knew tench were present. I adjusted my depth and shot pattern and fed small balls of mashed-up bread every few minutes until I got a bite. With regular feeding I caught four more tench, then it went quiet. I have had this happen before when carp move in and push the tench out of the swim, so, when the float next shot under, I was not too surprised to find an angry carp on the other end. Unfortunately, with my 6lb line and size 10 hook he managed to slip off.

From what I had learned from my time walking the lake as often as I could, I knew the carp ate lots of naturals, and as the other carp anglers on the lake were not catching on boillie, thought that this bread tactic may well be the way to go. I continued to feed and soon had another bite, but this was no carp. A black, old-looking bream was in my net at just over ten pounds. I caught two more bream soon afterwards, both doubles, so the bread tactic was working a treat. Again it went quiet and, yes, you guessed it, my next bite was another carp but again he managed to slip the hook. The lake is very weedy and so on my light gear I just could not keep them out of it. Just as it was getting dark I had what was going to have to be my last bite. Carp?

Oh yes! As soon as I struck, it tore off across the swim, so I jumped up the bank behind me and just kept the rod as high as possible. Twenty minutes later and the fish was still trying to find every weed bed it could; I saw it roll but could not tell how big it was. I eventually landed it and was over the moon to have what I knew was a new personal best English common carp. It weighed 36lb 2oz – not massive by modern standards but a fish that had never been caught before, from a tough lake that we still do not know exactly what it holds, and on good old bread and six Pound line and a float rod to boot.

Looking back at these captures and many others, I can say, yes, I have been lucky, lucky to have fished some great places, lucky to have met some great anglers who have helped me learn, lucky to catch some great fish, and, most lucky of all, to have a great wife who put's up with my obsession! So is it luck, judgement or skill? Personally I think that it is a mixture of all three, I have been lucky at times but, without the knowledge I have learned and hours and hours of hard work, studying other people tactics, studying the water and watching fish's habits, I would probably not have caught the lucky fish.

Above all, I think that passion and a will to succeed is most important: when I set myself a goal or a target I do all I can to achieve it; this does have to be balanced with work and family life but without the passion to achieve I do not think any of my successes would be possible. So next time you're on the bank and someone else is catching more than you, don't presume they are lucky, learn from them, what are they doing different, and use it to help you catch more.

I often describe Gary Newman as a young Dick Walker, so good is his angling prowess. His weekly Angling Adventures in the Angler's Mail are avidly read by thousands of anglers, as I and others did with Walker's Pitch back in the 1950s and 60s. Gary has an incredible record of quality fish. At the start of the 2010 season, editor Tim Knight asked Gary to go and try to catch big fish on the first day. He duly obliged with a cracking barbel of 12lb 10oz from the difficult River Colne. He also has a passion for the mahseer and travels widely to India and other foreign climes.

I emerge from the airport feeling exhausted and am hit by a blast of hot air, a cacophony of horns, a scene of chaos as taxi drivers hustle for business, and a variety of not altogether pleasant odours, which, when all combined, leave me with a sense of joy as I know I'm back in India once more.

The first time I ever walked out of Bangalore airport, in southern India, all of the things that I now associate with practically being back home, seemed alien and somewhat daunting to me. India is a country that gets under your skin and, for many, one visit is enough to keep them coming back, but the country does have a 'Marmite-like' quality in that you'll either fall in love with it or look forward to the day you leave to return to the UK – luckily for me it is the former that applies. For me, the overwhelming factor in travelling over 6,000 miles at least once, often twice a year, is the fishing, with a species called mahseer being the main attraction. But I have also grown to love the place and the people.

Mahseer are considered one of the hardest fighting fish, pound-for-pound, that you can fish for, and with their large, golden or silver scales, this species, that looks a bit like a carp, but is in fact related to the barbel, is an impressive sight to behold, especially as they grow to over 100lb. I first became aware of the mahseer many years ago when I was a kid and saw a BBC programme called Go Fishing, which featured famous angler John Wilson travelling to India to catch this mighty fish. At the time I never dreamt that one day I would get the chance to go and fish for the species myself, but 2004 saw me planning a trip to the same place that I'd seen John Wilson on TV fishing, all those years before – that place being the Cauvery or Kaveri River, depending on which version of the spelling that you go for.

I'd been invited along by a couple of friends, Spencer and Andy, who had visited the fishing camps on the river a couple of times before, so at least I had a good idea of what to take with me and what to expect when I got there. As it turned out, Andy (or more correctly, his wife) had managed to time the birth of his son rather badly, as the due date was slap-bang in the middle of our trip, so in the end he did the right thing and stayed at home with his wife.

My first taste of India was in procuring the necessary visa to go there, which meant a visit to the consulate in London. It was total chaos with little notion of queuing and staff that took bureaucracy to new heights – this turned out to be pretty similar to the experiences I had when dealing with any organisation in India.

Next on the list was obtaining the tackle necessary to land these incredibly powerful fish, and with a bit of advice from a few different people whom I knew had fished there themselves, I was

soon kitted out with everything I would need. Fishing was mainly going to be from coracles –
small, round, wicker-framed boats of about six feet in diameter that were covered in a tarpaulin;
so the 8ft rods that I'd acquired would be perfect. After a lot of thought, I opted to take my big,
pit carp reels, rather than multipliers, which I was completely unfamiliar with using, and the
Daiwa Tournaments that I took would hold enough line, hopefully! I'd had varying advice on
braid and monofilament so ended up going armed with 80lb Fireline XTS braid and 40lb Daiwa
Sensor nylon – strong and cheap enough to change every time it became scuffed by rocks.

Everyone I spoke to recommended Owner SSW hooks, so that was an easy choice and a bit
of searching soon found them in 6/0 and 8/0 sizes. Traditionally, the weight has always consisted
of lead wire wrapped around tubing, but having heard how rocky it was I much preferred the
idea of some sort of weak link with a conventional watch lead, and this is something that I have
stuck with ever since, as often, the lead comes off on the take, leaving you attached directly to
the fish with nothing on the line to get snagged. Other than that, it was a case of putting together
all the usual bits, including: scales and a weigh sling that could handle fish of this size, plus some
clothes suitable for temperatures in the high 20°Cs or low 30°Cs.

Reports from India were fairly encouraging and it appeared that the monsoons had finished
and the river would be dropping, and, with a bit of luck, would be ideal for fishing by the time
we arrived.

Finally, we were all set to go and a morning in early October saw us heading for Heathrow
Airport to board an Air Sri Lanka flight, which after several stopovers would eventually get us
to Bangalore. Having only ever flown as far as Spain before, I found the journey extremely
tedious, compounded by the fact that we had to stopover at Mali in the Maldives, and Colombo
in Sri Lanka, before finally arriving at Bangalore late at night. Thankfully, this journey is now a
lot easier, as British Airways fly direct to Bangalore in a shade over ten hours. In addition, I
have more experience of long-haul flying.

My first introduction to Bangalore airport was a bit of a culture shock and I was glad to be
travelling with someone who'd done it all before. Everything went smoothly and all our luggage
arrived in one piece. It wasn't long before we were seated in a taxi heading into the city to
spend a night in a hotel. The one thing that surprised me most was the noise, notwithstanding
the late hour, and it seemed to go on for most of the night. The hotel was pretty good, although
we were that exhausted, anywhere with a bed would have been welcome. Despite it being gone
midnight, some food was quickly acquired from a local restaurant and I had my first taste of
proper Indian cuisine; it was every bit as good as I'd hoped it would be.

The following morning we got a taxi and headed out of Bangalore – which was a mission
in itself, given the high volumes of traffic, all of which insisted on incessantly using their horns.
The roads were pitted with large potholes, and a collection of kamikaze drivers seemed intent
on advancing their passing into the next life, via reincarnation and total disregard of any road
markings or signs, including traffic lights. As we left the city behind, the roads got worse, and
despite the fishing camp only being 100km or so away, it took over three hours to get there,
including a quick stop for a cup of chai and a massala dosa at place by the side of the road, in
which I was very dubious about eating. The more time I have spent in India though, the more

Cauvery Sunrise. Credit Gary Newman

I have learnt that, as long as you are careful what you eat and don't drink the water, these sorts of eating places are generally fine, as all the food is freshly cooked. I have yet to be ill from the food.

Eventually, I caught my first sight of the river, and was surprised at just how wide it was and how many rocks, trees and channels there were – in fact, it looked a fairly daunting prospect. The river itself was still fairly high, swelled by the after-effects of the monsoon rains. After checking in to our tents at the camp and grabbing some lunch, it was time to set up the tackle ready for my first session on the river later that afternoon. I opted to spool up with braid as I could fit more of it on the reel, but ultimately this proved to be a mistake. By 4 p.m. when the afternoon fishing session usually started, the temperature had cooled slightly and I was introduced to my ghillie. His name was Dasa and, thankfully, we got on well despite his limited English and my total lack of the local language, Kanada. Since then, we have become good friends and he has helped me land many fish.

I'd seen photos of coracles but in the flesh they looked even more flimsy, and I had trouble believing that they were able to withstand the rapids and rocks that this river was full of. I soon learnt that they were the perfect craft, being stable, as long as the weight was properly distributed, and having the ability to flex, making them ideal when you did hit a rock that would have smashed a more rigid boat to pieces. We were soon out on the water and pulled up onto a half-submerged rock, casting to a spot where Dasa said the main channel was – until you get to know the river yourself you are totally reliant on the ghillie to tell you where the channels are, and it is essential that you fish with one that you get on well with, as, without their help, you will struggle.

Bait was ragi paste, with a tennis ball-sized lump moulded around my 8/0 hook. Ragi is a cereal similar to millet and a staple food item in the diet of local people; we'd seen it growing in fields on our drive to the camp. The seeds are ground into a flour which is then mixed with water and made into cannonball-sized lumps then boiled until it is cooked through. By breaking off lumps and kneading the outer crust together with the softer inner, a stiff paste is formed that will take a cast, but is still soft enough to strike the hook through.

The Cauvery is full of small mahseer and various carp species which all have a taste for ragi. I was getting plenty of bangs on the rod tip. Not knowing what to expect, I did wonder if it was mahseer having a go at the bait, but soon realised that it hadn't been when, after a while the tip slammed over and I struck into something that put up a far better fight than it should've done, given that it was only about 6lb and had easily managed to get the size 8/0 hook in its mouth.

Over the next couple of days I landed a few more fish, the best going 17lb, and was really enjoying the fishing, spending the mornings and afternoon/evenings on the river, with a few hours at lunchtime to eat, catch up with the other anglers at the camp, or take a rest. One morning, we headed right to the top of the stretch controlled by this camp, a place called Hattee Pool (hattee being the Hindi word for elephant) and tied up to a small bush sticking partly out of the water. Downstream, and slightly to my right, was a line of rocks and it was easy to see that the channel here kinked to the left to skirt round them. Towards the bottom end of these rocks was where I cast a ball of ragi.

Not much happened and the sun started to burn through the early morning mist. I started to get a few knocks and just sat considering whether or not to wind in and check that the bait was still on, when the tip suddenly hooped over and the reel screamed. Dasa was shouting, "Strike sir!" but I was having trouble just keeping the rod off the side of the coracle, such was the power of the fish. It started to slow and must have taken nearly 100 yards of line by that time, and, just when I thought it might stop, I felt the braid touch a rock and instantly go slack as it was sliced in two. That was the last time I ever used braid for mahseer fishing, it might appear tough but, under tension, it cuts far more easily than nylon when it comes into contact with a rock; ever since then, I have stuck to 40–50lb mono.

The next morning we were sat back in the same spot and, after landing a couple of smaller fish, once again I had a violent take, but this time after taking forty yards or so of line, the hook came out and another decent fish had got away. Both line cuts, due to sharp rocks, and hook pulls, caused by the mahseer's extremely hard mouth, are occupational hazards of mahseer fishing and there is little that you can do other than accept that it is inevitable that you will lose a fair proportion of those you hook. Still, I was less than happy at it currently being 2–nil in favour of the mahseer.

The fishing was fairly slow with not many fish being caught, and most of those that were landed were fairly small. This was partly due to the water level being at a height that made it impossible to fish many of the spots, as there were simply no exposed rocks or bushes that gave access to the channels to which the coracle could be moored. A couple of days later we were back in Hattee Pool again and this time Dasa wandered off and started turning over rocks before we started fishing. It soon transpired that he was collecting freshwater crabs, which were a big favourite with the mahseer and I soon landed a couple of small fish on them using the second rod.

But it was the ragi rod that put me in contact with something a lot bigger, as once again a fish tried to empty my spool of line. As it got lower, Dasa quickly untied us from the bush and we followed the fish downstream for a few hundred yards.

Once we had caught up with it we landed on a bank-side beach and I carried on playing it from there. Suddenly, it started coming in very easily but rather than having given up, I watched the line come level with where we stood and then carry on upstream before the fish started taking line again.

Luckily, it didn't go far, as with the force of the flow, it would have been impossible to follow it back upstream had it become snagged. Soon afterwards, a large golden fish lay on its side as Dasa expertly attached it to the stringer and, after giving it a rest and chance to get its breath back, we weighed it at 44lb. After a few photos I slipped it back. This was my first sight of a big mahseer and it was stunning, with large, golden-edged scales, orange-coloured fins and a massive mouth. By then it was around 11 a.m. and starting to get hot so we headed for a beach

44 lb Golden Mahseer. Credit Gary Newman

at a place called Balu where I'd previously caught a few smaller fish, and where there was a nice bit of shade where we could sit and eat breakfast. The rods hadn't been out for long when I had a take and, although it felt reasonably heavy, the fish wasn't doing much, so I was shocked when up popped a 32lb silver mahseer for the perfect end to the morning.

That was pretty much the last of the action, other than a few small fish, as it started to rain again and the river rose, eventually reaching a height where it was unfishable. After four days or so without a bite, we decided to head home a few days early, but even then, I knew I'd definitely be returning to try for a bigger one, and to catch up with all the friends I'd made at the camp.

Just over a year later I was once again flying back to Bangalore with Spencer, and this time, my friend Andy was with us as well. The journey this time was much easier with the British Airways direct flight. We arrived at Bangalore in the early morning, which was perfect for driving straight to the camp, as the chaos of Bangalore wasn't something that I wanted to experience anymore than was necessary. To try and ensure that we didn't lose any fishing to the rain or high water levels, this year we'd arrived towards the end of November and were greeted by the river looking in very good condition. Unfortunately though, the fishing proved to be pretty slow for some reason and no one at the camp caught any fish of any real size during our eighteen-day stay. Fishing with Dasa, we managed to land quite a few fish and tried some areas further downstream that I hadn't fished the previous year, due to the water being too high. My biggest catch, a nice golden fish of 26lb, was one of the better fish taken during my stay, with Andy landing a new PB of 32lb.

Despite the lack of any big fish being landed, or even hooked and lost, I still really enjoyed myself and was already planning my next trip back. That was to be the last trip for Spencer and Andy as they went off to fish for other things, or in Andy's case to raise his young family, but a few days before I left I bumped into another English angler called Joe who had been fishing the river for over fifteen years; we immediately hit it off and became good friends.

My Dad is also a keen angler and, after hearing about my exploits in India, he decided that he fancied having a go at catching a mahseer himself. Plans were finalised, the necessary visas obtained and various items of tackle procured, all of which was straightforward as I'd now done it several times before and knew the ropes. A cold December morning saw us both checking in at Heathrow Airport, and Dad commenting on how smoothly everything was going, which at the time I thought might be tempting fate. I was proved right: twelve hours or so later, as we were leaving the plane, there was an announcement asking several passengers, including my Dad, to contact customer services. It turned out that his luggage was still at Heathrow and wouldn't reach him until the next morning.

We were expected at the camp so, leaving Dad at a hotel in Bangalore, I caught a taxi and headed off to the river. As it happened, Dad missed very little by being delayed, and I only landed a couple of small fish that first afternoon, fishing with a ghillie called Corea. As we were returning to camp that night after finishing fishing, I spotted a lot of activity and lights, and it turned out that an Indian friend of mine, Junaid, had just landed a 56lb mahseer, which, at the time, was the biggest one I'd seen in the flesh.

For a few days we tried different parts of the stretch and landed a few fish to mid–doubles, which was nice, as it gave Dad a chance to see the river. He also managed to catch his first ever mahseer plus a few others. It then became apparent that a lot of the fish were at the downstream end of the stretch; they were probably waiting for the water to drop more before moving even further downstream, to the stretch controlled by the next fishing camp.

Along with my friend Joe, who'd already managed a few fish to over 30lb, we decided to concentrate on this area and managed to persuade the camp manager to let us spend a few nights down there as well. That first night I hooked into what felt like a better fish, just after dark, and after a decent fight landed one of 24lb, which, had I lost it, I would have sworn was bigger. We also spotted some lights further downstream where Joe was fishing. Soon after, he arrived back at the beach where we were camping, soaked from the chest down. It turned out he'd had a nice, silver mahseer of 52lb and that, when it came to doing the photos, he'd jumped out onto a sandy patch that looked to be in shallow water, but had turned out to be far deeper than he'd expected!

It was great to know that there were some bigger fish about, and later that evening my Dad got his first chance at a big one. I saw him strike, get dragged to his feet, then the line snapped with a noise like a gun shot. He'd got snagged earlier and had tightened his drag when trying to free his tackle but had forgotten to re-set it afterwards; the fish clean-snapped 40lb line.

We steadily caught fish into the high teens and a couple of days later I experienced my best-ever morning on the river. A few of the local villagers were sharing the beach with us as they were being paid to make ragi and to bait the river with it – one of the reasons why we'd chosen this beach, as the ragi water being poured into the river was definitely a fish attractant. I gave them a chance to supplement their income by collecting for me a load of crabs from under the rocks alongside the river, as I knew from past experience that mahseer love them. Corea paddled us downstream to a spot where the main channel in the river narrowed to just twenty yards or so, with a line of rocks sticking out of the water opposite the bank-side rock where we positioned the coracle.

A ball of ragi was cast well downstream towards the tail end of the channel, and the other rod was baited with a crab and gently cast towards the line of rocks, then allowed to swing round in the current. In the space of a couple of hours the crab rod produced five fish, the best two going 31lb and 20lb, and I had one on ragi of 17lb.

That evening after dinner, we all decided to have a cast from the beach as the water in front of it was pretty-deep and slow-flowing, making it the ideal place for a big fish at night. During the day, hordes of small mahseer of a few pounds make it impossible to keep a bait in the water for any length of time, but at night they all seem to disappear. It wasn't long before I heard Dad shout and saw he was attached to something that rapidly took line. After ten minutes or so he had the fish under control and his ghillie, Anthony, was soon slipping a silver fish of 39lb 8oz onto the stringer. After a ten-minute rest and a few photos she was returned.

With all the disturbance in this area, I decided to wander upstream 100 yards or so and give that a go. It was approaching midnight when I felt a bang on the rod as the tip flew round and line was taken from a tight clutch before I even had a chance to strike. The fish was moving downstream fast and I had to run along the beach to keep up with it, but eventually I had it under control and landed my second thirty-pounder of the day at 35lb.

After a couple of days back at the fishing camp, we decided to head back to the beach for a few nights as it was now approaching the end of our trip. We'd already had lots of fish, including a fair few over twenty pounds, but were hoping for one last big one. Unusually for this time of the year, the weather took a turn for the worse. It started raining and carried on for the next three or four days. We only had one small tent, which I let my Dad use, and I slept on the beach with a coracle propped up over me to provide a bit of shelter from the rain. It made little difference as everything was soaked anyway.

I managed a few more fish up to 34lb but the nights had been very slow with nothing to show for our efforts, despite the fact that I'd sat up until 3 or 4 a.m. fishing a couple of times. By now, it was our last night on the beach and I was keen to make the most of it, but very little was happening and I hadn't had so much as a tap, when the rod suddenly arched over and I was into a decent fish. I carefully played it all the way in to the beach and our shouts for a ghillie were answered by a new member of staff, who I didn't know it at the time but who had consumed a large amount of alcohol. He stood there in a daze holding the stringer and staring at the fish as it lay on its side in the shallow water. Then all of a sudden it shook its head and the hook came out. It wasn't a monster, maybe 35 to 40lb, but I was annoyed at losing it like I had, especially after getting it all the way in to the bank and knowing that it could be my last chance

Gary's Dad fishing near the coracles. Credit Gary Newman

of the trip.

I cast back out again and sat staring at all the millions of stars, many of which we don't see in the UK due to light pollution, reflecting on the loss.

Everyone else had gone to bed and I was feeling tired myself but decided to have another cast and leave it an hour or so before calling it a night as it was well past midnight. I had only been sitting there another twenty minutes or so when I felt the rod bend slowly over and struck into a heavy fish. It didn't charge off but steadily took fifty yards of line downstream and then used its weight. During the fight, which lasted about twenty minutes, it plodded around slowly, and steadily took line whenever it wanted to: I knew it was a better one. My shouts aroused my Dad and an Indian friend Sandeep who'd joined us for the night and they woke up Anthony, who is the senior ghillie. He made no mistake at all as he got the fish on the stringer first time, although my heart was in my mouth as I saw this big silver fish slowly sliding towards us across the surface. I knew that it was bigger than anything I'd caught before and the darkness seemed to magnify it further, leaving me with no real clue as to just how big it really was: on the scales it went 52lb.

The weather looked to be trying to brighten up for our final day on the river, but by mid-afternoon we could see a storm moving in quickly. We turned our coracle over on the rock we were sitting on, propping it up with the oar to provide some shelter.

Just before the storm hit I managed my last fish of the trip, a lovely 26lb golden mahseer. Minutes later, the heavens opened and after half-an-hour or so of torrential rain, it eased off just enough for us to get our gear together and head back to the camp. That proved to be a good decision as the river came up more than four feet overnight and much of the area where we'd been camping was underwater.

It had been my most enjoyable trip so far, with terrific fishing along with some great company. I knew that I'd be coming back for many years to come.

I love fishing the Cauvery in southern India as it is without a doubt the best place to try and catch a big mahseer, but if you are a serious mahseer hunter you just have to fish for them in the Himalayas. The fishing in northern India is far wilder than that on the Cauvery, with many rivers being difficult to access and the ever-present problem of poaching, which isn't controlled to any degree like it is in the south. If you can find stretches of river that haven't been stripped of their fish by poachers, then there is still a chance of something special.

In my view, the northern mahseer are also more impressive-looking than their southern cousins, being a slightly different species – barbus tor putitora rather than barbus tor mussullah – being more streamlined and a much deeper golden colour. There is a wide variety of different types of river in the north, from the mighty Ganges and its tributary the Kali, which is a big river in its own right, down to smaller rivers such as the Ramganga and Kosi.

The fish in these rivers won't have seen ragi and are far wilder, with lures or live and dead baits working best. There are a few places where they will respond to atta paste – a type of flour used to make chapattis. These fish are near to villages where they get used to cooking pots and the like being washed in the river where they can pick off any morsels of leftover food. I have noticed this myself when camping in the same place for several days: the fish start to gather where the washing-up is done, mainly small ones, but I have seen the odd double-figure mahseer doing the same.

Unlike the south, where there are purpose-built fishing camps, in the north you rely on finding the fish yourself, obviously with the help of a local guide, and camp rough by the river, taking all your own supplies.

My first trip to the Himalayas was with a friend, Chris Summers, who had visited the Ramganga the previous year and had caught fish to 32lb from one of the lodges in Corbett National Park. Our excursion though was going to be much more basic than the luxury accommodation he'd stayed in before. We'd be camping in small tents and moving between likely-looking fishing spots. Arriving in Delhi in mid-May was a real shock to the system, as the temperature was over 40°C. It took me a couple to days to acclimatise to it. We were met at the airport by Gaurav Kataria, the Indian tour operator who was organising everything for us, and he has since become a good friend – I even attended his wedding a couple of years back.

After spending the rest of the day catching up on some sleep at Gaurav's house, we drove to Delhi Old Station to catch the overnight train to a place called Ramnagar, right on the edge of Corbett National Park and where the foothills of the Himalayas begin. The station was a scene of complete chaos – luckily we'd booked tickets in advance, as, rather than an orderly queue like you'd find in the UK, there was a seething mass of people pushing and shoving to get to the ticket windows. The train itself was very good and we were in an air-conditioned sleeper carriage which was comfortable enough for the seven-hour or so journey.

We arrived around 5.30 a.m. and soon had everything loaded onto the vehicles we'd be using. After a quick stop for breakfast we headed off to the river. Initially, we were driving through typical Indian jungle, but as the road gradually wound its way higher up, the trees changed and in the far distance we caught glimpses of snow-capped mountains.

Finally, after three hours or so of driving along narrow mountain roads with little room to pass vehicles coming the other way (at times, if you looked out of the car window all you could see was the drop to the valley floor rather than the edge of the road, and there were no crash barriers!) we reached our destination. This was a tiny village, basically a small cluster of basic houses with one shop, and that was as far as we could go by road. All of the gear was unloaded from the jeeps and transferred onto ten or so horses and then we set off down the mountain into the valley, where, in the distance, we could see a shimmering ribbon of blue, which I assumed must be the river.

The path was very steep and zigzagged its way down the hillside in as direct a route as possible. It was covered in loose shale which made walking very difficult, especially as it was around 40°C. By that time the sun was blazing down. Finally, we came to a small village at the bottom and crossed a rickety suspension bridge over a lovely-looking river festooned with rocks. What didn't look so good though was the chocolate colour of the water after recent rain. We set up camp on a beach next to the river and spent the next couple of days trying everything to catch a mahseer, but all to no avail. This was down to the water colour. With just a few inches of visibility, nothing could see our lures, and the livebaits and chicken intestines that we tried, also failed to produce.

We decided to have a move, as it was also became clear that the villagers were doing a lot of netting on this bit of river. Moving was much more effort than it sounded as once everything – including a cooking tent and all our supplies – were packed away, we then had to walk alongside the river for a couple of hours over rocks, before climbing up a steep path for an hour or so, and then another hour down into the next valley, which, in the heat, was very tiring. The highlight of all of this was arriving in a little village after the steep climb and being met by locals offering us cups of sweet-tasting water that came straight out of the rocks, and despite not speaking the language, managing a conversation with one of them about cricket! For me, it is things like this that are just as important as the actual fishing.

The second spot we pitched camp looked really good, with a big, deep pool in front of our camp and several sets of rapids and boulder-strewn stretches of river.

The water was still coloured and the first twenty-four hours produced nothing – if anything it was now even hotter, making it difficult to fish during the middle of the day. Our ghillie, Asharam, persisted though and on the second day, whilst we were sitting in the shade, he hooked and landed a nice fish of around 15lb, the first Himalayan mahseer I'd seen.

The river was starting to clear and things were looking good, and that evening we headed a short distance downstream. I'd had a couple of casts with a Mepps Aglia spinner and nothing had happened, but then I moved slightly and cast right behind a rock. Before I could even turn the reel handle it was taken. It wasn't a big fish, around 5 or 6lb, but, after several days with no action, it was very welcome. I went on to add a couple more of a similar size that evening.

We were due to move the next day and fished for an hour or so in the morning, as the staff were packing away the camp, but to no avail. What I did spot though was a fairly innocuous-looking snake, about as thick as your finger, with a pointed head, sitting under a rock a few feet below the one I was standing on. I described it to Gaurav and he said it was a saw-scaled viper, one of India's most deadly snakes! After that, we were all a bit more careful to look where we were walking!

The final place we were to fish, before heading back to Delhi, was a temple right next to the river. After what we'd been through over the last few days, it was a relief to see that we could drive right to it. We were made very welcome by the priest and given rooms in the temple to stay in. It was nice to be able to get out of the sun and to be somewhere with a ceiling fan. It was quickly apparent that there were quite a few fish in this stretch. From vantage points on a couple of big rocks we were able to see them, and best of all, there were a few that looked very big. During the first couple of days we managed to catch a few more fish between us but nothing over 10lb and it quickly became apparent that the fish soon became wary and knew that they were being fished for.

So, we decided to fish for a few hours in the morning from first light onward and then give the stretch a rest until the evening and fish for a couple more hours then. This also had the advantage of fishing when it was a bit cooler. On the third morning, I was fishing slightly downstream of Chris, who was in a big pool where we'd seen the bigger fish. Within ten minutes of starting, I heard him shout that he'd hooked a big fish. I made my way up to him and saw he was standing in mid-river with the rod bent double, but after ten minutes or so he had the fish under control. Asharam grabbed it first time and got it on a stringer. After letting it rest for a while whilst we got the camera and weighing gear ready, Chris lifted it out and we could see that it was a very good fish, turning the scales round to 42lb.

Chris decided to go back to the rooms and get some sleep but I carried on fishing and was just about to give up, as the sun was now fairly high, when my Mepps was hit right on the crease where water coming through a small rapid met the slower water of the pool. The fish tore off downstream and I ran through the water, slipping and sliding on submerged rocks, to get a better angle on it. I could see that I was attached to a very good fish, of a similar size to the one Chris had landed or maybe bigger, but then it suddenly charged towards some rocks and cut me off. I was gutted and, with just one more day remaining, felt that my chance had gone.

Things didn't look good the next morning as the monsoon rains looked to have started. It was hammering it down when the alarm went off at 5.30 a.m. but I decided to give it a go anyway. Third cast in the pool where I'd lost the fish the previous day and I had a strike, this time I managed to land it. It was nowhere near the size of the fish I'd lost but at 18lb I was more than happy. I carried on fishing but the river was rising rapidly and starting to colour up and it didn't look good. I wandered down to another pool where we'd seen a big fish the day before and tried various lures but all to no avail. It was getting towards the time where I had to stop to go and pack my stuff up ready for the journey back to Delhi, so I said to Asharam that I'd have three more casts, and on the second one something hit the lure hard. It was instantly obvious that it wasn't the big fish I wanted and I quickly landed a mahseer of about 4lb, but it was a nice way to finish.

Himalayan Mahseer. Credit Gary Newman

I first met Scott Richmond from Oregon when he arrived with his lovely wife Barbara for a stay with Kate and I in our home, after winning the auction prize we had donated to Oregon Trout. Scott learnt lot about our coarse fishing, even catching a River Teme barbel. The following year we were back in Oregon with Scott and Barbara when I got Scott involved in carp fishing. Today he fishes with the same enthusiasm that I had back in the 1950s and 60s.

Sooner or later every angler has a jinx – a species of fish that just refuses to be caught, no matter how hard the angler tries. My current jinx is redfish, a semi-tropical saltwater fish that typically grows to 5–10 pounds. Redfish live in shallow water along America's Gulf coast. They're good sport on a fly rod – or at least so I've heard, since I've never actually caught one. Every time I've angled for redfish something happens: I'll make a great cast and presentation, and the target fish completely ignores me; or a puff of wind comes out of nowhere and sends my fly off course, or a tiny ripple rocks the boat and some small object falls on the deck and the noise scares the fish away.

One time, I made a perfect cast followed by a perfect presentation. Not one, but two redfish rushed my fly. They ran into each, and the resulting collision scared them both off. My guide said he'd never seen such bad luck in his life. It wasn't bad luck; it was a jinx. When you have a jinx, you wonder what sins you've committed, what gods you've offended, to be treated with such cruel disdain. You can call it fate, karmic retribution, whatever. It's something you have to work your way out of it. I'll keep trying with the redfish. I know that perseverance pays off – eventually – because I was present when Martin James finally overcame his personal jinx.

Martin is the finest all-around angler I've ever known. He has travelled the world, and his knowledge and experience are vast. It seems he can catch any fish with any gear. But when Martin came to my part of the world, the state of Oregon in the Pacific Northwest, he had a steelhead jinx. Steelhead are a sea-going rainbow trout, one of seven anadromous salmonids in the Northwest. Averaging seven to ten pounds, but going as large as twenty or more, steelhead are greatly prized by anglers for their superb and often acrobatic fight. Fly-rod tactics are similar to those for Atlantic salmon, and some of the flies bear a resemblance to classic salmon patterns. Steelhead are not plentiful in my home waters, at least not any more. If you get more than one or two hook-ups a day, you count yourself lucky; and only half of all hook-ups are landed.

Martin had been to Oregon a couple of times before I met him. He was desperate to catch a steelhead and had been fishing with some of the best anglers in the sport, people who were not just good but legendary. And while he'd hooked a couple of steelies, he had not landed one. So I took him on a four-day float trip on the Deschutes River, one of our finest steelhead streams, during prime season. I was confident he'd catch several fish. But I wasn't counting on the power of a major jinx.

I put Martin in a prime run at the top of an island. He expertly cast his fly, mended line, let the fly swing across, then took a step downstream after the swing ended. This is the classic

Author and Kate taking time out for lunch on the Deschutes

steelhead tactic. You might have to do it 500 times before you hook a fish. Just as Martin was getting into the best water, an idiot in a canoe came shooting out of a side channel, ripped through the water he was fishing and spooked the bejabbers out of any fish that might have been in the run.

I've never seen anyone in canoe on the Deschutes before or since that moment. Yet, there it was, at precisely the wrong time. That's how a jinx works: you do everything right and something beyond your control spoils it for you.

Later that day, Martin was in another excellent steelhead run when he got a 'zip'. That's what we call it when a fish plucks your fly and pulls the free line from your hand without getting hooked. On the Deschutes, most fish that zip you will come back and take the fly aggressively if you present it to them one more time. So I told Martin what to do and watched with eager anticipation as he prepared to cast. Suddenly a boat with three people cut out of the river, and passed directly over Martin's run. I stared open-mouthed at the bad manners of the boater, and offered him a brief phrase that questioned both his intelligence and the legitimacy of his birth. There was no point in casting further. The boat would have scared off any steelhead.

And so it went. For four days. We floated the river in my boat, camping on the bank each night, and casting to the best steelhead water on the river. I landed a few fish, and Martin hooked a beautiful one that came unbuttoned fifteen minutes into the fight. At the end of four days, Martin's jinx had triumphed and he had no fish. To top it off, he'd forgotten to pack his favorite Yorkshire Gold tea. "For four days," he told people, "we had nothing to drink but water and herbal tea!" He said it like he'd just gone through the Blitz one more time.

Martin was uncomplaining, although it was clear he was disappointed. But one thing I'd learned about Martin James: he doesn't give up; he'd be back. And the next year he returned, ready for another crack at the elusive steelhead and a chance to banish the jinx.

Mark Bachman, a local fly-shop owner and fishing guide, had met Martin the year before and was convinced he could find him a steelhead. He volunteered to take Martin and I out on the Deschutes. Mark was brimming with confidence. Maybe he didn't realize the extent of

Scott Richmond, preparing dinner

Martin's jinx. I didn't enlighten him; no sense destroying his confidence, I figured.

So, 5.a.m. one morning in early August, Martin and I met Mark at the Rattlesnake boat ramp on the Deschutes and set out in Mark's driftboat.

We fished one run without a pull from a fish and moved down to the next good run: Crow's Nest. Crow's Nest is a shortish run on an inside bend of the river. It's what we call 'transition water', with a gradual change from fast water on the outside of the bend, to slow water on the inside. It doesn't look like much, but it's a productive run because somewhere in that spectrum of current a steelhead is sure to find a spot that it likes. We split the run, with Martin taking the downstream portion and me above him. We weren't five minutes into the run when I saw a deep bend in Martin's rod. Sure enough, he'd hooked a steelhead! I reeled up and got out of the way. I had one hope, one prayer in my head: "Please, fish, don't come unhooked. Stay on, stay on!"

And it stayed on! Ten minutes after hooking up, the fish was in Martin's hands. It was a beautiful wild hen of about seven pounds, with bright silver sides which had a hint of a red stripe. I snapped a couple of photos and Martin released the fish to continue on its journey. We punched the air, and there were high-fives all around. I don't think Martin cared two hoots about the rest of the day. For him, one steelhead was enough, because it was the one that broke the jinx. That day I learned a lesson: every fish is catchable, eventually. Just keep at it, just keep believing in yourself, and you can banish the bad mojo. So I'm ready: take me to the redfish!

Mark Bachman, who guided Martin to his first Steelhead

Trevor Bross fishes salt and freshwater. He is married to lovely Christine and they have three children: Adele, eighteen months-old, Ethan, five-and-a-half and Autumn who is seven. As well as being an keen angler, Trevor plays a good game of tennis. His work at Thomas and Thomas gives him the advantage of fishing with the best fly-rods in the world and often fishing with some of the best fly-fishers. When dining out he enjoys fried squid.

My introduction to Martin was in Lapland Sweden for the World Fly-fishing Championship. Martin was covering the event for the BBC and I was representing Thomas & Thomas, the supporting rod company. The World Fly-fishing Championships are where the best anglers from competing countries come together to battle for top country – a title the anglers take seriously and with great pride. Teams receive daily points in several categories: number of fish, total length of landed fish, and top angler of each beat. Awards are given for top country and best angler.

My insides were doing back-flips with excitement from the time I departed for Sweden. I had spent the previous weeks readying – rods for demonstration, charts for rod actions, literature for new rod development, and most importantly, my fly-fishing tackle. I knew I was headed for the pristine waters of Lycksele in Swedish Lapland. My primary responsibility was representing Thomas & Thomas, both as a supporting rod company and angler.

Yep, I was also competing in the sponsor's tournament, a tournament the organizers offered to the sponsors to fish, sightsee, whitewater raft, and socialize. We fished similar 'beats' to the competing countries and the anglers were awarded points in similar fashion: number of fish and total length of fish. I was given flies by my opening guide, and the Norwegian Team, a young group of anglers that had no fear and who were, in my mind, a group of skateboarding, fly-fishing thoroughbreds. They were fearless on the rivers: many times wading halfway across a raging river with water boiling over their shoulders to present a fly to an unobtainable seam, only to be washed down river, but persevering and retracing their steps, until perfection was achieved.

It is a humbling experience, fishing foreign waters – not to mention competing. We fished vast river systems, small intimate streams deep in the forest, and large, still lakes. I was alone with the world's best anglers, some of whom I knew. Their purpose was to represent their country. I was skunked that first day, but proceeded to fare better, with the help of Martin's fly suggestions and most importantly, samples! That weekend, I also discovered a valuable life lesson from Martin: compassion – a simple word that has far-reaching meaning – his ability to demonstrate kindness and empathy.

Dinner was always a memorable experience. The hall would be buzzing, with anglers talking about the catch, beat, and their secret fly. Many of the teams came with an official tier who would be readying the team's boxes with the appropriate flies, and tying flies to the team's request. I learned more that weekend about fly-tying than I had from the many years of having my nose stuck in books and videos.

I learnt about some unique knots: knots that swing a fly river-left and a reverse knot that would swing it river-right, to mention a couple. Each night, the evening commenced in the hotel bar; it was the one place where every team member seemed to let down their guard and socialize with their fellow competitors. The entire bar would partake in singing and dancing, the ultimate release of the day's nerves and stress.

I was deflated when my shuttle arrived that morning for the airport; I was leaving the meeting point for the world's elite anglers. I had experienced one of the cleanest and most beautiful places I had ever been to, and made many lifelong friends.

Martin has been associated with Thomas & Thomas for over a decade. He has given the company insightful forethought to some of our best rod tapers. Much of Martin's knowledge comes from his many hours on the stream and his devoted teaching schedule. I have fished many places with him, but none more memorable than my home waters. On one trip, Martin was travelling with a close friend, David. They had a free day to visit the rod factory and possibly fish my backyard, blue riband stream: the Deerfield River.

I was excited to show Martin some of my hidden gems, I promptly called my father to help set up a day's fishing. After a quick factory tour with Martin and his friend David (many of the photos he has taken at the factory have been featured in our yearly catalogues and website), it was off for an afternoon fishing on the no-kill zone of the Deerfield River. This section of river runs through the town of Florida which is secluded and isolated, not to mention pristine. The Deerfield is the most heavily dammed river in the Northeast with six hydroelectric dams that span from the headwaters in southern Vermont to where it empties into the Connecticut River in Greenfield, Massachusetts.

Trevor Bross on the Deerfield River

These dams provide clean power for the area and a unique habitat for trout – unique in that, each dam uses bottom release flows, ensuring a cool, well oxygenated climate for the trout: brown, rainbow, and brookies. Martin and I fished a section of the river we call 'pole 29', a dry-fly specialist pool, while my father went downstream with David and swung wets and streamers. Impressively, Martin fared well, landing several rainbows, but most notably a large brown then we were forced to leave the river. One hazard of the Deerfield is the unpredictable rising water levels caused by dam releases. We met up with my father back at the truck to discuss the evening's fishing. This is where the story gets interesting. The easiest access routes to the river are along the train tracks that run parallel with it. We have used the tracks to access our favourite spots since I was in my youth, with never an issue.

That afternoon, an officer approached David and my father, questioning them of their purpose in being there? After September 11 security has tightened. As they were dressed in waders and felt boots, and carrying fly rods, the officer feared 'terrorist'. He promptly asked for identification. David brought forth his English licence which instantly raised suspicions and questions. "What are these black dots on the back?" asked the officer. David said, "Oh, nothing, they're speeding violations." The officer appeared perplexed, but after reading my father's licence he realized he was a past student of my father from the local college! A sigh of relief; this would end with no one travelling to the police station and phone call to the wife asking for bail! Telling the story, we all can laugh now – thankful for law enforcement, but that evening there was no hatch to fish.

During another visit, I took Martin off to Cape Cod. The charter was scheduled for early afternoon allowing us a late morning departure. After a couple cups of coffee – of course tea for Martin, we headed east. Traffic was unusually heavy that morning, causing delays and thus making us tight for time in meeting with Andrew. The fog was heavy and the tide was leaving. We could hardly see the ocean as we approached the harbour.

Andrew, who was visibly agitated at our tardiness, hurried us to the dock where his boat was running. I soon realized that the harbour was just about dry. Cape Cod sees 9–11' tides and we just barely crawled out; this was one of the few times I witnessed Andrew having to use GPS. The fog was so heavy we could barely see in front of us, making fishing all but impossible. Martin used this time to interview Andrew.

He stuffed the ice cream cone of a microphone towards him and asked about the stripe bass fishery, blue-fin tuna and his aquaculture. Suddenly, Andrew shouted, as he killed the motor, "Grab that rod!" We quickly realised there were fish everywhere, we hadn't even noticed the fog had lifted. At the time, Andrew ran a 'skiff', stealthy, quiet and unusual for the Northeast, which allowed the boat to draft just six inches of water and which got us into some phenomenal fishing situations. I recall sitting on the poling platform and seeing fish under the boat and thirty yards out, a feeding frenzy. We came upon school after school of fish. Each school could be seen on the horizon, a black cloud in the water, which allowed us time to get our bearings and tackle straight between pods. I have spent countless days on the water and have only experienced a handful of situations like this. It seems Martin has a guardian angel hovering over all his fishing trips! We had a banner day for both weather and fish.

Salmon is the poster fish for many government-funded projects. The Cronin National Salmon Hatchery and the Silvio O Conte fish laboratory are both located in Western Massachusetts. The Silvio O Conte fish lab studies anadromus fish: shad, American eel, short nose sturgeon, and Atlantic salmon. The Cronin fish hatchery raises salmon fry from eggs gathered from returning Atlantic salmon running the Connecticut River.

One summer evening, Martin and I met up with Micky Novak, managing director of the Cronin fish hatchery. Timing could not have been better. Micky reported several dozen salmon were lifted over the Holyoke dam and there was a strong possibility we could experience a transfer at one of two dams, the Westfield (tributary of the Connecticut) or Turners Falls, the last dam on the Connecticut the salmon can cross. Micky called late that afternoon stating there were two captured fish at the Westfield dam, a salmon and a grilse. Martin and I rode in Micky's one ton pick-up, equipped with a live well and oxygenator.

Martin used this time for an impromptu interview with Micky: a stout, weathered man with a dry personality; the conversation made for an entertaining drive. As we approached the dam, Micky abruptly stopped the truck and hopped out to move a helgramite from the road – years of protecting salmon carried over to every facet of his life. Martin and I descended the staircase into the dam and through the catacombs to the viewing window. The dam was primarily used by shad and the American eel, but on this day two salmon ventured up. Martin and I, with the help of Micky, gently netted the fish and transferred them to the live well on the truck. The salmon where then brought back to Cronin where they were given antibiotics and will be raised to maturity and to breed, thus preserving the delicate cycle of the salmon.

Martin and I would be sitting at the table and it would be filled with fried foods, cheeses, breads, and desserts, most of which were off Martin's menu. After years of a reckless diet, my doctor discovered I had high cholesterol and that it was inherent in the family. Diabetes was a path I did not want to go down, nor pass on to my children. One of Martin's favourite breakfast discoveries was eggbeaters, an egg substitute that looked and tasted like a real egg. Unavailable in England, Martin and I spent countless hours tracking down a source and a possible distribution channel. Here's a product that brought normalcy to someone's life, but which is unobtainable outside the US. Martin and I contacted the manufacturer with no success, even pursuing the possibility of exporting to the UK. Funny how much time was devoted to incidents that seemed trivial but have far-reaching effects. This was my first introduction to the importance of a healthy diet and the impact it has on one's family.

Rod Designer, Tom Dorsey, flaming bamboo

Martin, editing another programme. Credit Ian Chapman, Anglers' Mail

Throughout my lifetime carp fishing has seen dramatic changes. Having said that, carp can still be caught on floating crust, potatoes, brown bread, honey paste and lobworms; though modern baits are often more effective. Even so, floating crust will often out-fish other floating baits, and of course it's cheap. I was probably eleven years of age when I got the carp-fishing bug, along with my school friends Billy Race, Peter Burstow, John (Stinker) Carole and Bill Hall – and that's some sixty-one years ago!

Since then there have been many changes: some rather drastic. When I started, it was with an old World War II tank aerial rod, with either a Bakelite or Walnut star-backed reel. The preferred line would be made of silk but they were far too expensive for us boys. Instead, we used a brown, thin, twisted flax line which I believe went under the name of 'cuttyhunk'. When we wanted to fish floating-crust, I reckon we spent as much time greasing the line with Muciline to make it float as we did fishing. Our first hooks to gut were rather crude, known as eel hooks.

During those early days (1948–49) much of our carp-fishing took place at Apple Tree Pond at Wainscott, a short cycle ride from home. This small pond got its name from the single apple tree on its bank, and each year it had a big crop of Worcester apples. The carp there were 'wildies', long, lean, common carp averaging 2–3lb: these fish really did scrap. Sometimes, during a long, dry spell, the pond would shrink to a fraction of its size when it looked as if all the fish would die: they didn't – they just disappeared. After a few days of heavy rain the pond quickly filled up and the fish were still there to be caught. Me and my mates reckoned they buried themselves in the soft, liquid-like mud – if they didn't, I don't know where they went to. Sadly, Apple Tree Pond was eventually filled in for housing.

One day when Peter Burstow and I were fishing Leybourne Lake we were told about another lake at Snodland that held big carp, and that the fishing belonged to Gravesend Kingfishers Angling and Preservation Society, a club that had some waters on Cliffe Marshes. I decided to cycle out there and look at the lakes – and I soon found them. The two lakes, which were separated by a dirt road that ran across the marshes to the coastguard houses, were not far from the Alpha Cement Works. It was a place that Charles Dickens had written about in Great Expectations, and on a black night it was a creepy place to be on your own.

Here I saw an angler fishing what I learned was Windmill Lake, and I watched as he caught several big rudd. My appetite was whetted and I decided to try to join the club. I chatted with the club member and obtained the address of the secretary. That evening I sat down and wrote a letter in my best handwriting, asking if I could join. I received an application form which I filled in and sent off with a postal order for five shillings. A few days later, equipped with my new membership card, I was on my bike to Paddlesworth Lake, a flooded clay-pit owned by the local cement works and leased to the club. This pit contained carp, rudd – thousands of them, but which all seemed stunted: some roach and a few perch. It was the carp that interested me – in fact they became an obsession; I just had to catch one of these magnificent fish.

Two-thirds of the bankside of this three-acre pit was covered in trees and bushes. At the roadside end of the lake the banks were steep and, being of clay, treacherous when wet. One false slip and you were in ten feet of water from which it was difficult to get out. At the opposite

BB (Denys Watkins-Pitchford MBE) and friend

end there was a large reed-bed and a small island – in fact the island was the home of millions of biting red ants. Black ants I have never found to be a problem, but every time I waded out to that island I was bitten to pieces.

The bottom of the pit was littered with all manner of rubbish, including rusty cable – a real trap for tackle but a favourite place for fish to swim around when hooked. There was also an old truck, that was a favourite place for busting tackle on. There were fallen trees and masses of Canadian pond-weed but the one good thing about the water was that it was sheltered from the wind most of the time.

It was the type of lake that Dennis Watkins-Pitchford MBE had described in Confessions, a book which had just been published. Two types of anglers fished the pit in the late 1940s. There were those who wanted to catch anything, which in this case meant mostly stunted rudd, or if they were lucky, a carp of four or five pounds, which was considered a good fish but hard to catch. And then there was the dedicated carp angler who fished for nothing but carp throughout the summer months. The carp angler fished in three ways: the first method was to use a float with gentles, worms or a paste bait flavoured with honey; the second approach was to use unweighted, floatless tackle with just a large hook tied on the end of the line and baited with plain, white bread paste, usually the size of a bantam's egg, but on occasion even as big as a chicken's egg. Our special bait of the day was brown bread and honey paste, but that was only if granny would give me some honey. Mum would not often let me have honey, but sometimes I managed to take a bit when no-one was looking – there was trouble though if she found out!

My walnut star-back reel

The third way was with a matchbox-sized piece of crust fished on the surface, and very exciting it was too, to see a carp weighing five pounds come up from the depths towards the bait, circle it for up to thirty minutes, often nudging it with its lips, and then leave it alone.

The pit had a carp of about ten pounds, which to us youngsters was huge. It consumed many of my waking hours – and probably all of my sleeping ones. This big, common carp would roll on the crust bait hitting it with its tail and, as the bread drifted away on the surface, feed safely on the small pieces.

Early in 1949 I had been given a tank aerial about 14ft long. My Uncle Eddy helped me to make it into a fishing rod, but a success it was not. So after a rethink, the aerial was cut down to 9ft and made into a nice spinning rod, which caused the downfall of several pike. The reel was an old, walnut, star-back reel of 3½in diameter. It was fitted with a check, and came with some antique line, very thick and of dubious breaking strain. Attached to the end of the line was a length of thick, cat gut to which I could tie a hook. It had been used for pike-fishing all through the previous winter.

From the start of the season I had been going to Paddlesworth pit at every opportunity, either fishing, watching the carp, or talking to other anglers. For most of the time I was fishing I could see that the carp were coming close to my bait but I just couldn't get one to pick it up. It was exasperating to say the least, and I used to get very angry because I couldn't catch a carp... that was until late July. It was a Friday, and I had cycled to the pit with Peter Tillitt. Our idea was to camp for a few days so that we could fish day and night. We chose as our pitch the top of a high bank on the western side of the lake. The tent was a small white one known as a pup tent, and there was just enough room inside for the two of us. Our cooking stove was an old paraffin Primus, and for light we had a hurricane lamp. We had no sleeping bags or camp beds, just a couple of old army blankets and some big safety-pins.

We arrived in the rain, pitched the tent and wrapped ourselves in our old gas-capes to keep dry. Soon the sky cleared, the sun came out and it turned very warm. We watched an angler on the other side of the pit catch a carp. I was envious and wished that I could catch such a fish. Then, looking down from the high bank where the tent was pitched, I spotted a mirror carp of about five pounds. I grabbed my rod bag and tackled up. It was with fumbling fingers and a fast-beating heart that I threaded the line through the rings and tied on a hook, all the time frightened that the carp would swim off.

I baited with a piece of brown bread and honey paste, pulled a few feet of line from the reel and dropped the bait into the margin about twelve inches away from the nose of the fish, which was still rooting about in the bottom. There was no reaction from the carp as it continued to dig into the mud, causing the water to colour up. Only the occasional bubble appeared on the surface – something that Richard Walker in his Still-water Angling called 'smoke screening'.

Through the murky water I watched as the fish straightened up onto an even keel and moved towards the bait. My heart thumped, my mouth was dry and my hands were shaking as I willed the fish to pick up my bait. It tilted its head downwards and the bait disappeared. With no more thought I struck upwards; there was a boil in the water, the fish shot out into the lake and my old wooden reel screamed as line disappeared off its spool. Then everything stopped – the fish had buried itself in the weed.

Peter suggested trying to pull the line from side-to-side. I did, but nothing happened. Then one of the senior members came around from the other side of the pit. He also told me to try pulling the line in a seesaw movement. I did, and the fish started to move, taking more line off the reel. The older angler said, "Lay the rod over to the left, lad." I did as he told me, the fish turned and I started to take in some line. But how was I going to get the fish out of the water without a landing net? This problem was soon solved when the older angler told Peter to go round and get his net. I don't think Peter had ever run so fast in his life. He was back in no time, and with the fish wallowing on the surface, the older angler took the net and scooped out my first carp! I was a happy boy. The fish was put on the club scales: it weighed 4½lb exactly. I left Peter and cycled off home to tell my Mum the good news, and then pedalled all the way back to continue our carp-fishing. I continued to fish for them for many, many years.

One nice place I fished was called Laughing Waters. There were two lakes alongside the London A2 near Cobham in Kent. The larger lake of some six acres was gin-clear with lots of weed, and it held a good head of perch, roach and rudd, plus a few good pike; we often wondered if it could produce a twenty-pounder. The smaller lake of less than two acres had rhododendron bushes around its banks, and contained lots of common carp which could be caught on floating crust. Sometimes we would catch up to eight in a night session.

I fished with floating bread crust, using 10lb Luron line and a size 6 Allcocks Model Perfect hook. I used to grease the line to make it float, and cast out the bread so that it drifted under the rhododendron bushes. Then I would pull off some more line from the reel and fold a piece of silver paper from a Player's cigarette packet over the line as a bite indicator.

My friends and I would sit quietly watching the water birds, and sometimes a carp would appear near the bait. We would sit there, mouths dry, eyes bolting out, willing the fish to take our crust. Sometimes they would cruise around the bait for twenty minutes or more, but as soon as the crust disappeared in a swirl we would be on our feet striking hard over our shoulders. The rod would be pulled down towards the water as the fish fought hard to get in among the tree roots. We never gave much line – it was like a tug-of-war in which sometimes we won: other times it was the fish.

On the A2 just outside Laughing Waters there was a mobile coffee-stall, and during our night-fishing sessions we would go there to buy hot pies and coffee. It was all good fun, and some evenings we would have these good-looking women walking around the lake in the evening

after dinner at the lakeside restaurant. You can imagine what thoughts we seventeen and eighteen year-olds had. In fact I had a romance for a few weeks with one of the waitresses. She would bring me tea and sandwiches to the waterside, and if the carp weren't feeding then it would be cuddles in the back of the restaurant. They were good times!

In those far-off days, and for several years, there were three

Lobworms – a good bait   men who taught me so much.

Their knowledge was awesome – they told me things I shall never forget. They were: Len Cuckoo, a newsagent, Dennis Trim, an engineer, and Harry Rowlands who owned a snob's shop, or shoe repairer's. In those days you called a shoe repairer a 'snob'; a 'snob' was the name for a cobbler; you don't hear the word 'snobs' or 'cobblers' very much these days. I was lucky to have a Saturday morning job in Harry's shop, where I would spend my time cleaning his four-legged seat basket and numerous rods and reels. I would then sort out and tidy up all the other bits and pieces of tackle. Having finished these tasks I would go off to Gammon's tackle shop in Chatham to collect Harry's bait order that he would need for his next day's fishing. It usually consisted of two pints of gentles, a pint of hempseed, perhaps some worms, and Sprats silver groundbait. Back in the shop, after being cleaned, the gentles were put into fresh bran. I got half-a-crown from my Saturday morning job.

Harry, Dennis and Len never missed a Sunday fishing-trip whatever the weather. All three men were extremely good, match-anglers, winning many competitions between them. They also caught their share of big fish including carp. Harry often fished Windmill Pond where he was very adept at catching carp on floating crust. What made us all smile was whenever Harry was fishing Windmill pond on a Sunday, a good-looking woman from a nearby house would deliver a roast-beef lunch and a bottle of beer to his swim. Lunch over, Harry would say, 'Keep your eye on my gear I'm going for a walk' (nudge-nudge, wink-wink) and we didn't see Harry for two or three hours! All three men taught me so much and it was through these gentlemen that I got into match-fishing myself, winning my share of the money and trophies.

It was Harry who gave me my first hooks to nylon. They were far superior to the old cat gut. A few months after I started using these I met Brian Bannister, a carp angler from Croydon, at Windmill Pond. He showed me some Allcocks Model Perfect hooks; they were so much better than anything I had seen or used before. With the money from my Saturday job, plus what I made from selling bundles of firewood around the village; the money given by granny, aunties and my pocket money, I soon had enough cash to buy some. I also got an Allcocks Wallis Wizard rod with an Ambidex reel filled with Luron 2 line. The only thing missing was a large, landing net so my uncle Eddie made one for me from some netting he used for shrimping, and the metal rim from the wheel of a child's pram. It was heavy and cumbersome but it did the job. My carp-fishing baits were floating crust, bread paste, lobworms and boiled potatoes. Floating crust and potatoes were the top two baits. Me and my mates really did think we were proper carp-anglers; these days I often wonder what we would have caught if we

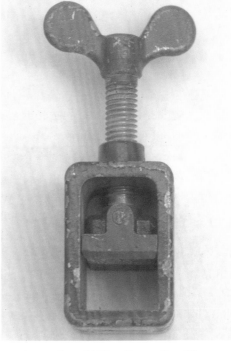

My well used Milbro Lesney Bread Press

could have used modern baits such as boilies, casters, gentles, boiled wheat and hemp. My special bait of the day was brown bread and honey paste but it never proved as good as potatoes – the small fish could soon whittle it down.

We moved on to catching carp from Windmill pond, Laughing Waters, Mote Park, Badger and Paddlesworth Lakes. It was from this latter water that I caught a lot of my carp, a spot where I learnt so much about the fish which often proved so exasperating. Paddlesworth Lake was the water where I caught my first double-figure carp – a big highlight in my life.

I had borrowed a small pup-tent that was supposed to be big enough for two people – I reckon they meant pigmies! It was so small that we could just about move in the confined space. John Barnard, another angler who loaned me the tent, never seemed to have any problems making love to his many girl friends in it. He seemed have a different girl at the lake whenever we met. On a couple of occasions we even exchanged girl friends, but I never did see him fishing. One summer's evening he was caught out in the open making love to the current girl friend, with her stockings, suspenders and knickers scattered close by. They didn't seem bothered and just carried on. That was JB for you. John called the small tent his 'love nest.' For cooking we had our old paraffin Primus cooking stove, with a hurricane lamp for light. There were no camp beds or sleeping bags; we made do with an old army blanket. The most important items of equipment we were never without were the kettle, teapot and frying-pan.

With the wind blowing towards the deeper water at roadside end of the lake, we pitched our tent on the west bank, an area that often proved a favourite spot for carp as they patrolled in search of the loose pieces of crust. Having sorted out our home for a few days, we put together our tackle. We both had an Allcocks Wizard rod, and, as we were fishing floating-crust, we chose centre-pin reels with 10lb Luron 2 line which was given a good covering of Muciline grease so it floated. Our hooks were Allcocks Model Perfect pattern – there wasn't a better hook. With everything in order we threw some chunks of crust on the water then sat back to wait for the appearance of our quarry.

After an hour, with no sign of the carp, we decided to have something to eat and drink. Soon the frying pan was full of sizzling sausages, bacon and beans, while Pete buttered some bread. We then sat and stuffed ourselves full of food. With our meal finished, Pete put the kettle on for a brew and minutes later we sat back enjoying our mug of tea, smoking and talking about carp; the latest rumours of who was catching what and where from – even in those far-off days there was a lot of secrecy. As usual we discussed Walker's Pitch, the weekly column in the Angling Times. What a great paper it was in those days; I don't know of anyone who now buys a copy. Today I have the Angler's Mail which gives me enough news on a weekly basis.

Just after dusk had settled over the pool, and with thick cloud cover, conditions looked excellent. Then we heard the first 'cloop' as a carp sucked down a bit of crust. It was time for action. I baited my size 6 hook with a chunk of crust, lowered it into the water under my rod tip, then folded a piece of silver paper over the line between reel and butt ring. Meanwhile, further along the bank, Pete was doing the same. I sat back waiting for another 'cloop' that showed a fish was close to my bait, or better still had sucked in my crust-baited hook. An owl hooted from a nearby beech tree, otherwise all was peaceful.

An hour later Pete came by to announce that he had just missed a fish, and was going back to the tent for a smoke and to make a brew. Ten minutes later the silver paper moved in determined fashion. Picking up the rod I made a firm strike, a good fish was hooked. The reel screamed into life, I called to Pete, 'Fish on, can you get the net?' He was quickly beside me. Thankfully the fish powered away to my right which was up to the main body of the lake away from the roots of several large beech trees on my left. For ten minutes it was a bit of give-and-take but slowly I started to gain some line. After what seemed a lifetime a big boil appeared on the water some five yards away. Slowly I pumped the fish towards the waiting net. Pete didn't need a second chance as the fish went head first into the deep mesh. He said, "It's a good one".

Well away from the water's edge we laid the net on a hessian sack and then parted the wet mesh. It was a mirror carp which to me looked huge. While I took out the hook, Pete soaked another big hessian sack in which we would keep the fish overnight – we couldn't get the club scales until next morning. Then, having made sure the fish was on an even keel in the sack, I put the kettle on for a brew. Within minutes I was pouring boiling water into the teapot, and soon we were sipping hot tea as we discussed what we thought the fish would weigh. We both agreed it was over ten pounds. An hour later with no more sounds of 'clooping' carp we got our heads down until dawn. It was around six in the morning when I crawled from the tent. The first priority was to get the Primus stove going for a fresh brew. While waiting for the kettle I had a smoke then checked on the fish, everything was in order. At eight o'clock Pete went across the road to collect the scales and weights; in those days we weighed our fish on a set of greengrocer's scales which had a brightly-polished brass pan. Pete found a level bit of ground, set up the scales and put on weights totalling twelve pounds. I then took the fish from the sack and placed it carefully in the pan. Nothing moved: too much weight. Pete tried again with a few ounces less: still nothing moved. On the third try the scales stirred then settled on an even keel: the fish weighed in at 10lb 12oz. Pete took some pictures on my new Kodak bellows camera and we slipped the fish back into the water. We watched it swim off strongly then shook hands and entered the weight of the fish in the book.

In those early days I fished a short stretch of the Higham canal and Mote Park Lake. I never caught a single carp from either of these venues – though I did catch some big eels from the canal, which I would take home to granddad. I was often rewarded with some of granny's apple pie, plus a shilling piece; if I was very lucky it would be half-a-crown. One water I fished a lot was Paddlesworth Lake; it was alive with masses of tiny rudd, perch and many carp, with enough good, double-size fish to make it interesting. It was where the lucky angler had the chance of a big fish weighing ten pounds or more. At this time my mates and I were really into carp-fishing. We would study the articles by Water Rail (Richard Walker) whose pieces in Fishing Gazette were read and re-read dozens of time. We devoured anything on carp-fishing. As we had many discussions regarding the best bait to use, one book we all owned and avidly read was Sheringham's Coarse Fishing, especially his experience of fishing the Red Spinners water at Cheshunt Lower Reservoir, and the use of potatoes as bait. He wrote about how small fish would ignore them.

It was through his writings that we decided on a baiting programme with potatoes. I, or one of my mates, would visit the water as often as possible to throw in a pound or two of boiled potatoes. Whatever the weather I don't think we missed a baiting session. After about four weeks the carp were addicted to spuds. In many of the old angling books, authors describe fishing with par-boiled potatoes – how they caught carp I will never know! It would be very difficult to pull the hook through such bait – remember, some carp anglers in those days even used a treble hook. I suggest you give it a try! In my opinion, potatoes should be boiled so they are quite soft. That's what Sheringham told us on page 180 of Coarse Fishing. He writes:

Potato on Crust Pad

> "A small new potato boiled till it's soft and stripped of half its brown skin so as to show white on the bottom".

We then used a baiting needle to pull the line through the potato bait before tying on a size 4 hook. The hook was then pushed through a piece of crust, which sat on the bend of the hook to act as a pad for the potato to rest on. The bread pad helped stop the hook pulling through the soft bait. In those days the only weight we used was the bait: back then, lead was taboo.

I can remember one special occasion as if it was yesterday. I had thirteen double-figure carp in a session: the smallest at 10lb 3oz, the best at 12lb 10oz. Bill Cutting, Brian Long, Peter Burstow, Bill Hall and I had pre-baited a water with boiled potatoes for nine weeks leading up to the start of the season. We never missed a single day of baiting. It got to the stage where we could throw stones in the water and the carp would appear – looking for the spuds!

Bill Cutting and Brian Long had arrived on the Thursday for a midnight start to the season, I wasn't allowed to miss college on a Friday, and we really did expect to catch lots of fish that night. It was a disaster: Bill and Brian didn't catch a single fish, or even get a bite, and it was the same on Friday. All through Saturday we sat behind silent Heron bite indicators. At around six

o'clock in the evening I cooked eggs, bacon, sausages and beans for our tea. As we sat eating I turned and said, "We'll catch tonight, can't you smell water mint?" There was a strong smell of mint in the air, and from experience, whenever this mint smell was noticeable at the water's edge, we have, more often than, not caught fish.

Back in our swims nothing happened. We sat through the dark hours talking in low tones, smoking

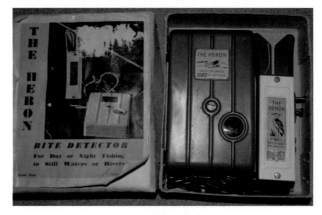

Heron Bite Alarm

our pipes or nodding off, then waking with a start. The first light of dawn appeared: still nothing. Half-an-hour after dawn I had a screaming run on my right-hand rod; as I was playing this fish the left-hand buzzer sounded. Opening the bale arm on the reel of the fish I had already hooked, I put the rod back on the rest and struck the other rod; I now had two hooked fish. I got the second fish in then picked up the rod on which I still had the first fish, and got that in the net. Bill quickly got the two carp into hessian sacks while I re-baited both rods, and then cast out. Within minutes one of the rods was away – another good carp was landed. It continued in this manner until around

Never without my Jack Knife

eight o'clock in the morning. While all this was going on, my other mates collected all the hessian sacks they could get hold of so we could sack up the fish. Meanwhile, Bill was alongside me landing and unhooking the fish, making tea and generally being a great help. At nine o'clock we got hold of the club scales. After weighing each fish we released them and watched as they swam off strongly. It was without doubt my best-ever carp-fishing session up to that time in my life. I have had much bigger fish and more fish in a session, but never such an exciting time as that morning. The pre-baiting paid off in great style.

I almost lost our secret of boiled spuds as bait. It was during the second week of the season, and the second week of our two-week session, when the secret was nearly discovered. I had hooked a good mirror and for several minutes slowly had the fish coming towards the landing net. Then I noticed the potato had been blown about three feet up the line. Another member watching the action said, "What's that on your line?" In an instant I said, "It's a balanced weight that sits on top of the weed." Seconds later I asked him to go across the lake and collect a sack from my friend Brian Long, thankfully he agreed to do so.

While he was away I got the fish into the net then crushed the potato. When he got back the fish was weighed – a nice mirror of fourteen pounds – he then asked about the balanced weight. I just said, "After taking out the hook and cutting it off the line, before I tied on a new hook, the weight slipped down the line into the water." Thankfully he believed this tale. That season we caught a lot of carp on potatoes when other anglers were failing to catch on their pigeon-egg size bits of bread paste. In those days we didn't have bivvies, just our white pump tent, though usually we would sit behind a small bush or screen of reeds, waiting for some action. We would often make the screen using camouflaged netting. Anglers, moving quietly around the water, would often say to one another as they passed you, "He's a carp angler," often in a hushed voice and reverent tones. Such was carp-fishing in those days where our target fish were carp over ten pounds.

Some years later, probably 1969–70, I again commenced a heavy baiting programme with potatoes on a north Kent gravel pit. It really pulled carp into a small area between two islands, a place no-one bothered to fish; I had those carp to myself. I caught lots of double-figure fish, with the odd twenty-plus pounder. Should another angler come by he would see other bait scattered around. I had those fish so turned on I could often predict to within an hour when they would start to feed.

I well remember Mike Harris, who built some great, top quality rods, a man who caught the first thirty pound carp from Kent and one of the nicest guys I had the privilege to know and fish with. (Mike, like me, also loves to fish for big roach.) One July afternoon in 1970 or 1971 Mike joined me for a carping session. Two hours into the session I said to Mike, "I reckon we should get a take at about a quarter to five". Minutes later the silver paper moved to the butt ring. I glanced at my watch: it was 4.45 p.m. After a good scrap Mike netted a nice double-figure mirror carp for me. Then he said, "I don't mind you catching these bloody carp but you don't have tell me what time you will get a take!" I would visit the area every day between four and five o'clock in the afternoon, then throw in three or four tins of spuds. If anyone was around I would chuck in some crusts in another area.

Back to 1956 when I was a dedicated carp fisher – I suppose you could call it carp fever – I had two Richard Walker MK1V rods, two Mitchell 300 reels and a Richard Walker landing net with laminated cane arms; I was using Sportex nylon. I had been using the Heron bite alarms for some time, having been asked to field-test a pair and report on their performance. They

Another Carp on potato bait

were not very reliable in damp weather; I found silver paper folded over the line a far better proposition. On damp nights I would often sit with the silver-paper indicators in the palm of my hands – should I nod off, the movement of the paper would usually have me alert. No way did we get inside our tents and wait for the bite alarm to sound.

To keep dry we used an army cape on four sticks. If we wanted to sleep, we did so in a small white tent, bringing in our tackle before we settled down. It was considered rule-breaking to leave a rod unattended; unlike nowadays when anglers are often fifty yards away from their rods – it has been known for some carp fishers to go off for a pint or visit the local Chinese or Indian restaurant for a curry. These days, I have even seen them watching TV inside their bivvies. I find this rather horrid; surely we want to sit beside the water and watch what is going on.

From 16 June until the first frosts of October, carp were king, though I still fished for other species both in fresh and saltwater. My granddad often took me on fishing trips in his Ford 8 car so I got to fish carp-waters further afield. I also had a beat-up BSA Bantam motorbike from my uncle Eddie, which helped me reach all those out-of-the-way secretive fishing spots. One such place was Wadhurst Lake in East Sussex which contained lots of wild carp. I heard tales about carp that could weigh twenty pounds though I didn't see any evidence. I did see a carp of fourteen pounds get caught one night. There were plenty of signs that the water contained double-figure fish though the best I can remember was about eight pounds. It was a difficult water to fish.

Some of the great carp-anglers of the day fished Wadhurst. They were the late Fred J Taylor and Dick Walker and other anglers, like rod builder Tony Fordham, and Derrick Davenport who I believe lived or worked in Faversham, Kent and was responsible for the manufacture of the Heron bite indicator. I still occasionally use one today for old time's sake. Bill Keal, who lived in Woolhampton and worked on the Financial Times, and who died so tragically in a motorway accident, also fished the water. Bill was a great all-round angler: I can recall him fishing at Paddlesworth. He fished the Medway on many occasions in winter for the roach. He was also a great fan of the River Kennet, and up to the time of his tragic passing, lived a stone's throw away from the river – even today he is sorely missed. Alec Lewis and Jack Hilton, the man who gave us that great book Quest for Carp were among other great anglers who walked the banks of Wadhurst.

In the 1950s me and my mates were the disciples of Walker: he was our guru. Walker taught us we could catch big fish by design and not by luck. Through his writing, Bernard Venables of Mr Crabtree fame, gave us the mystery and magic of carp-fishing, while Walker welded on his experience of a being a naturalist, engineer and mathematician. His scientific knowledge gave us not only the tools for the job of catching big carp, but also the technical know-how of how to do it. Walker and the Carp Catchers Club pooled all their knowledge, and then passed it on to us – his disciples through articles in the angling press.

In the early 1960s a twenty pound carp was the target fish and we were using new ideas and baits. Many hours, probably hundreds, were spent experimenting with baits and end rigs. My friends and I devoted a lot of time trying to work out new ways to present a bait, or thinking up ideas for paste baits. We tried various bait mixes which were then boiled to give them a hard skin – hopefully to stop the rudd, roach and skimmer bream from nibbling away at them, but I don't think it really worked as the bream still took the baits.

Rods, using various rigs, were cast out a few yards onto the grass; the rod then put in a pair of rests, while someone pulled the line. We noted how much pressure was needed to move the silver-paper indicator. Perhaps a couple of times a week we would get together and discuss carp. Women were often considered a distraction in our quest for the big fish. I remember catching one twenty-pounder. As I sat in a coffee bar with Mary my girl friend at the time, Paul Bailey said, "Shall we go bowling?" Most of the couples said, "OK." Blasting from the jukebox was Bye Bye Love by the Everly Brothers. Picking up my crap hat (crash helmet) I said, "Not me, I'm going carping." Mary said, "No, we're going bowling!" I turned, said, "Bye-bye Love." Then I walked out. You could easily pick up a girl friend: carp were more difficult to catch.

I arrived at a large gravel pit that evening, conditions were perfect. Two mates, Bill and John, were fishing either side of a stream that entered the northern end of the stretch of water. I chose to fish a channel on the western bank, where the water was about seven feet deep. I had been baiting the area with cooked potatoes for several days; during a previous visit I had seen the carp eating those spuds. As I sat feeding the line through the guides of my MK1V, a big fish rolled over the baited area. The chances of catching a carp were looking good. Having got all my tackle sorted out, I positioned the Heron bite alarms. I was now ready to bait the size 4 hook. With a baiting needle I pulled the line through the well cooked potato then tied on the hook. Before sliding the spud down onto the hook, I placed a piece of crust on the bend to act as a cushion, stopping the hook from pulling through the bait when casting.

Ten minutes later with both baits in position, I put the kettle on for a brew. Around midnight the left-hand rod was away. I turned the reel handle and waited as the line started to tighten; the firm but controlled strike encountered strong resistance – the fight was on! I quickly realised it was a good fish; after several minutes I had the feeling I was winning this contest. Sliding my giant-size Richard Walker laminated cane arm landing net into the water I crouched, watching the direction of the line from the rod tip against the darkening night sky, knowing I didn't have to worry about obstructions. The fish was nearly beaten; I cramped on the pressure and started drawing it towards the submerged net. It was a big mirror: within seconds it was

mine. Taking out the hook, I transferred the fish to a well-wetted hessian sack which I had previously soaked in the water.

Rounding up my mates I said, "I think I've got a twenty." Bill and John quickly wound in their tackle then followed me back to my pitch. John tried lifting the sack, commenting, "Bloody hell you old bugger, this sack's heavy." Our scales were nothing like those in use today. I had a big, brass Salter spring balance; we hooked the sack on the scales and took a reading. We then got a picture of the fish – this nearly didn't happen as the first two flashlight bulbs didn't work. Thankfully, the last

A Kettle was part of my kit

one did the trick. Having released the fish we weighed the sack, and then deducted the weight, the fish weighed 22lb pounds 8oz, give or take an ounce or two. I spent the rest of the night smoking my pipe and drinking tea. I was elated. It certainly beats bowling and girls – the latter can be caught anytime. One super bait we often used was floating crust. To defeat the gulls we would cast out an anchored crust then feed line until the crust appeared on the surface. When a gull appeared we would pull the line dragging the bread below the surface. It worked every time.

The middle of the 1960s was a time of change in the carp-fishing world. Overnight we moved from bread in various forms, worms and potatoes, to boiled-paste baits. It was the start of a new bait regime. I think it was 1967 or '68 when we first used Kit-e-Kat: we also started to use a weight on the line. I don't know who thought of using cat food but it certainly switched on the carp. I remember pre-baiting a swim for several weeks before using it. Sadly, the bream and tench also loved the stuff. The cat food was stiffened with Pomenteg, a ground-bait produced by a London company Efgeeco. Fred J Taylor who worked for Efgeeco was the guy who had done the experimental work with this ground-bait. Mixing it with Kit-e-Kat we made a firm paste, and then boiled it to get a hard skin.

At first we boiled the baits indoors, until our parents or wives said, "Get that horrid smell out of the house!" I then got hold of a Baby Burco clothes boiler which I installed in the garden shed. After a season some of us stopped boiling baits as we didn't think the flavour leaked out of the unboiled samples. Despite my success with cat food, I still used and continued my baiting programme with spuds. Another successful bait was sausage meat paste; I first used it for tench, but it caught good carp. The late Gerry Savage had a lot of carp on this bait. I am still using it today, for tench, chub and barbel; occasionally I catch carp on it. Other paste baits in the late '60s and early '70s were made from luncheon meat, cod roe, sardine and finely-minced liver, all mixed with Pomenteg. I rated this latter bait very highly for a few weeks; we didn't boil these baits. It was also was a very secretive world; we would only bait our hooks when no one was around and would always make sure we had some other bait partially hidden to throw curious anglers off the scent.

Up until the middle 1960s, I only used a weight on the line when legering bread crust. By the end of the '60s things had changed and we were using weights on the line, often in conjunction with weighted bite-indicators known as 'monkey climbers'. Little did we know how effective a weight could be. We caught a lot of carp, using a standard link leger, 15in hook link, with a 4in lead link. We had gone from no weight to an ounce or more. To make matters more comfortable at the water edge, we now used a brolly. Then the late Bill Keal, a journalist on the Financial Times, gave us the sun lounger, known as a bed-chair purchased from Woolworths. It was not that reliable; suddenly you would hear the tearing of material as you were dumped on the ground, perhaps the legs would collapse, and anglers were sometimes thrown into the water. Our season was 16 June until the first frosts in October. We didn't think carp fed in the winter.

In the late '60s early '70s, the man who made the big breakthrough with modern baits, and who must be given full credit, was London docker Fred Wilton with his HNV(High Nutritional Value) baits. Fred is the man who created today's modern boilies. I couldn't be bothered getting all the ingredients and spending time in the kitchen, so I stayed with the baits that I've previously mentioned. A man who was using the modern baits and catching a lot of big carp was Kevin Maddocks, author of Carp Fever: if you're a budding carp angler then read this book. I quote a recipe from Kevin's book for a Sodium Caseinate Paste: 5oz Sodium Caseinate, 2oz Pym or Yestamin, 4oz Milk Powder, 4oz Wheat Germ. In the early '70s I was using sweet corn, which was known as 'the golden grains', and red worms – an excellent bait for close-in work for bubblers. Air-injected lobs were another success.

I remember catching an eighteen pound mirror carp about a foot from the bank on a free-lined lob. As I was playing the fish, a guy in the next pitch came out of his bivvy. On seeing me playing, then netting the fish he said, "Where did you catch that?" "Under my rod tip," I answered. "No you didn't, you can only catch carp on that gravel bar," he said as he pointed out towards the lake. No way could I convince him otherwise. As mentioned, potatoes were still a good bait. To the best of my knowledge I was then the only one who continued using them, as they were considered old-fashioned – or so other anglers told me. Potatoes continue to take carp today.

Discussing baits such as potatoes, cat food and the new HNV baits and the boily revolution which changed the face of carp angling with fellow enthusiasts, I got the impression that carp-fishing was now more about baits than water-craft. During the 1980s I spent a lot of time carp-angling up-and-down the country. Estate lakes and old, mature gravel pits were the waters I chose to fish. I was also fortunate to have the right to fish on a gravel pit in Gloucestershire which had originally been dug in the late 1930s to provide gravel for a nearby airfield. The stocked carp were the Leney strain (the same fish that were stocked in Redmire). I would spend three-days-a-week carp-fishing, though if my work schedule allowed I often had a full week at the waterside. I was fortunate to have a caravan on the Gloucestershire water, on the other waters I fished I, like everyone else, had a bivvy.

I was now using the latest, bite indicators, bait-runner reels and various rods designed for carp-fishing at long range. Of course I still used softer-action rods for close-in work or when fishing with floater baits. While many of my carp-fishing friends made their own baits I couldn't be bothered. I used Ritchworth baits, and I didn't notice that my catches were below those of my mates with their home-made recipes. Thankfully, I was single, didn't smoke or drink so I could afford to buy lots of boilies which I fished on a hair rig. In those days most of us supported the Carp Society which certainly catered for the carp-angler. The society organised meetings up-and-down the country, with an annual conference each year. All of them were very well supported. I thoroughly enjoyed these events where anglers from all over the country met up and discussed carp, which was then the number one fish; it was also a very profitable business for many people.

I can remember fishing a carp water in Sussex when, as I was having breakfast on 3 August 1985, an old friend from Warwickshire hunted me down to tell me Richard Walker had passed away. Even though I knew Richard was very ill, I was still shocked to learn of his passing. I am not ashamed to say I shed some tears for the great man. I suppose it was about eleven o'clock

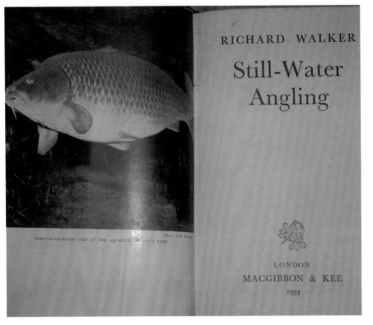

RICHARD WALKER

Still-Water Angling

LONDON
MACGIBBON & KEE
1953

in the morning when my right-hand rod indicator crawled to the butt ring. The strike connected with a carp which was soon netted; it weighed about ten pounds. It was a replica of Richard's forty-four pounder caught back in the 1950s. I glanced skywards muttering a few words of thanks to the master. On Sunday, 20 October many of us travelled to St Andrews Church, Biggleswade for a Service of Thanksgiving. The Thanksgiving Address was given by Fred Buller. It was very moving and I doubt if there was a dry eye in the church that morning. I recorded the service which was broadcast by the BBC. Following Richard's death I spent several years trying to get him honoured in Westminster Abbey.

Without doubt the great event in the eighties was the Carp Society Conference '88 in Dunstable to look back over the past fifty years of carp-fishing and to remember Richard Walker and his enormous contribution to angling. I recall getting a letter from Mike Kavanagh, conference organiser on 27 October my fiftieth birthday, asking me to host the chat show. His final words were, "Please say yes?" I immediately called Mike to say I would be delighted. I considered this a great honour to be asked. As I said to Mike, "It's a bigger honour doing this to celebrate the memory of Richard Walker, than getting an award in the New Year's Honour's list." Three anglers couldn't attend: BB (Denys Watkins-Pitchford MBE), Maurice Ingham and Dick Kefford. I told the Carp Society I would be prepared to visit these great anglers and video an interview with each of them at no cost, not even my expenses. The video was done and shown at the Conference. When I interviewed Maurice Ingham, I was shocked to learn that he didn't have a copy of the book Drop Me a Line that he and Richard Walker had written. I said, "Don't worry Maurice I'll get you a copy." Within a week,

Martin with the late Dick Kefford of Suffolk,

after numerous telephone calls, I managed to find a first edition which I sent to him. It was a thank-you gift for the knowledge he had passed on to us young carp anglers in the '50s. During the preparation for the Conference, my multiple sclerosis was giving me a lot of trouble, I had to use both my wheelchair and Zimmer frame, but it was worth all the effort.

On the day of the Conference, to say I was nervous would have been an understatement – I even had to get a friend to put my cuff links in my shirt. Standing in the wings waiting to be introduced by Fred J Taylor, I thought back over the past years and the job I had agreed to do in Dick Walker's memory. Once on stage everything went without a hitch as I introduced and interviewed the famous names from the past fifty years of carp-fishing.; everyone was so kind. Once the memorial for Richard Walker and the main part of the Conference were over, a friend took me back home to Lancashire. My late friend Len Head stayed on for the auction with instructions to make sure we put in the highest bid for the first week's fishing at Redmire.

The next day I got a call from Len to say, "We can't fish your lake on June 16th for a week."

"Why not?' I asked.

Len then announced, "Were going to Redmire."

I shouted, "Yes, well done Len on getting Redmire, I'll call you in the week." Turning to my current girl I said, "We've got Redmire, let's celebrate, is it out for dinner first or a tumble in the bed?" We chose the tumble – thankfully she wasn't hungry! "We've got Redmire." It cost us £750 and it was worth every penny.

My visit to Redmire Pool was a dream comes true: I had wanted to visit this historic carp-fishery since 1951 after reading a feature in the Fishing Gazette. My two companions were Dougy Wood and the late Len Head. We agreed to meet in Ross-on-Wye at eleven o'clock in the morning. As I pulled up early at the arranged spot Len and Dougy appeared. Seeing them,

The Gang L-R Len Head, Les Bamford, Vic Cranfield, Author, Len Arbery, Dougy Wood
Credit Len Arbury

I said, "I thought we were meeting at eleven?' "Yes,' said Len, "but we couldn't wait." We then went off to a café for tea and toast. Arriving on the dam at Redmire, we met up with Len Arbery, Les Bamford and Vic Cranfield who had been at the water for the previous three days, they were leaving as we arrived.

Len and Dougy bivvied up and fished with bait-runner reels, carbon rods, bite alarms and boilies. I fished with Richard Walker designed cane MK1V rods, vintage 1953 Mitchell 300 reels which had rollers in the bale arm designed and fitted by Len Arbery in the late 1960s.

I used silver-paper indicators when fishing in the darkness, with free-lined soft paste baits. The old ways worked for me but sadly, my companions didn't catch. I spent a lot of time in the shallows looking for feeding fish, and then casting soft-paste bait just ahead of a moving, rooting fish. I managed to get a few pick-ups. One night I fished Walker's Pitch in the famous willows, not daring to sleep. I sat up all night watching my indicators. Then in the false light of dawn the silver-paper indicator on the left-hand rod crawled slowly to the butt ring. The answering strike connected with a powerful fish.

The MK1V and Mitchell 300 reel were working perfectly. After some five minutes – perhaps ten – the fish slipped the hook. Winding in my limp line, I leant the rod against the willows then made myself comfortable on the rushes and went to sleep, waking up in the rain some three hours later. Our week was a great success. Each morning I would go into Ross to buy fresh vegetables and meat, each evening I would serve a three-course dinner. We even celebrated with a bottle of red or white wine depending on if we had chicken, fish or meat. I shall never forget my days at Redmire, with two great friends, and walking in the footsteps of giants.

After Redmire, I went off to the River Charante region in South West France, to write some features on the fine cognacs of the region, make some programmes on travel, boating holidays and wines. I also spent some time carp-fishing. In fact, so good was the fishing, I spent a lot of time in the region, where I rented a cottage for just a few francs. I also made many friends, two of whom had been in the French resistance; without a doubt, brave men who not only had to fight the Germans, but many of their own kind. Despite the atrocities carried out by the Germans, these courageous men and women of the French Resistance continued to take up arms against the German Army. After the war General Dwight D. Eisenhower wrote:

"Throughout France the Resistance had been of inestimable value in the campaign. Without their great assistance the liberation of France would have consumed a much longer time and meant greater losses to ourselves."

I recommend Ian Ousby's book, Occupation: The Ordeal of France, 1940-44 Published by Pimlico 1999 ISBN 0-7126-6513-7.

I had two more years of serious carp-fishing then bowed out. I didn't like the drinking, drug-taking and general behaviour that was taking place, more so when five people moved onto the water I was fishing. I had to witness groups getting together for a 'social' as they called it. Relying on bite alarms to tell them when a fish had hooked itself; often they were a hundred yards away from their rods.

At times they went off to the pub or for a curry, leaving one person in charge of the rods. Good luck to those who want this. It wasn't for me. I returned to my old ways of carp-fishing, doing short sessions. I still occasionally fished behind a couple of rods when I was trying to catch fish that were feeding well out on a gravel bar, but the week-long sessions are gone. My last two carp were both twenty pound fish from under my rod tip on a lake in Dorset. Today I fish in fresh and saltwater for anything that swims. But I wouldn't have wanted to have missed my carp-fishing days and nights, especially those of the 1950s and '60s.

Early on a Saturday morning in 2007, Martin Salisbury, a solicitor from Leyland, picked me up at six o'clock for the trip down to Redmire Pool in Herefordshire where we had arranged to meet Martin Mumby, a bailiff, and Eddie Price, who caught a 40lb 12oz carp on a cold September morning in 1959 and whose Fishing Diaries were soon to be published. Within three hours of leaving Lancashire, Martin Salisbury, Will Carter and I were sitting in a café at Ross-on-Wye having breakfast – after a visit to Wye Angling to get information on the fishing. We then went off to Redmire, a place I had last been to in 1987: it still had its magic, mystery and beauty. I suppose we spent about two hours at the pool where the highlight was meeting a giant of carp-fishing, Eddie Price. He was one of the pioneers back in those far- off days.

While Eddie sat on the dam looking up the Pool, and no doubt thinking back to the grand old days of carping, Martin Mumby and I walked the banks of this romantic pool as he told me about his love for the place and his previous meeting with Eddie, who he described as a charismatic figure and one of the greats of carp-fishing. After chatting with Martin, I rejoined Eddie who then told me about the day he caught his huge fish – at that time it was the second largest carp ever caught. I recorded the conversation and it was broadcast on Radio Lancashire. As I recorded the interview with Eddie, Martin and Will walked around the Pool taking many pictures and enjoying the flavour of this place which is so special in the hearts of so many carp-fishers.

Ten days Later, I arrived at Aquatecs Lakes in Berkshire, after a brew, I went off looking for carp. My baits today are bread, sausage meat paste and lobworms. I would just walk slowly moving around the lake scanning the water surface for signs of feeding or moving fish.

On this occasion I found a fish in a small area of open water among some dense weed, it could best be described as a 'smoke screening' fish, a name given by the late Richard Walker to describe a carp disturbing the bottom as it feeds. In doing so it creates an area of cloudy muddy water. The next minute this fish moved from rooting, to an upright position: a good mirror carp. On hands and knees, indian-fashion, I moved as close to the fish as I dare, no more than ten feet from it. I then lowered a worm-baited hook into the clear water about a foot in front of the fish. I could see its gills and pectoral fins occasionally moving. As the worm slowly drifted downwards then settled, wriggling on the bottom, the fish moved forward tilting as it did so. I controlled my breathing as if I was on a rifle range. This was as close an encounter with a fish as was possible. My heartbeat must have increased as the fish slowly moved its mouth over the bait.

The line twitched – and then twitched again; the fish righted itself and I could see the line going in the direction of its mouth. A controlled strike set the hook; suddenly the water was swirling and boiling as drops of water and weed seemed to go everywhere. The rod tip pulled down savagely, my reel screamed like a scolded cat as the fish tried to put as much distance as possible between itself and me. The fight was on. I reckon some thirty yards of line went in that first rush. Ten minutes later I had the fish in the landing net. It went 15½lb. It was some of the most exciting fishing I have had in a long time. As I sat having a fresh brew, my mind went back to the far-off days of the 1950s when we stalked fish, rather than sitting behind our rods. Back to the current day, I caught three more doubles, another mirror and two commons, one on floating crust, two on slowly-sinking bits of flake.

After an hour I found some carp, rooting and feeding in a corner where a stream trickled water into the lake. When it rains hard the stream resembles a raging torrent. To my left in no more than a foot of water close to some Norfolk reeds, I could see a common carp, about eighteen pounds, might even go twenty.

I flicked a small piece of sausage paste in the direction of the fish. Within minutes it upended, then sucked in the free offering. The next piece of paste had a size 8 hook hidden inside it, ten minutes later the fish moved forward then tilted downwards and took the paste-baited hook: I set the hook. Where once the water had all been calm, there was now a big boil as the surface erupted, bits of weed floated up – suddenly a big tail shaped like a huge paddle waved above the water. The fish righted itself then shot across the shallows creating a bow wave as it did so.

My old Mitchell 300 1953 vintage screamed and growled as line was torn from the spool. There wasn't a lot I could do at this time but wait for the fish to slow down: forty yards away it did just that. Collecting my senses, I proceeded to play the fish then get the line back on the spool. Ten minutes or so later, I had the fish wallowing in the shallows as I waded out with landing net in hand. Soon the fish was engulfed in the mesh. I reckon it was one of the most interesting scraps I have had with a carp. On the scales it weighed in at 19lb 12oz.

Nice Common Carp caught in the margins on freelined flake

I reckon tench are one of the nicest fish to catch, at perhaps the nicest time of the year. In my book it's hard to find a better time in the angling calendar. A warm June morning, as the first rays of the false dawn show in the east, is, I reckon, a beautiful time to be at the water's edge. Just looking at a tench makes you realise how beautiful these fish can be, especially those lovely yellow-looking fish with their orange red eyes. When you see that big paddle-shaped tail and those pectoral fins, you realise why these are such a powerful adversary.

During the 1980s I spent a lot of time at a pool in Gloucestershire in search of a double-figure tench, the water also contained quality roach and rudd; occasionally, I caught a rare bream including my first double-figure fish of 10lb 6oz taken as I recorded a Hook, Line and Sinker programme for BBC Radio Lancashire. This was a tough period in my life through having multiple sclerosis, a time when I had to use a wheelchair or Zimmer frame. I might have contracted MS, a rather horrid disease, but nothing was going to stop me from my chosen sport, pastime or passion; you see, I reckon it's a bit of all three, with a chunk of good luck thrown in when we get a big fish on the line!

Nightingale Pool was an old and very mature gravel pit, having been dug in the late 1930s to extract gravel which was so badly needed at that time for the building of airfields. Around the pool, were many willows and alders, in some areas these hardy waterside trees would lean right out over the water, offering shade and sanctuary to both fish and birdlife. Along the western shore were some big oaks, the odd beech and some tall sycamore trees.

Author with a Tench at Dawn

In the marginal shallows eres branched bur-reed, blue and yellow-flag iris, clumps of real bulrush – not those with the brown, fluffy heads, often called bulrush, they are, in fact, reed mace. Growing in the shallow, clean gravel were various sedges which attracted lots of damsel and dragon flies. In the deeper water were areas of white and yellow water lilies, plenty of Potamogeton natans, a floating, broad leaved pond weed, greater bladderwort and spiked water-milfoil, with lots of Canadian pond weed. As in most mature pits, I had plenty of snags to contend with; in this one they were along one bank. On the north bank, some fifteen feet out from the bank and in about ten feet of water, there was some 50-60 feet of three inch thick, rusty cable, along with several large trees that had crashed into the pool over a number of years, creating a haven for fish and waterfowl. I reckon my pool in this small area of the English countryside was as near to an angler's paradise as I could wish for.

Depending on my work schedule, I would sometimes spend two or more weeks at the pool, sleeping in a small cabin that had been put up some years previously close to one of the big oaks whose spreading branches offered coolness from the summer heat. Badgers visited my cabin home in the evening looking for food; often I would put out a chicken carcass or peanut butter sandwiches for these persecuted animals. Occasionally a fox would come by looking for some easy picking. I waged war on the evil, cunning and savage mink with trap and gun, eventually wiping them out from the immediate area. Waterfowl once again nested in a more peaceful environment.

Though my tackle requirements were quite simple I had rods, reels and lines to cover any eventuality that might happen at the pool. My rods were 12ft with a soft Avon action, designed for 4–6lb lines, these I used when seeking the roach and rudd using 4lb line, often with a 2lb hook link. I had a pair of rods for 8–12lb line, these I used for tench with 8lb line, sometimes I would step up to 10lb line in some swims. Two rods were a pair of Avons designed to handle 15lb line. These 'whopper stoppers' were chosen in case I spotted a very big tench in the area of the fallen trees and wire hawser. If I hooked a fish there I would need power to lug the fish out of the danger area.

Apart from rods designed to be used for legering or free lining, I also had a float rod, designed for lines of 5–8lb. My Mitchell 300 reels were fitted with line rollers by Len Arbery, back in the late 1960s, hence the reason they sound a bit like a coffee grinder, as Alan Roe calls them. I still reckon these reels work as well today as they did when purchased back in 1953, I cannot fault them. I had a couple of Shimano bait runners and two centre-pin reels. In my large rucksack were boxes of hooks, spools of line, weights and split shot in various sizes, spools of braid, swivels, Beta lights, and bite alarms, in fact, everything a long-stay angler would want.

I fished Nightingale Pool for several years, in the hope of catching a double-figure tench. It never happened: I caught a lot of tench, many over 7lb, my best weighing-in at 8lb 7oz, not a spawn-bound fish, but one in perfect shape. I always made sure my work schedule enabled me to arrive at Nightingale Pool several days before the season opened on 16 June. My last visit to the pool had been in early March when the trees and bushes were leafless,

1953 Mitchell 300's with bale arm roller fitted by Len Arbery

Nightingale Pool – Author with a nice Tench

the reeds around the margins withered and brown. Arriving in June, I could see a huge transformation: gone were the bare, lifeless banks, leafless trees and bushes; the oaks, sycamores, willow and alder trees, bushes and brambles were looking lovely in their new cloaks of green. Along the bank side were a profusion of wild flowers: purple-loosestrife, poppy, common dog-violet, red campion, cow parsley, common forget-me-not in a delicate blue, and hogweed. In the woodland were lots of wood-sorrel, with brambles, dog rose, hedged bindweed and a profusion of sweet-smelling honeysuckle. The small cabin proved ideal if I took a girlfriend to the lake for a few days.

In the gravel shallows were various aquatic plants looking resplendent, as the dragon and damsel flies flitted to and fro, often settling on a bulrush stem or yellow flag iris. Sometimes, I would cast my mind back to previous summers' days, when float fishing, and seeing the delicate damselflies settle on my red tipped float. I marvel at the flying display of dragonflies as they chase smaller insects for food.

At Nightingale I could often hear the hum of a million insects on those hot, windless, airless days. Pigeons would coo from the branches of the sycamore, beech, hawthorn or oak trees. Quarrelsome coots would do as they have always done down the ages, quarrel and fight among themselves. The clucking moorhen sometimes called a waterhen, goes about its business, with its constantly bobbing head, flicking tail feathers in a quiet fashion. Groups of ducklings on fast-moving paddle feet, chase and grab many of the aquatic flies hatching-off. Suddenly, the water erupts in a shower of spray as dozens of small fish leap skywards, no doubt from the toothy jaws of a pike, though it could be one of the big perch that inhabit my pool. Sadly, today, far too many waters are fished all through the year with no consideration for the fish and wildlife. Too many people these days are quite happy to take a selfish attitude and continue to fish, when fish, birds and wildlife need a rest from those who want another kipper on the end of their line and a fishery owner who wants more cash. As a committed naturalist and environmentalist since I was a young boy (I even got involved in protesting when DDT was a major problem) I've always wanted to improve and protect what we have. It's our duty to ensure that kids not yet born have a beautiful environment in which to enjoy the same pleasures we have had.

Arriving at Nightingale Pool, my first job is to rake and pre-bait some swims in readiness for 16 June, when my mate, John Bodsworth, would travel up from Sussex a couple of days before the opening of the coarse-fishing season, for our planned fishing together. Our best fishing times were usually either side of dawn and dusk. The latter session often lasting into the early hours of the morning, the dawn session was usually over by 8 o'clock. If it was an overcast day the fish would feed in short spells through the day. A strong wind blowing across the pool often encouraged them to feed.

I used a mixture of brown crumb, sweet corn, casters, hemp and lots of chopped lobworms to bait my swims, the baiting-up took place at dawn and dusk with a top-up in the two deep-water swims around midday. What did amaze me during the baiting period was the number of big roach and rudd that often appeared with minutes of baiting the shallow swims; I would sit and watch the fish move up the gravel bank, pushing through the weeds to get at the food.

In fact, as Len Head, author of that delightful book simply titled Tench often remarked, "I have never seen roach and rudd so aggressive in trying to get at food." On one occasion Len arrived just as I had finished putting in a pile of casters and hemp. As we stood chatting, a shoal of between ten and thirteen big roach appeared. As soon as they were over the bait they started to feed with gay abandon. The roach, we reckoned, weighed between one-and-a-half pounds to well over two pounds – in fact we thought one of those fish might push three pounds. Not just big fish, but giants in my book. Remember, this was taking place in about two feet of very clear water. I told Len how this often took place after baiting, but I couldn't get the fish to pick up my bait. After chatting about the problems for some time, we decided to fish the area with a single caster super glued to a short hair of 1lb BS and a size 16 fine wire hook. Then, having got everything sorted out, we waded out and dropped our baited hooks onto some clean gravel at the edge of the sloping bank leading into the deep water from where the roach usually appeared. Having spread about half a pint of casters over and around our baited hook, we moved back to the bank covering the line as it lay on the bottom with some fine gravel and bits of weed.

With our rod tips pointed downwards, the top guide resting on the gravel bottom, lines carefully camouflaged and with nothing else to do but wait, I put the kettle on for a brew, while Len went off to the cabin and made some sandwiches. Sitting in the afternoon sunshine, we discussed these incredible roach, I told Len about the big rudd that inhabited Nightingale Pool saying, "I've had several three pound–plus fish up to 3lb 5oz." Some three hours after baiting and setting our hooks, the roach appeared and quickly started feeding as they had done previously, with no thought of danger.

We sat hunched over our rods, just waiting for the line to move when we would spring into action. Twenty minutes later, the fish, along with all the free casters had gone, leaving just two baited hooks and two very frustrated anglers! That weekend the roach appeared on several occasions, we didn't catch a single one, but we didn't complain as we had some good tench to just over 7lb, Len also had a personal best rudd of 2lb 12oz.

Throughout that summer I continued to fish for a big tench, also hoping I might catch one of those big roach. I did catch several big rudd on legered crust. I remember Tony Farquarson and me visiting the pool for a few days; I was having a rough time with my health, using my wheelchair for most of the time. It was about 8 o'clock in the morning when I got out of my sleeping bag. Tony had been up for a few hours, and after I had finished getting dressed, he helped get me to the water's edge. A good wind was blowing in our faces.

Martin with a fine Rudd

Ten minutes later I spotted a rolling fish, saying to Tony, "That looked like a big rudd." I baited with a chunk of crust on a 2ft tail, allowing the bread to sit just above the weed. Within five minutes the dough bobbin moved purposely to the butt ring. Striking, I felt a good fish which put a lovely bend in my soft action rod. Soon Tony and I were looking at a big fish in the landing net. He said, "That's a big rudd Mart." I had to agree – it was well over three pounds.

Though it's been above average rainfall this season, I reckon it's been a good summer, the trees and bushes look wonderful, and the green conkers on the horse chestnut trees are starting to fill out, probably due to the wet summer, which is far better for the countryside. How I hate those hot summers with no rain, the countryside looking parched and dry; rivers full of weed and rubbish, streams down to a trickle.

What amazes me when the sun shines, are the hundreds of thousands who flock to the beaches to get a tan, often getting burnt in the process and ignoring the warnings of skin cancer, when they could be enjoying our wonderful countryside. There are some brilliant wild flower displays, pigeons coo in the nearby trees, blackbirds wrens, robins, blue and great tits, and other birds, hunt for caterpillars and other food items. Green woodpecker with their dipping flight and maniacal laugh are a welcome sight, and the coots are still as quarrelsome. The flora and fauna mean as much to me as the fish I catch. In fact the whole ambience of my surroundings is most important. No way could I fish the modern, still waters with their cafés, bars and all the other trappings of modern life. I just love the pristine wilderness of the English countryside.

On this trip, I chose a swim where the southwesterly wind had been blowing for the previous few days. The water averaged six feet. Dotted around the water's edge were areas of water lilies – a text book tench swim. Raking a swim near the lilies, I baited with Pallatrax method mix containing sweet corn, hemp, dead gentles, and casters with some molasses. It was then time to put together my gear; I chose to float fish using a 13ft rod, centre-pin reel and 6lb Gamma line, with a waggler float set-up.

During the dark hours I would use soft Avon rods, Shimano reels and 6lb Gamma line, my end rigs were Drennan feeders with a short fluorocarbon hook link and Pallatrax hooks between sizes 6s and 14s, depending on the bait being used. This could vary between corn, gentles, casters, flake or lobworm. I then left the baited areas alone for an hour or more, it's most important to do this as I reckon the fish will feed with more confidence. I wasn't in a hurry to get started as I had two days and a night in front of me. With everything sorted out I went off to the cabin for breakfast.

As I walked back to the cabin I spotted a smoke-screening fish in front of some reed mace. I watched it move from rooting to an upright position. A good carp, and there were two other fish in the area; I decided breakfast could wait. Making my way back to my car, I collected an 11ft rod and centre-pin reel with 12lb line, and a box of red worms.

I tied on a size 6 hook. Crouching down, I slowly moved to where I had spotted the carp, it was still feeding. I crouched lower behind some reed mace and watched the fish with bated breath. With trembling hands I put four worms on the hook, a bunch of these often proves more attractive than a single lobworm. On hands and knees I crept along the footpath to a gap, a big cloud of coloured water appeared five feet in front of me, I could make out the shadow of a fish; the bait was dropped into the muddied water a few inches in front of the fish.

I tried to control my heart beat which must have increased considerably, the fish slowly moved forward. The line twitched, twitched again and then moved away. I set the hook, my rod tip was savagely pulled down and the reel screamed – the fight was on. Though I have caught literally hundreds of carp, I am still amazed at the speed and power of the fish when hooked in the shallows. Fifteen minutes later I had a mirror carp in the landing net. I reckon this is the most exciting fishing one can experience.

A few days later I was joined at the waterside by Jon King. As I was helping him to get tackled up, I heard my buzzer bleep. Moving off to my swim, I heard a crack then fell in a heap, with pain searing through my body: it was my left leg. I headed off to the hospital where I was informed I had torn the muscles. After getting it strapped up I was told to rest; within three days my leg from ankle to knee was black and blue. Sadly, no fly-fishing, but I could sit beside a lake and try to catch some good fish. Three days later I was forced to return home.

A week later I was on different water with Anthony Morris for a two day session. Anthony had some good fish including a 2lb 6oz rudd. My best fish was a 2lb 9oz perch. After a few days at home I was off again with Martin Salisbury who caught rudd of 1lb 12oz, 1lb 14oz and 1lb 15oz. Both Anthony and Martin were extremely helpful in getting me to the waterside and my tackle to my swim while I hobbled along.

On my third session at the waterside I put in five droppers of red gentles and chopped worms. On both of my Avon rods I attached an LG shot, baiting the size 6 hook with a large lobworm, one bait was fished close in, the other into deep water. An hour later the bite indicator moved upwards, the strike connecting with a good fish. A few minutes I spotted the dorsal fin of a good perch which was soon netted. It weighed 3lb 1oz and was in excellent condition. Martin shot some excellent pictures.

Last season Martin Salisbury and I fished a water near Oxford, a mature gravel pit of about fifteen acres. I suppose it was mid morning when we started fishing for tench in bright sunshine, though heavy showers had been forecast. My hook was baited with four red gentles or lobworms, sometime a cocktail of worm and corn, fished two rod lengths out from the bank. I had my first

One of my prettiest Tench waters!

tench within twenty minutes, an old black fish about four pounds. After several hours I had taken a small perch and seven tench, the best at 5lb 15½oz, also a bream of 8lb 1oz. Sadly, I lost several fish in a dense bed of spiked water-milfoil. In my book there is nothing that beats catching fish with nicely balanced float tackle – except a wild brown-trout on a dry fly.

Within thirty minutes of the bites ceasing, the rain sheeted down, it was some of the heaviest rain I have ever experienced in the UK. Fifteen minutes later we were fishing in the gloom as the sky turned a greyish colour with patches of purple and masses of black clouds. In the distance I heard the rumble of thunder, then a flash of lightning. Winding in our tackle and covering our baits up with a ground sheet, we hurried off to a local waterside tavern for dinner. Back at the lake the storm raged overhead, sounding like a war front, with the rumble of thunder, and flashes of lightning? I said to Martin, "Bugger the fishing tonight, let's get our heads down!" Safely tucked up in our sleeping bags, we listened to the storm as the rain hammering the thin, tin roof.

The alarm on my phone went off at 7 o'clock. Rubbing my eyes, I peered out of the window; a thick mist covered the lake. The impression I got was, as many writers have said before, "It's a tench-fishers dawn!" Martin was already off and fishing; with all the rain during the night it was going to be very wet walking and pushing through the long grass and bushes, so I pulled on waterproof trousers, jacket and boots then made my way to the swim we had fished the previous day. My swim was fizzing, it looked as if I had baited with a box of Alka-Seltzer tablets, though Martin described it as a jacuzzi. There were patches of bubbles from the size of a pin head to a five-pence piece. Martin was fishless, I thought, how I can fail, but I did! Having tried different baits and getting nothing, just lots of slight movements on the float, the penny dropped! These fish have noticed that the baited hook doesn't move like the free offering. Remember: tench usually hoover up their food rather than picking up single morsels with their lips. I needed to counteract the weight of the hook.

I reckoned the answer was to bait with some black casters, I said to Martin, "Do you have any casters in your bait box?" He said he had and so I baited with four red gentles and two black casters. I dropped it into the mass of bubbles; a minute or two later the float disappeared. Soon, fish number one was being unhooked. In five casts I had five good bites yielding five nice tench to nearly six pounds. After a break of about ten minutes, I had three more fish. Martin broke his duck with a nice male tench of 5lb 1oz which certainly tested his tackle. The idea had worked. I remember many years ago when the fish got finicky with sweet corn. I would pick out the inside of the corn and replace it with a piece of polystyrene to counteract the weight of the hook. When you're having problems with finicky bites think about counteracting the weight of your hook. After a couple more fish, I couldn't get another bite. An hour later, with no bites or bubbles, it was time to move on. Why not go out and target the tench.

For many years it's been a well known fact that the River Ribble is the jewel in the crown of Lancashire, it's a river that can offer the angler good coarse and game-fishing. In the middle and upper reaches of this delightful water you can enjoy some excellent fly-fishing for salmon,

The float at a drunken angle as a tench picks up the bait

grayling, sea and brown-trout. Downstream of Calder Foot you can expect to catch barbel, chub, roach, and dace, further downstream you will find some good pike-fishing, with the chance of a thirty-pounder.

I want to tell you about another jewel in the crown. Tewitfields, a twenty-year-old, mature, ten acre limestone lake that contains specimen roach, rudd, perch, tench, carp and pike. Yes, the water contains some cracking fish – it's not easy water so don't expect instant success. You will have to spend time learning all its moods, remember, fish are not spread around like currants in a pudding. As we all know, fish move around following the wind, and this is certainly true of carp; tench will often do likewise. Not all swims contain big fish, it's all down to learning from experience of fishing during all weather and water conditions.

My first visit to Tewitfields was with Leyland solicitor Martin Salisbury to record a programme for my At the Water's Edge programme on BBC Radio Lancashire. Then, later in the week I would return to the water with Bolton photographer Ian Chapman for a feature in the Angler's Mail. It was late in the afternoon when Martin and I arrived to find the sun shining brightly, this certainly surprised us as the rest of the county was having heavy rain. In some areas, hailstones were giving the impression that winter was upon us. The fishery looked great in this rare glimpse of summer. Walking around, we met bailiff Frank Squirrel catching quality rudd. Many fish over a pound-and-a-half graced Frank's net; he had some forty, perhaps fifty fish during this latest session. He was float-fishing Ringer pellets. Walking along the far bank, we spotted several good tench rooting in the bottom, certainly the chance of some of those I thought! After recording my programme and talking with some other anglers, it was time to fish.

Martin chose a swim on the west bank while I picked a spot along the bank that separated the two lakes, the smaller, coloured water has produced some big carp and perch. After giving my swim a good raking, I made up some method mix adding sweet corn, hemp and liquid bloodworm. I then fed the swim with three cricket ball-sized pieces of bait. I chose a 13ft rod, matched with a centre-pin reel and 4lb Gamma line with a 6 BB shot waggler and size 14 Pallatrax hook, I was ready to go. Plumbing the area, I chose to fish my bait on a ledge in 8ft of water. In the gin-clear water I would often see several tench moving through the swim – one of these could have been eight pound-plus. For three hours fish rooted around in my swim, masses of tiny pin-head bubbles appeared on the surface; still no bites.

I asked myself the question, "What are they eating?" Eventually it was time to leave the fishery. When Martin arrived he said, "I had fish feeding and bubbling in my swim but couldn't get a bite." The same for me I said. We both returned home wondering why we couldn't catch.

Arriving at Tewitfields on Tuesday, I chose a swim a few yards along the west bank. Having raked and baited with brown crumb hemp and sweet corn, I made up two legering outfits using my Grauvell Specialist 1.2 rods, Mitchell 300 reels with 6lb line and Stonze weights. On the right-hand rod I chose to fish a hair rigged Jungle boily on a size 8 Pallatrax stumpy rig.

The other rod was baited with three grains of popped-up corn to a 15in braided hook line. Despite feeding little and often, not one fish stopped to feed in the baited area. Having fished for some twelve hours, where I had plenty of fish passing through my swim, I didn't get a bite. I made the decision to wind in my rods and have some food. I had only eaten a piece of cake and sandwich with a few mugs of tea. After my break I recast the rods, still choosing to fish with popped-up corn and Jungle paste.

At 2.15 in the morning the boily-baited rod was away; soon, a tench was in the net, the only bite of the night. I thought I might catch at dawn – no such joy. Then the wind changed. It was time to take a walk along the windward side where I spotted the odd feeding tench. I took the decision to move. Soon, I was sitting in a new swim with the wind in my face hoping above hope the fish would feed. About ten in the morning Ian Chapman turned up all smiles as usual and said, "How many?"

"Just one." I answered. Soon, Ian was sitting next to me float-fishing hair rigged corn. Apart from an odd fish, nothing wanted our baits, though further along the bank Frank Squirrel had four tench. As I have always recommended, seek local advice on where and how to fish a strange water. I had done that but it didn't help me on this occasion. As previously said, the tench had

Tench in the Net

sex on their minds – I suppose I wouldn't want to eat on those occasions! By noon, Ian had his Angler's Mail feature and was on his way home. Packing all my gear away I had a few hours sleep, I wasn't in any fit state to drive. Nine o'clock that evening I was back home having a shower. In the words of the later General Douglas MacArthur, "I shall return". Then, hopefully, after a few visits, I will have sorted out a way to defeat those big tench, which could weigh ten pounds, when they haven't got sex on their minds!

It's been another tough two-day session on Tewitfields. For my latest effort to try and crack my big tench target on this water, I ordered four pints of fresh casters from Gerry's of Morecambe. It's been some time since I visited Gerry's, I was most impressed with the well-

The Author with another fine Tench

stocked shop. Having collected my casters and the odd item of tackle, I was back in the car for the short journey to the tench lake.

Tewitfields is, without doubt, one of the toughest tench-fishing waters I have fished, not helped by the unseasonable weather. I've had fish rooting around in my swim just inches from my bait, still they refuse it. If I use worms they are immediately seized by small perch; using gentles, it's tiny roach, rudd and perch that snap them up. Bread is soon shredded to bits. Yes, I can catch a few tench but not the big ones that I seek – fish in the eight and nine pound class, I reckon I have seen a couple of fish that might push the scales to ten pounds. On this trip I would bait heavily with method mix containing hemp, tiny pellets, casters and corn. I would be using a bait dropper to get most of my casters in one swim, hoping the small fish wouldn't take them.

Having spent some time walking around the lake, I fed a few handfuls of method mix into three spots; I then went off for a late breakfast and a mug of tea. An hour later, still no signs of fish in the baited areas. I chose to fish the roadside bank towards which the southwest wind had been blowing for a couple of days. Choosing this area knowing fish often follow the wind, I picked two swims: one situated fifty feet from the bank where fish had been rolling, this is often a prelude to feeding. Plumbing this area, I found ten feet of water between two weed beds which I baited with twelve, cricket-ball sized lumps of bait containing mini pellets, casters, hemp and corn, I then added a pint of casters using a bait dropper, I reckon throwing balls of bait in by hand at this distance, is better than spodding.

My other swim was under the rod tip with eight feet of water, in among the hundreds of small rudd, perch and roach I would occasionally see the odd tench move through. They averaged four pounds, not the fish I was interested in, but at least fish did visit the area. Hopefully, one of the big ones would pay a visit later; with a bait dropper I put in half-a-pint of casters, a can of sweet corn, three pints of mini pellets and a pint of hemp.

I wanted a bed of bait down there to keep a big fish occupied. Both swims were left alone for some time, I didn't want to take the chance of spooking any fish before they became confident in feeding on the bait. I fished two 12ft Grauvell rods, Shimano 3500 reels and 10lb Gamma line; some readers might reckon this is over the top on tackle strength: I don't. Tench can be tough fighters and I may have to pull the fish through a weed bed. I might also hook one of the big common carp. My end rig was the Pallatrax in line Stonze with a 4in fluorocarbon hook link with a size 10 hook and a short hair; I wanted the two bits of hair rigged imitation corn tight to the hook shank. As we know, chub often pick up the bait in their lips, I have seen tench do the same. With too long a hair, this usually means a missed bite. I made sure the balanced corn would be popped up about an inch above the light covering of silkweed by pinching a small bit of tungsten putty on the hook link. My second rod had a Pallatrax in line Stonze system, again with a 4in fluorocarbon hook link with a slightly longer hair on the size 8 hook. Bait would be a popped-up boily.

My other outfit was a 13ft rod, centre-pin reel with 6lb Gamma line; I rate this line excellent for all types of coarse-fishing; it has excellent abrasion quality and knot strength. I chose a 3 swan shot waggler, 2 swan shot locking the float, with two AA pinched on the line halfway between float and hook with a BB shot some 6in from a size 12 Pallatrax hook which are extremely strong. To the bend of the hook I tied on a ½in of ½lb breaking strain line. When the time comes to fish I would superglue two or three imitation casters on the hair.

By using these imitation casters, I would know I have bait on the hook at all times. Having plumbed the depth, I set the float so about 8in of line was on the bottom. Having baited my swims, I left them alone for a couple of hours, I didn't want to start too early and spook the fish before they got their heads down. Having made up all my tackle, I sorted out rod rests, bite alarms, bobbins, landing net, weigh scales and weigh bag. When I am on a two or three day session I have a large plastic box with cooking and brew gear, spare gas bottle, water, tea bags, and tins of soup, tuna pasta, fish and chicken. In my big Chillers cold box I have sandwiches, milk, diabetic fruit cake and biscuits, and breakfast cereals. I don't use a bivvy, making do with my waterproof gear should it rain, though if the rain is persistent, I will erect my umbrella.

With everything sorted I sat back with a mug of tea, I spotted a rolling fish over the fifty foot swim, sometimes a tench rooted around in my swim close to the bank. I left them alone to settle on the feed. Suddenly a streak of forked lighting appeared to my right. I immediately grabbed my paper, mug of tea and disappeared towards Les Bratby's cabin. If you're caught out in the open during a storm the best place to be is in your car. Don't do what I have seen some idiots do, carry on fishing! No fish is worth a life.

The storm lasted an hour, and then it was blue sky with some small, white fluffy clouds. Back in my swim, I could see several tench feeding, though none were the size I wanted to catch. I topped up the swim with a can of corn. I put six droppers of casters in my fifty foot swim then had a walk around the lake, checking out some of the close-in swims where I had put in some bait. About halfway along the opposite bank I spotted two big tench rooting around in the bottom, tight up to the bank under the grass. Normally this would be a firm bank but with all the rain this summer it was under water, giving the fish an extra feeding area.

I immediately went and got my float tackle, then adjusted the float so the bait would just be on the bottom. I lowered the two hair rigged imitation caster quietly in the water. Still the two big tench, which I reckoned would weigh seven pounds-plus, continued to feed. For an hour or so the fish moved in and out of the area, often only inches from the bait. For a few seconds I took my eyes off the float to look up the bank when I heard a big swirl. Disaster, something had picked up the bait and moved off fast towards the centre of the lake. As I heard the reel screech, I grabbed the rod in a panic. The line jammed where it was taken off the reel too fast. Suddenly the rod hooped over, and then it was gone. I had that sickening feeling as the limp line fluttered from the rod tip. I was gutted. Those few seconds when I had taken my eyes off the float had caused me to lose a big fish.

After dropping a ball of method mix containing casters and corn in the swim, I walked back along the bank towards my base for a mug of tea. As I did so it looked as if it was raining, the lake surface was dimpled where hundreds of small rudd, roach and perch were feeding, probably on Chironomids. Having made a mug of tea, I cut a slice of cake then settled down in my chair. I looked across the water to my fifty foot swim, a good tench rolled, my hopes were getting sky high. Perhaps tonight I would get one of the big ones.

After a break, I went back to the lost-fish swim. A good tench and two common carp were feeding. Picking up my rod and bag, I moved well back from the water's edge then tied on a new hook and hair to which I glued on two imitation casters.

Creeping back to the water's edge, I could see the tench, but the carp had gone. I lowered the baited hook down tight to the bank, twelve inches in front of the fish; I watched the fish as it inched closer to my baited hook. Soon, it was perhaps only an inch from my hook. Occasionally, the float dipped slightly, probably caused by the fish touching the line. I was ready to spring into action. Half-an-hour later the fish was on an even keel and slowly swimming off towards the centre of the lake. I spent another hour or more waiting to see if it would return, it didn't. I collected my gear and went back to base.

At six o'clock I decided it was time for dinner of potatoes, venison, peas and gravy followed by a slice of cake and mug of tea. I was then ready for the evening session. It was time to position my leger rods, one with a popped-up boily, the other with imitation corn. With some method mix moulded around the Stonze weight, after casting out, I placed both rods in the rests then clipped on the bite indicators, switching on the buzzers. I then float-fished the close-in swim with various baits: corn, small pellets, caster, bread flake and worms; no tench, but a succession of small roach, rudd and perch. I fished until dark with nothing better than small fish.

Throwing in some crusts for the ducklings, I was amazed to hear fish swirling at the bread. I quickly took all the shot and float from my line then baited with a piece of crust which I dropped on the water; there was a swirl. The line pulled through my fingers. The strike connected with a nice fish; soon a rudd was in the landing net. Realising it was a good one, I got the scales out, the fish weighed 1lb 8oz. Between darkness and midnight I had twenty, perhaps thirty good rudd with two at 2lb 2oz and 2lb 3oz. These fish looked as if they had just been minted: fin and scale perfect.

At midnight the fish stopped taking crust off the top, then disappeared, it was time for a bowl of soup to keep me going through the night, and I still expected to get a decent tench on one of my leger rods. Up till now I hadn't had a single bleep; I sat watching motionless bite indicators until about two in the morning. With no sign of action I decided to get my head down for a couple of hours. I was woken up by heavy rain around 4 o'clock. Before putting on the kettle, I recast both rods, clipped on the bite indicators, then made a brew; I was thankful for my waterproofs. Within fifteen minutes the right-hand indicator moved slowly to the butt ring. Soon, a tench about five pounds was netted. I rebaited and cast to the same spot, and then fed in three, cricket ball-sized lumps of ground bait. In the half light of dawn a big fish rolled over the baited area. The buzzer bleeped twice, the bite indicator shivered; five minutes later the indicator hit the butt ring. Fish number two was powering away, several minutes later a good tench was netted. On the scales it went 6lb 4oz.

Still it rained: it was monsoon conditions. I put up my umbrella, and by seven o'clock I had caught nine tench averaging about five pounds. At nine o'clock the rain ceased and soon I had blue sky and bright sunshine with a strong southwesterly wind. Time for breakfast. During the day I roved around the lake looking for big tench but without success. I went back to my baited swims and sat it out until about seven in the evening then called it a day.

For some years I have been fishing a gravel pit in the Midlands; I first got to know about Rookery Lake when I visited the area to record an At The Water's Edge programme for BBC Radio 5. During the recording I was told about the good fishing available on Rookery Lake and I soon got hold of a syndicate ticket at just £350 for the season.

Unlike many of today's coarse fisheries, the lake is not a hole in the ground, over-stocked with fish. It's a mature gravel-pit with lots of trees, bushes, reeds, water lilies, wild flowers, aquatic and wildlife. Birdlife is plentiful: you will have the chance to see or hear green woodpeckers and various owls including the barn owl, If you're extremely lucky it's even possible to hear the nightingale in June. Blackbirds, thrushes, robins, wrens, warblers and blackcaps can be sighted. It's always interesting to watch and be entertained by the great crested grebes. As you sit quietly at the waterside you will see foxes, rabbits and often a badger.

The best carp taken from Rookery lake weighed in at 36lb 8oz, several seven pounds-plus tench have been caught, and if it's big bream you fancy, you couldn't chose a better water. From what I have seen, I feel you have the chance of catching fifteen pound-plus fish. Roach-fishing can be good, with a very realistic chance of catching a two-pounder. It's possible to catch big crucian carp, and perch topping four pounds.

I have fished many gravel pits on-and-off for over fifty years; one fish I could always rely on was the tench. It's a great fish of the summer and autumn, a powerful, beautiful-looking fish that can grow to sixteen pounds or more, with the present record tench weighing-in at 15lb 3oz 6dr caught by Darren Ward from a southern still water. In the 1950s my target weight for tench was four pounds, in the 60s it was a five pound-plus fish.

Having caught tench to eight pounds-plus, my target size fish these days is seven pounds, but a tench of five pounds is still a good fish in my book. I enjoy every tench I catch, whatever the size. The swim I had chosen to fish had five feet of water under the rod tip, going to a depth of twelve feet some thirty feet out from the bank. On my left were some water lilies with lovely white flowers, others had pink-coloured flowers. Along the bank to my right and left was reed mace with its furry-brown head. It gets its name from its mace-like appearance, and is often mistaken for the bulrush. There was plenty of bank-side cover from willows, alders and bank-side vegetation. Having raked my swim I had a good clean area of gravel between the Canadian pond weed I baited this area with some ten pounds of groundbait. It was a mix of brown breadcrumb from a local bakery, to which I added some cooked hemp, sweet corn, chopped boilies, dead gentles and chopped worms. Within thirty minutes of raking and baiting the swim, a few tench could be seen feeding.

I chose to float-fish using a powerful 13ft rod, centre-pin reel and 6lb line to which I attached a size 10 barbless hook. The chosen float was a peacock quill with a red painted 2in fine insert to take two AA shot, I used double rubber to fix the float in place. After plumbing the depth I positioned the float to fish 1ft over-depth, then lightly pinched on a BB shot some 8in from the hook, a further 2ft up the line I lightly pinched on the 2 AA shot. I baited with a lobworm which I injected with a small amount of air, so the tail would be just off the bottom.

I then added a grain of corn. With an underhand cast I dropped the baited hook down among the tench. Within minutes I had my first fish of about four pounds. This was quickly followed by three other fish averaging four pounds. After a quiet spell lasting about thirty minutes, I had a sail-away bite with the float burying itself. I set the hook and the rod tip was pulled savagely down towards the water; I was forced to give line. After a tense tussle I had a super-looking tench in the net. It pulled the scale needle down to 6lb 9oz: I punched the air with delight. On a trip two weeks previously my best tench weighed 7lb 7oz. On that occasion I was float-fishing with a lobworm.

After an hour with no more bites, though I could see tench moving around in my swim, I decided it was time for a bait change. Within minutes of changing the bait from worm to corn on a size 14 hook, I quickly had another tench of 5lb 12oz, this was followed by five fish around the four pound mark and two more good fives, 5lb 10oz and 5lb 14oz. The bites then dried up, the swim was barren. I couldn't see a single fish. I decided to push the float up the line another two feet and fish further out. Within minutes I had a good roach of nearly a pound, this was quickly

17 ½ ft Pole, another option for Roach

followed by five other roach, all around the pound mark with the best at 1lb 6oz. These were top quality fish and a complete surprise. I was over the moon.

Roach have always been one of my favourite fish, but sadly, over the past fifteen years, quality roach-fishing has been thin on the ground. Even on my lovely River Kennet, roach are often very hard to find. With the light fading I decided to pack up. Supper and a mug of tea were the order of the day. Over breakfast the next day, John Bodsworth and myself discussed the roach fishing, I said, "Let's have a serious go for roach." John agreed. At the water's edge, it was time for a tackle change, I chose to fish a 3lb line and size 14 hook, with the same rod and float set-up, choosing sweet corn as bait. For the next couple of hours I caught a lot of roach, between ten ounces and a pound-and-a-half. It was like roach fishing back in the 1950s and 60s.

After lunch we carried on catching roach, I was keeping a score of my pound-plus fish. An hour after lunch, John, who was fishing the next swim, stopped by to give me a mug of tea and some more corn. We discussed the quality of the roach fishing and how nice it was to catch on the float. As we talked, the float disappeared. I struck and hooked a fish, which made me give a few feet of line.

"Small tench," I said to John, I then spotted a flash of orange and realised it wasn't a small tench but a special roach. As I pulled the fish over the landing net I said to John, "That could be a two pounder!" The scales gave a different story it weighed 1lb 15oz. This was a picture fish, my best roach to date from the water. John shot a couple of pictures before we released the fish.

About 5 p.m, the bites ceased; for an hour I was biteless, I changed over to a size 16 hook and fed half a dozen casters every couple of minutes. For half an hour I couldn't get a bite. Suddenly, the float disappeared, on striking I found myself attached to a signal crayfish. In the next half a dozen casts, I hooked four more signals. A quiet fifteen minutes followed. I then had a sail-away bite, connecting with a powerful fish. It was a A tench,

Author with a nice Crucian Carp

which pulled the scale pointer round to 6lb 3oz. A few more tench followed together with some roach and small perch. With a storm brewing, I called it a day and headed off for a brew.

With storms forecast on my final day, I decided I would head off home early. It was half past eight in the morning when I arrived at my swim, I couldn't see any tench, roach or crayfish; the swim looked dead. I threw in a handful of gentles and casters, then sat peering intently into the crystal-clear water. Suddenly, from my right, a crucian carp appeared and started hoovering up the loose food items. I decided to change over to a size 16 hook on 2lb BS hook link. I plumbed the depth allowing just 2–3in of line on the bottom with the BB shot some 12in from the hook. I then buried the hook inside a single caster before dropping the baited hook among the free offerings. For over an hour the fish continued to appear, pick off some free offerings, then disappear under the water lilies.

I could see a hole the size of a tea plate in the lilies about two feet in from the outer edge of the leaves. I said to Phil, "If I drop some free offerings through that hole in the lily pads, perhaps the fish won't be quite so spooky." I spent fifteen minutes or more dropping half a dozen gentles and caster in the hole then, hoping the fish was still picking up the free offerings, I dropped the baited hook into the hole with some more freebies. If the fish picked up the baited hook, I could pull the tackle and fish to my right, then hopefully beat it in the open water. For ten minutes I stood with bated breath peering intently into the water, I could just see far enough under the pads where my baited hook was. I watched the fishing moving into the baited area, then take a few free offerings. Suddenly, the crucian up-ended – head to hell, tail to heaven, right over my baited hook.

The float slowly submerged, I tightened then pulled hard to my right, shouting to John "I have the crucian!" I was lucky: everything happened as I had planned. I quickly had the fish out into the open water. Provided it didn't dive into some reed mace, I was confident it was mine. As John arrived I pulled the fish over my landing net. I felt elated; the planning had worked. On the scales the fish weighed 3lb 3oz, a personal best. I went across to Phil and said, "I've just caught that crucian." He came across and shot some photographs on my digital and SLR cameras. We then watched the crucian swim away, hopefully to grow into a four-pounder.

My friend John Bodsworth from Sussex and I were visiting some gravel pits alongside the Old Bath road near Newbury, as a guest of Kevin Rolls, who I had got to know when he invited Tony Farquharson and me to fish the Wasing Estate water for tench some years ago. I caught a lot of fish during that visit, not only tench but carp and some nice perch. I was also told that bread and corn were blown baits. Thankfully, the fish hadn't been told this – they were eating both corn and bread!

Kevin called round to my swim on the second day to ask if we would like some fresh mackerel I said, "Yes please." Tony and I enjoyed a plateful of fried fresh mackerel for tea that day. Since that first meeting, Kevin and I have remained good friends, as have our wives.

On one occasion, John Bodsworth and I got Kevin's wife, Julia, to try fishing the Kennet where she enjoyed a few hours catching dace and grayling. Later on, Kevin helped her catch a double-figure barbel. Having parked up my car, and John's van – which would be home for a couple of days, we took a slow walk around the bigger of the two pits, deciding to rake and bait a small bay on the roadside bank. We chose this bank as the wind had been blowing into it for several days.

The lake bed comprised pea and marble-size gravel, with some larger stones, and sloped down from about two to eight feet, then plunged to around sixteen feet. Having raked and baited the swim with brown crumb containing: molasses, sweet corn, hemp, chopped boilies and worms, we left it alone for an hour to give the fish a chance of finding our free offerings where, hopefully, they would start to feed and gain confidence.

We then took a walk around the lake to try and find some feeding fish; at the bottom end of the pit was a weedy bay. Crouching low, we crept forward until we could hide behind some rushes. We both peered intently into the water, spotting several carp; we counted three commons and seven mirrors between twelve and sixteen pounds.

Occasionally, one would stick its head in the bottom. We both agreed, "Those carp were for catching." Back at the car, we tackled up with identical outfits: 12ft Avon action rods, and Mitchell 300 reels with 10lb Gamma line to which we tied on a size 4 hook.

The Author cooks some fresh fillets of mackerel caught from Chesil beach by Kevin Rolls

Choosing a loaf of bread and a box of lobworms, I chucked them in the bait bucket, then, collecting my landing net, John and I walked back round to the weedy bay. The carp were still in close to the bank; further out we spotted another group of fish. John chose to fish bread flake; my first choice was crust. Tearing a piece from the loaf, I baited the size 4 hook then cast out, dropping the bread close to the reeds, ten yards along the bank. Minutes later I watched a nice common moving towards the bait. Seconds later it nudged it, and then moved away a foot before circling the bait, then coming in close and nudging it once more. It slowly moved away – a minute later it was back, this time a bit lower in the water. As it came in close it sucked in the crust. The answering strike connected with an angry fish which moved off along the bank then out through the mouth of the bay into the main lake.

John called, "Fish on!" I could see the fish moving round and round in the centre of the bay. Meanwhile I moved down the bank and started to win some line, drawing the fish back from the main part of the lake into the weedy bay, I didn't have a worry about the weed as it was a soft variety that wouldn't cause a problem. I heard John call, "Fish Netted."

I was more than confident in my tackle as I cramped down hard, stopping the fish in its tracks. Slowly, I bullied the fish back through the weed, finally netting a nice common of about thirteen pounds. Once more the old baits had proved that they work, despite me being told bread was blown bait.

During the next hour, moving around the lake looking for feeding carp, we caught several more low doubles. They might not have been twenty or thirty-pounders, but it was great fishing.

Two hours later we were back in our baited swim; after a brew and some food we both made up sliding float rigs, baiting with lobworm and corn. After five hours of fishing John had two tench, I had a big perch of 3lb 4oz and one nice tench, with two missed bites. We called it a day. Before leaving, I raked the area, while John made up a bowl of mix. After dumping it into the swim we went off for a meal in John's van.

Paul Smyth with a fine catch of rudd from Aquatek's lake fishing waggler tackle and gentles. Credit Paul Smyth

Next morning, we were back on the Aquatec lakes. I chose to fish my previously-baited swim in the roadside bay, while John fished a swim on the opposite bank. I was going to fish a Pallatrax in line Stonze weight with hair rigged corn. On the other rod I chose a sliding float rig, which would be baited with lobworm and corn cocktail or bread flake. After putting in a bowlful of groundbait containing: molasses, chopped worms, red gentles, corn and hemp.

In the first hour I had several bites where the indicator moved about three inches, I missed them all; I don't think they were crayfish, the bait wasn't marked. Rebaiting and casting out for the eighth time, the bobbin lifted – this time the answering strike connected with a powerful fish which went off to my right, staying deep as it did so. "Is it a tench?" I said to myself. A minute later I thought, "Could this be a big perch?"

For a couple of nervous minutes I played the fish gently, suddenly my heart was in my mouth as everything went solid; the fish had found a snag or weed bed in some fourteen feet of water. I put pressure on from the right, then the left, still it wouldn't budge. After a minute or so of intense pressure the fish moved off to my left, I was now able to get some line back on the reel. Peering into the crystal-clear water, I spotted the fish for the first time. It was a big perch, in fact a very big perch, even more so, as it was a summer fish. A minute or so later, with its prickly dorsal fin erect, it appeared on the surface. Then the danger moment as it shook its head, twisting and turning as it did so. I pushed the landing net out as far as possible and, with a gentle lift of the rod, drew the fish over the waiting net, then lifted. It was mine.

On the scales it went 3lb 13oz, a new personal best. It was a fish that could well go four-and-a-half pounds in February. After a couple of quick pictures, I watched my prize swim off strongly. It was also time for the rain to sheet down. I just sat there as happy as could be. In all, I had a dozen good perch, but no tench. After a quiet hour I went off, chasing carp in the small lake. I found them feeding in the shallows. Fishing small bits of free lined flake within a dozen feet of the carp, I caught three nice commons, all between 12lb and 14lb. John had a good mixed bag of bream, tench, carp and rudd. We both agreed it had been a good session. John left for home, while I went off to fish the Kennet.

I had 20 perch like this one over 3lbs from Aquateks lake in a season

*I*t never ceases to amaze me how often I catch fish, when all the books reckon I shouldn't – due to water or weather conditions. Then I get told the baits I am using are useless on this or that water. I well remember fishing a gravel pit in Berkshire, catching some nice tench, also the odd carp.

One of the members stopped for a chat saying, "You're catching some good tench, what bait are you using?" I said, "Corn and bread." As we chatted I said, "You've got lots of carp in this water and I'll have a go for them tomorrow morning." My new-found friend then said. "What bait will you use?" I said, "Corn or bread."

I was quickly told that corn was blown bait, bread wasn't any good. "Is that so," I said, "and when did you last use these baits?" He said, "It must be ten years or more since I've used corn and I've never used bread." What a stupid remark! I then told him that I had already caught the odd carp on both corn and bread flake. Today they are still excellent baits.

He said, "You're lucky." Thankfully, no one had told the carp. During the following days I caught several carp on both baits – enough said! As corn or bread hadn't been used for some years, how would this gentleman know that these were blown bait? Let's be honest, fish don't follow rules, and they certainly don't read books or magazines.

I will never understand why some anglers just won't believe me and my mates when we say we are catching barbel on bread, from various rivers such as: the Stour, Kennet, Swale, Wharfe, Loddon, Severn, Avon, Ribble, Wye, Thames and Teme, to mention a few. There have been many occasions when we get told, "You only have bread with you to cover up the use of a secret bait" What rubbish! Barbel, like all the other coarse fish, eat bread. I reckon they have done so

Colin Culley on the River Kennet with a nice Barbel that didn't give a 3ft. twitch!

since bread was first used on a hook. I've used it since the 1950s and it still works today.

For several years I kept telling Thatcham Berkshire angler, Collin Culley, to use bread, suddenly, he thought he would try, and started catching barbel when he was failing to do so on his other baits: another convert to bread. Blackpool angler, Alan Roe, a great all-round fisher, joined me for a session on the Teme; I put him in a prime swim, suggesting how he should fish, and I left him with two loaves of bread. I went upstream and found another suitable swim. At lunchtime Alan turned up in my swim as I was tying on a new hook, having just lost a fish in a snag. "Have you caught Alan?" I said.

"No, not a bite."

"Are you using bread?" I said. "No," was the answer.

"That's why you're not catching, that swim's full of barbel who just love bread!"

As I baited with a chunk of crust Alan said, "Are you really using bread?"

Dropping the bait in a gully, I said "Nothing else."

Within thirty seconds I had a slight pluck, then set the hook into a good fish. A few minutes later Alan netted a barbel of 8lb 8oz. We then went off to the local inn for lunch. Alan now doesn't question the value of bread as bait for barbel.

On my many visits to the water's edge, I see lots of anglers with a pair of rods pointed skywards. Often, I will ask the question, "Are you catching?" and often get told. "Nothing, just a couple of knocks or small plucks on the rod tip." I reckon some of those knocks or plucks were fish the anglers missed by not holding the rod. If they had been holding the rod, those 'small plucks' could have been turned into fish. Last winter the water temperatures were low, barbel were hard to tempt, though I did catch my share of fish, as witnessed by, Brendan Ince, Mick Holgate, Colin Culley and Will Carter. There was only one occasion when I had a savage pull on the rod tip. I would sit holding the rod, feeling a little pressure on the line caused by a light, soft pluck. Pushing the rod forward, I watched the bow in the line start to tighten some more, then set the hook.

Often, when I felt a pluck on the line, I would resist striking, and bring in the bait, as I wanted to check if a fish had mouthed it. It nearly always had. With soft paste I would notice it was either partially flattened or had a piece missing. This showed that a fish had picked up the bait. With crust, it was either gone or had been nibbled. If you watch barbel feeding, you will see they usually pick up the bait then either move sideways or upstream to another food item. I use the lightest weight possible, which is one or more LG shot, often as many as six LGs, depending on the water flow. The distance between hook and weight when fishing paste baits varies between 1ft and 3ft, with crust bait it's about 5–6in, unless the water is a few degrees below 40°F, then it's just a couple of inches.

If you choose to fish a big weight and a hair rig using pellet or boily, then you will often get those big whacks or the so-called 'three foot twitches' as the fish either feel the weight or get pricked by the hook, then bolt in fright.

Don't be sheep-like or blinkered by following the others who are often fishing with their two rods pointed skywards, as previously mentioned. Try fishing with one rod and feel for those plucks, knocks, and slight taps and see what happens. You could get some pleasant surprises. Last

Never underestimate the power of Corn!

winter, Len Arbery often fished slack-water swims on the River Thames with a small dough bobbin, getting slight movements but turning those bites into double-figure barbel.

I often did likewise on the Kennet, Thames, Loddon, Ribble, Teme and Wye, using a dough bobbin just heavy enough to counteract the pull of the water on the line. It was a successful method when nothing else worked. Barbel are not always in the streamy water; in fact you would be surprised how many barbels get caught from slack-water swims.

We must never forget the power of corn. In the fifties and early sixties I used a lot of stewed wheat (often called creed wheat, a strange name, as the dictionary defines creed as a statement of a religious belief, though in this case it means to soften by soaking). Wheat was certainly a top roach-fishing bait until sweet corn appeared on the supermarket shelf, then called by a few anglers in the know as the 'Golden Grains'. If I was fishing still-waters for roach, casters would certainly be on my list of baits. It is the choice of many still-water roach anglers.

During the past three seasons I have noticed more and more roach being caught from two rivers. The first is the Wyre, a lovely Crabtree type water, with lots of inviting swims that really do scream out, "Come and fish this spot!" The other river is the Ribble, Lancashire's premier river, where I have taken fish to 1lb 14oz this season, sadly caught when trotting for chub with 6lb line and a size 6 hook with a big chunk of bread flake. At the time I was recording one of my At the Water's Edge programmes for BBC Radio Lancashire, the listener could certainly hear the excitement in my voice when the fish rolled, in midstream.

I reckon the time to target Ribble roach is when the river is fining down after being bank-high – but they are not spread around like currants in a pudding. You can fish twenty good-looking swims and find roach in only one of them. You also need to keep your mouth shut regarding the location. Tell no one, otherwise, you'll find the swim occupied when you next visit the water! If you can find the Ribble roach in mild weather conditions, I suggest you float fish; my rod of choice would be 13–15ft with an all-through action, matched with a centre-pin reel with 3lb BS line. I would attach 3ft of fine hook link, 2.5lb when fishing casters or gentles, 3lb if its corn, bread or red worms. If fishing corn as bait, I would suggest a size 12 hook, for bread flake, which I rate highly. I would choose a size 8 hook. Fishing with casters or gentles as bait, and depending on the clarity of the water, I might use hooks sizes 14s and 16s.

It's most important when float fishing to choose a float that takes some weight, the minimum I use would be 6AA, often it's a float taking 10 AA. I bunch most of my shot 12–18in from the hook, with a BB shot some 6in from the hook, though this might change at various times during the day. When mending the line, you don't want to be moving the float; you need something that takes some weight so you can boss the stream. Once I have chosen my swim I will introduce a golf ball-size piece of finely mashed bread, repeating the process every fifteen minutes for the first hour, but I won't attempt to fish for perhaps fifty minutes to an hour. Every three or four minutes I will introduce two or three pieces of hook-size bread flake.

Having plumbed the depth, I will start off by fishing the bait a few inches off the bottom, if nothing happens I will try fishing a little further up in the water. Should nothing still show, and I feel I have fish in the swim, I will trip the bait along the bottom. I will make sure I put in a chicken egg-size lump of finely mashed bread every fifth cast. If the water is high and coloured, why not fish a lobworm on a size 6 hook? It's accounted for a lot of big roach over the years.

My first choice is often stret-pegging. Having plumbed the depth, I set the float about 2–3ft over depth, the shot is bunched about 18in from the hook. Having cast out across the river and downstream, I hold back the float on a tight line, the float will then settle at an angle. After a few minutes with no sign of a bite, I lift the rod tip, allowing the float to move a few feet downstream before once again tightening down to the float. I repeat the process until I have hooked a fish or the tackle is so far downstream that I need to repeat the process.

If I have been trotting and find the fish hard to tempt, I will switch to laying-on. All you need to do is move the float up the line so the bunched shot are resting on the bottom. Holding the rod and using a rest, I tighten down to the float causing it to lie at an angle. A bite is usually signalled by a sharp dip of the float or the float moving across the flow and slowly submerging. Both these styles of angling are a good way of fishing at dusk and into the darkness when I illuminate the float with a torch beam. Why not give it a try.

A great roach-fishing venue on the Hampshire Avon, close to Salisbury, is the Britford water, controlled by the London Anglers Association: day permits cost just £10, a season permit only £42, excellent value for money. The river keeper is Stuart Wilson, a very knowledgeable guy. You won't find a better river-keeper. The LAA in 1965 had the foresight to purchase the fishery for, I believe, £65,000 which included a house. It probably cost £1 for each member of the association in those days. Today, I suppose that fishery would fetch millions.

The current Chairman, Dick Hodges, follows in the footsteps of a long list of chairmen who have guided the association over many years – and long may they prosper. Looking through rose-tinted glasses, I suppose the great days were those after the Second World War when, up until the end of the 1960s, many of the affiliated clubs would run coach trips to the various LAA venues. We learnt so much in those days which has helped us catch more and bigger fish these days. Pike, perch, chub, dace, roach, barbel, trout and grayling are spread throughout this delightful fishery at Britford. It comprises some carriers, the old river and the new, the latter built to alleviate flooding in Salisbury. Roach are what most anglers seek these days and you have a chance of a three pound fish, they are caught each season. Of course, they don't get taken often.

Lots of chub to five pounds-plus, with a good head of perch to three pounds, but I reckon there is a chance of a four-pounder for someone who is prepared to target this species for a season. Pike are abundant, as are dace, pike going thirty pounds. Fly fishing for trout and grayling can be quite exciting in the lower reaches. I defy anyone not to get excited when they see a brown trout sipping down olives on a May evening.

*I*t all started when I got a telephone call from a fellow presenter at BBC Radio Lancashire who told me that comedian singer song-writer, Phil Cool wanted to meet me. I said, "Tell Phil to give me a call." Now this comedian is the world's only 'Stand up Chameleon' who is armed with a controllable rubber face which he's not afraid to use! Phil's body, too, seems to be able to defy the normal anatomical laws.

With this unique weaponry, he can be anyone or anything instantaneously, from international celebrity to intergalactic alien. He can be shockingly funny, even doing a good impression of Martin James! Phil is one of the most original and unique comic talents to come out of Great Britain. During the 1980s and 90s Phil was a familiar face on BBC and ITV television, working with some great artists of the day: Rolf Harris, Jasper Carrot and fellow angler Chris Tarrant OBE. Phil's escape from this hectic life is with his wife Beverley and their three children; he certainly enjoys the peace and quiet of angling and the countryside.

A week later Phil called and we chatted as anglers do; it transpired that Phil wanted to spend a day fishing with me. We arranged a chub-fishing session on the River Ribble in late February; it was a day of heavy rain with a gale force wind, what I call horrid weather, not really suitable for catching fish. I guided Phil up and down the beat, urging him on with encouraging words. Just downstream of a weir pool I suggested he bait with a fresh chunk of crust and cast on the edge of a large boulder, in fact a mini-car size boulder which created a nice crease. Within minutes the rod tip pulled over with a perfectly timed strike, Phil was into his first chub of about four pounds. He followed this up with a couple of other nice chub. I was impressed. It was time for a fresh brew of Yorkshire Gold tea in the sanctuary of the cabin away from the sheeting rain and gale force wind.

When the trout-fishing season started I called Phil to invite him to join me on my stretch of the River Ribble for a day's dry-fly fishing. We met up two days later on a delightful May morning, with a light but warm south westerly wind with fish sipping down a variety of insects, mainly buzzers, which were hatching off in big clouds. I didn't ask him to fish a buzzer pattern, but suggested he fish a size 14 Grannom pattern on a 12ft leader, the reason for this is that I have found better quality fish will often take the larger pattern of fly. I matched a 5 weight floating line with a Thomas and Thomas 9ft Whisper-Lite rod. His casting was spot on; during the session he caught some fine brown trout, while other fly-fishers that day went fishless, through concentrating on that ridiculous method of down and across with a team of wet flies.

On our last fly-fishing trip in May, Phil mentioned that his lifelong dream was to fish the River Kennet; I invited him to join me for a few days and he accepted with boyish enthusiasm. In late June we drove south from Lancashire for a few days fishing on his 'River of his Dreams'. That first evening's fishing was on the Wasing syndicate water of the Warren beat. Having fished several likely spots we arrived at the Rockery just on dusk; during the next half-an-hour, Phil had two rod-wrenching bites. Both fish were hooked, putting a good bend in his rod, but sadly, he lost the two good barbel in an alder tree hanging down in the water. After an hour into the darkness, with no more bites, we headed off to our accommodation.

Next morning I cooked, his favourite breakfast of kippers, toast with tea; breakfast over we were ready to go fishing. After stopping off to view the Rivers Enborne and Kennet, we paid a visit to Tadley Angling, where the first question your asked is, "Is it tea or coffee?" Soon, Kevin's delightful wife Lynne, produced two mugs of tea, in this shop you even get offered biscuits. As I chatted with Kevin, Lynne and some customers, Phil looked around the shop. As anglers do, he couldn't resist purchasing a new item of tackle, in this instance a Grauvell 12ft two piece rod designed for big river fish. After more chatting with customers, then buying some tackle items that we probably already had, but couldn't resist, we finished our tea and went off fishing.

Conditions were rather horrid, sunshine and clear blue sky, it was looking like it would be tough going to get my guest a good fish. As we roamed the river bank on the Wasing fishing syndicate beats of Dalston, Warren, Woolhampton and Aldermaston I pointed out various swims that produced roach, perch, chub or barbel. I explained how I fished for the various fish in the different swims. On one area that is little fished, we pushed through head-high nettles and brambles, getting stung several times and scratched to bits as we did so.

This was jungle-type fishing, but I felt this undisturbed stretch of river bank might just yield a fish for Phil. I found a good swim with an over hanging tree offering shade, peering into the three foot deep swim over gravel and silt close to the bank, I could make out lots of cabbages. (These are submerged water lilies with curled leaves hence the name.) From many years of experience, I have noticed that big fish find these areas very attractive as they provide plenty of food nymphs and invertebrates. Another attraction for perch and chub along with jack pike, occasional a big pike, are the swarms of small fish that seek sanctuary in these areas. If big roach are your quarry I suggest you target these areas. As in catching all big fish we need a bit of luck, despite John Wilson who tells me there isn't any luck.

I pointed out to Phil an area where big chub could sometimes be found, suggesting he fish legered crust. Creeping away from the waters edge so we didn't spook any fish – remember chub are easily spooked, they disappear ghost-like. While Phil put together his gear, the new Grauvell rod, matched with a Shimano fixed-spool reel, 10lb line and a size 6 hook with 2 LG shot lightly pinched on the line 5in from the hook. I handed him a chunk of crust which was impaled on the hook, he was now ready to go. I told him to drop the crust alongside some reeds showing just above the water. Phil made five casts, each time the bait was taken, the rod tip pulled round and the bites missed. I couldn't believe how lucky he was to get so many takes without the fish getting spooked.

I then suggested he hold the rod, and as the tip moves, strike a bit more firmly.

Phil Cool pictured with his 14lb 15oz River Kennet Barbel, even bigger than his best River Spey Salmon

Phil Cool with guitar surrounded by those who helped out at fund raising concert. Credit David Bleazard

Within minutes of making cast number six the rod tip pulled round once more. This time Phil made a firmer strike, it worked beautifully. The rod took on its battle curve; picking up the landing net I knelt down holding the submerged net in the water. Phil was in control and soon was drawing a big chub over the net, I lifted, then said, "Yes it's a big one, in fact it's very big!" on the scales it went 5lb 13oz – now that's a big summer-chub. Later in the day he eclipsed this with an even bigger chub of 6lb 7oz, this time on a piece of Platinum soft paste bait. What a great way to start a trip. On another day we fished a different Wasing syndicate water; after fishing for about half-an-hour Phil had a barbel about six pounds. After a mug of fresh brewed Yorkshire Gold tea, I recorded a session with Phil playing guitar while singing a comical fishing song for my At the Water's Edge programme on BBC Radio Lancashire. It was time for some food. After clipping the leads of my microwave oven onto the car battery, I soon heated our cottage pie which, as always, tasted good in the open air. It was time to start fishing again. As the sun dipped below the riverside trees we cast out our baited hooks. Within the hour Phil astounded me and everyone else when he hooked a big barbel, after perhaps ten minutes I was able to net a fish that many of us only dream about.

As I tried to manhandle this great fish up the steep bank one of the landing net arms collapsed. I grabbed the net mesh, saying to myself, "If need be I will go in the water!" I was determined this fish wasn't going to escape. Eventually I had the fish safely on the soft sponge mat where I slipped out the size 8 barbless hook from the scissors of the fish. Moving along the bank, I found a spot where I could peg the fish safely in the water.

Next job was to sort out camera gear, scales and weight bag. Having zeroed the scales, I collected the fish which was placed safely in the weigh bag. Hoisting it on the scales, we watched the needle go round to 14lb 15oz. Bigger than Phil's previous best fish, a salmon from the River Spey. Again it was caught on Platinum soft paste bait made by Jim O'Hearn, what a winner. Phil had a grin a mile wide with two big sparkling eyes. The tackle set-up was 10lb line, size 8 hook using the Grauvell rod he purchased on the first day of his trip, from Tadley Angling matched with a Shimano fixed-spool reel, with 1½oz of inline stonze stopped 15in from the size 6 hook by a small swivel.

At the end of the trip Phil said, "What do I owe you Martin?" I said, "Just make a cheque out to one of my charities." After a few minutes Phil said, "I'll do better than that, I'll give you a free concert!" For my kindness in guiding Phil on his incredible trip, my two charities: Ribble Valley Crossroad Care and the Army Benevolent Fund, will benefit. What a great gesture. While fishing at Tewitfield Lake I told Les Bratsby, the fishery owner about the concert, he immediately said, "Our band, O'Connor's Fusiliers, will give an hour."

The event took place on Friday, 13 November at the Grand Hotel in Clitheroe. It was an evening of fun and music with O'Connor's Fusiliers and Phil Cool. As master of ceremonies I welcomed the sell-out audience. Then followed by a minute's silence for those lost in Iraq and Afghanistan wars. After introducing the first half entertainment of O'Connor's Fusiliers I was able to relax; this group really did put on a first class act and a great show. During the interval, I welcomed representatives from Crossroad Care and the Army Benevolent Fund to give a five minute presentation on their work. This was followed by asking all serving and ex servicemen present to stand up and let the audience show their appreciation.

I then introduced Phil Cool, Old Rubber Face, who kept the audience in stitches; I don't think there was a dry eye in the audience. Everyone was ecstatic over the entertainment. Before we all departed I asked everyone to stand for the National Anthem, something sadly missing today from many entertainment venues. Two weeks later I was able to present two cheques to my chosen charities for £1,300 each.

Martin James centre presents cheques to Liz Parkinson, Treasurer, Ribble Valley Crossroads Care and Lieutenant Colonel Philip Aindow MBE Army Benevolent Fund. Credit David Bleazard

Last week I visited the river for just a couple of hours each day to check on my mink traps and scare off the cormorants, though I did check the water temperature, which over the past few days has been 34°F. On Sunday, Brendan Ince joined me for a short session of chub-fishing.

Snow and ice was everywhere, from a distance the river looked black against the white, snow-covered banks, the surrounding white hills were shrouded in mist, it was a slippery journey down the long ice-coated track to the river, in driving conditions more suited to a four-wheel drive than Brendan's Ford Focus. Eventually we pulled into the car park.

As we did so half a dozen mallard shot skywards, a few years ago I would have had a loaded twelve bore, and no doubt I would have got off at least one shot, if not two. I shivered in the easterly wind.

Unwinding the cord from my thermometer, I dropped it into the ice rimmed margin of the river, five minutes later I got a reading of 34°F. Chub were our quarry. As we waited for the kettle to boil, I put together a 12ft Avon action rod, Mitchell 300 reel, 1953 vintage, but still perfect for the job. Blowing on my cold, shaking fingers and hands, I attempted to push the end of the line through the guides, occasionally wiping tears from my eyes, caused by the cold wind. Finally, I managed to tie on a hook after three attempts.

As I get older I find the simplest of jobs becoming difficult.

Standing the rod against the fence, I turned to see steam coming from the spout of the kettle, soon, Brendan had a mug of coffee, for me a mug of tea with a piece of fruit cake, the day suddenly seemed a lot better. I could see flocks of fieldfare and starlings, and then a robin appeared, I gave it some pieces of cake which were greedily eaten, as if there was no tomorrow.

Finishing off the last crumb, he puffed himself up then flew to the shelter of an ivy-clad beech tree. Please make sure you have some ice-free water in the garden for the birds and don't forget all the table scraps. No doubt you will have some stale cakes left over from Sunday tea or a birthday party. The birds will love them.

A group of long-tailed tits suddenly appeared in a nearby willow tree, their restless activity and acrobatic actions resembling those of other tits as they worked to-and-fro through the branches seeking tiny flies and other insects. The excellent eyesight of these delightful birds never ceases to amaze me.

Tea finished, I chucked a loaf of bread into my small shoulder-bag, along with some soft cheese and sausage paste, adding a towel, my JetBoil stove, a small bottle of water, tea bags, powdered milk and mugs. I slung my chair over my back followed by the bag; picking up rod and landing net we headed off upstream for a couple of hours fishing before dark.

Walking alongside a small copse, two small roe-deer suddenly appeared, then a pheasant shot skywards in panic. After fifteen minutes of brisk walking we arrived at our chosen swim, a dark deep-looking swim overhung by a big ivy-clad oak tree, many of its roots plunging deep into the water offering a sanctuary for fish from the marauding cormorants that have invaded our rivers.

The first thing I noticed was the ice, covering the very slow flowing area of water which extended several yards up and downstream, a quarter of the way across the river we had a perfect crease with a steady flow on the outside going from left to right. From many previous experiences of fishing the area we had six foot deep swim over small stones and gravel.

Let me say this once and once only. Forget all the rubbish you read about fishing small baits and light tackle for winter chub it's a lot of nonsense, I use my normal gear which includes 6lb line and size 4 hooks. My first bait is bread, either crust or flake, I always start with crust. I also have some cheese and sausage paste as extras. If lobworms are available, I will have a few.

Bites usually are a light tap then a good pull. Only about one percent of bites are usually small pulls. Most bites will pull the rod in, if given the chance. What I usually do on feeling or seeing a light movement on the rod tip is to push the rod forward, giving a bit of slack – then it's usually a good strong pull.

We both lightly pinched on one LG shot about three inches from the hook then baited with a piece of crust. A slight underhand swing had the baited hook settling in the right spot. Watching some line come off the spool, I banged over the pick-up, and then settled back, holding the rod with the butt resting on my thigh, at the same time I held a loop of line and watched the rod tip.

Within minutes I felt a savage pluck. I released the line then, as the line tightened, I made a firm strike. Nothing, I thought, "How could I miss a perfect bite." I made another cast to the same spot, ten minutes later the line went slack in quite a dramatic manner. Another fish missed, this time I reckon the fish must have moved six or seven feet upstream.

We fished on for another fifteen minute with no more bites, and decided it was a time for home. As we walked across the snow covered fields, I tried to work out how I had missed some

Martin with a fine winter Chub

perfect bites. I didn't have an answer. Sadly, Brendan, who sat next to me and fished the same swim, didn't get a touch. Fishing can be a strange game but we both reckon it's still the greatest sport.

I suppose it was about three o'clock in the afternoon when I came off the ice-free road for the long drive down an ice-covered track, one false move and I would be down the bank, I drove at no more than ten miles an hour. Automatic cars are not the vehicles for driving on sheet ice. Eventually I was in the car park, heaving a sigh of relief. Climbing from the car, I pulled on my windproof arctic smock, certainly an excellent garment for this weather. Taking the rod and shoulder bag from the back of the car, I then put together my landing net then picked up a rod rest. I was ready for another chub-fishing session in wintry conditions.

I went off downstream for half a mile, choosing to fish in the area of an alder tree. I wanted to fish a slightly deeper channel; twenty feet out from the tree and fifteen feet below it, there was a three foot wide side-stream which flowed into the river, creating an ice free area. In front of me, and for some fifty feet upstream, was a length of ice-covered water extending ten feet out from the bank.

My downstream swim had an estimated five feet of water over silt, sand and gravel with the odd football-size rock. Baiting with a piece of crust, I dropped the bait into some steady water on the outside of a crease; minutes later the rod tip moved slightly then pulled round in a savage manner.

I set the hook into a fish that dived towards the margins, no doubt seeking the sanctuary of the tree roots. Pulling the rod over and upstream I bullied the fish away from the danger. Suddenly a chub of about three pounds swirled on the surface where it was quickly netted. Taking out the barbless hook, I lowered the net into the water and watched the fish swim away.

I fished on until darkness with no more bites, though I did get the rod tip pulled round on a few occasions as chunks of ice floating down river hit the line. By now my rod was frost-covered, landing net frozen to the ground and my feet were starting to feel the cold. I called it a day. Walking across the fields, I disturbed a skein of Greylag geese, and then spooked two hares. Back in the car, I listened to the weather forecast, hearing the announcer say that the "Arctic conditions could be with us for a week-to-ten days." Not good news. It was a slow drive up the ice covered track, but within the hour I am indoors.

Today, Tuesday, it's snowing hard; no buses are running from my village into town, certainly not the day to be driving, my car stayed in the garage. I kitted myself out with walking boots, a good pair of waterproof trousers, my arctic smock, trilby hat; then, with haversack on my back I walked the six-or-seven miles into town.

Despite the heavy snow storm, it was an enjoyable walk, some of it alongside the river, other times, through a small wood where I watched several fieldfare feeding on some hawthorn berries. After a quick walk around town, picking up my Angler's Mail and a few items of shopping, I walked back home. Looking at all the snow that has fallen and the forecast of frost tonight, I don't think I will be able to get on the river tomorrow.

Opposite – Chub fishing on the Avon at Britford. Credit Ian Chapman, Anglers' Mail

The River Bain flows through the Lincolnshire Wolds. It's a delightful part of England with rolling hills surrounding a flat Fenland landscape of dykes, ditches and huge fields. It's a part of the world where for many years, I hunted pheasant, duck and geese with the same passion as I hunt fish today.

I first got to know the River Bain through the pages of 'Drop Me a Line' by Maurice Ingham and Richard Walker in early 1953. Maurice also lived in the small, market town of Louth, where you can buy great pork pies, oven-ready pheasants, excellent sausages and trilby hats – hats made from pure felt with a genuine leather band.

The River Bain is a tributary of the River Witham, which of course was one of the top match-fishing rivers up to the 1980s, being known for its huge shoals of bream, with the Boston and Lincoln anglers catching their share of the fish. Let's not forget Boston tackle dealer, Jack Clayton, who gave us the swing tip, and anglers such as Fred Foster, who made it work so well on the Witham and similar waters.

The river was once more in the news in late 1953 when Richard Walker fished the second of a three-leg series of matches on the River Bain against Tom Sails, the Lincoln AA team captain on 31 October near Coningsby.

In the early 1980s I often shot pheasant and ducks, my dog sometimes retrieving a bird from the Bain. From the first time I set eyes on this small, twisting, flowing river, it looked attractive, as it flowed through the Lincolnshire countryside. It is a tiny river averaged some three feet in depth; on the inside of bends, I sometimes found five feet of water, often with an undercut bank. What made these bends so attractive, as a fishy place and to the eye, were the willow, hawthorn and brambles overhanging the river bank, making these spots look dark and secretive. I said to myself on several occasions, I must start to fish the River Bain and walk in the footsteps of Walker and Ingham, two authors who had given me so much pleasure through their writing, and the knowledge they passed on about catching better than average fish. Somehow I never found the time.

In October 1986 I was on my fifth trip to Lincolnshire in three months to visit June, an old girl friend who had moved from London to a village near Louth. It was my chance to fish the river for a few days. I had no problem in finding some water to fish, through my friendship with several landowners who had invited me to fish the river whenever I was in the area. I could also purchase a Boston AA membership book which offered me some good water in the Coningsby area. It was time I started to catch some fish.

In early September I had been on a duck-hunting trip. From my stand at the edge of a wood alongside the river, my attention was drawn to some movement in the water. It was then I spotted a couple of big pike, probably twenty pounds-plus; these were in fact, huge fish for such a tiny river. At the time, I was shooting as a guest of Paul Evans; Paul and I had worked together in South America. Over dinner that evening I mentioned the pike to my host who said, "You're welcome to come and fish anytime." (Sadly, Paul later died during an incident in the Middle East.)

It was just perfect for me: June would cook breakfast, then put together an interesting lunch box before going off to work at nine o'clock while I went off to the river, often arriving home an hour or two after dark. Some evenings I would take June out for dinner; on other occasions, I would arrive home, take a shower then have dinner, sharing a bottle of wine. After the dishes were put in the washer we would spend the rest of evening, and much of night, making love. June was a great cook with a good knowledge of wine, and a good-looking woman who certainly dressed to thrill a tired angler. What more did a guy need.

On my first visit to fish the river, it was about ten o'clock when I arrived and parked about a mile upstream of the wood. Pulling on my boots and picking up my binoculars, I walked slowly downstream in the hope of finding those pike. As I slowly trod the bank I peered intently into the clear water. Not only did I not see the pike, I didn't see any small fish. I was disappointed, even more by the shallow depth of the river; it probably averaged around three feet. After walking perhaps a thousand yards and not seeing any fish, I could see the river was taking a sharp right turn. I walked a few more yards, coming close to the bend in the river. I could see the bed of the stream gradually shelving down to create a deeper pool on the inside of the bend. It was just possible to see the bottom through the crystal- clear water. I didn't see any pike, but I could see three big chub, probably the biggest chub I've seen in such a small river. Creeping away, I walked slowly back thinking about those fish and trying to decide on the best approach. Back at the car I put the kettle on for a brew, and while waiting for it to boil, I put together my Bruce and Walker Avon rod, a centre-pin reel, then threaded the 6lb line through the guides before tying on a size 4 barbless hook.

Steam was coming from kettle and I made a brew then sat in the warm sunshine enjoying my tea and a beef sandwich. My mind was on those chub – they were not just big, they were huge! Finishing my break, I chucked a loaf of bread and some cheese paste, along with scales and plastic bag, into a small shoulder-bag. Picking up my rod and net, I walked off downstream to the wood. This time, as I approached the bend in the river and the chub swim, I got down on my stomach and slithered forward until I was close enough to peer over the bank into the water. My three fish were still slowly cruising around. I said to myself, "Those fish are for catching," as I threw in a piece of flake. Ever so slowly, it sank down through the water, settling on the bottom. Slowly, one of the chub moved across the stream then sucked in the flake; in the blink of an eye it spat it out then sucked it back into its cavernous mouth.

Fifteen minutes later I baited with a chunk of flake, at the same time and quietly as possible, I slightly lifted myself off the ground and cast the bait upstream; it landed with a faint plop. Holding the rod with just a couple of feet of it sticking out over the water, I laid back

These two reels cover all my needs on the River Bain

on the ground. I watched with bated breath as the flake moved a few feet before slowly sinking as it travelled downstream.

I could see the chub with their black tails and cavernous mouths slowly cruising near the opposite bank. One moved out into midstream, the other two followed. The first fish then spotted the flake; I watched it move into position to intercept my bait. Seconds later it moved forward sucking in my baited hook. I tightened into the fish, the water boiled as it rolled on the surface. Meanwhile the other two fish shot off down the river. By this time I was on my knees playing a big chub. Probably within five minutes – no more than six, I had the fish in the net: it was mine. After zeroing the scales I placed the fish into the plastic bag and hoisted it onto the scales, it weighed 6lb 4oz, my biggest River Bain chub, at that time also my personal best. I made several more trips into the area seeking out the roach and chub. With a heavy workload and some new fishing interests I moved on to other waters.

In 1988 I was back in Lincolnshire, to make a series of programmes about the countryside, its characters, the wildlife, and hopefully do a bit of fishing. This was my chance to pay tribute to a couple of great anglers, Ingham and Walker. It worked out well; I also met up again with my old girl friend June.

I made several exploratory trips into the Wolds, talking with local characters, learning about the local crafts and interviewing interesting people. During one of my many visits to Lincolnshire I stopped off at Horncastle to seek advice on what fishing might be had in that area. I was told about a short stretch of river available near Coningsby. My informant said, "Just take the A153 and you will get to the river." Not quite true. After driving for several miles up and down the A153, I spotted a garage at Haltham, where I stopped to seek further information. I was in luck. The garage proprietor, Alan Gunn, was an angler himself, he soon told me where to fish and said, "The only permit you need is an EA rod licence." Thanking Alan for his help, I made my way to the river as instructed.

The tiny River Bain, was more like a stream than a river. It really did look great in the bright sunshine; after several days of rain it was high, coloured and fast-flowing. I do enjoy fishing a river carrying some extra water. In a short hour-long session, legering crust and flake baits, I caught five chub averaging some two-and-a-half pounds each. I got bitten off by one fish,

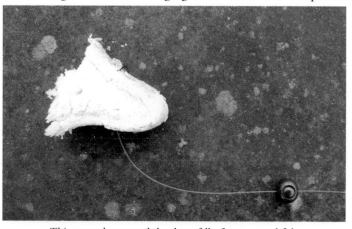

also pricked two others and caught a big brown-trout probably going three pounds; I was more than happy. Close by was a red telephone box, I called June to see if she wanted to go out for dinner.

After chatting for a while, she suggested we should eat at home then have an early night. What a good idea I though. As I was staying with June I

This set up has caused the downfall of many good fish

stopped for another hour on the river, while she cooked dinner. I caught two nice chub, one weighing in at 4lb 14oz, on cheese paste.

On the drive back to June's home I decided to visit the river the next day for a longer session, before visiting two planned filming locations. I now had a warm, comfortable base to stay during my visits.

The river Bain isn't an easy river to fish; it's very narrow, shallow and steep-banked in many areas with several small weir pools. The river is often less than twenty feet wide with a depth of three feet but it can offer such exciting fishing. Forget all about catching big bags of fish; don't take tackle boxes, umbrellas and bags of ground bait. This river is a roving water: catch one or two fish then move on. It's not a river where your friend can fish ten yards up or downstream of your swim, he needs to be four hundred yards or more away.

I have fished the river on many occasions with great success, catching roach to 2lb 3oz, bream 9lb 6oz, chub of 6lb 4oz, pike of 18lb and rudd of nearly two pounds, my best was 1lb 14oz. Yes, that was a lucky fish; I was trying to catch chub at the time. Then, I was chub fishing when I had the big bream; I didn't complain, it was an experience I loved. That's one of the beauties of this sport of angling; you never know what you might catch.

This river is so small it could easily be called a stream. It has a lot of wildlife on and around its banks to keep the most avid naturalist happy when the fish are not biting. One Sunday morning I sat working a bit of cheese paste down the swim, when a stoat appeared on the far bank, it was out on a hunting trip. I watched the stoat, at the same time feeling for a fish to pick up my bait. I was fascinated and enthralled studying this ferocious hunter go about its business. When it eventually got hold of a small rabbit, the scream of its prey was certainly blood-curdling. I have heard it plenty of times, but I reckon it would have given a few dog walkers a fright. Pheasants, partridges, geese, yellow and grey wagtails, robins, wrens, coots, little grebe or dabchick and moorhens are in profusion. Kingfishers, blackbirds, thrushes and many more birds can also be seen. On three occasions I have seen several foxes as I have arrived at the water around dawn. On my latest trip I witnessed a big skein of pink-footed geese, probably five or six hundred, no doubt heading for the Wash estuary. How my mates and I enjoyed our days on the Wash marshes hunting geese with McKenzie Thorpe as our guide in the 1950s. What great days they were.

Having left the BBC Radio Lancashire studios around 6.0 a.m. after a very early morning recording session, I headed off to Lincolnshire. It was a grey, soft morning with a light drizzle in places but, with just the odd lorry and a few cars on the road, it was a pleasant enough journey, listening to the Beach Boys and Buddy Holly; the miles were soon eaten up.

Dawn appeared and with it, on the horizon, a small open area of light-coloured sky, quickly changing to a light golden yellow, tinged along the right-hand side with soft shades of pink. It was a wildfowler's dawn, and hopefully, an angler's dawn. In the next hour the sky continued to change to various shades of yellows, golds, pinks and blues: it was quite dramatic. I felt that if the day stayed fairly overcast and warm, then it would be good for fishing. I mention the weather being warm; it was far warmer than it had been the previous week when I had been on the Teme with temperatures below zero some nights.

A typical River Bain winter chub

After parking in a quiet lay-by, I put the kettle on for a brew, then set up my other stove to cook breakfast of bacon, sausage and eggs, I could eat meals like that in those days. Half-an-hour later I was ready to put my gear together, nothing special – in fact it was a simple set-up: An 11½ft Avon rod, Mitchell 300 reel, 6lb Masterline Illusion and a size 4 hook. I then lightly pinched on 2 LG shot some 6in from the hook. My baits today were soft cheese paste, bread crust and flake; all three baits had produced good fish over the years.

With bait bag over my shoulder, I walked off upstream to a small weir pool which, a couple of years previous, a friendly farmer had given me permission to fish when I met him on a pheasant shoot. It included nearly two miles of other water. All it had cost me was a good bottle of brandy for him and a bouquet of flowers for his wife each Christmas. At one time an angling club had the rights, but litter had become so bad he stopped them fishing. I usually start off at the pool as it looks so inviting, despite the locals saying, "There wasn't much to be caught." I suppose that might be true if you're fishing small hooks with those small white grubs. I haven't found it difficult catching good fish; I reckon chub find it hard to resist a good chunk of bread or cheese paste drifting seductively through the swim, if you haven't spooked them.

Having cast out a chunk of crust, I put the rod in a forked stick while I got the camera set up, in case I got a good fish. Just as I focused on the rod tip, it pulled around, bite one missed. Rebaiting, I cast again and immediately had another bite: this was also missed. Baiting for a third time, I cast the bait up close to the white water. I was ready for anything. As the tip moved, I hit, feeling a good fish. For a couple of minutes I wasn't sure who was winning this tussle – no way could I get any line back on the reel.

Then, as usually happens, the fish started to tire and after another minute I was able to get the fish below me. A minute or so later, it suddenly dived in towards the bank becoming fast in a snag. I couldn't get any line, then all went slack; the fish was gone. I was gutted. I had been too casual. It was a very good fish – perhaps a good five. Sitting, watching the rod tip, I thought over the events of the past hour, realising I had taken too much for granted. In fact I told myself I was a bloody idiot for being so cocksure, confident and blasé. I had no one to blame for those missed bites and lost fish except myself. I fished on for another two hours without a bite then decided it was brew time.

After a brew and a sandwich I rebaited with a big bit of crust then cast out towards a spot on the far bank where the current swirled backwards towards a small pool. Half-an-hour later the rod tip moved just fraction of an inch, I struck, just knowing it was a bite, connecting with a good fish. After a few minutes it was netted: a lovely-looking winter chub in perfect condition. It weighed 4lb 10oz I slid out the barbless hook and quickly released it.

A light rain started to fall but the weather remained quite warm, the water temperature was 42°F, with conditions still quite good. I was confident of more fish. An hour passed without a bite. It was decision time. "Should I move?" I asked myself. Five minutes later I was winding in. I had decided to fish the Bridge Pool, some 800 yards downstream. After pulling over onto the grass strip alongside the road, I stood on the bridge looking down into the pool wondering what it held. With an hour of daylight left, I settled down behind some reed mace.

I baited with bread flake and quickly hooked a chub of about three pounds, this was followed by another fish of about two pounds. Another quickly followed about the same weight. In the three casts I had three more fish averaging about three pounds. With darkness enveloping me I decided to have a brew and a sandwich then fish on until at least 10 p.m. Half an hour later, feeling refreshed (it's surprising what a mug of tea and sandwich will do to revive one's spirit) I made my way back to Bridge Pool, where, in the next hour, I got four more chub, like peas in a pod, weighing around two pounds each. I felt it was time for a move, I didn't think I would get a good fish from this pool today.

Chucking all the gear in the car, I drove a couple of miles upstream to another bridge. I had often caught good fish, either just under the bridge, or downstream of it. I chose a swim sixty yards downstream with an overhanging tree on the far bank which had several of its branches trailing in the water; this helped create a big raft of reeds and other rubbish which had got caught up on the branches. I just love these areas. I suppose the river was about thirty feet wide at this point.

In the gloom, I cast a piece of crust upstream of the raft letting the bait drip down under it. I then sat, trying to see the rod tip in the darkness, having forgotten my torch. Twice I was sure the tip had moved, but no, it was just my imagination. After a few minutes I wound in then rebaited with another big chunk of crust, casting again so the bait would roll under the trailing

branches and rubbish raft. This time I held the rod. Within seconds I felt a pluck on the line. Striking, I set the hook into what felt like a good fish.

As it twisted and turned into the current, seeking the sanctuary of the tree roots, I was glad I had chosen 6lb line. I wasn't going to give this fish any chance of escape and stepped into the water. No way was this fish going anywhere except my landing net! I heaved the rod back over my right shoulder dragging the fish

Another winter chub on on bread flake

towards the net; I cramped on the pressure then bullied it into the net. Lifting the net I could feel it was a good fish.

As I parted the net mesh I was surprised how big a fish it was, "Must go five," I thought. Out with scales and weigh net. I zeroed the scales and placed the fish into the soft mesh netting then heaved the scales skywards. By this time I had retrieved my torch and I shone it on the clock face, I could see the needle give me a reading of 5lb 4oz or 5lb 5oz. I settled on the weight of 5lb 4oz. I was a happy angler – in fact I was very happy angler! I punched the air and shouted, "Yes, another five." And this from the River Bain where, they tell me, it's not worth the effort. It was then back to Louth for a shower, some well-cooked food with an old flame from the 1960s.

Parking the car in a lay-by close to the banks of the River Bain in Lincolnshire, I looked towards the river and the mist-shrouded flat fenland landscape, and realised I had the river to myself. Though the snow had melted, the ground was still rock hard. A few cattle stood forlornly in a tree-sheltered corner of a riverside field. Everything was quiet, it seemed as if death had gripped the surrounding countryside, there wasn't even a pheasant to disturb the stillness. It's very rare not to see or hear this beautiful game-bird which was imported into Britain by the Romans some couple of thousand years ago.

Walking up-river towards my chosen weir pool near that delightful market town of Horncastle, I could see ice along both banks. A moorhen, its red beak adding a spot of colour to the drab day, was spooked from the straw-brown riverside reeds. Legs trailing just inches above the smooth green-tinged water, it flew low to the opposite bank where it dived for the sanctuary of a willow bush. A grey heron rose skywards, its great wings flapping as it made a harsh call which sounds like the word "fraank" – I often say to my friends, "there goes Frank." Slowly, it gained height, making its way up-river to another resting or fishing spot. Either my presence or the moorhen crashing into the area had frightened off old Frank, which had been resting or seeking its breakfast.

Herons might not look very graceful when flying and it's also quite amazing to think of these long-legged birds nesting in tall trees. Their nests are called heronries, though they have been known to nest in tall reed beds, but it's quite rare for this to happen. The diet of the heron is varied: from ducklings to fish; it's said the eel is its favourite meal though I don't know what evidence has been produced to prove this statement. I reckon its favourite meal is the one that is most readily available and easy to catch when it's hungry. Frogs, toads, fish of all species, voles and other small mammals, all go to make the heron's diet a very varied one. When the weather is cold and frosty why not purchase a couple of pounds of sprats from the fishmonger, then, on your next fishing trip, you can spread the sprats around the river bank in an area where you have seen herons feeding at the water's edge. We must do everything possible to help our wildlife when weather conditions make it hard for them to get any food. I probably spend a hundred pounds every six weeks on food for the birds that visit my garden.

Over the past few weeks I have often had between fifteen and twenty blackbirds in the garden at any one time. Altogether I have had thirty-six species of birds visit, long may it continue. It's not only herons that have a varied diet – fish are no different, they also eat most things, in fact chub, trout and other fish will eat anything, provided they have not been spooked. Most fish when spooked quickly disappear in a shower of spray, ripples or swirls. The chub just disappears, ghost-like, without any trace. If you hadn't seen the fish you wouldn't have known it had been there.

The greatest aid to catching chub is not the tackle or bait: without doubt the most important thing is to approach the water as quietly as an owl approaches its prey, at the same time making sure you don't create a shadow on the water, which is easily done in the winter time when the sun is low in the sky. Always remember, you're the hunter after the hunted.

When we were kids we used to see how close we could get to the rabbits sitting outside their warrens on a summer's day. Sometimes one of us would get close enough to grab a young rabbit with our bare hands, and not use our catapults. I reckon it's all those hunting days of my youth that have helped me become a successful chub-hunter. There have been many times when I have spent twenty, perhaps thirty minutes or more, getting into position, before dropping the bait to an unsuspecting chub. To be successful at hunting them you need to know their habitat in a given set of water and weather conditions. I can assure you, chub will move from one location to another as the river flow changes, they don't stay in one spot.

Today, I have new bait: cocktail sausages, lightly fried then given a coating of curry powder. When I'm chub fishing I like to have a couple of different baits, apart from my usual and very successful bread, such as cheese or sausage paste which have accounted for a lot of chub over the past sixty years. Some days, a new bait will encourage a chub to eat when all else fails. Curry-flavoured sausage is a new bait for my chosen weir pool today.

Looking upstream through the gloom, I could just make out the outline of my chosen pool with its alder tree and some silver birch on the far bank; in the gloom the trees were my landmark. Another couple of hundred yards, then one more stile, and I should be able to see the turbulent, swirling, creamy, foam-flecked current below the weir, then the slower-flowing water towards the tail of the pool.

As I poked my head over the bank, three ducks and five mallard jumped skywards. My mind went back to my duck-hunting days, saying to no one in particular, "That would have been a right and left." In those days of the past, I would have had the pleasure of watching my labrador working. Today, it wasn't a shotgun, but an Avon action rod, centre-pin reel loaded with some 50yd of 6lb Masterline fluorocarbon line, with a Partridge barbless hook in size 2, 4 or 6, depending on the size of bait. The banks of my chosen pool were very slippery so I decided to go down the bank on my backside, it was safer this way.

As I sat there looking at the various fishing spots available, a kingfisher flew low to the water up towards the pool, then came to rest on a small willow bush. Opposite my chosen spot was a big raft of rubbish, mainly floating weed, where a grey wagtail (which in fact is quite yellow with a black bib) its tail continually on the move, was walking about, pecking here and there at some item of food. For some three hours I fished various spots up and down the pool with crust, flake, cheese paste meat paste and those curried sausages, without a bite, not even a tremble on the line.

After some lunch and a fresh brew I decided to feed three big balls of mashed bread into the fast swirling water and see what happened. I imagined the bread would get swirled around with various sized pieces eventually floating downstream over a period of time – hopefully the chub would wake up and start to feed. I sat there until dark without a bite. It was time to head off for home, a drive of 150 miles. As I walked down river to my car I suddenly realised why the fish didn't want to eat: the river was carrying lots of 'snow broth' which, in my book, is the kiss of death.

With mild weather and heavy rain I decided to head off to Lincolnshire and the River Bain, the prospect of an extra foot of water with rising water temperatures was encouragement enough to drive 150 miles. Apart from tackle and bait, which included some excellent lobworms, I loaded up with food, cooker and sleeping bag. If the fishing was good I wanted to spend as much time at the waterside as possible.

Disaster struck a few yards from home – the front offside tyre was punctured. Changing over to one of those silly spare wheels, which can only be described as a doughnut and about as useful, I headed off to the garage where I was given the news that the punctured tyre was scrap. The mechanic then checked the other front tyre, and gave me the news that it also needed replacing. The bill was £102.93. Where would we be without our plastic cards?

I set off once more, in the gale force wind and driving rain hoping both might ease a bit during the long drive. It was around 2.00 p.m. when I arrived just upstream of Horncastle to find the river windswept but at what looked like normal level. I quickly climbed into my chest-high waders and waterproof jacket, and then tackled up with a 12ft Avon action rod, centre-pin reel, 6lb line and a 2 swan-shot cork-on-quill float with a size 6 hook. My bait bucket contained two large loafs of bread, some lobworms, cheese and meat paste. Time for a quick brew before heading off downriver to seek, what I feel is the perfect winter quarry, the chub.

My first swim was some two hundred yards below a small weir pool where a tree hung over the river, some of its branches trailed in the water and rubbish had collected, creating a small raft. I chose a spot ten yards upstream, sitting down on the low bank covered in dead reeds ripped from the river. I set the float at about two feet then baited with a large bit of flake. Casting out, I then guided the float downstream. After about twenty feet the float dipped; the answering strike connected with a nice fish, which put up a good scrap all the way back to the net. It was a good chub which was quickly weighed and turned the scales to 4lb 10oz.

Three times I guided the float downstream, introducing an egg-sized lump of mashed bread with each cast. At the end of the third cast I held the float back, causing the bait to rise at the edge of the raft. Seconds later the float had disappeared, pulled under with a violent savage jerk: another good fish was hooked! Cramming on a lot of pressure, I soon had the fish twisting, turning and wallowing all the way to the net, another good one that weighed 4lb 12oz. After four more casts and no sign of a bite, it was time to move.

Moving on downstream, I came across a small area of water which had created the perfect crease. It's a spot that usually means a bite. Again, sitting down low, I cast out, then trotted the bait downstream to the crease and held back the float – it quickly disappeared. The strike connecting with another good fish, after a brief struggle it was netted then weighed, turning the needle to 3lb 12oz. I decided on another cast to the same spot, in fact, I fished the swim for some fifteen minutes but no sign of a bite; it was time to move on. Back at the car I loaded my tackle in the back, then made a brew before driving a few miles to a very small weir pool. An hour or so without a bite, I packed in then moved off to another area of the Bain. This time I was choosing a swim on a long straight stretch, I had to slither down to the bottom of a steep bank, as far as I could see, up and downstream, there wasn't a tree or bush in sight.

The wind was a real hooligan, blowing upstream creating some good size waves. Every now and again they would be crested by white foam – it was more like fishing the ocean. I introduced two handfuls of mashed bread, and then plumbed the depth: it was about two-an- a-half feet. I set the float at two. Baiting with a lobworm, I cast out then guided the float down the stream some twenty yards. With no sign of a bite I retrieved the line. Four or five more casts, still no bites. I decided to lie on. Setting the float at about four feet, I bunched the shot about fifteen or so inches from the hook, baited with a piece of flake and cast out towards the far bank.

After the tackle had settled, I chucked in a handful of mashed bread. Several times the float was swamped by a huge wave, often disappearing, though it wasn't time to get excited. Also, it was the first time I have seen white horses rolling up the Bain, several times the rod was blown from the rest or the tip was bent facing upstream, so violent was the wind. After about twenty minutes the float disappeared. I couldn't decide if it was a bite or if a big wave had swamped it, then the rod tip pulled round.

I struck, finding I had hooked a good fish – or it had hooked itself? This fish really did put up a good scrap all the way to the net. Often, when you hook a fish in these shallow rivers, they will roll on the surface. I didn't see this fish until I pulled it over the waiting net. It was a good one, probably a good five. The scales told a different story, it was certainly a good fish but not as heavy as I thought. It weighed 4lb 15oz, certainly a great fish on a gale-swept tiny river. Next cast with a lobworm accounted for a nice roach which weighed 14 oz, certainly a welcome sight; with so many cormorants on the river it's surprising this roach had survived.

In the fading light, with darkness approaching, the float was becoming difficult to see. I rebaited with a big bit of flake and this time I cast further downstream, allowing the tackle to settle in mid-stream. Within minutes the float had gone; a good fish was hooked and landed, it weighed 4lb 3oz. The chub then decided to feed with a vengeance! I quickly hooked and landed three more good ones all over the four pound mark: 4lb 6oz, 4lb 14oz and 4lb 12oz. Then the bites ceased as suddenly as they started. It was really difficult to see the bobbing bouncing float in the torch beam so I discarded it. For an hour or more, while I was being battered by the wind and rain, I thought, should I call it a day, but, ever the optimist, I thought, perhaps they'll come on again in a minute.

It was time for a bait change. I decided on two big lobworms which really did wriggle as I tried to get them on the hook. I then had to push the hook through a tiny square bit of rubber to keep the worms in place. Having done all this, I cast out towards the far bank and sat holding the rod.

The wind was so strong it was impossible to keep the rod in the rest. Suddenly I had a violent thump on the rod and found myself hooked into a hard-fighting fish. With the rod being knocked about by the wind I was getting worried about the hook pulling loose but I didn't want to bully the fish more than was necessary. Slowly I gained line, bringing the fish closer to the net. I then had it wallowing under the rod tip. It was certainly a good one I thought, as I pulled it over the net. Parting the wet mesh, I could see in the torch beam a splendid fish, fin and scale perfect. The scales gave a reading of 5lb 3oz.

Rebaiting with another couple of lobworms, I cast out towards the far bank and sat holding a wind-battered rod which sometimes resembled a figure S. Suddenly the rod tip, which had been pointed upstream, was pointed downstream. I felt a good fish which had hooked itself and which I quickly bullied to the net. The fish was quickly netted and pulled the scales down to 4lb 12oz. I was cold, wet and the wind blew. All I wanted now was to get back to the car for a mug of tea, so I called it a day.

Picking up my rod, sponge seat and bait bucket in one hand, the landing net and rod rest in the other, I attempted to climb the bank. It was impossible. It was a climbing job on all-fours, I chucked the landing net, rod rest and bait bucket up the bank, and slowly crawled and slithered up the bank, pushing the rod in front. At the top, the wind really was fearsome, nearly bowling me over. It was certainly a long hard struggle back to the car; often I had to sit down for a long rest and get my breath back.

After about an hour I eventually arrived, a journey which normally would take ten minutes. I was shattered. I tried to light the stove but found it impossible the wind was far too strong. Chucking all the gear in the car I headed off to a local café. It might have been a rough wet day

Another winter caught Chub for the author

but what a cracking fishing session: ten chub, best at 5lb 3oz and a nice roach. I then went back to a quiet area of the Bain where I could park up for the night. Having cleaned my teeth, I crawled into my sleeping bag. It was nearly midnight.

Next day I was back on the river just after dawn, conditions were still rough. I fished hard until darkness for only one bite, which accounted for a nice chub of 4lb 10oz. I fished an hour into the darkness, no bites; I headed back to the car for a mug of tea and bacon sandwich. I had a long drive home. Reaching the M180, the rain sheeted down, driving was horrendous. As the service station came into sight I pulled in for a break from the extremely poor driving conditions, hoping the rain would cease: It did.

The driving was so much more pleasant two hours later. I passed over the River Aire. Stopping to have a look, I could see the river was bank-high; no doubt it would be over the banks by the next morning.

I was once again in the Lincolnshire Wolds to record a programme for my At the Water's Edge series on BBC Radio Lancashire; I would also have a few days fishing on the tiny River Bain just a few miles from Louth. Wednesday 14 February was a day made for photography rather than for angling; with spring-like weather and a wind coming from an easterly direction, blue sky and bright sunshine. To make matters worse, there had been a very heavy frost overnight, though I didn't think that would stop the chub from feeding as the river would be high and coloured from several days of rain.

Ken Greenall, a retired engineering fitter, was my companion on this visit and he also offered to do the driving; Ken is a match angler who usually fishes with a pole. It would be interesting to see how our differing methods worked on this tiny river. Stopping off in Horncastle, I picked up two loaves of bread, some luncheon meat for the fish, and a couple of pork-pies for Ken and me. The florist's shop was having a busy day, and then I noticed the sign: St Valentine's Day. Oh, that's the reason why so many guys were out buying flowers. For me it was going to be a day of chub chasing!

Travelling up the River Bain valley is a nice experience when like me you do not have to drive. I could look around the countryside. Pheasants, rooks, pigeons and herons were everywhere, looking for food. No doubt the herons were stalking frogs and toads which are on the move at this time of the year, making their way to the

ponds of their birth. For the rooks though, it wasn't just food, they were also nest building. Snowdrops were about in profusion and there were odd groups of crocuses. Many of the well-sodden fields had small ponds due to all the rain. The ducks just loved these new feeding grounds. After several miles of driving we turned off the busy A road on to a minor B road then once more pulled into Haltham Garage for a chat with Alan Gunn, who filled me in with a lot more information on the river and its fishing? A more helpful guy you couldn't wish to meet. We shook hands, I thanked him once more for his help and bid him goodbye.

Having left the main road we drove several miles along twisting country lanes to the spot where Alan had suggest we should park up, I immediately thought we were in luck as there were no other cars around; we had the place to ourselves – perhaps everyone was out buying flowers! Pulling on our boots, we trekked across the fields to the river. We had all the swims with bushes or trees and a small weir pool to ourselves, just as I thought. As expected, the river was still highly-coloured and flowing fast. The gauge gave a river height of three feet. I checked the water temperature, it was 43°F. good enough for chub I thought.

I decided to start off fishing the weir pool then slowly work my way upstream, chucking baits into all the likely-looking spots. Ken chose to pole fish further downstream in the slower water. My tackle choice was quite simple; An Avon action rod, centre-pin reel, 6lb fluorocarbon line and a size 4 Partridge barbless hook I would pinch shot on the line as and when I needed to. After so many years of talking and thinking about the River Bain, I was ready to fish it for the second time in two days. I spent probably some ten minutes or so looking at the swirling water trying to work out where the chub were likely to be waiting for food to be swept down to them. I picked a small area of water about the size of a decent kitchen table close to the far bank, and fed in a small ball of mashed bread. I pinched two LG shot on the line 3in from the hook and baited with a big bit of crust. An underhand swing dropped the bait into my chosen swim.

Within seconds a good fish was hooked and bored powerfully upstream in the fast swirling water. For a couple of minutes it was give and take between us but the combination of balanced tackle and skilful handling soon had the fish beaten. This was a good fish, I thought, as it was netted. It pulled the scales down to 3lb 6oz. Not a bad fish from a tiny river on a February day. I cast again with another chunk of crust. Within seconds I noticed the line had gone slack. I tightened into another fish, which again bored powerfully upstream. After some three or four minutes I had the fish coming towards the net. This must go four pounds I thought as it was engulfed in the folds of the net. I weighed this one and it went 4lb 10oz; I was more than happy! I was like a kid with half a dozen Christmases all in one. To make the session even better, it was beautiful spring-like day.

After a nice break in the warm sunshine, I resumed fishing, once more casting big bits of crust upstream then letting them roll downstream, watching the line like a hawk and feeling for anything that might be a take. Several casts later and with no bites, I made my way over the river by the way of a small bridge then settled in close to the weir apron. Once more I cast a big bit of crust into the fast swirling water that was flowing up towards the weir and sat holding the rod feeling for a bite.

Perch of this size can offer good sport on float fished worm

Suddenly a voice behind me said, "Caught anything?" I turned to see Alan. "Yes. Two nice chub, best at four pounds ten ounces both on bread." As we sat chatting I felt the line tighten, the answering strike connected with a heavy fish. "Got a good chub this time Alan, must go five pounds or more, it's a heavy fish!" After a couple of minutes I had my first glimpse of the fish. No chub this, it was a bream – but not a skimmer – this was a big fish. In fact, when I got another look I realised it was a very big fish indeed! After a couple of minutes I had it coming towards the net, then it was mine as it sunk into the folds of my big landing-net. It looked huge and completely out of place on this tiny river.

Turning to Alan I said, "That's a bloody big bream; we'll have to weigh this one." Out with the scales and the weigh net was zeroed. The fish pulled the needle round to 9lb 6oz. I found it hard to believe and said so to Alan. We re-checked the scales to ensure they were accurate. They were. We weighed the fish once more; the scales gave the same reading. I told Alan who had guided me to the successful swims, "That's my best-ever river bream in England."

I left the BBC Radio Lancashire studio for the 150 mile drive, arriving in Coningsby Lincolnshire around 12 noon. It was time for a brew. Sitting on the grass verge close to the water controlled by Boston AA, I waited for the kettle, after which I cooked-up some bacon and eggs. I looked downstream to the now disused bridge supports of what was once a railway system, sadly destroyed by Dr Beeching and company. I loved those days when it was possible to jump on a train and arrive at the waterside without all the hassle of driving.

How many of you remember those coach trips? The juniors would sit at the front, the older members at the back, telling jokes, smoking and reading the smutty stories in the News of the World, sometimes planning what swim they would fish.

An hour later, the rod tip trembled then pulled over, that's not weed, I thought, striking into what felt like a good fish. The reel grudgingly gave line as the fish moved upstream into the fast,

Members of the Barnes and Mortlake Angling Society in the 1950's

white, creamy water of the weir pool.

Every now and again I could feel the fish turning and twisting in its bid for freedom. I had some anxious moments knowing there were snags the fish could get into, including a large tree that had crashed into the pool during the January storms. My anxiety was short-lived as I started to gain line by pumping the fish up towards the water surface away from any snags. As it rolled on the top I could see it was a big chub, it looked magnificent in the bright sunshine all silver, gold and bronze coloured. Slowly, I pulled the fish towards the sunken net, within seconds it was mine. Swinging the net ashore, I laid it down on the soft straw-coloured rushes then parted the wet mesh. It was a good fish one that perhaps would go five pounds. Quickly adjusting the scales to zero, the fish was weighed at 5lb 2oz, my twenty-third chub over five pounds this winter. I then lowered the net into a quiet bit of water where, after some seconds the fish was off, swimming strongly into the fast turbulent water.

After my fresh brew and a bacon and egg sandwich it was in the car for another stretch of the Bain. After parking up, I spent fifteen minutes clearing away litter and junk left by anglers, motorists and dog walkers, ending up with a dustbin liner full of rubbish. After getting dressed up in chest-high waders and jacket , I chucked two large loafs of thick sliced bread, some cheese paste and meat into my canvas bucket. Picking up my tackle, I headed off downstream to a private weir pool. I walked slowly, well back from the quite clear low-flowing River Bain so as not to spook any fish. It looked perfect for chub fishing with crust as bait, but I would have liked to have seen it with an extra foot of water.

The pool looked delightful in the winter sunshine, creeping close and low, I slithered on my bottom down the steep bank to a clump of reeds and an overhanging willow bush, where I could sit and comfortably cast to all areas of the pool. My first two casts accounted for two big chub, both on crust. The first fish just upstream of the tree snag, weighed in at 5lb 12oz, my next fish was caught about five yards down the stream, weighing in at 5lb 13oz. The first fish gave a light pluck. The second chub bite was a tiny flicker on the rod tip, which then slowly pulled over. The strike connected with a good fish which stayed in the fast water. I had to use a lot of pressure to get that fish moving upstream where it was quickly netted.

For my third cast I baited with a chunk of well-matured cheese paste which was cast upstream into the white foaming water. Within minutes I had a drop-back bite, the line suddenly went slack. Taking in the line, I set the hook into what felt like a good fish, it surprised me with its power. After some minutes I eventually got the fish in the net, I knew immediately that it was probably a new personal best River Bain chub for me, sadly, on the scales it went 6lb 3oz.

The long journey had certainly been worth it: a brace of five pound chub and a six-pounder in three casts; I was certainly a happy angler. Sitting in the warm sunshine, I held the rod feeling for a bite at the same time trying to watch a stoat on a hunting trip. I then spotted a grey wagtail that was probably its intended prey, I stood to frighten off the bird or stoat. They both disappeared.

I fished on for another hour or so without a bite then decided to move further downstream, fishing every likely-looking spot. I was in luck, catching four more fish, all on legered crust, every fish coming from the centre of the river. The fish weighed in at 3lb 10oz, 4lb 8oz, 4lb 14oz and 5lb 4oz. I was most surprised to catch these fish which gave quite savage pulls on the rod tip; they felt like nervous fish.

I can only imagine they would dash out from a weed-bed, grab the bait then dash back to cover. I fished on in the darkness for a couple of hours but without any more bites so decided to call it a day. Before heading off to my B&B I went off and found a quiet lay-by where I stopped and heated up a pot of stew. After my meal I headed off to Pitchaway Guest House in Woodhall Spa for a hot bath and a good night's sleep.

Back home, the Ribble and Aire had burst their banks, Grindleton Bridge was impassable and cars were stranded in flood water, I was told riverside fields were looking like lakes. On the River Bain it was at normal level and flowing clear! I decided to fish a weir pool.

For three hours I didn't have a bite, and moved off downstream, fishing several spots on the way. The next couple of hours can only be described as a minor disaster. I had three good pulls and hooked three fish which were all lost; one was certainly a big five. I had it close to the net when the line just parted at the knot, my fourth bite of the session was missed.

This is all you need when roaming the banks of the River

Around 1 p.m. I made my way back to the car for some lunch and a fresh brew. It was very nice, sitting in the warm sunshine listening to a blackbird singing its heart out. In fact it was great to be alive. After lunch I moved off further up river to a small wood where the river made a right-hand sweep. Fishing various swims, I caught three chub, 4lb 6oz, another about two and a half pounds with the best at 4lb 13oz, all on cheese paste. I fished on into the darkness staying until around 8 p.m. when I called it a day.

Back at the car I heated up a saucepan of stew which I devoured as only hungry angler could, I then made a fresh brew. Sitting in the darkness I decided to go and fish a bit of water near Louth. It was certainly the right decision as I caught five good roach all over the pound on crust fished on a size 10 hook to 3lb line. My best roach weighed 1lb 12oz. About midnight I called Bob to see if he was at home. I was in luck; I was offered a bed for the night – far better than sleeping in the car!

Next morning after a good breakfast I went and dumped my overnight bag in the car. I then realised it would be tough on the river. I would described the wind as being a bit of a hooligan. The taller trees in the Grove were getting a real buffeting.

Back on the river I fished several of my previous spots without any sign of a bite; I had to hold the rod to stop it being swept out of the rest. I then decided to move off for the river near Horncastle. I stopped off on the way close to a big gravel pit, spending some time watching the water fowl. A few yards from where I was sitting were large clumps of snowdrops looking beautiful; it was very nice to hear the birds singing in the warm February sunshine. I don't need to catch fish to enjoy our countryside.

David Foster with winter-caught Chub

After a while I moved up-river where I fished a straight stretch, taking a chub of 3lb 15oz on float-fished bread flake with a size 6 hook. For two hours I fished this stretch without any more bites, it was time to move on. The next spot I chose to fish was where a feeder stream flowed in. Fishing with float tackle and lobworm bait, I quickly caught a nice perch of about twelve ounces. It was a most beautiful-looking fish, straight out of the 'Crabtree' book. I fished on until dusk without another bite then called it a day. Back at the car I made a fresh brew then headed off for home.

I've been lucky in being able to fish the Wye since the 1950s. In those days much of the river was controlled for salmon-fishing, but coarse-fishing was available in a few areas: today it's a different picture.

A club with excellent water is Ross-on-Wye Angling Club which controls fishing in and around the market town of Ross. I first visited this delightful market town in 1953 with Brian Watkins, as a pillion passenger on his 350 Matchless – I was also carrying our fishing gear and some clothes! In those days we stopped in a B&B. I reckon Ross was then a more picturesque place than it is today, as now some parts of the town look quite shabby; having said that it's still a nice area to visit.

Though salmon was king in the 1950s and '60s, coarse-fishing anglers had the opportunity to fish for chub, perch, pike and roach. The latter in my book were far more important than salmon, though I still caught my share of this fine game-fish. Through several friends, and my love of shooting, I got to know many of the river and gamekeepers who put me on to some good beats of the river when the salmon season ended. I targeted the roach, catching lots of pound-plus fish and some two-pounders: the best at 2lb 5oz.

Occasionally I caught good perch, up to 2lb 14oz. As I roach-fished, I would float-fish a live roach for pike, my best pike weighed in at 24lb 8oz. Upstream of Hay-on-Wye I sometimes fished for salmon with spinning gear, but I never did see a coarse fish; no doubt a few pike might have escaped the eagle eyes of the riverkeeper. Back in those early days, coarse-fishing anglers fished the river from Hereford downstream to Symonds Yat, yielding some excellent catches, especially during the mild days of winter when the river had an extra foot of coloured water.

To the best of my knowledge it wasn't until 1970 that coarse-fishing anglers started fishing downstream of the book town of Hay, where dace, perch, pike and chub could be caught. I was privileged to watch an angler catch a pike of twenty-eight pounds just upstream of the toll bridge. It looked huge; and in fact it was a giant-size fish. Today, I am told it's possible to catch barbel in this area.

These days, between Ross and Symonds Yat, you have the chance of catching barbel, chub, roach, perch, pike and carp, the latter fish going thirty pounds-plus, I reckon these fish are escapees from the Mecca of carp anglers: Redmire. Those I have caught look very much like the Redmire commons. Today the roach-fishing isn't as good as in the 1980s, this is due to the large number of cormorants that target these beautiful fish. At Symonds Yat as you fish for roach, you also get the chance to see peregrine falcons.

I have been fortunate to catch the river at its best for big roach; that was back in the 1980s. I caught more than my share of big fish, with many two-pounders, during a four-year period of autumn and winter-fishing, my sessions often lasting for a week-or-two at a time. I was lucky that my then girl friend Janice, lived in a small, white painted, riverside cottage within walking distance of some good roach-fishing swims. Janice was also a good cook and ever-willing to please. Even when I didn't get back from the river until gone midnight she was always in a loving mood. Life was pretty perfect; often I would leave my gear on the bank and return home where Janice would quickly sort out some lunch. Sometimes we would make love before I went back to the river. Some evenings she would join me on the river and if the fish were feeding we would stay late – if the roach didn't bite she would make me an offer I couldn't, and didn't want to, refuse! Also in those days I liked my food.

My two top baits were bread flake and crust, with a lobworm or cheese paste in coloured water. If the river was at normal height or carrying six inches of extra water then either stret-pegging or laying-on were the successful methods. In high and coloured water I found legering to be most successful. Occasionally I would get the chub feeding, which proved exciting on light, roach-fishing gear; I reckon I lost the odd barbel – though when I reported such an event I was told the Wye didn't hold barbel. I wasn't convinced.

Another long weekend at Ross springs to mind. It started with a visit to Redmire Pool to interview Eddie Price, one of the carp-fishing pioneers from the 1950s. Having completed this enjoyable task I said my goodbyes to Eddie and his family and travelled to the White Lion at Ross, close to the lovely-looking Wilton Bridge. After booking in, I chose the room with the double bed, giving the other room with twin beds to my fellow anglers, Will and Martin. They are both avid football fans: one supports Southampton, the other Preston. They were determined to have some fun. After a quick lunch, it was off to the Ross town stretch of the river. I walked some distance looking for suitable swims, and just upstream of Wilton Bridge I found two vacant spots which I gave to the youngsters (it was said I had given them duff swims – not true). I decided I would sit behind Martin and have a brew while listening to the football on the radio. An hour later I went for a walk in the hope of finding a suitable swim. I was in luck: an angler was packing up, and I decided to move into his swim even though he told me it was useless, as he hadn't caught.

For half-an-hour I sat feeding in bait-size pieces of bread flake and the occasional handful of bread crumb. I chose to fish with a 3ft long tail with two LG shot and a size 4 barbless hook to 6lb Gamma line for chub. My other outfit for barbel was 12lb Gamma line, a size 4 barbless hook and one LG shot about 3ft from the hook. Baits were sausage meat or bread flake. I chose to use 1953 vintage Mitchell 300 reels with one of my own-design Avon action rods. In three chucks I caught three chub, including a fish estimated about four pounds eight ounces, all on bread. Half an hour before dusk I noticed the tip of the heavier rod, baited with a chunk of bread flake, move slightly. Picking up the rod, I pushed it forward to give some slack. The line tightened, the tip slowly dipped; I set the hook, and was rewarded with a beautiful gold-coloured barbel. In fact we all agreed it was one of the best-looking barbel we had ever seen. I ended the session with seven chub: best at 5lb 1oz, and three barbel: best at 8lb 6oz.

Martin with a nice Barbel on bread when others failed to catch

Back at the White Lion we showered and changed our fishing clothes for something decent to wear for dinner – I even had a glass of red wine. After dinner I noticed Martin and Will chatting up a good-looking blonde. It transpired that they were suggesting she should visit my room after I had gone to bed, so they could then shoot some compromising photographs. Sadly, they gave her so much to drink she couldn't climb the stairs! After chatting with 'Mine Host' about the fishing, we watched the Rugby World Cup semi-final, France v England, on a big screen. When Josh Lewsey scored the first try I nearly punched the ceiling with joy – though I must admit, the last few minutes of the match were probably some of the longest of my life. It was great seeing our boys put one over on the French. I reckon it was another Agincourt without longbows; let's hope they can do the same to the South Africans. After making a few telephone calls I went off to bed, but Martin and Will were on the river until around two in the morning.

Next morning I was up and dressed before the alarm call on my mobile sounded its strident note. Downstairs I met Will Carter, Martin Mumby and Martin Salisbury for breakfast, after which we would be off to the River Wye at Holm Lacy to seek more chub and barbel. We finished breakfast, paid the bill and said our goodbyes. In a convoy of three cars we made our way through the Herefordshire countryside, down lanes we could just squeeze through. It was great being back in this county on the Welsh border where I have had some very enjoyable times – and some tough ones, but whatever I was doing, it was all good fun. The weather couldn't have been better for angling: mild, an overcast sky and a light wind. After Saturday's fishing on the river at Ross I was full of confidence. Hopefully today my two mates would also catch.

After several miles we stopped on a grass verge in a deserted lane which seemed miles from

Martin, with 5lb 12oz Chub

any habitation, though I expect there would have been a farmhouse nearby. As I got out of the car I heard the croaking of a raven, I wasn't sure if I wanted to hear this bird of ill-omen – supposedly the harbinger of death. Still, as I don't believe in any of the old wives' tales, it wasn't a problem. My problem was the long walk with a big rucksack, rods and all the other gear we anglers reckon we need at the waterside. What I did need were stove, water and food. Once over the first stile it was fairly good walking. As we moved downstream I met a local guy with a black labrador who said, "Are you after barbel?" I said, "Yes." He pointed out a good area half-a-mile downstream. Thanking him profusely, we carried on our way. The area he had pointed out was on a wide, sweeping bend with the main flow on the far side of the river. I decided I would let the two Martins and Will choose their swims; I settled down in an area that looked quite good, with a crease about a third of the way across the river.

After sorting out my gear I put the kettle on for a brew. While I was waiting for it to boil, I fed in several cricket ball-sized lumps of mashed bread and some bait-size pieces of bread flake and sausage meat. Tea made, I sat back watching the buzzards working the thermals and listening to the ravens, occasionally one would appear on the far bank, then a pheasant would glide over the river, or the ravens would give me a fly-past.

In the first hour several kingfishers put in an appearance – it could have been the same couple of birds. Looking downriver I could see Martin Salisbury playing a fish, a minute later he picked up the landing net and netted it. Meanwhile, Will, fishing upstream of me, was catching chub on bread. Martin Mumby had gone off to Redmire Pool for a couple of hours.

It was time for me to start fishing. The swim had been rested for about forty minutes which had given the fish the chance to feed undisturbed on the free offerings – they should be well primed by now. I chose my favourite Avon action rod with a Mitchell 300 reel and 6lb Gamma line to which I tied a size 4 barbless hook, then pinched on two LG shot 6in from the hook, baiting with crust. A long cast was made, dropping the bait a foot from the tree-lined far bank. I then bounced the bait downstream: three, four, five, six yards it had gone, when I felt a light pluck – I gave some slack line. On feeling a good pull I made a powerful strike pulling the size 4 hook into the mouth of a hard-fighting fish. On the line was a chub of four pounds-plus which was unhooked in the water and released untouched by hand.

Everyone tells me you need to use heavy weights when fishing the Wye, and you need to fish with pellets. Even with a couple of feet of extra water on the river I can usually get away with using LG shot. Pellets I don't need to use, I catch enough fish to keep me happy on bread and sausage meat. The magazines might tell us we need pellets but the fish don't read magazines! They seem happy to eat my bread and sausage meat. You could call me a poor customer of the tackle shops when it comes to bait. I occasionally buy a pint of gentles, though I do often purchase fifty or a hundred lobworms for bait, and feeding as chopped worms. In the session before lunch I had seven chub and one barbel about seven pounds – all fish taken on flake or crust. The barbel was taken on the chub outfit, but I quickly had it in the net. Over lunch with Will, we discussed the prospects of fishing the river on future occasions, both agreeing we would like to join the Ross-on-Wye angling club. This would give us some interesting-looking water to fish in the future.

I reckon it's a good bet for some exciting pike fishing, and as it's only a three-hour drive, it's possible to have a good weekend with only one night's B&B. The Wye has been a lucky river for me over the years: chub to 6lb 7oz, common carp 18lb, pike 26lb 8oz, salmon 13lb, a lot of two pound- plus roach and some excellent brown trout on a dry fly. As we sat having lunch, Martin came up for a chat while I kept feeding in crumbed bread and pieces of thumb-size flake. I reckon the salmon just upstream of Will, which swirled on the surface three or four times, was putting the chub off in Will's swim. I don't like to see a salmon in or close to the swim that I am fishing. With lunch over, I cast out a chunk of crust. It had only travelled three feet down the swim when I set the hook into a nice chub. Martin said, "You only just cast out!" I rebaited and cast again, and soon had another chub. Martin looked disgusted and said, "I'm going back to my swim!" I suggested he bait with chunks of sausage meat then rest the swim for a while, "You might even have a kip!" As Martin trudged off downriver Will said, "The red mist has descended on Martin!" For the next couple of hours I caught a few more chub and lost a barbel. I then got a call on my mobile from Martin to say he had a big chub. Grabbing scales, weigh-bag and camera, Will and I went off downstream. Martin certainly had a super chub, I said, "That's a big five-pounder!" It was, weighing in at 5lb 10oz – a personal best for Martin; we were all pleased for him, and he was fishing just as I recommended, catching the fish on sausage meat paste. The following week the picture appeared on the front cover of Angler's Mail.

The afternoon session was probably better than the morning, with several chub on flake or crust. Late in the afternoon I lost another barbel, then, just as I was packing my gear away, I pricked what felt like a heavy fish – but within seconds it was gone. Martin Mumby returned late in the afternoon, and choosing to fish with meat, he quickly caught some nice chub. Further downstream, Martin of big-chub fame caught a couple more nice chub then, as the light was fading, he had a big whack on the rod top which was missed. Packing up, we made our way back to the cars, arriving in the darkness, all of us feeling relaxed having spent some quality time in the peaceful Herefordshire countryside. Martin and I arrived back in Lancashire about 10.45 p.m. after a good drive with no hold-ups.

Recently, Brendan Ince of Leyland and I travelled down to fish the Wye for a couple of days. During our stay we witnessed some of the most appalling behaviour by a person catching fish that I have ever seen – I refuse to call him an angler. The person in question was fishing the Ross day-permit water just upstream of Wilton Bridge on the right-hand bank. He was catching fish then dragging them up the bank. The poor creatures were then unhooked and thrown back into the water from the top of an 8–10ft steep bank. At one stage he dragged a keepnet up the bank, spilling the poor fish out onto the muddy bank where they were just chucked back into the net in the same way that you and I would chuck rubbish in the bin. I thought such horrid scenes were a thing of the past in these more enlightened times. Perhaps keepnets should be banned, except for match-fishing. Thankfully I have never seen this type of behaviour for many years.

Just after lunch on day one, two responsible pike-anglers called my attention to a person on the opposite bank who had dragged a pike from the river and smashed it over the head before dumping it in a plastic bag. I walked over a mile from my side of the river to check out these people, they were not youngsters or East Europeans. When I asked where they were from I was

Bailiff, Mike Evans, isues a day permit to David Foster

told Hereford, though I reckon they were from the Ross area. I then asked for a rod licence, they said, and I quote, "Where do you get those from?" I asked to see their day-permit; one answered, "It's in the tackle shop." I quickly moved them off the water, a stiff verbal warning ringing in their ears. I am not a bailiff – just an ordinary member; I would like to see all angling club members check on those who are fishing their waters. In my many trips this season to Ross I have removed nine people who were fishing illegally. How many are on your club water when the bailiff isn't around? Remember our hard-working bailiffs cannot be on the water twenty-four hours-a-day. Most have a full-time job and a family. It's up to all of us to assist the bailiff. The Ross-on-Wye AC Bailiff, Mike Evans, does an excellent job, but he can't be around 24 hours a day. We all have to do our bit.

Visit any tackle shop or discuss River Wye fishing with most anglers, and they will tell you about chub, barbel and pike with hardly any mention of the other species. Yes, the chub-fishing can be excellent with a realistic chance of a seven pound fish; I reckon a twelve pound barbel is a huge fish for the Wye – and they can be caught, but I believe you need a big chunk of luck. This also goes for pike if you are seeking a thirty-pounder. Please remember these huge specimens are rarities indeed, and very fragile, but the chance of catching a big one is a possibility somewhere on the River Wye. Today, two species of fish which hardly get a mention are the perch and roach. When I first fished the river we wanted to catch roach, perch and chub, probably in that order. Until the birth of commercial fisheries which are predominantly stocked with carp, the roach were our most popular species of freshwater fish; now, roach are conspicuous by their absence from many of our rivers. Many die from cormorant predation. That's the position on much of the River Wye, but there are some reaches where you can certainly find quality roach. I have seen some nice specimens caught this season close to Ross town.

What do I mean by quality? It's roach of a pound-plus. A two pound roach is a giant, with a three pound fish a veritable monster. The other species that most anglers don't talk about or fish for is the perch. I reckon in some of the deeper, slower-flowing, quieter stretches of the river with overhanging willows and alders you'll find the places to fish where you have a realistic chance of a four pound fish. A river fish of that weight is certainly a monster.

The two most popular ways to fish for the roach or perch are legering and float-fishing: both styles work, though for roach I reckon the latter is the better bet, even when the river is carrying ten feet of extra water. Roach-anglers, fishing some beats on the River Wye, are handicapped by not being able to fish on into the darkness. The rule which states, no night-fishing on much of the river, only affects the honest angler – the poachers will

My well used float fishing set up on rivers

just fish the waters at will anyway. It's been my experience that on waters where night-fishing is allowed, the poaching is cut right back. I find this especially true with reference to East Europeans who continue to fish our water where they catch, kill and steal our valuable fish stocks. Most, when asked for their permits usually say, "I don't have a permit, I want a day ticket," knowing full well that tickets are not issued on the bank.

When allowed, and the conditions being suitable, I will seek the roach after dark. I either fish laying-on or stret-pegging with bread or lobworms. I have lost count of the number of occasions when, seeking the roach with lobworms, I have caught quality bream, perch, chub and barbel – even decent pike have been landed when fishing with lobworm. The reason we can land pike on this tackle is that most fish are hooked in the scissors, so they are not able to bite through the line. I've had many fishing days in winter, when the roach just wouldn't bite, then as the light started to fade, they would start rolling and swirling. I call it the 'magic hour'. Often it's the time when my float, dough bobbin or rod tip, will show a bite. Roach being one of my favourite species, I am more than willing to sit in the darkness for several hours catching these delightful fish, using either a torch beam to illuminate the float or a Starlight fixed to the float by a short length of rubber tube. A Drennan float with an insert is a useful item to have, as the insert can be replaced with Starlight.

My top roach-fishing baits are bread in various forms. Ask the majority of anglers what bait they use when roach-fishing and the answer would probably be gentles, casters, bread, red worms and corn. In my book, bread in various forms would be the first choice bait – a piece of bread flake, between the size of a ten and fifty-pence piece on a size 8 or 10 hook, has accounted for a lot of big roach over the years. Bread is a bait that will work in coloured water, though I often switch baits around, during a day's fishing, from flake to crust. Lobworms, paste and sweet corn also account for lots of big roach.

In cold water conditions I often pinch a shot within an inch or two of the crust. During the past sixty years I have read many thousands of words where authors have said that the bait for coloured water is the tail of a lobworm – yes, it's good bait, but I disagree with the authors when they say it's the only bait, also: why choose only the tail end? A pound roach is quite capable of swallowing a whole lobworm on a size 6 hook with ease. Many write about keeping worms in moss to toughen them up. What nonsense! The roach doesn't look at a lobworm and think, "I can't eat that one, it's not been toughened-up!" The only reason I keep worms in moss or damp newspaper is to keep them alive and nothing more. If your struggling for a bite on bread or worms, try soft cheese paste; remember cheese isn't just for coloured water it works

Brendan Ince with a nice roach on legered crust

exceedingly well in clear water.

On one trip to the River Wye with Brendan Ince, conditions were not their best, with heavy frost on the previous few nights and a water temperature of 41°F. Despite the conditions, Brendan fished legered crust, catching some lovely roach up to 1lb 6oz – a personal best, while I had a catch of chub, the best at about four-and-a-half pounds, again bread was the chosen bait. I couldn't get a bite on meat. At dusk we moved to the riverside cabin at Huntsham Bridge where I clipped the leads of my microwave oven onto Brendan's car battery. Within minutes we had hot pasties and soup, followed by freshly-brewed coffee. With the rain hammering down and a gale-force wind blowing we moved off upstream of Huntsham Bridge where we could legally fish on into the darkness in our attempt to catch a few chub. In an hour's fishing I had one chub of about three pounds, on meat. With the weather getting worse, we called it a day and headed off to the White Lion where Brendan had a couple of beers, while I had a glass of red wine.

Then it was off to our B&B, Copperfield House in Wilton Lane, Ross-on-Wye: email. fran@copperfieldhouse.co.uk. Copperfield house was clean and warm, and Fran proved a friendly hostess. After a shower we had some coffee and within minutes Brendan was fast asleep while I listened to us getting battered in the test match.

I was more than happy to lose, when we have an arrogant South African as captain of an English cricket team. I find it rather crazy that we pick foreigners to lead our national side. The following morning Fran cooked us an excellent breakfast – the lady even makes her own wholemeal bread; I can recommend the accommodation, which is within walking distance of the White Lion and the river. After breakfast we went off to fish the same beat that we had fished the previous day. Conditions were slightly better with a water temperature rise of 1°F.

I chose a different swim in the hope that I might find some perch and roach. My tackle set-up was a light Avon action rod, fixed-spool reel with 4lb Gamma line with 4 LG shot and a size

6 hook. The swim was over gravel and silt with quite a lot of water crowfoot. To my left I had a very snaggy area, making me think to myself, "If a fish gets into that lot, all will be lost." To my right I had a row of willow bushes; there was a fast pace of water. I decided to start off fishing lobworms as bait, which turned out to be the right decision, as I soon started catching some good pound-plus perch, with the occasional roach. Sadly, by lunchtime I had run out of worms – no more perch. Still, I had a dozen or more fish with the best at 2lb 6oz.

After our lunch of fresh coffee and beef sandwiches we went back to our swim, this time I changed my hook to a size 10 with 2 LG shot about 15in from the hook. My bait was bread flake: bite indication, a dough bobbin. Within half-an-hour I had caught several 12–14oz roach in pristine condition. About three o'clock the dough bobbin sailed up to the butt ring, the answering strike connected with a good fish – seconds later it was off the hook! I reckoned that it was a big roach possibly two pound-plus, I was quite gutted. Around four o'clock the river came alive with rolling, swirling roach from a few ounces to a pound-plus. It was exciting to see so much activity. I fished on, catching a couple of nice roach around the pound mark. Sadly, like all good things, it had to end, it was time to pack away our gear and leave the river. On the way home Brendan and I listened to the Brazilian Grand Prix hoping Lewis Hamilton would win. Thankfully, after giving us both some heart-stopping moments, he clinched the World Championship.

Brendan Ince waiting for the pull from a big barbel

Despite the low and gin-clear rivers countrywide I travelled south to fish the Hampshire Avon and rivers Kennet and Enborne. I chose to start on the Kennet Wasing Estate water. Despite being told that very few fish were being caught, I felt I was in with a chance. At Dalston I met up with Jon King, his brother Tom and son Peter. As we chatted, Peter caught a barbel about seven pounds – certainly a good start for the teenager.

An hour later I was on the Warren beat. I parked my car and grabbed a loaf of bread and some Platinum Maple cream paste bait before making my way downstream, putting crumbed bread in some swims, and paste in other spots. With only one member on the beat, I had plenty of swims to fish. Back in the car park I put the kettle on for a brew, and then connected my microwave to the car battery and heated up a cottage pie for dinner. Twenty minutes later I'm sitting at the water's edge with a hot meal and a fresh brew – it certainly beats sandwiches or a can of soup!

My plan of action was to move down river, fishing all the baited spots, then repeat the process on the way back, planning to fishing until about midnight. No chair, just a piece of sponge – I would hold the rod feeling for the bites; I find this method of fishing so exciting – all your senses are at a high pitch as you sit in the darkness waiting for a slight pluck or a violent wrench on the rod, in this case a 12ft Avon for lines between 10 and 12lb BS, my reel, a centre-pin. I tied a size 4 Pallatrax hook onto 12lb Gamma line. Weight would be one or more LG shots, sometimes just a chunk of paste. I chose a swim a few yards downriver from the car park. An old alder tree lay at an angle from the far bank creating a nice crease. Within ten minutes I had a chub of about four pounds. Half-an-hour later I moved downstream to a bend opposite a riverside cottage. In the first ten minutes I had two barbel, about five pounds each.

Thirty minutes later I moved downstream to the Pipe Swim. Two LG shot were lightly pinched on the line 15in from the hook, baited with a pigeon's egg-size chunk of Maple cream paste. Sitting in the darkness waiting for a bite, an owl called somewhere downstream. Hearing a sound behind me I looked around, finding a muntjac deer ten feet away.

Minutes later the rod whacked round, a bite I couldn't miss, a barbel about seven pounds. Half-an-hour later, with no more interest, I move downstream to the Black Cabin run. I fished crust and paste baits, searching the swim from top to bottom. Just as I was thinking of moving I felt a slight pluck, not sure if it was weed or a fish I gently lifted the rod tip. Feeling tension on the line I struck, connecting with an angry fish which dashed around the swim. Eventually, I netted a barbel of about eight pounds on paste.

Moving upstream on the other bank, I fished a quiet area downstream of some poplar trees that had crashed in the river three years ago. Thirty minutes later, with no signs of interest, I moved off upstream. I chose to fish the shallow water above the green footbridge. An owl hooted from a nearby oak tree, and then two roe deer entered the river for a drink. Ten minutes later the deer had gone. I was on my mobile talking to Brendan Ince when I felt a pluck then another pluck, the line tightened, I set the hook, saying to Brendan, "Got to go, I've got a good fish!" Minutes later I netted a barbel about eight-and-a-half pounds. I was ready for a brew, so packed up for the day.

The next day, Sunday, I suggested to Will Carter we should fish the Wasing Woolhampton beat of the Kennet and that he should try a swim where I have had a lot of success, I chose a new swim downstream. An hour later Will called, "I've got a good fish!" Reeling in my rod, I went up to Will and picked up his landing net. For five or ten minutes the fish battled away not giving Will a chance to gain line, then, as always happens, the fish started to lose some power. Soon the fish coming towards the net which was sunk deep in the water. With the fish over the net I lifted; a good barbel was enveloped in its folds. It looked big, we both thought perhaps thirteen pounds-plus. The scales gave a different story: it weighed 12lb 8oz, a personal best for Will. Back in my swim I had two bites, a chub of about two pounds and a bream of about a pound. Still, that's fishing.

Without doubt, one of the toughest rivers around must be a certain Thames tributary, I fished for three days, the first day I had just one bite on sausage meat paste at about seven o'clock in the evening, catching a barbel weighing 10lb 13oz. On that high note I decided to leave. Tuesday, I am back, trying various other beats, taking two fish of 9lb 10oz and 8lb, both on sausage meat paste. Wednesday, I fished for about seven or eight hours without a bite – in fact I didn't see a fish! Hence, it's an Enigma.

Thursday, I fished the Britford fishery on the Hampshire Avon near Salisbury, owned by the London Anglers Association. A card for all their waters will cost just over £40 for a season ticket or £10 a day, certainly excellent value for money. My guest for the day was Mark Cannon from London who was achieving a lifelong ambition of fishing the Avon. In the car park we met Stuart Wilson, the river keeper, who really does an excellent job of, not only keeping down the vermin such as mink and cormorants, but also, through working with the local police, defeating the poachers who use rods and nets, and also snag fish.

I chose to fish a pool below a small footbridge, while Stuart took Mark off downstream to fish for dace, grayling and chub. I used a bait dropper putting in a pint and a half of red gentles and twenty chopped lobworms. I left the swim alone for about an hour. Around 12 noon when I commenced fishing, I used an Avon rod, Mitchell 300 1953 vintage, 4lb Gamma line with a size 6 Pallatrax barbless hook. Using 2LG shot pinched lightly on the line 15in from a hook baited with two lobworms; I added a small piece of rubber

Will Carter with a Personal Best barbel of 12lbs 8oz

band on the hook to stop the worms wriggling off. Within ten minutes I felt a light pluck, then a more positive pluck, I lifted the rod, feeling the heavy weight of a fish then the head shaking so reminiscent of a perch. Slowly I gained line. Then all went slack, the fish was gone. I realised I hadn't set the hook with a firm strike.

In an hour I caught nine perch averaging a pound and a half, all on double lobworm. Then followed a quiet spell. I put together a 13ft rod, centre-pin reel with 4lb Gamma line and a size 8 Pallatrax barbless hook. With a float taking 7 bb shot which I set at 5ft, I put about ten gentles on the hook, then made a long cast across the pool. The float slowly moved downstream, it dipped a foot further down the flow, then it dragged across the flow – I realised it was a fish and set the hook. Minutes later I netted a very good roach, which I thought might weigh two pounds. The scales said 1lb 14oz, a great Avon roach. It was a happy angler who stopped for lunch and a brew.

After lunch I had two perch of about a pound, followed by fish of 2lb 4oz and 2lb 7oz, I then pricked two fish, thinking, "This will spook the perch." It didn't: I quickly caught three more fish averaging a pound and a half. Three o'clock, a cold wind ruffled the water surface, the bites ceased. I couldn't get a single pluck. As the light faded I got a couple more fish. It was time to pack up. As Mark and I compared notes on our way to the car park, we both agreed it was a great day out on the Avon. Mark had six chub averaging three pounds and several good grayling to a pound and a quarter.

Friday afternoon, I met Will Carter on the Woolhampton beat. Will chose to fish the swim of the previous Sunday. I did the same, quickly catching two barbel of six pounds apiece on sausage meat, and a mirror carp about twelve pounds on two lobworms. Prospects of a good session looked good until a crazy barge owner tried to turn his boat round in the narrow confines of the canal right in my swim, he had run aground. For an hour the engine was well and truly revved up, the roaring sounded something akin to an aircraft getting ready for take off. At the stern, the water was being stirred as if a giant washing machine was at work. Silt and other rubbish was spread up and down the canal, the water turned a horrid muddy colour. The fishing was ruined through the actions of an idiot. As I sat thinking about my next move to another beat, the barge moved downstream, peace reigned. I decided to stay and give the swim an hour before attempting to fish. The hour turned into about three, before I had a fish – barbel about seven pounds. At eleven o'clock I thought I would give it another half an hour. It was a good choice. I had a 5lb 10oz chub on sausage meat paste. I then packed up thinking what might have been without a crazy bargee. It was time to go home; I did the journey in about four hours.

Before the mid 1960s up until the early 1970s many coarse-fishers wouldn't bother going fishing after the first frost, unless they were pike-fishers. In fact in those days many clubs had a crazy rule which stated that pike-fishing couldn't begin until 1 October.

Other anglers would say, "It's a waste of time fishing for pike if it isn't frosty." Even those anglers who did fish, targeted roach, dace, perch and chub. It was considered a waste of time to fish for barbel, tench, bream or carp. If you did catch one of these fish, you were considered extremely lucky. Unbeknown to them, some of the best bream-fishing in the south of England was to be found during the autumn and winter.

Thankfully, my mates and I realised we could catch plenty of bream on our local rivers. Even tench were caught frequently enough by us to make fishing for them worthwhile. It was well worth the effort to fish both the Hampshire Avon and Dorset Stour in search of barbel, where bread often proved the best bait. We rated winter bream-fishing very highly on both the Medway and Beult – as good if not better than during the summer months. Every year during the Christmas holiday I would go off fishing or rabbit-shooting, something I had done since I was about ten years of age. Opening presents on Christmas morning meant nothing to me; I could do that in the evening when it was too dark for me to be out in the woods or at the waterside. I probably put fishing just ahead of shooting, but it would have been a close thing.

On Christmas morning 1953 I left home, long before daylight, for the twelve mile cycle-ride to the River Beult at Hunton. I arrived just as the sun came up; the river was a dull, yellowish-brown colour and bank-high. As I walked downstream to the 'Big Oak Swim' in the light drizzle I thought, "It's a perfect day for catching bream." Several hundred yards further on, I got to my chosen spot where the river made a sweep to the left. The sweeping bend had created a deep, quiet pool, overhung by a big oak tree – hence its name. It's a spot I've fished on many occasions, with some success. I sat on my basket and put together a 15ft rod built by Clarkson of Rochester. It had a Tonkin cane butt and middle section with a split bamboo top; my reel was a Rapidex centre-pin with 6lb line. I then attached a large, swan quill and bored bullet, finally tying on a size 6 Model Perfect hook. I checked the depth, and found 10ft of water. I set the float at 12ft then stopped the bored bullet 15in from the hook with a split shot.

Four cricket -ball sized lumps of bread and bran with chopped worms were dropped into the swim. With keepnet in the water and everything sorted out, I was all set to start, but not before I had powered-up my Primus stove. Soon, a billycan of boiling water was ready for tea-making, followed by a fried egg and bacon sandwich. I was now ready to get on with the fishing; my bait was a big lobworm. Making an under-arm cast, I dropped the tackle on the edge of the crease, put the rod in its two rests and sat back to wait for a bite. I suppose fifteen minutes had gone by when the float slipped away, it was a perch of about twelve ounces, quickly followed by three more of similar size. Then a bream about four pounds followed by a pound-plus roach and three other bream around the four pounds mark.

After this I had a biteless spell of an hour or more, and then – just as I put the billycan on for a brew – the float moved out into the flow, slowly submerging as it did so. The answering

My First Basket

strike connected with a powerful fish. I was forced to give line and for several minutes I thought I'd hooked a pike, which often happens when fishing with lobworms. Slowly I started to win back some line; I was now at that stage when I had the feeling that I might just win this fight with my unseen adversary. Gradually, foot-by-foot, I got more line back on the reel: then the float appeared. I pushed the landing net into the water, and carefully worked the fish towards me.

I gasped when a big tench swirled on the surface, it was a big one, and I very carefully pulled the fish over the net, then lifted my prize catch, now safely enveloped in the wet mesh. I well remember saying to myself, "Bloody hell, that's a big tench – and its mine!" On my brass, spring balance it weighed in at 3lb 9oz, my best ever at that time – in fact, to me, it was a giant tench. I placed it in my keepnet, re-baited with another lobworm, and cast out to the same spot, allowing the float to settle in the crease. Within minutes the float was gone, this time the rod tip was pulled downstream. As I picked up the rod I realised the fish had hooked itself, so I just kept a tight line, thinking, "I bet this is another tench."

After a long fight, during which I was worried in case the hook pulled out or the line broke, I eventually netted another giant-size tench. It weighed in at 3lb 8oz: the float-legered lobworm had done the trick again. I thought, "What a great Christmas present, catching two giant-size tench." Even one would have meant a red-letter day. Wingets Angling Club had a specimen-fish trophy: I needed a witness. With no anglers on the river, I made the long walk up to the Bull Inn knowing the landlord was an angler and that he would have the club scales. He was most surprised to see me, but more than happy to come to the river to witness and weigh my fish. After weighing them both, he filled in the club form with his name and address and signed it as a witness.

The landlord went back to the pub and his Christmas lunch while I carried on fishing, catching few more bream, perch and another tench of 3lb, until it was too dark to see my float. I emptied my keepnet, watching the fish swim off strongly, none the worse for wear, and after packing-up I started the long cycle-ride home – it was well worth the effort, having caught my two biggest tench. In those days, tench of that size were considered specimen fish; for my brace I was awarded the Wingets Angling Club Specimen Fish of the Year Trophy.

Winget Engineering was the company where my Dad worked, so I was allowed to join the work's angling club. Apart from trips to the club water on the River Beult at Hunton, we also went on coach trips to other venues on the River Medway at Yalding, Wateringbury and Teston, also Kentish Stour at Grove Ferry and Plucks Gutter. Each year the club would have a presentation evening in the work's social club. Several years later I would report on those presentation evenings for the local paper.

We reckon we had some of the best bream-fishing in the country on the River Beult, and River Medway up and downstream of Yalding. I suppose the two top big-fish anglers in those days on the River Beult were Tony Howe and Brian Holloway, they certainly taught me a lot, including how not to drink beer. At the time, I was sixteen, they were in their early twenties. We had gone to Hunton for a weekend's fishing in late October. Having pitched our tent and sorted things out we went up to the Bull Inn where Brian asked me what I wanted to drink.

I said, "I'll have an orange juice."

"You'll have to have beer; otherwise it's an insult to the landlord!" said Brian.

Not knowing otherwise, I said OK. I was given a pint glass of some horrid-looking, brown liquid with froth on the top. I took a sip, it had a bitter taste.

I said, "What's this rubbish?"

"Brown and mild," Tony said. I slowly sipped the evil-tasting, smelly stuff.

When it was finished I was given another one. I was now feeling terribly ill. What I didn't realise at the time was that I was probably getting drunk. On the way back to our tent I fell over; Tony and Brian said, "Get up you drunk!" Then they just left me in the field. I woke up sometime later, wet and cold, wishing I was at home. Staggering back to the tent, I flopped on my groundsheet and went to sleep. After a couple of hours I woke up feeling cold and wet. I had a mug of tea and some breakfast and began to feel slightly better, but I wasn't in any mood to fish with Brian and Tony – and they could stuff their brown and mild! Having got myself sorted out, I went off fishing on my own at the top of the field. The fishing proved good with several bream averaging four pounds. I also caught three pike into double figures. Since that day I've never drunk beer. The nearest I get is half-a-pint of shandy on a hot day.

Our style of fishing was quite simple. 15ft and 16ft rods built by Clarkson of Rochester. Three-piece rod with a whole-cane butt and middle section with a top joint of split bamboo. Reels were Rapidex centre-pins, filled with 6lb line, usually with size 6 hooks. Bait was a big piece of crust, flake, or a lobworm. Fishing style was usually float-legering, laying-on or stret-pegging. Most times our float choice was a big quill, either swan or goose, with a bored bullet stopped about 12–15in from the hook.

Favoured swims were the slower water on the inside of a bend, a big eddy, or places where the water flowed deep, fairly fast and smooth, without those whirlpools that you often find when the river is in flood. Having plumbed the depth, our floats would be set about two feet over-depth. I reckon one of the reasons for our success was baiting our swims quite heavily with mashed bread, bran and chopped worms, made into cricket-ball size lumps. To start, we would

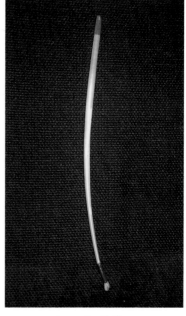

Swan Quill Float

introduce three or four balls into the chosen swim, then a couple more balls of bread and bran each time we caught a fish. I lost count of the fish I caught that weekend.

A very special day's fishing was in March 1954. My current girl friend Carole, suggested I stay-over at her place while her mother was away for a few days. How could I not accept such an attractive offer? I also wanted to fish the last day of the season, 14 March. I said to Carole, "I'll have to get up early on Sunday morning."

She said, "No problem, we can stay at home, then I can kick you out of bed early and cook your breakfast!" She wasn't only good-looking: she was also a great cook. Though we missed our Saturday night out at the Pavilion dance hall in Gillingham, Carole made sure I got lots of cuddles and attention: just what a guy needed. We had an early night, though I don't remember getting much sleep – perhaps it was the excitement of looking forward to fishing the next day! What more can I say! Carole was one of those gorgeous women who really did have sex appeal, with a super, trim body to match. Next morning, it was a half-asleep angler who staggered off to Halling station where I caught the train to Maidstone.

As the train pulled in I picked up my six-legged basket and rod holdall ready to alight. As we came to a halt I was off and up the stairs. From there it was just a short walk down the hill and over the bridge to the bus station. An hour later I was in a small copse about half-a-mile upstream of Hunton Bridge, where the fishing was controlled by Linton Angling Society. Dumping basket and holdall on the ground, I smoked a cigarette and stood watching the bank-high water flowing from left to right, thinking how lucky I was to get this well-known bream swim.

I tackled-up for laying-on, with a 15ft cane rod, centre-pin reel with 4lb line. A swan quill float and a bored bullet stopped some 18in from a size 6 hook completed the tackle set-up. My number one bait in coloured water was lobworm. After feeding four balls of mashed bread and bran with chopped worms into the swim, I placed my keepnet and landing net in position: I was ready to fish. Baiting with a big lobworm I made a cast, dropping the float into the fast water on the outside of the crease or seam. Having controlled the tackle until I got the float lying at an angle downstream of the rod tip, I put the rod in the rest. I thought "time for a brew" as I put the kettle on my small, methylated spirit stove. I lit a cigarette and sat back to await events. Two hours later I had my first bream, about four pounds – a couple of pound perch followed. Thirty minutes later I had three more bream around the four pound mark; I was having a good day.

A while later the float sank slowly out of sight. Lifting the rod, I tightened into a good fish – river bream really could pull the string and bend the stick. After a fair bit of fighting and boring the fish swirled on the surface; I quickly netted a good bream.

"That's my biggest-ever bream." I said to myself. I placed the fish in the keep-net and went off to get the weighing scales from the local riverside tavern, The Bull Inn. It was a long run across the field to the pub, it was a breathless teenager that arrived, saying to the landlord,

"Can I have the scales please, mister?"

He said, "What have you caught this time?"

I said, "A big bream."

Drying his hands on a bar towel he said, "I'll be right with you."

He fetched the scales and we made our way back to the river, where the friendly publican set them on a level bit of bank while I got the net from the water. "That's a big 'un, boy," he said. It weighed in at 5lb 4oz – my best ever bream at that time and caught on the very last day of the season. During the afternoon session I caught quite a few more bream and some good perch, plus a pike about eight pounds. I couldn't stay until darkness as I had a bus to catch for my train connection, otherwise I might well have had a few more fish.

At the bus stop next to the pub was a telephone box. I called Carole with the good news about my big bream, saying, "I'll take you out for dinner tonight." Her answer was, "Just get a bottle of wine, I'll cook dinner, then we can celebrate with lots of loving." What more could a guy wish for? Ten minutes later the bus arrived for the journey to Maidstone railway station. On the station platform I met some of my friends from Bermondsey who had been fishing the

Medway. They too had caught some nice roach and bream. Since that day I've had quite a few good fish on the last day of the season, including a three pound-plus perch, double-figure barbel, a 6lb 5oz chub, a 22lb pike and a 2lb 9oz roach. I never did get that bottle of wine.

Another day's fishing on the River Beult was with Bill Hall. It was one of those weekends when only the keen anglers ventured forth to the river bank. In those days if you didn't fish on your weekend off work or college you had to wait until the following one. Back then, there was no way that could I go without my fix of wildfowling or fishing. We didn't get paid if we were off work or college – our only chance was at weekends, bank holidays or annual holidays, and the odd chance when we could grab an evening session in midweek. This particular weekend the weather was horrid, snow covered the fields and footpaths, some roads were considered dangerous through snow and ice, but good old South Eastern Railway Company were still running trains and the Maidstone and District bus service was still operating.

Bill and I caught the train to Maidstone, and then a bus to Hunton. The bus journey involved negotiating a very steep hill; our driver was up to the task and we arrived at the Hunton Bull only ten minutes late. Trudging along the snow-

My bamboo pike rod

FG Pike Bung

covered fields with a big basket and holdall wasn't the easiest of task. Finally we arrived at a small, wooden bridge downstream of Hunton Bridge. Bill stopped off at the first swim below this while I walked on to a small group of trees. We both planned to fish one rod with herring bait while we searched for roach, fishing stret-pegging style using bread flake as our first choice bait followed by stewed wheat. If that didn't work it would be a switch to a lobworm, in the hope there might be some perch.

It was just after twelve o'clock when Bill showed up, saying, "Are you catching?" my answer was, "No not a touch." We decided to go up to the pub to try and get warm. After a game of bar billiards and a mug of coffee it was back on the river. Half-an-hour later the snow sheeted down, the visibility was so bad that we could just about make out the opposite bank. Soon everything was snow-covered. As we sat trying to boil some water on Bill's stove, my pike float disappeared. I picked up the rod and could see the two pilot floats going across and down river. Winding down, I gave a hefty strike, then felt the power of a good fish, the small, bait-casting reel grudgingly giving line.

Bill picked up my big Richard Walker landing net, and stood sentinel-like with the net deep in the water ready for me to draw the fish over it. Slowly, foot by foot I gained line; then the pike went skywards, crashing back into the water, taking line off the reel. Bill said, "That's a big one." I said, "Yes, and that's probably his last gasp." It was. Soon, I had the fish moving over the waiting net; Bill lifted and the pike was mine, it weighed 17lb 8oz. An hour later we called it a day, and after packing-up we headed off for the bus stop. A good covering of snow was on the roads, and though the bus was late it did arrive. Our trip back to Maidstone was a tough struggle for the driver: at the bottom of Hunton Hill we all got off the bus and put our shoulders to the back of it. I don't think we really made much difference but the driver did negotiate the hill, albeit very slowly. In Maidstone the snow was still falling but the trains hadn't stopped, though again a bit late.

On another occasion Bill Hall and I went by train to fish at Yalding. On the journey we could see the river was bank-high and many riverside fields were flooded. We arrived at the cut and found we had the river to ourselves. While I chose to fish just inside the cut, off the main river, Bill walked downstream to fish Horseshoe Bay. As I sat on my basket watching the water, trying to choose where to put in some groundbait, a fish rolled by the far bank closely followed by another rolling bream. To reach the far bank was an easy cast with my Richard Walker MK1V Avon rod, Mitchell 300 reel filled with 6 lb Sportex Perlon line and with a 1oz Arlesey bomb stopped about 2ft from a size 6 hook. Often I would use a swing tip but today I chose to use a dough bobbin to detect the bites. Two or three more bream rolled, I was very excited, knowing that if I didn't make any mistakes, I would have a good catch of bream.

I put six balls of mashed bread and bran containing lots of chopped worms into the swim. Having put all my gear together, I placed my basket in the correct position, and then went off downstream to see Bill. He was fishing the top end of Horseshoe Bay and netting his second bream of the day at about three pounds. Roach were topping and the occasional bream rolled in his swim. At the opening of the bay were some big piles, certainly not the place to fish in these conditions. After chatting with Bill and sharing a cupful of lukewarm tea I went back to my swim. I lit a cigarette and sat on my basket, then baited my size 6 hook with a big lobworm. Making an overhead cast, I dropped the bait in the area where I had seen the rolling bream.

Within minutes the bobbin moved in a determined fashion, fish number one was hooked and quickly netted. I placed it in my keepnet, rebaited then cast to the same spot. Very quickly I had another good pull; fish number two was being drawn away from the shoal and was soon netted. I lobbed in another ball of mashed bread and bran. As the swim was about ten feet deep,

Martin with a Bream

I didn't feel throwing in groundbait would disturb the fish. In fact I reckoned the more feed I put in the longer the fish would remain feeding. Soon, another fish was netted and put in the keepnet; they were averaging about four pounds.

After about three hours of fishing, I decided to rest the swim and have something to eat. In those days we carried a small stove, about the size of a two pound golden syrup tin, it had a small pot with a series of holes around the top with a screw lid so that we could carry enough methylated spirit as fuel for a brew – we just unscrewed the cap and were ready to go. These small but efficient stoves were sold at Woolworths and Millets.

I opened a can of beans and put them on the stove, occasionally giving them a stir. Once the beans were heated up I had them with my cheese sandwiches, while the kettle was put on for a fresh brew. Half-an-hour later I was ready to fish again. The bream continued to feed and it was some of the best fishing I had enjoyed to-date. What surprised me was that I didn't get a perch or roach: just bream. About five o'clock, as the darkness enveloped us, we stopped fishing, it was one of the darkest nights we had experienced and there was a train to catch.

As I released my bream from two big keepnets, Bill counted them, I had twenty-two fish averaging about four pounds. We reckoned I had between eighty and ninety pounds of fish, Bill had fourteen fish on the float from his swim, of a similar average size to my haul. Considering the small size of Horseshoe Bay, Bill's catch had been exceptional. It was two happy anglers who slowly made their way up the river bank and onto the road to the station. The biggest catch of bream I heard about on that particular stretch of river was 140 pounds, by Bill Simmonds, a welder from Gravesend, who was fishing the high bank about half-a-mile downstream of Horseshoe Bay. On the day of Bill's big net of bream he had fished a swim-feeder rig with worm and caster cocktail on a river that had three feet of extra water after being in flood.

Winter bream-fishing in the South East was fantastic and it wasn't rare for an angler to make a 100 pound catch of fish from the high bank on the River Medway. In fact, so good was the fishing on the Medway and Beult, that Dick Walker, who had a weekly column in the London Evening Standard, casually said to me one Friday, "I would like you to write my column next week on "bream-fishing in the South East". I've told the editor he will have your column on Tuesday morning."

I spluttered and stumbled over my words as I tried to say, "I can't do that!" Dick wouldn't take "no" for an answer. The feature was published in the following Thursday evening's edition. This was in the days when the London Evening Standard probably sold some five to six million copies. I kept the copy in my wallet until it just faded away, brown with age.

In the '50s and early '60s the Dorset Stour was a great venue. I will never forget Newman's

Cane Pole with whalebone tip

boat yard at Wimborne where you hired a punt for the day, then spent the time trotting with bread crust and flake. One good swim was just downstream of the viaduct, a few hundred yards below Newman's. Some days, three or more two-pounders would be taken. A friend of mine, Owen Wentworth, a postman in Wimborne, was the guy who put me right on this river. Sadly Owen has passed on, and Newman's is no longer there. When I last fished in this area it was during the 1980s, but the roach were not there in the numbers that I had enjoyed in the '50s and '60s. Through Southampton Piscatorial Society I did have a nice stretch of river further upstream above and below White Mill Bridge where I caught some nice roach. Downstream of the bridge on the opposite bank to the Southampton Piscatorial water, the fishing was controlled by the Red Spinners, the water where Ray Clark caught his 4lb 3oz record roach.

A summer and winter venue I enjoyed fishing was the Waveney in the Geldeston lock area; in summer it was very clear but weedy. In winter, after rain, and with the river carrying an extra foot of water and some colour, it was a great roach-fishing venue, with bread flake the top bait. In summer or winter at dusk I would often see big roach, fish of two pounds – perhaps pushing three pounds, rolling on the surface. When the river flowed clear I could spot roach moving in-and-out of the swaying weed or drifting over the clean, sparkling gravel. Often I sat spellbound at the sight of these magnificent fish, occasionally one would dip its head downwards 'head to hell' then pick up some food item. No doubt a caddis or nymph of damsel or dragon fly had just been eaten.

Close by was a delightful pub where I stayed for the price of five-shillings-and-six pence a night. This included a good breakfast as well as a pot of tea and cake when I returned, well after darkness. Unbeknown to the landlord and his wife, I even had a fling with their daughter Jean during my various summer and winter visits. During the summer Jean would bring me a pot of tea and sandwiches – that's when fishing stopped for an hour or more! Well, how could I not reward this delightful girl with my undivided attention – it was summer time!

After two or three nights of heavy frost, the river flowed gin-clear. I could often see roach swimming to-and-fro over the gravel, or holding station alongside the dying, swaying, water crowfoot. In these conditions I would sit well back from the water's edge, fishing a cane pole with its whalebone tip. I would then lower a size 16 hook, baited with either two gentles or a caster, to the fish. If I used a float the fish would be spooked.

My best Waveney roach went 2lb 7oz, taken in the dark on a small, red worm. Sometimes I arrived late on a mild, damp Friday evening to find the river high and coloured. I would then have a couple of hours legering with bread flake crust or lobworms, often catching a dozen or more quality roach with the odd, two pound fish.

If the river had been coloured through heavy rain with warm days and nights for a while, then I really could expect some good roach-fishing. On these occasions I would be up well before dawn heading off upstream to one of my stret-pegging swims. I would use my 15ft Clarkson's of Rochester, hand built cane rod, centre-pin reel with some 3lb line, and a cork on quill float taking 7or 8 BB shot.

I had one excellent swim where a nice promontory pushed well out about three feet into the stream. There, I could sit low behind some brown-coloured sedges, often working a bait up to fifteen yards downstream before the water started to shallow up quite dramatically, going from five feet to about eighteen inches. On these rare occasions I often had thirty or forty quality roach with one or two, two-pounders. Once I had five fish over two pounds with many pound-plus roach as a back-up. What I wanted was one of the three-pounders; I didn't even hook or lose such a fish to the best of my knowledge. I had two years fishing this water on-and-off, enjoying some great roach-fishing. Saturday evenings were often spent in the local dance hall – which was equally entertaining.

Another good roach-fishing venue in the late 1950s and '60s was the Little Stour near Mersham where I had access to some great roach and dace-fishing. Here was roach-fishing where you had a realistic chance of a two-pounder. Through a wildfowling friend of mine, a retired

Brigadier, I got to fish this delightful stretch of water up and downstream of Mersham Mill near Ashford, which was in those days a working mill.

At weekends when the mill wasn't working, I could adjust the water flow to suit the fishing and stop overnight in the mill. Upstream, the water resembled a small canal which held some huge gudgeon. We never ever weighed them but they were certainly bigger than any we caught elsewhere. Some weekends we would fish for the gudgeon until a couple of hours before dusk, then switch to fishing for roach and dace below the mill. While we fished for the gudgeon, two or three pints of little yellow grubs would slowly escape into the water from a biscuit tin with holes punched in the bottom which I suspended over the weir pool, it certainly attracted lots of fish into the area.

The creamy, foamy water going into the pool would flow a few yards downstream before swinging right under some far-bank trees. I well remember a warm, overcast day when I caught a 2lb 3oz roach and a 1lb dace. It was one of those days when we could do nothing wrong. Dennis Williams and I both used 11ft cane rods made by Clarkson's of Rochester, centre-pin reels with 2lb line and size 16 hooks. Our floats were cork on quill, made by myself, taking 4 BB shot bunched together about 12in from the hook.

Wearing waders, we would stand side-by-side in the water, trotting our floats down the stream, probably no more than two feet apart. Many times the floats virtually disappeared in the same instant. I suppose the average size that day was fourteen ounces to a pound, and we both caught a 2lb roach. For me the icing on the cake was taking the 1lb dace to go with my 2lb roach. That dace is still the best I've caught up to the present time. Another advantage of fishing during the autumn and winter was being able to sleep at the mill on a Saturday night. Sometimes we would visit Ashford for a night out, though usually it was one of the local village dances. On one occasion Angling Times accompanied us to shoot some pictures for the 'Spot the Float' competition. I shan't forget my days at the mill and its super gudgeon, roach and dace-fishing.

In the early 1970s we enjoyed some great roach-fishing on the Stour at Wye, upstream of the village, opposite a small copse close to a small sewage-works. The 'sewage swim' was either on or off: you either caught a netful or nothing. If it was the former you would probably get at least one or more, two pound roach. The Little Stour at Wye gave several of my London friends their first ever two-pounders. Baits were annatto gentles, casters and hemp, red worms and bread flake. For some strange reason, bread crust just didn't work like flake did. The most successful method was trotting, tight to the far bank with light float tackle, though we did catch the occasional big roach by laying-on or stret-pegging on the outside of bends where we often had some deeper water. I often fished float tackle in the dark with a cycle lamp to illuminate the float. I remember one session, fishing with Lou Page and John Larraman. We chose to fish downstream of Wye Bridge where I caught some lovely pound-plus roach on trotted bread flake.

I can recall that day as if it was yesterday: Lou and John were having trouble walking a thousand or so yards alongside the ploughed fields of heavy, dark-brown coloured Kentish clay that stuck to our boots like glue. To make matters worse, it had rained for the previous twenty-four hours. Seeing my mates struggling I grabbed their baskets and with my basket plus rod holdall, I just walked on. Lou said, "Look at him, just like an old mule" – or words to that effect! In those days I was fit – in fact very fit. I also did a lot of cross–country running and wildfowling on the tidal marshes, where I would often walk a mile or two in thick mud that really did cling to the boots. Walking to work became an easy task and I could dig lugworm for several hours without a break. That day on the Stour at Wye I got my reward with those nice roach while the other two struggled for a bite.

I spent a lot of time fishing in the Wensum Valley, probably the greatest roach-fishing river available anywhere in England, when I had the privilege of fishing it back in the late 1950s, '60s, '70s and '80s. (Note: I said 'in England' as I reckon the roach-fishing on the Tweed was even better in those far-off days.) Not only did we catch some great roach from the Wensum, we also caught big chub. After the roach-fishing deteriorated, the chub were still available to be caught. I remember catching a brace of chub weighing 6lb 2oz and 5lb 7oz on cheese-covered bread, with consecutive casts, back in the 1980s. My roach-fishing in those days was done mostly by trotting the stream, laying-on or stret-pegging, I usually legered only if the river was bank-high but that was only on rare occasions.

A lot of my fishing was done at night when I used a cycle lamp to illuminate the float. I will state now: "lights don't bother our coarse fish, they only bother some anglers!" I have on many occasions stood on the bank with a powerful flashlight, illuminating fish feeding in the margins. Did they move away? No, they just carried on feeding! If you are using a torch to light up your float, make sure it doesn't interfere with another angler who might be on the opposite bank. I am still using a lamp at night to light up my float or rod tip. A fish I caught in the 1980s, not available in the early days on the Wensum, was barbel. Though I caught plenty of these fish, I just couldn't get a double, but I did see other anglers catch them. In the '70s and '80s many of the big-fish anglers of the day fished this once great roach river. Two such men were Trevor West and Tony Miles. I feel privileged to have known these guys and many others who gave their time and knowledge freely.

During my angling career of over sixty years I must have fished the Rivers Medway, Kentish Stour, Thames, Kennet, and Beult more than any other venues. These rivers also provided me with some good roach-fishing, sometimes great fishing, and more often than not I felt I had a realistic chance of a two-pounder, though as always our target fish were pound roach which I still rate as a quality fish. These waters offered us good sport throughout the autumn and winter – and I also had the big, London reservoirs which I often fished, especially in the 1950s, but nothing beats a river roach.

I don't think it's difficult to catch roach, if you follow the simple rules of keeping quiet, fishing the bait on or near the bottom, and

In the past I had many fishing days under arctic conditions, such as pictured here

One just like Walker would catch. Credit Mick Holgate

choosing to fish when conditions are right. Yes, we had our blank sessions, but they were probably fewer than those experienced by most anglers. My most-fished venue was probably the River Medway. Sadly, I believe it was in 1967, a terrible pollution caused by the ICI plant at Yalding wiped out the fish from Yalding downstream to Maidstone.

The Medway under normal conditions was deep, slow-flowing water with big shoals of quality roach and bream, with probably the best fishing from East Peckham downstream to Tovil. It wasn't a river of clear-flowing water over a gravel bottom with swaying water crowfoot, that delightful aquatic plant with its lovely white buttercup-like flower that we see on the southern chalk streams; the Medway flows through Kentish clay. Very little weed flourishes, though there are many areas where you will see water lilies, and sedges that line the margins in many places. In some areas you will find occasional clumps of bulrushes; which makes it an attractive area for roach and perch.

On the railway side of the river, from the high bank downstream of the Yalding Cut to Nettlestead, we anglers enjoyed some great bream and roach-fishing during the autumn and winter months, especially when the river had an extra two or three feet of warm, coloured water after being bank-high for a few days.

On one occasion I was fishing the high bank, 200 yards downstream of Horseshoe Bend, the river just a few inches off the top of the bank – in fact many areas were flooded. Having arrived just after dawn, I had the pick of swims where I was lucky to find what I reckon was the perfect slack with some twelve feet of water. It was ideal for laying-on; my baits were bread crust flake and lobworms. I suppose I had been fishing about an hour when a group of London anglers marched along behind me looking for a suitable swim.

One old guy said to his mate, "What would Walker catch today?" As he spoke I struck into a fish, they stopped, waiting to see what I had caught. Soon I was able to net a good roach about a pound. Setting my net on the bank I turned and said, "Walker would have caught a dozen like this." Two hours later both anglers returned, not having found a suitable swim; they sat behind me for the rest of the day. I caught some nice bream and roach, which surprised them – remember, these River Medway bream often went four and five pounds, with the occasional six pound fish. That didn't surprise us regular Medway anglers, but it did the London anglers who might only visit the river a few times each year on their club outings. If the river was up and coloured with warm water, the fish would have it. Two weeks later they joined me for a day on the river where I helped them catch some good Medway roach and bream.

Another area where we had some great roach-fishing was the first bay above Teston Weir pool . On 27 December 1963, using a 14ft cane rod, centre-pin reel with 3lb line, with a porcupine quill float fixed on the line with double rubbers, I chose to fish laying-on style with

bread flake or crust on a size 10 hook. The water was around eight feet deep. After introducing some mashed bread as groundbait I waited about thirty minutes before making my first cast. I tightened down to the float after it had settled; within seconds there was a slight movement, and then the float was gone. I struck, and the first fish of the session was hooked – a lovely roach of over a pound. Things were starting

Teston Bridge

to look good; I felt better already. The fishing that day was excellent; every roach was over the pound mark, the best going 1lb 14oz. I caught thirty-two fish, while all those around me struggled for a fish or two.

Another good stretch of river was from Teston Bridge downstream to Barming Bridge. It was from this area where I lost a big – no huge chub on a live-roach bait meant for a pike. How big? I don't know but we reckon it was well over seven pounds if not eight, certainly a giant fish from any river. But remember, the Medway wasn't known for its big chub. A four pound fish would have been a good specimen. I also had permission to fish a couple of fields downstream of Maidstone Victory Angling and Medway Preservation Society water at Teston Bridge, on the right-hand bank looking downstream. Much of the bank was tree-lined with willows and alders with lots of brambles and the occasional elderberry trees; I often had to push my way through head-high nettles.

I also loved to fish the weir pools at Yalding, Teston and Farleigh. At Teston Weir, on the right-hand bank of the pool, there were some old ruins where we used to camp in the summer.

Downstream of the weir was a lovely, old stone bridge that carried the B2010 road over the river. I would often stand on the bridge in summer watching shoals of fish: roach, dace, bleak and chublets darting for scraps of food.

About thirty yards downstream were some hawthorn bushes, an area known for its wonderful roach-fishing, where on some days we caught lots of pound-plus fish, and the occasional two-pounder. Legered crust was the first method and bait we would try, followed by bread flake, then lobworms. Sometimes we would fish casters and gentles, but to be honest, bread was number one bait.

Medway roach-anglers eagerly looked forward to the first floods of autumn. The surging muddy water would sweep away all the rubbish left by summer visitors and hop pickers. This was the land of hops, and just upstream of Yalding at East Peckham were Whitbread Brewery's oast houses where every year hundreds of East Enders came to pick hops and have a good time. Lots of those hop pickers were roach-anglers who brought their black, wooden seat boxes and Sowerbutts roach poles, most of them used hemp for feed and bait.

There were many brief love-affairs between the East London girls and us Kentish lads. One of my mate's (Albert Smith) parents had a small apartment in Wateringbury where we used to stay at weekends. When we were fishing during the hopping season our teddy boy suits went with us. After a day's fishing, we would change, then go off to find the East End girls, who in those days wore stockings and suspenders, far more glamorous than the tights of today. We would meet in the pubs or at one of the dances around East Peckham, Yalding, Nettlestead and Wateringbury, sometimes catching the train into Maidstone.

Enough of this talk about our weekends with the women, let's get back to the roach, a favourite fish not just of the Kentish anglers but also of Londoners who came in coach-loads on Sunday mornings. You would see them sweeping across the fields to their favourite swims – lovely people, always willing to help and share their knowledge with us. I made many friends with the London anglers. Sometimes a couple of them would fish with me during Saturday then stay overnight at my house, where Mum would usually cook a load of chips, eggs and sausages. Then it was off to the Pavilion dance hall in Gillingham, and from there down to Chatham Station coffee-stall for hot pies, coffee and to chat-up the girls (if we hadn't been lucky enough to pull a girl at the Pavilion!).

Sunday, it was back on the river. This way the London boys got two day's fishing for the price of one. The following week I would go up and fish the tidal Thames and stay with one of the London boys. Saturday evening we would all go off to one of the coffee bars, the 2 I's in Old Compton Street being our favourite. There would always be lots of pretty girls, with good rock and skiffle music. The coffee bar at the 2 I's was in the basement of an old building, it was supposedly owned by a professional wrestler. It was a place where we could chat to and listen to some of the great names from rock and skiffle, musicians like Joe Brown, Tommy Steele, The Vipers and Lonnie Donegan to name just a few. In those days we would often go to the coffee bars, chatting and listening to the music from the jukebox. I wouldn't like to guess how much money I put in those machines – thankfully, I was earning well from my various jobs. They were certainly great nights – and all on coffee. We also spent a lot of time in the jazz clubs and going to concerts, Count Basie concert being one of the favourites. I am not sure if it was at the Albert Hall or the Festival Hall.

In the 1950s, five styles of fishing were popular with Medway roach-anglers: swimming the stream, legering, float-legering, laying-on, and stret-pegging. The latter was a great way to catch good fish; in fact it's as good a way of fishing today as it was fifty-or-more years ago. Go and give it a try! Stret-pegging is often described as an old-fashioned method of catching fish – that it might be, but it can still be deadly effective, Editor of the Angling Star, Jim Baxter, uses a very similar method where he fishes over-depth with an over-shotted float when fishing flooded rivers. I use a similar method, but I often replace the shot with a bored bullet. I cast out into the stream and allow the tackle to straighten downstream of my position. It's certainly a winning method on the River Thames, Beult, Ouse, and Suffolk Stour, Wensum and Waveney and similar waters. Even when fishing the Sixteen Foot river in Cambridgeshire it works when the water is being pumped, often proving a winner when all else has failed.

I was first instructed on how to stret-peg by the late Harry Rowlands, a match-fisherman from Northamptonshire, who spent a lot of time helping us newcomers to match-fish in the late 1940s and early 1950s. When seeking bream and roach on the Thames, Beult and Medway in winter this style of fishing was most successful. Many anglers could be seen fishing the laying-on style, which they would confuse with stret-pegging. When I asked if they were catching they would usually say, "I'm catching a few roach stret-pegging with gentles or flake," when in fact they were laying-on. Laying-on is usually done with the same float-tackle as used for trotting or swimming the stream. What often happens is, the angler trotting or swimming finds the fish shoaled up in a small area. He then moves the float two or three feet up the line, bunching the shot together about 12–18 inches from the hook, and then casts out so the bait is anchored in the chosen spot. Laying-on can also be used on canals and still waters whereas stret-pegging is used only in flowing water.

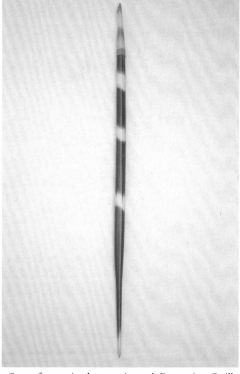

Stret-pegging is a searching method, one I suggest anglers try before knocking it. There is a big advantage in using a long rod, 15–17ft, matched with a centre-pin reel. This type of reel can be very efficient, giving excellent control of the tackle. Line strength and hook size will depend on the fish one is hoping to catch. I find a big, porcupine quill float to be a good choice – not one of the modern plastic types, but an original one about 12in in length, or alternatively, a swan quill. A large traditional cork or balsa-bodied float will also be found suitable.

One of my prized possessions. A Porcupine Quill Float, given to me by Mr Crabtree.

Having ascertained the depth, I move the float another 3ft further up the line, bunching the shot 12–15in from the hook. If I am using crust, which is very buoyant, I ensure a shot is pinched gently on the line 3–4in from the hook. Having put together the tackle and baited the hook. I cast out at right angles to the bank and a few feet downstream, allowing the tackle to straighten, so everything is in a straight line. You can put the rod on a rest, but I don't advise it, as you will miss many bites which can be quite sharp, often moving the rod tip. Having fished the bait in an area for five to fifteen minutes I then lift the rod allowing the bait to lift off the bottom, and with the reel giving a few feet of line, the baited hook settles further downstream. I repeat the process until I find I am fishing as far downstream as is efficient or I have had a bite.

The top baits were bread crust, flake and paste, gentles and lobworms, although occasionally we did use such baits as hempseed, stewed wheat and cheese. When the river was carrying two feet of extra water, anglers would fish with 10ft or 12ft rods and centre-pin reels, but now and again you could see someone with a fixed-spool reel such as the Omnia – a reel that looked like a cycle dynamo lamp. Thankfully I had a Mitchell 300, but a centre-pin was always my first-choice reel. With the river at its normal winter level we used float tackle, either swimming or trotting the stream, although some anglers still fished with the old Thames-style roach pole with great success. I enjoyed watching them as they fed with hempseed and fished the seed or with an elderberry on the hook. I too had a Sowerbutts roach pole, which I still use today.

A method many of us used was known as 'dusting and crusting'. We would drop a hazel-nut size lump of fine ground-bait into the swim then drop a piece of crust on a size 10 hook into the slowly sinking dust. The whalebone tip of our pole would be inches from the float as we followed it downstream. If the float moved we quickly lifted the rod just a few inches.

I had some great bags of pound-plus roach on lobworm bait when the river was in flood.

Martin on frozen snow

One February day I was at Teston downstream of the bridge. The river was over the fields, and the road on the approach to the bridge was under water. I fished laying-on style with lobworm bait in front of some half-submerged hawthorn bushes. My total catch was seventeen roach, all over the pound mark, the best making 1lb 12oz, as well as several bream around the three pound mark and a few eels.

Another time I had gone by train to Yalding and walked downriver to the start of the trees on the high bank. It was a frosty November morning; the river had some flow and colour, and the puddles on the field were thick with ice. I didn't think much of my chances. The swim I chose, in front of some withered, brown sedges, was around eight feet deep. I fished laying-on, with a 16ft rod, whole cane butt with a split bamboo middle and top joint, Rapidex centre-pin reel and 3lb line. 4 BB shot were bunched 12in from the hook, and my bait was flake on a size 8 hook. It was not until around two o'clock in the afternoon that I had my first bite, a pound-plus roach.

This was followed by a couple of bream and then six bites and six good roach. The frost was coming down now and my fingers were getting numb. Rooks, crows and pigeons were going to roost; there was the occasional sound of gunshot. The sky overhead was electric blue; in the direction of the setting sun it was pink and orange – a sure sign that there would be a heavy frost. A pheasant crowed from the tree behind me as it went to roost. I decided to stick it out until dark, and maybe do an extra half-an-hour with my cycle lamp beamed onto the float.

Changing to crust I moved the shot down to within 3in of the hook; in a magnificent couple of hours fishing into the darkness, I had a succession of pound-plus roach and two 4lb bream – every cast brought me a fish. I ended the day with twenty-six big roach, the best weighing 1lb 14oz. I didn't want to pack up but the cold was so intense that I couldn't stand it any longer. I was a happy angler as I trudged up-river to Yalding station thinking of the warm train carriage and checking my football pools when I got the evening paper at Maidstone.

I used the same method on another chilly day when the banks at Nettlestead were covered with frozen snow, and ice fringed the margins. Brian Long and I had gone off to fish the River Stour at Canterbury. When we arrived, all the swims in the weir pool were taken and I suggested we went back to the Medway, Brian agreed and it was just after two o'clock when we arrived at Wateringbury station. I suppose it took double the usual time to walk up-river to a favourite roach swim, as we slowly slithered up the snow-covered, icy bank.

We both chose to fish laying-on style with our 14ft Apollo Taper Flash tubular-steel rods (I was to field-test this rod by the manufacturers, Accles & Pollock from Birmingham – I reported back favourably) and centre-pin reels with 3lb breaking-strain line. I fished a cork, on crow quill float taking 5 BB shot pinched on the line about 1ft from a size 8 hook. Plumbing the depth, I found 8ft of water. I find that fishing around 2ft over-depth is perfect for laying-on to work effectively and so I set the float at just over 10ft. The swim I chose was in front of some dead water-lilies, my hook bait was bread cube. For a long time we saw not a sign of a fish, and to help us contend with the cold, I had a bottle of brandy.

As we chatted, the level in the brandy bottle fell steadily. Eventually my float slowly slipped from sight, the answering strike brought me a good roach. By the time it got dark I had caught several nice roach including three which were over the two pound mark. It had been a good day. Brian, who was married, had invited me back to his home for a meal, but it was gone 10.30 p.m. when we staggered up the garden path, a little worse for wear having consumed all of the brandy. Brian knocked on the door, it was answered by a woman who screamed, "Here's your bloody dinner," and then threw it at him. I decided not to stay! About fifteen minutes later I was in a taxi heading for home after a great day's winter roach-fishing.

Another venue I loved to fish was the Kentish Stour in and around Canterbury, which I fished on many occasions from the early 1950s until the mid-sixties. Much of the river was free fishing, around and downstream of Canterbury. You could catch some stunning roach and dace within the perimeter of the City itself. We even caught some very big, brown trout to four pounds–plus, which we captured when we were float-fishing annatto gentles; in those days we purchased them from Don's of Mexborough in Yorkshire. We would send off our postal order on a Monday, the bait arriving by train on Thursday or Friday. Over a period of several years we were never let down either by the bait or railway company. A lot of businesses could learn from the service industry of those far-off days.

Just downstream of the city centre was Barton mill, I am told it was the last, working water mill in Canterbury. I believe it started life as a paper mill, ending up as a corn mill. I am not sure if one or two water wheels drove the millstones. At one time, when I was fishing the pool, I got told by some workers that the millstones had been replaced by rollers.

I was fortunate that, as my grandfather often shot with the mill owners, they gave me permission to fish the pool. It wasn't a summer venue; in fact you would struggle to get half-a-dozen small fish. Autumn and winter were a different matter: it was stuffed with big dace and roach, which moved upstream from the more streamy, weedy water downstream. Some Sundays you couldn't get a swim, as it was a popular venue with London anglers. Though they were not allowed to fish, it wasn't usually a problem on Sundays when the mill wasn't working. On several weekends, three of my friends from Bermondsey and Blackheath and I, booked digs for the Saturday night in Canterbury. Those weekends on the banks of the pool were full of fun with fished-filled keepnets. A couple of us had thigh-high waders allowing us to fish in the better spots where the water poured through the centre of the pool creating some nice, streamy runs, ideal for trotting. In those days not many anglers could afford waders. I can remember my first pair of green, thigh waders with studded leather soles, costing a small fortune.

In the early 1950s my gear was a 12ft bamboo rod built by Mr Clarkson of Rochester, a Tonkin cane butt, middle and top joint of split cane. Clarkson built me several rods in those days for various aspects of angling. I, along with many of my friends, also used the new, tubular steel rods from Accles & Pollock. We rated the Taper Flash for roach, dace and bream.

In those days we wouldn't be seen dead using a fixed-spool reel when trotting the stream laying-on or stret-pegging, it had to be a centre-pin. Although some of my friends rated the Hardy reels, I wasn't a fan, being keener on S Allcock & Co tackle. One of the nicest reels I had was an 'Allcock Aerial', sadly lost when I was fishing for tench on a big gravel pit in Gloucestershire in the 1980s. It was a scorching hot day; I baited with a lobworm and cast out. I lay the rod on the bank and picked up the box of worms then walked to the hedgerow to put the worms in some shade. Returning to my swim, I noticed that the rod was missing. Thinking my mate Derek Green was a playing a joke, I walked along the bank and said to Derek, "Let's have my rod back." He looked puzzled and I quickly realised the tackle had been pulled in by a tench or carp grabbing the worm. Though we took the boat out, spending several hours dragging the area, we never did find the tackle.

I was quite gutted. I reckon the wide drum 'Speedia' my grandfather gave me was nearly as good as the 'Aerial' though my friends would disagree. Other reels I used were 'Perfection Flickem', 'Rapidex', and 'Trudex'. I think it was 1965 when the 'Match Aerial' (not to be confused with the 'Aerial Match') came on the market. I reckon I wasted my money with the purchase of this reel, even the position of the knob on the side for switching on and off the ratchet seemed all wrong. Like the 'Flickem', 'Rapidex' and Trudex, I felt the drum was too narrow. Today I have various centre-pins, probably the best are my Richard Carter, and wide drum 'Purist 11'. Both work extremely well, I see no need to change.

Our floats were home-made using cork or balsa on goose quill taking a barleycorn or barrel weight; in the fast-moving water we wanted our bait – usually a bunch of gentles on a size 10 hook – down deep, even the dace would be taken on this rig. What we did use was a lot of gentles, usually six pints, though there were occasions when we would go through a gallon of the little white grubs. We tried bread, worms and stewed wheat, but annatto gentles were the top bait. We would hold the float back hard, slowly easing it down the swim. I reckon, even through my rose-tinted glasses, that the dace would average ten ounces, the roach around the pound mark.

During those winter sessions we had our share of two-pound roach which were usually caught after dark, fishing laying-on style at the tail of the pool. Some good perch around two pounds, bream averaging four pounds – with the odd five pound fish, plus lots of brown trout were caught. Sadly the fishing on the river took a turn for the worse in the 1970s, in fact it got so bad I stopped going. Another winter venue on the river Stour was the tidal stretch at Grove Ferry, a top place for quality roach with many pound-plus fish and the occasional two-pounder; this kept us going back time-after-time. We also fished Plucks Gutter which often produced some good bags of bream, but nothing of size to get excited about. Occasional, if you caught the right tide with the fish feeding, you could have some enjoyable roach and bream-fishing, though eels could prove a nuisance.

One of my nicest sessions on this delightful River Beult, where I have had many, was in the 1970s when Jack Hilton and Tom Mintram joined me for a day's winter chub-fishing. Jack was not just an extremely good carp-angler, he was a great all-rounder, even today many of us still mourn his loss. Without doubt Jack's book A Quest for Carp, published by Pelham, was and remains one of the finest books on the subject. I believe it's still available from Little Egret Press. Tom was another one of the great 1960s carp-anglers who fished Redmire and Ashley Pool, among other carp-fishing venues. Tom has sadly passed away. Meet a group of carp-anglers from the 1960s and 70s, and you will find he is still held in high esteem by them all.

Our chosen river was the Beult at Benover near Yalding, a water I've fished for some sixty years. It was known for the quality of its chub-fishing both during the summer when we free-lined slugs, flake, meat or floating crust, and for its winter-fishing, which was done usually with a short-link ledger – crust being our first choice bait. The stretch of the river we chose to fish had a weir pool at the top end and then flowed downstream for about a mile-and-a-half often through high, clay banks with shallow, gravel runs and deep pools, lots of bulrushes and patches of water lilies and water cabbages.

It was arranged that I would meet up with Tom and Jack at a café in Yalding. After breakfast we headed off for the river. We pulled into the car park and realised we had the river to ourselves. I could see it was carrying an extra twelve inches of water, the previous day it had been up two feet. As we stood on the road bridge looking upstream towards a small waterfall I pointed out a good chub spot on the left-hand side of the river, where a small, side stream flowed into the river. Downstream of the bridge was a nice pool, from where the river flowed over clean gravel with lots of bulrushes between the high, clay banks. Four-pound chub were considered good fish, a five-pounder, a giant among River Beult chub. Thankfully, a few giants were caught during the course of the season. Tom and Jack tackled-up with what I thought was identical gear, both rods were of Avon action in honey-coloured glass with Mitchell 300 reels and 6lb line, choosing size 6 hooks with a 3 swan shot link leger. We all had a crusty loaf and some lobworms as bait. After pointing out some spots for Jack to try from the waterfall downstream, I took Tom off upriver to a weir pool. Weir pools are few and far between on the river. This one had a reputation for big bream and chub. I well remember a match organised by A.C.T. fisheries on a hot summer's day, which I won with some forty-odd pounds. This included four, six pound-plus bream. I also had my share of big chub from the venue, my best at 5lb 6oz.

Tom, on his second cast, had a nice pull, accounting for a chub of about three-and-a-half pounds, fifteen minutes later he had another fish of the same size. Half-an-hour later, with no more interest, we moved downstream. Tom quickly caught two more fish of about two pounds, both on bread flake. I left Tom and went off down-river to see how Jack was doing. I found him in the 'Big Oak' swim; he told me he had several bites accounting for three chub, one of which he thought was a good four-pounder.

I then went off well downriver, fishing my way back upstream where I found Jack and Tom having a cup of tea. It seemed we had all caught. As Jack told me, "it's a nice bit of river with plenty of character". I called my wife to say I was bringing two guests home for dinner.

"What do I give them?" she said. No problem, Chips, eggs, bacon and beans. Most anglers enjoy that food. Within fifteen minutes of getting home we all sat down to a good meal and a mug of tea. On leaving, Jack and Tom told Kate it was a good meal and they would be back for more. So ended a great day with two of the giants of carp-fishing: true sporting gentlemen.

During the late 1970s early '80s I spent a lot of time fishing the Fens and Norfolk Broads, enjoying some good sport and the company of great anglers like Martyn Page, Vic Bellars, John Bodsworth, Pete Bannister, and Arthur Sayers who was with me one winter's day on the River Medway in the 1950s when I lost a very big chub that grabbed a roach live-bait.

A water where I spent a lot of time fishing, both day and night, was the River Wensum, where I caught a lot of good roach and chub, though I never had a barbel from the Wensum. It was from this river where, in 1983 or '84, I caught a magnificent brace of chub on the last day of the season. I had been on the river for a few days fishing hard for a three-pound roach, often well past midnight. I then went off to Kath and Arthur Sayers' house for a couple of good night's sleep and a welcome shower. I planned to fish with Arthur on the last day of the season. Over supper that night we discussed where to go for the last day.

"What about Swanton Morley on the Wensum?" I suggested. Arthur agreed, and the next morning we struggled down to the river with all our tackle. I picked a straight stretch below a bend where the water was about four feet deep. About five yards below my chosen swim was a small bay, but at first I ignored this fishy spot. Chub were far from my mind. It was the Wensum roach I had come to catch. I tackled up with a light, quiver tip rod, a thirty-year-old Mitchell 300 reel, a paternoster rig and a size 22 hook baited with a bronze gentle. The main line was 1½lb breaking strain, and the hook length just on1lb. In the next four hours I had six bites: I missed three and was broken by three fish.

The bailiff turned up to check our permits, saying the area was good for chub, I immediately thought that those breaks could have been bite-offs, and I soon had another rod made up, baiting with crust and smearing it with cheese paste. I quickly caught a chub, and minutes later I had another fish. This one was different, it fought like a demon, head-shaking and taking the occasional foot or two of line. Eventually it was netted. It weighed 5lb 7oz. I put it in the landing net to rest before taking some pictures.

What a way to end the season, I thought. I flopped into my chair and said to Arthur, "I think I will sleep for the rest of the day." Then, as an afterthought, I added, "If I'd caught a six-pounder I would have done a streak across the river." I relaxed, thinking about the pictures we would be able to take of the fish a little later. After a rest I felt refreshed and decided to have another go. I baited once more with bread flake smeared with cheese spread. Within ten minutes the rod pulled round and my answering strike saw the tip pulled savagely down to the surface. Line flew from the spool, sounding like a scalded cat. For a while it was a battle with neither side winning. Then the fish swirled on the surface and soon I was easing it over the landing net; it was mine. Adrenaline was pumping through my body as I realised that I might have managed a brace of five-pound chub in a single session. Out came the scales again, only this time they bumped down at 6lb 2oz.

We rounded up witnesses, weighed both fish a couple of times, and then took some pictures. The chub were returned to the river, hopefully to grow into seven-pounders. I felt the water and decided that streaking was out of the question – perhaps when I catch a seven-pounder! Two weeks later the weights and measures inspector in Blackburn told me the scales were weighing two ounces under, but I was more than happy to leave the weight at 6lb 2oz for my best chub to-date. Since the day of the 6lb 2oz chub I have had lots more six pound-plus chub, the best six-pounder weighed in at 6lb 15oz. My fish have come from several Rivers: Kennet, Loddon, Ribble, Aire, Bain, Wye, Teme and Ure, with my biggest-ever chub coming from the River Ribble at 7lb 10oz – truly, an awesome, winter fish. On the same day I had a 10lb 10oz barbel. The water temperature was 34°F with cat-ice in the quiet, shallow water.

A winter scene, such as this, was often viewed by the author in the 1950's and 60's

I have always found the perch to be an interesting fish, ever since I was a lad fishing *Laughing Waters* at Cobham Kent. I liken the perch to the swaggering teddy boys of the 1950s: I was always reminded of them when watching perch cruising around in search of food; the perch is the bully boy of the aquatic world. Having fished for over sixty years, I don't reckon there has been a better time than today to set out to catch a big perch, it is certainly a magnificent-looking fish – both in and out of the water.

The late Richard Walker intimated that perch are, 'the biggest fish in the net'. What he meant was, put a carp, tench, bream, roach and rudd alongside a perch, all of identical weights; the latter would look far bigger than the other species, and he was right, they certainly do. In the 1960s, perch disease struck and eventually wiped out most of our perch countrywide. It wasn't until the early 1980s that big perch once again started to appear in a few waters.

I remember fishing various venues in Suffolk and Essex with the late Len Head, where we caught our fair share of good perch. Back in those days, Len and I would often fish Ardley reservoir in Essex. Not only did we catch some great perch, but also big pike. I recall the time, back in the 1980s, when two members of the Perch Fishers, I think it was Pete Rogers or Steve Burk, were either trolling or working a big plug at Bewl Water, when a brace of three pound perch got hooked on a single plug at the same time.

If my memory serves me correctly one perch was hooked on the front treble, the other perch on the rear treble hook. A picture was published in The Book of the Perch: by the Perch Fishers, whose authors, Pete Rogers and Steve Burke, are both extremely experienced perch anglers. Today, Steve Burk runs the very successful Wingham Fishery in Kent. What is a big perch, you might ask? In my book it's a perch of over three pounds. It doesn't matter where you live in the UK you have an excellent chance of catching a good perch, and they are not a difficult fish to hook. Somewhere in many of the nation's rivers, lakes, gravel pits and canals a big perch or two will be in residence.

One area worth seeking them has to be the commercial fisheries which are often over-stocked with small silver fish – an ideal food for the perch to grow big on. Most of these waters are predominantly carp-fishing venues, where most of the anglers are targeting the carp – which means that the perch are left free to grow large. From my experience of many years of angling, I have always found that predatory fish will thrive on neglect. Long live the carp-fishers!

Today, many of our rivers hold big perch-stocks that we could only dream about back in the 1950s. Carp are the number one fish in still waters, with barbel the number one fish in our rivers. Once again the predatory fish in our rivers are being neglected, allowing both pike and perch to thrive, you have a realistic chance of catching a big perch from many of our rivers. Over the years, the Kennet, Wye, Teme, Ouse, Thames, Ure, Hampshire Avon and Dorset Stour have been rivers where I have caught big perch; and let's not forget the Suffolk Stour. I haven't caught a big perch from this water, my best being 2lb 10oz, but others have caught larger fish. It was rumoured that a 4lb 3oz fish was caught at Bures in 1986, but I couldn't find any proof of such a capture. I do reckon that in some of the quieter waters four-pound perch roam around striking fear into the smaller fish.

Whilst fishing the River Teme many years ago for barbel, as I sat peering into the crystal-clear water looking for the barbel to move into my baited swim, I kept seeing a number of good perch swimming to-and-fro. How I would love to have a box of lobworms, I thought. As I sat there waiting for the barbel to put in an appearance, I suddenly remembered that my fly-fishing vest was in the car. Bringing in my rods, I made my way upstream to the car park. After rummaging through the vest, I found what I needed – some big, Walker beaded Mayfly nymphs. Back in my swim, the perch were still present. I suppose there must have been two dozen or more ranging in size from twelve ounces to perhaps two-and-a-half pounds. Stripping down my barbel rig, which was nothing more than 4 LG shot and a size 4 hook, I tied on the nymph. Sitting well back from the water's edge, I lowered the nymph down into the water then worked it, sink and draw. On my third lift I felt a hit. Striking, I hooked my first perch. Amazingly, it was one of the bigger fish, probably weighing two pounds. I was amazed at how easy it was. In about three-and-a-half hours I caught seventeen perch, the smallest weighing about a pound. The best fish weighed in at 2lb 13oz. Eventually they drifted away, no doubt thinking it strange their mates were disappearing. Each fish I caught was moved well downstream then released.

As I have written before, I have caught big perch on lobworms, nymphs and streamer patterns, but this predator can be caught on a variety of baits and lures. Spinners, plugs, nymphs, streamer flies, dead and live baits, crayfish, gentles and poppers, even sweet corn has caused the downfall of some big perch. A 3lb 2oz perch was caught from Aquatecs Lake in Berkshire on corn – though a small fish might have been eating the corn as the perch grabbed it. I reckon perch have eaten virtually everything that we anglers have put on a hook to catch them, but the one bait I would always want whenever I go perching would have to be a box of lobworms. I reckon worms will outfish all the other baits. They can be fished on a float rig, free lined or legered. Back in the 1950s I sometimes watched a Thames angler spin a lobworm on a two hook Stewart rig with a small celluloid or Perspex vane, which proved quite effective for perch around the pound mark, but I didn't ever see him catch a fish of two pound weight – though he did catch some big brown trout.

When you next go perch-fishing, try nipping off the end of your lobworm and feed with lots of chopped worms. I use those new triple-bladed scissors and chop my worms until they resemble a thick stew or soup which I often put into a PVA bag. This is then quickly dropped inside another PVA bag which is then attached to the hook, but you need to be fairly quick in getting it into your swim. Many successful perch-anglers feed with lots of red gentles to attract the perch into their swim; I find chopped-worm soup a better attractant.

If you want to catch a big perch, you need to fish with tackle that causes the least amount of resistance. I use 11ft soft Avon action rods designed for lines of 4–6lbs, using both centre-pin and fixed spool reels; I use the latter for fishing at distance on big, still-waters; sadly you get more resistance when having to fish with more weight on the line – something that perch hate, and so it's not a thing I often do. When I use a centre-pin for my fishing on rivers, I have far better control and presentation, be it float, leger or free-lining bait. I get sick-and-tired of being told they are a fashion accessory. They are a superb piece of equipment that have helped me be more proficient, and so I catch a lot more fish. I have used them since the age of six when I was allowed to use my grandfather's Allcock Ariel.

I always fish my lobworms on a size 6 or 4 barbless hook, I will say this: I have never lost a fish through using a barbless hook, but I have lost them through a mistake on my part. For the past few years I have been experimenting with Circle hooks; my problem is I have to keep telling myself not to strike: but I often do. I reckon the jury is still out on these hooks. When float-fishing I use the lightest float possible, with most of the shot 2ft from the hook with just a BB shot some 5–6in from the hook. This only applies to still water, slow flowing rivers or canals. If you are fishing fast, pacey water then you need a float that will allow you to boss the stream.

My floats for powerful river-fishing often carry as many as 10 AA shot bunched about 15in from the hook. I will then have a BB shot 6–8in up from the hook. Though I am using this type of heavy float tackle, it's still well-balanced and quite sensitive. Using this set-up will allow you to mend the line when you're fishing well out into the river.

Most of my legering on still waters is done with just 1 Swan or LG shot about 15in from the hook. When legering I use extremely light bobbins with a 2ft drop from the rod. Often perch will play around with a worm for some time before taking it, in a smooth lift to the butt ring. Hopefully you're not like me: I sometimes get a series of perfect bites where the bobbins glide smoothly up to the butt ring; I miss everyone of the takes – I don't even prick a fish. It certainly can be exasperating.

Let's not forget the country's canal venues, which are often given a wide berth by those seeking big fish. If you want a big perch then look at the canals near you. One way of checking them out is to watch the match result for clues on where the fish are being caught. If you're interest is in big eels then canals can be some of the best places to seek your quarry. Two that spring to mind are the Leeds and Liverpool, and the Kennet and Avon. Both have produced perch over four pounds and most lengths can be fished for the price of a day permit costing just a couple of pounds, or a season ticket. Some successful canal anglers have been using the long pole with lobworms and they have enjoyed some great fishing.

On the occasions when I fish the canals, I either float-fish or free-line lobworms. Some of my friends use small live-baits, gudgeon being their favourite. The problem you will find when fishing live or dead bait will be the pike, I haven't yet found wire that's fine and flexible enough to use, so if I am fishing water where pike are present I only use lobworms. Yes, I get my share of pike on worms but most are hooked in the scissors and landed. Three waters worth fishing for big perch are: Aquatecs in Thatcham, Berkshire – chance of a five-pounder; Wasing Fisheries, Aldermaston, Berkshire, lakes and River Kennet, plenty of three pound fish with four-pounders being caught, and Tewitfield Lakes, Carnforth, Lancashire: the small lake is the better venue.

My best perch session in sixty-odd years of angling started off fly-fishing for pike on the River Kennet. I was with solicitor Stephen Collins from Hungerford, Berkshire and Mike Osborne of Carlisle. First cast, a three pound perch on a 6in long fly designed for striped bass, known as the Black Magic. Apart from a couple of pike, I had no more interest. An hour later as I enjoyed a mug of tea, I looked towards the spot where I had caught that perch, saying to myself, "If there's one big perch, there should be others around."

I put together a 13ft rod, centre-pin reel, 4lb line with a 5 AA cork on quill, Avon float; a size 6 barbless hook completed the set-up. Having plumbed the depth at 5ft I set the float at 6ft, and then baited with two lobworms. As the float went downstream it bobbed, I thought that's a fish, it bobbed again, once more I said to myself, "That's a fish, not weed." Ten feet further downstream the float moved sideways, slowly submerging. My strike connected with a good fish. Soon, a second three pound perch was in the net.

After weighing the fish, Stephen shot some pictures. He then said, "I'm going to watch you fish today and shoot a few pictures.' Stephen netted, unhooked and weighed each fish if they looked over two pounds. Those weighing three pounds-plus were photographed. All I had to do was bait the hooks, cast, watch the float down the swim, then hook and play the fish. I fed two swims with chopped worms; it worked like a charm, the perch continued to feed. Having caught a couple of fish from the near-bank swim, I would switch to the right-bank swim. As the day wore on I started running short of bait; Stephen was quickly beside me with all his worms and gentles. I was able to keep the fish in the swim and feeding. I caught a total of thirty one perch between 1lb 12oz and 3lb 11oz with nine, three pound-plus fish. I lost one fish which I reckon could have been a big four pound-plus fish. I had a good look at it before it slipped the hook. Was I gutted? No! It had been a magic fishing-session.

A 500 mile round trip for two day's fishing on the Wasing estate fishery, on the river Kennet was worth all the effort despite the icy-cold nights, bright, sunny days and low water temperature though I must say, at the age of seventy, as I was then, it was getting tough, roughing it at night – even more so now at seventy three! But, I have always said: If you don't put in the effort you can't expect good results. Through working at my fishing, I sometimes get lucky and catch a whacker. As I tell my listeners, if you want to catch, then put in the effort – don't complain about those who do catch.

Despite the low water temperature and icy-cold easterly wind, it was a one of those days when nothing moved, even the birds were absent on this trip – I didn't even see the friendly robin. By lunchtime, several anglers had packed in, usually with the words, "It's a waste of time today, Martin". After several hours fishing, with Will Carter of Burfield, Berkshire, we began to think that perhaps we should have done the same thing. Yes, conditions were grim, but if you have a bait in the water you have a chance. After covering some two miles of the River Kennet, trying probably 15–20 likely spots, we arrived at a swim where a poplar tree had crashed into the river during the previous winter. Behind the tree was a dinner-table size area of virtually still water creating a nice crease either side of this slack. I turned to Will and said, "Hold on a minute, I'm going to chuck some lobs in that

Author with a brace of 3lb plus perch from the River Kennet

slack, I reckon it's good for a perch." I was using a soft Avon action rod, centre-pin reel, 6lb Gamma line with a size 4 barbless hook. Weight was an LG shot lightly pinched on the line 15in from the hook. To keep the three lobworms on the hook I used a small square of rubber band to stop them wriggling off.

Within thirty seconds of the bait entering the water and rolling slowly down the swim, I felt a light pluck, then a more distinct pull. "That's not a crayfish," I thought. Striking, I felt the typical head-shaking of a perch. I shouted to Will, "I'm in, bring the net." Down in the clear water I could see a good perch, fin erect, diving and twisting as it sought the sanctuary of various snags and submerged tree branches. Cramping on pressure, I slowly pulled the fish upward; in seconds a big perch, with dorsal fin erect, thrashed on the surface. I applied side strain and pulled the fish towards the net, it was quickly gathered in by Will. I punched the air with relief. On the scales it weighed 3lb 4oz, and after a couple of pictures by Will, we watched it swim off with that swaggering attitude so reminiscent of big perch. Twenty minutes later in the same spot I had a 3lb 2oz caught while attacking the bunch of worms as I dragged the bait across the surface to make another cast. It's a pity I didn't retain the first fish in the landing net, but then I didn't expect another one. Also, I don't like to keep perch in a net as they are very fragile fish. Driving all those miles, roughing it and living mainly on porridge, wholemeal sandwiches and tea had been worthwhile.

For probably forty-odd years I've targeted coarse fish with dry-flies, streamers and nymphs. There isn't a fish that I know of you can't catch on an imitation fly. Barbel, perch, chub, rudd, dace and pike are my usual target fish. Apart from barbel, the other species will avidly take a surface or sub-surface pattern – pike and perch being my favourite fish, but in this chapter I am writing about perch. They can be caught from a variety of waters, spate rivers, chalk streams or lowland slow-flowing, clay-based waters.

Dry-flies, nymphs and streamers have accounted for lots of good perch (fish of two-pounds plus) over many years from various rivers: Wharfe, the Great Ouse. Rivers, Wye, Kennet, Teme, Enborne, Hampshire Avon and Beult It was on this latter river I caught my first fly-caught perch in the 1950s; sadly the river doesn't seem to have the head of perch it did in those days. Cholmondeley-Pennell mentions fly-fishing for perch in the book Fishing (Badminton Library: 1893). While John Bickerdyke writing in the Fur and Feather series, Pike and Perch writes on page 256 "Now-and-again, perch will take an imitation of natural flies, but can hardly be classed among fly-taking fish". How wrong he was.

Looking back over the years I have had many happy days with a fly rod, but none can beat the day on the Kennet when I had a series of very good perch, using nymphs and streamers by sight-fishing. I started the day by putting together two outfits, a 9ft 5 weight rod, floating line, 12ft leader with a 3lb tippet, this outfit was for upstream nymphing. For fishing streamers I chose a 9ft 6 weight rod, floating line with a mini sink-tip of just 7ft to which I attached a 6ft leader with a 6lb tippet. I chose to use a stronger tippet in case a jack pike should hit the streamer.

I suppose it was around ten o'clock when Stephen Collins and I split up to fish our separate beats. I walked to the bottom to fish my way upstream, while Stephen walked half-way up the beat before starting to fish his way to the top, hopefully, meeting-up in time for a late lunch. I tied on a weighted dragonfly nymph and crept, low and quiet, towards the water's edge. I peered intently into the crystal clear water, it's at times like this you need good quality, polarised sun-glasses. Mine are made by Optilabs, who have matched my prescription lenses. Slowly, I made my way upstream. After about fifty yards I spotted a good, brown trout, tight against some swaying water crowfoot with its lovely daisy-like flower. After watching the fish for five minutes, I aerolised enough line to drop the fly ten feet upstream of the trout. It landed with a tiny plop and descended in the stream down to the trout. In a split second the fish moved forward then engulfed the nymph. A few minutes later, having been unhooked in the water, the fish returned to its old hunting spot. It was as easy as that.

I suppose it was midday when I spotted the first of many perch. I had cast the nymph upstream to a trout, which ignored my offering. As I worked the fly back downstream, I spotted a good perch moving from under the water crowfoot – by its action I could see it intended to hit my fly: I gave two, quick, six inch pulls, which increased the speed of retrieve. The fish shot forward, engulfing the fly. There followed a spirited fight, I netted a cracking perch, scale and fin perfect: it just fitted in the landing net. After a couple of quick pictures I watched the fish swim strongly off back to the cover of the swaying weed. In the next half-an-hour I had five more fish; all on the dragonfly nymph. It was time for lunch. Back at the small cabin overlooking the river, Stephen and I enjoyed our lunch as we discussed the morning's events, while watching the river flowing left-to-right. It was great to be alive in the warm sunshine.

After lunch we fished our way downstream catching some nice trout. Arriving at a right-hand bend, we saw the water flowing fast along the sedge-lined opposite bank over-hung by willows and alders. I decided to make a long cast upstream, dropping a streamer close to the far bank; hopefully a big trout would fancy this large mouthful! On my second cast, as I worked the streamer downstream, I had a hit – this wasn't a trout I thought. Suddenly, the water boiled, a good perch, fin erect, swirled on the surface then dived towards the sedges and swaying weed, I cramped on the pressure. This powerful outfit should control anything I might hook on this beat. Minutes later a good fish was in the net. I quickly shot a couple of pictures then slipped out the barbless fly, sliding the perch back in the water. I would love to have known its weight but when trout-fishing I don't take any weighing scales. During this afternoon session I caught more perch than trout, finally catching my last fish as Stephen appeared in view – so I got a trophy shot! Why not go fly-fishing for perch: it's an ideal way to fish some of the canals. One such water is the Kennet and Avon which holds some stonking perch of four pounds-plus.

The Kennet starts life in Avebury Wiltshire, in the same area as Stonehenge, the prehistoric temple to the sun. On its way to the River Thames, it flows through the most delightful of Wiltshire countryside, taking in the town of Marlborough, then through the Savernake Forest, Ramsbury and Littlecote, and on to Berkshire. At Hungerford, a rod for trout-fishing could cost £3000 a season, sadly, these days some of the stock fish are horrible, bloated rainbow-trout that have no place in our chalk streams.

It's in Berkshire around Newbury where this lovely chalk stream changes to clay, and really does become a coarse-fishing river – best described as a Crabtree River. Bernard Venables, the author of Mr Crabtree Goes Fishing, certainly captured its many moods in his magnificent paintings and in his descriptive writings. Thankfully, today we still have landowners who are prepared to keep their property in private ownership, retaining the format of a sporting estate.

One such estate is Wasing which has been in the same family since 1759; it has matured gracefully over more than 250 years, surviving many of the crises that have beset other country estates throughout England. The Wasing Estate covers three villages and several thousand acres of prime Berkshire countryside just one hour from London. It's an oasis of calm with twisting, flowing, winding rivers, where you will find dozens and dozens of diverse swims, and fast gravel runs, so beloved by dace and trout. There are deep holes under overhanging willows and alders, where you have the chance of a twenty pound pike, a fish that today seems sadly neglected, as fishers rush past in search of the new, fashionable fish: the barbel.

Alongside swaying water crowfoot you will often see a few big, pigeon-chested roach intercepting invertebrates and nymphs as they drift downstream. In a quiet backwater you can spot, if you're careful, half-a-dozen basking chub – make a false move and they will disappear, ghost-like. Alongside a fallen tree you might catch a glimpse of a perch perhaps pushing three pounds, again, ignored by most people as they seek the barbel. You will find beautiful oaks and

beeches hanging over dark, secretive chub and barbel swims. There is a weir pool that can put fear into the faint-hearted; it's a great 'fishing hole' where you don't know what the next bite will bring.

Various species of deer abound on the estate: from muntjacs to roe. You will find several lakes, including two in Wasing wood that anyone would enjoy fishing. The lakes support some incredible fish including double-figure tench and bream that might push twenty pounds, carp of fifty pounds-plus, big perch, rudd, pike and roach. The estate supports an incredible variety of flora

Wasing Estate Manager Ian Lindsay and the efficient office staff

186   AT THE WATER'S EDGE WITH MARTIN JAMES

John Butler, Fishery and Game Shooting Manager
on the Wasing Estate

and fauna, having matured gracefully over 250 years coping with the many problems that have beset country estates, especially since World War II. Not a day has gone by when I have not heard the maniacal laugh of the green woodpecker, remember the 'Woody Woodpecker Song'?

Today, Wasing has a fine bill of health – it is not just the landscape that has a dazzling breadth of diversity, it still maintains its traditional farming, sporting and property base, with a striking portfolio of activities and businesses. In recent years, apart from boasting one of the UK's finest coarse-fishing estates, it has further diversified into conservation.

As a full member of the Wasing Fisheries Syndicate you get to fish several lakes and miles of the rivers Kennet and Enborne, a Wasing syndicate ticket for the rivers will cost just £260-00 – far cheaper than most golf clubs or Premier Soccer club season tickets. You don't have to be a millionaire, to have a millionaire life style. It's a fishery where John Butlers bailiffs are friendly and helpful; members are more than willing to offer you advice and help. For me, it's a return journey of over 500 miles to fish the delightful waters but its worth very penny, even if I do moan about the price of petrol and some of the B&Bs. For further details telephone 01189-71140 or write John Butler Fisheries Manager Wasing Estate Office Wasing Berkshire RG7 4NG

Mike Osborne of Cumbria and me were on a two-day fishing trip in search of chub and barbel. Pulling into the Wasing Estate fisheries syndicate car park, patchy fog was keeping visibility down to about a hundred yards in some places. Before putting together our tackle, Mike put the kettle on for a fresh brew, I checked the water temperature. It was 40°F, the river was low and gin-clear, not the best of conditions. It looked as if it was going to be rather difficult to catch fish from the River Kennet today.

The riverside trees and bushes were frost-covered, looking beautiful in their silvery foliage which seemed to blend in nicely at this Christmas period. The robins added a dash of colour, as did the rose hips. A pheasant flew low over the river, no doubt to escape the estate shooting party. As Mike was my guest, I suggested he fish the weir pool and then try a swim on the side stream and three fishing spots upstream of the bridge.

Meanwhile, I was going roving. I would be chucking baits in lots of likely fishing spots. After a mug of tea and putting together our tackle, I walked with Mike upstream to show him where I thought the better fishing spots were. In the weir pool I pointed out the area he needed to fish his bait. Sadly, close to the hot spot was a large length of tree trunk making casting difficult. Leaving Mike in a good area for barbel, I made my way off downstream. Everywhere I stopped to fish, blackbirds and robins quickly appeared. I reckon there must be more robins per acre on the Wasing estate than any other area of the country. I didn't have just one robin; sometimes three would come and feed. I was surprised at this behaviour as robins are very territorial.

I fished every likely-looking spot; before moving onto the next one, I would introduce some crumbed bread. After two hours of fishing with no bites, I moved into what was possibly my tenth fishing spot alongside an ivy-clad tree trunk which lay at an angle in the water, creating a nice slack. Dropping a size 6 hook baited with a small cube of crust in the seam created by the fast and quiet water, I sat holding the rod, hoping above hope I might get a bite. A minute or so later, I felt the line tighten on my finger. Striking, I hooked into a nice fish, a brief struggle followed before I netted a barbel about four pounds. Success at last I thought. Releasing the fish, I made my way upstream to the car park for lunch, fishing the same spots I had fished on the way downstream.

One of my chosen swims screamed 'fish'. The river curved to my right, a stream flowed into the river from the opposite bank. Close to the stream mouth stood a large ivy-clad oak tree with several of its great roots plunging into the water. A big slack was created at the junction of the stream and river – certainly a place one would try for a perch. Baiting with two big lobworms, I cast across the river, dropping the bait into the fast-flowing water. By lifting and lowering the rod and allowing the reel to give line, I worked the baited hook into the slack. Within seconds there was a good rod-wrenching pull. Striking, I connected to a fish which I thought must have been a barbel. Every now and again the rod tip was savagely pulled downwards, forcing me to give line. The fish fought hard for about five minutes in the fast water. The pressure of the Avon action rod and 6lb breaking strain line were able to subdue a good chub of about four pounds.

On the way back to the car park I had two more chub averaging three pounds apiece, one on cheese paste the other on flake. In the car park Mike was waiting with two mugs of tea and the news that he hadn't had a fish. This surprised me, as Graeme Cook of Lancaster, fishing under identical conditions a few weeks before, had brace of barbel weighing 8lb and 8lb 8oz from the pool. I reckon there must have been half a dozen robins in the car park waiting for some morsel of food. The fog had gone; everything looked wonderful in the countryside. The sun shone down from an azure blue sky giving out it warming rays. The silver frost-covered riverside trees and bushes were regaining there normal, drab winter colour. As the frost melted, it looked as if a thousand water droplets were dancing on the water. Looking skywards, I could see a sparrow hawk being dive bombed and harassed by a couple of crows.

Lunch over, I started off in the swim above the bridge, quickly taking two chub about three pounds apiece on cheese paste. A biteless half an hour followed; time to move on downstream. I missed out the first swim dropping into the next one. Immediately, I had a good pull on crust and missed, then hooked and lost a fish minutes later and moved on. In the next spot I missed two bites then connected with a nice chub of 4lb 8oz. Introducing some mashed bread, I moved on upstream. As I was fishing the next swim David Hallet called me on my mobile, whilst chatting with him, I had a real savage take. Striking, I felt a good fish move off fast downstream I had to give line. "David, I have to go, I've got a good fish on!" Dropping the phone in my bag, I started to get the fish under control. It tried to get into some tree roots; I cramped on the pressure but I lost out, as everything went solid. After some minutes I had to pull for a break.

It was time for a mug of tea. Sitting in the car park, I marvelled at the beauty of the countryside, the trees might be bare, the vegetation brown and straw-coloured but it could easily have been a spring day in the warm sunshine. I probably had half an hour before the sun went below the riverside trees and the temperature would plummet. There would certainly be a severe frost tonight. Picking up my tackle and bait bag, I made my way upstream to fish my last swim of the day. I met up with Mike who was going for a brew. He would then fish the next swim upstream from me. At dusk a wren chattered loudly among the dead brown sedges, frost started covering my rod, bait bag and clothing. I missed four good pulls, caught two chub around three pounds. Mike had one chub he estimated at about three pounds. We stayed on the river until 8 p.m. then went off to Mrs Ingle who has a B&B in Midgham just a couple of miles from the river.

Lying in bed, I switched on the wireless for the latest on the cricket from Sri Lanka. It was good news for England as Trescothic and Vaughan were scoring runs. An hour later it was the same old story as wickets were falling. I cannot understand why we keep picking old has-beens like Hussein when we have guys like Paul Collingwood. Looking out the window, the prospects for a good day's fishing looked like the England batsmen – hopeless! There had been a heavy overnight frost, everything was white. It was foggy and drab-looking, and the cricket news was as dismal as the weather. After breakfast I cleaned the ice from the car and collected my bag, then Mike and me said our goodbyes to Jan and departed for the River Kennet just a mile or so away.

Pulling into the car park, visibility was down to fifty yards. It was teeth-chattering cold. It looked hopeless. I checked the water temperature, it was down to 37°F. An hour later the sun was shining, birds were chattering and the fog had gone. Mike decided he was going to fish the weir pool. Before he did so he waded out and removed the tree trunk that was causing problems in casting to the right spot. Collecting his tackle and some bread, he walked up the side stream to a likely-looking chub spot.

In ten minutes he had his first fish of the day, a chub about three pounds on legered crust. Meanwhile, I had gone off downstream, fishing several spots without success. At noon, the sun was shining; most of the fog had disappeared – it was a nice day to be in the countryside. As I walked downstream with the river on my left, I came across a small copse on my right. Among the dark, damp, dying trees and stumps, some laying at crazy angles, the ground was moist, with rough brown ferns, brambles, dead nettles and decaying reeds.

Frost and fog remained in the sheltered areas of the copse giving it a ghostly and eerie appearance. Suddenly, the quietness was dramatically shattered by the clattering of wings, as a cock pheasant soared skywards just a few feet in front of me. Crossing over a narrow bridge, I walked downstream some ten yards then checked the water temperature. I was amazed to see it was 40°F. Thinking I had made a mistake, I checked it again; it was the same reading, a rise of 3°F. Making my way downstream, I came across what looked a good fish-holding area. It was a well-worn spot. I decided on fishing this spot from an area some fifteen yards upstream. Any fish I hooked, I could then pull away from where I expected the fish to be shoaled up and, hopefully, I wouldn't spook the other fish which might be in the area.

Having fished several spots with crust and getting no bites, I decided this time to use a small piece of sausage meat. Within thirty seconds of rolling the bait downstream, I felt a slight pressure on the line. Striking, I connected with my first fish of the day. It turned out to be a barbel of about five pounds. I called up Mike and suggested he might like to try meat. He said he was already fishing that bait. In my next five casts, I had five bites which resulted in five more barbel all about five pounds. They were like peas in a pod. I fished on for another half-an-hour without a bite, and then decided it was time for lunch.

Back at the car park over Tuna Twist and sandwiches followed by a mug of tea, Mike and I discussed our morning's fishing. Mike told me he had caught two chub and three barbel, best at 9lb 12oz, on three small bits of meat, fished on a size 4 hook. Mike certainly deserved his fish by sticking it out in the area I suggested he try. A month ago I had three doubles from the weir pool. Then, of course, conditions had been perfect, with a high water temperature and a river with a foot of extra water with some colour. Mike's barbel was a magnificent fish, equal to a good double under such tough conditions.

After lunch I made my way back downstream and Mike walked back to the weir pool. Back in my swim, where I had caught the barbel before lunch, I threw in a dozen bits of meat. Within half-a-minute of casting out a meat-baited hook, I had a powerful pull on the rod tip connecting with a good fish. I didn't think it was another barbel. As I pulled the fish towards the net I could see it was a good chub. I thought it might go five pounds. Out with the scales and weigh bag. The chub went 5lb 3oz. I called Mike who said, "I'll be down in a minute or so." After a couple of pics, the fish was returned. I again checked water temperature: it was 40°F.

Having caught that good-size chub, I decided to bait with a big chunk of crust. Within minutes I had a chub in the net which weighed 5lb 10oz. Switching back to meat and rolling the bait downstream, I made four casts, connecting and landing two more chub both at 5lb 8oz, but sadly, losing two fish close to the net through the line breaking – or were they bite-offs? As dusk started to settle over the countryside, pheasants were going to roost; from the reeds, nettles and ivy-clad trees I could hear the wrens and robins chattering. I fished on in the darkness for half an hour until, with the mist closing in, I thought it was time to leave. I walked back alongside the copse where it was dark, dank, misty and cold;

A very successful and experienced angler Fred Haskins pictured with 15lb barbel from River Kennet.
Credit Fred Haskins

the frost was back with a vengeance. Back at the car, Mike told me he had caught some more barbel and chub. It had certainly been a very successful day for both of us in some of the most delightful countryside in England. We had certainly been more successful than England's batsmen in Sri Lanka.

The tackle I used was an Avon action rod, centre-pin reel, 6lb line and a size 6 or 4 hook, the weight I used depended on the flow of water. It was 1,2,or 3 LG shot lightly pinched on the line. Mike used a John Wilson quiver-tip rod, fixed-spool reel and 8lb line. His hooks were 6s and 4s. Mike often used 5 LG shot in the weir pool. Our varied baits were: bread crust, lobworms, sausage meat, luncheon meat, cheese paste and pellets. It was very noticeable that there was always a quite hectic feeding spell at dusk lasting some fifteen minutes.

Early on Wednesday morning, Will Carter called to say conditions on the River Kennet were looking good, I told him I would be down later in the day. Having sorted out some clothes, tackle and food, I loaded it all in the car. Indoors, I put some new Gamma 12lb line on one centre-pin reel, 6lb Gamma on my other reel. I rate these reels as the best for my type of fishing on small rivers. There isn't a spot on the Kennet where I cannot put bait.

When it comes to playing a fish I find the centre-pin reels are perfect, any pressure I want to put on the fish I can do so by using the pressure of my thumb on the reel. Should the fish dive I can easily slacken off. One item of equipment I decided to take on his trip were my chest-high waders. When the Kennet is over the bank you need them to help you to reach some swims, but you must wade with extreme caution and use a wading staff. I said to Kate, "That's it, I'll be home in a few days time. I'll give you a ring." About five hours later I was in the Warren car park on the Wasing Fishery. Having placed the thermometer in the water, I put the kettle on for a brew, at the same time warming up some food in my microwave, which works off the car battery. Conditions looked good: in many areas the river was over its banks, even flowing into the nearby woods. Checking the thermometer I got a reading of 47°F.

Lynne and Kevin of Tadley Angling
Berkshire

Colin Colley was catching barbel from a swim further upstream; Jon King and his brother Peter were in a swim near the car park, where Peter had a nice chub. By roving and trying several spots, I caught a few barbel, averaging six pounds, on sausage paste. At nine o'clock, with the rain sheeting down, I called it a day and went off to a local pub for dinner and to plan my next day's fishing.

Next morning, I called into Tadley Angling Centre for a chat with Kevin, a fresh brew and to collect a box of lobworms. On my way to the Warren beat on the Kennet, I passed over the River Enborne. It was bank-high and coloured. I thought to myself, "Any more rain and it will be over the bank." It was about 10 o'clock when I pulled into the Warren car park on the Wasing fishery, checking the water temperature I got a reading of 48°F. My plan was to fish my way downstream to the salmon hut, fishing all the likely-looking spots with sausage, cheese paste crust and lobworms. I would then fish my way back upstream on the opposite bank, again, trying all the interesting spots.

Tackle was a 12ft Avon rod, centre-pin reel, 12lb Gamma line. I tied on a size 4 Partridge F7 barbless hook. LG shot would be lightly pinched on the line, the number depending on the swim being fished. Without chest-high waders, many of my chosen swims would be off limits. I had a shoulder bag containing hooks, weights, scales, weigh net, bait and piece of sponge to sit or kneel on, along with my landing net. Wading through thigh-high water, I managed to reach a swim known by many as the 'Straight Run' – a stretch of water twenty yards long over gravel, with the occasional clump of water crowfoot with depth normally averaging three feet: today I had five to six feet. It's a swim where in the past I occasionally caught a good barbel. I baited the swim with a few pieces of cheese paste.

What made this swim look exceedingly good was the huge tree which had crashed into the water last winter; it lay at an angle of about forty-five degrees downstream, creating a lovely crease. I went further off downstream looking for other likely spots; I found five more spots I could try during the day and dropped in a few hook-bait samples at each spot. An hour later, I'm back at the 'Straight Run'. Pinching on 3 LG shot, I baited with cheese paste, and then cast out. Having found the weight staying put in the crease, I leant the rod against a tree trunk. Within a minute the rod tip pulled over. Striking, I connected with a fish, and after a short struggle I netted a barbel about eight pounds. In the next hour I had five more fish of between five and nine pounds. Thirty minutes later with no more bites, I moved off downstream where I had to wade through thigh-high water to reach my next swim.

An ivy-clad beech tree, with some branches trailing in the water, protruded well out over the river. I dropped a sausage paste-baited hook just downstream of the trailing branches and close to the bank. Fifteen minutes later I felt a light pluck, suddenly the line fell slack, and as I took line back onto the reel, I felt a savage pull. A powerful fish went off downstream. I followed it for a few yards then realised the fish was trying to get into some sunken tree branches. I cramped down on the fish, the rod bent as it's never bent before, and I could feel the line grating on some snag. I kept on as much pressure as I dare; this did the trick, as the fish moved upstream then stopped, sulking on the

Jon King

12lbs 6oz Barbel

bottom. A bit more pressure had the fish moving as I slowly gained line – sometimes just a few inches, but I was winning. Ten minutes later I had the fish coming up through the water. I grabbed the landing net and thrust it out into the flow where it was immediately pushed downstream and back to the bank by the force of the fast-flowing water.

Pulling the net towards me, I tried to lift the fish; slowly it came up and eventually it was on the surface; suddenly it dived and I was forced to lower the rod tip. Again I lifted. Once I had the fish on the surface again, above the net, I let it drop downstream into the net – then it was mine! After unhooking the fish, I placed the landing net in the water; I stuck a rod-rest between the V of the handle and net frame while I set about sorting out scales and weigh bag. Having zeroed the scales, I lifted the net from the water then placed the fish in the weight bag. The scale needle went to 12lb 6oz. After a couple of pictures, the fish was released.

With the water rising, I dropped some free offerings of hook baits into the swim, and then slowly made my way upstream to the car; it was time for a mug of tea and a sandwich. In one or two areas wading proved quite difficult, I made a mental note to keep a watch on the river level, should it rise a few more inches it would be too dangerous for wading. Back at the car I met Paul and John who were fishing the 'Fallen Tree' swim where they had both caught barbel on garlic-flavoured luncheon meat.

Half an hour later, I made my way back downstream to my last swim. In an hour I caught three more barbel, losing one through a hook pull. I then moved upstream to the 'Straight Run', within minutes I had a cracking barbel of 9lb 7oz quickly followed by a fish of 8lb. With the flow speed increasing and the river rising, I decided it was time to move upstream. A twenty minute walk upstream to the car, turned into a thirty to forty minute struggle through the rising, swirling water. In some spots I had to physically push my way through floating rubbish including some big branches. Back on terra firma I heaved a sigh of relief, it wasn't a walk I wanted to do again in a hurry especially in the darkness – it could prove dangerous.

As the river was fast-rising, I lost some of the swims I had planned to fish. I chose to fish the 'Salmon Hut' swim and walked down the gravel track; I was thankful I had chest-high waders. Just upstream of the 'Salmon Hut' I spotted a small eddy where the water was hardly moving. Kneeling down, I pinched on 4 LG shot 15in from the size 4 hook. Baiting with a chunk of cheese paste, I lowered it into a small eddy. Within thirty seconds I was hooked up to a good fish. After some heart-stopping moments, I was ready to net my catch: it went 10lb 3oz. Fishing several other likely-looking spots, I caught and lost some barbel – nothing big, probably the best around seven pounds.

I crossed over the river and moved upstream to fish a quiet bay, catching two more barbel about five pounds. With dusk falling, I cast a chunk of cheese paste behind a sunken hawthorn bush. Minutes later I had a light pluck, the line tightened and I soon had a good chub – no, a big chub! In the landing net it looked a six-pounder, when weighed it went 5lb 15oz. If it had been a six it would have given me a dozen six-pounders from the Kennet. It was time to call it a day; the rain was now sheeting down, the wind had increased to gale force – the going was certainly tough on my way upstream to the car. Occasionally, a big branch would fall from a tree. Back at the car, I chucked my gear into the back, and headed off for a hot shower some dinner and a mug of tea. Then it was bedtime.

I suppose it was around three in the afternoon when I arrived on the bank of the River Kennet; it carried a few inches of extra water. Far better than last year, when I refused to fish the rivers for much of the summer months, until there had been some appreciable rainfall – in fact, I did most of my fishing on the coast or in still waters. Thankfully, this year we are having, what I would best describe as, a normal summer; long may the rain showers continue!

All the trees were cloaked in their new coats of green, wild flowers were in profusion including some beautiful foxgloves. Pigeons cooed in the nearby trees, blackbirds wrens, robins, blue and great tits were hunting for caterpillars, while the green woodpeckers, with their dipping flight and maniacal laughing call, were going about their business. The flora and fauna mean as much to me as the fish I catch. In fact the whole ambience of my surroundings is most important to me. It was lovely to be back in the pristine wilderness of the beautiful Wasing Estate where the fishery manager John Butler and his staff have worked wonders in repairing all the damage and destruction caused by the storms of last winter. The only thing that saddens me are the number of people these days who bivvy-up on the banks of such delightful, small rivers.

I chose to fish for barbel, which is not the most difficult of fish to catch. I usually adopt the roving approach through the fishery, dropping sausage meat, bread crust or Pallatrax Jungle paste baits into every likely-looking spot. I matched a centre-pin reel holding Gamma 10lb line, with an Avon action rod designed for lines between 8 and 12lb. I reckon it was the perfect match for these fish. Having tied on a size 4 Partridge barbless hook with a five turned tucked blood knot, I lightly pinched an LG shot on the line some 15in from the hook. I was ready for the off.

Will Carter with one of his double figure fish

A hundreds yards upstream of the car park I could see the perfect crease, as the water flowed under some overhanging alder branches. Creeping slowly into position, I sat down then baited with a pigeon egg-size bit of sausage meat. I quietly lowered the bait into the swim and sat, enjoying my surroundings and the bird song. Ten minutes later I felt a light pluck, that wasn't a crayfish I thought. Suddenly the tip whacked round I was hooked up to my first barbel of the season. After a brief struggle I netted a nice fish of about six pounds, ending the session with three fish to about eight pounds. Back in the car park, I sat enjoying a mug of Yorkshire Gold tea thinking, nothing beats this great pastime. Tea finished I zipped up my sleeping bag, I thought about my next day's tench-fishing, then drifted off to sleep.

I left home around four o'clock in the morning for the two hundred-and-forty mile trip to Newbury. Pulling into the Wasing syndicate car park, I found I had the river to myself. Out with the gas stove and on with the kettle, at the same time I clipped my microwave oven to the car battery and warmed up some porridge. With breakfast over, it was time to get on with my chores before starting to fish.

On the Wasing water are several wooden bridges which I decided to cover with chicken wire. During the autumn and winter months these bridges become very slippery and dangerous. Two hours later the job was finished, members could now feel safe when crossing over the river. Back in the car park, I enjoyed a fresh brew with some buttered toast. Will Carter turned up to tell me about his successful barbel-fishing which included catching two doubles in less than thirty minutes.

We then parted company, Will went off to the Aldermaston beat on the Kennet, while I fished Woolhampton. On the advice of Will, I fished one rod with feeder and hair rigged pellets. As the feeder landed with a splash I imagined all the fish fleeing from the immediate area! My other rod was baited with a chunk of sausage meat, fished tight to the bank. In a three-hour session I caught seven barbel on meat, the average weight about six pounds. I had just one chub pick up the pellet-baited hook. Enough said.

The next day, Will and I fished the Aldermaston stretch of the Kennet. The weather was atrocious: gale force wind and heavy rain. We stuck it out for several hours, and then decided we were wasting our time. Will went off home; I made my way to a cafe where I had some dinner before making the long trek home. What made the journey home more enjoyable was the football on the radio.

A few days after arriving home from a trip to the River Wye, I got a call to say the River Kennet was well over the bank in many areas; roads were flooded, making driving dangerous – idiots driving far too fast in the prevailing conditions and not caring for other road users made things even worse.

Next day I left home at four in the morning, ensuring that I missed a lot of the rush hour. I was on the river bank at eight o'clock after a good drive, despite the rain and areas of flood water which occasionally slowed me up. I had the river to myself. During the day I roamed up and down the fishery trying my best to get a hook-up. I suppose it was just after 1 o'clock when I got my first fish weighing about six pounds, this was quickly followed by another of the same weight. About 3 o'clock I had a nice barbel of 8lb 5oz. At about 4 o'clock, Will Carter turned up for a couple of hour's fishing; as we sat in the darkness it started to rain, it didn't just rain, it sheeted down, it was like sitting under a shower. Very quickly Will and I looked as if we had been dunked in the river. Thankfully we were wearing good, waterproof clothing so we remained dry.

About 5 o'clock I had a light tap on the rod tip, I then felt another more positive take and struck. A powerful fish moved off downstream; the well-balanced tackle was able to master the fish which I quickly had under the rod tip. I slowly lifted, making sure I didn't jerk the line. (I see more fish lost when they are being lifted towards the net than any other time.) Pushing the landing net into the water, I gently raised the rod and pulled the fish to the surface. Then it was mine, the fish weighed 9lb 7oz; Will shot a couple of photographs before releasing the fish back in its watery kingdom. Half an hour later I packed up and went off for some hot food. The rain continued to sheet down for the next few hours, the wind increasing to gale force. I spent the evening reading the Angler's Mail and a novel.

Next day I found the river extremely high; the weather was spring-like with a light wind and warm sunshine. I roamed down through the Warren and Dalston beats, trying all my usual fishing spots, plus a couple of new ones that might hold fish. I was pleasantly surprised to catch one fish from a spot where there is normally just a few inches of water flowing under a willow bush; today the depth was probably near three feet. From having seen the area many times, I knew the bottom was fine, pea-sized gravel, it looked a good spot to try. In the first half-an-hour, I had a couple of barbel estimated at about seven pounds, both fish on sausage paste. I then moved downstream, where I chose to fish a bait under the bridge.

Within minutes I was hooked up to a fish that wanted to get back into the River Thames. After a ten minute struggle I got my first glimpse of a barbel. A couple of minutes later I had the fish in the net, it weighed 12lb 2oz: a very welcome fish in difficult conditions. I caught a few more fish averaging, I suppose, six pounds. With no more fish in the next hour, I made my way back to the car, then drove off to the Woolhampton beat.

After a break for a sandwich and a mug of tea, I was ready to go roving and try a few likely areas that might hold a fish. I was in luck. Within an hour of starting to fish, I hooked up to a big one; I thought it was a chub, or was it a foul-hooked fish? For ten minutes I played the unseen beast, and then suddenly, the hook slipped – I was gutted. I fished on for another hour catching two chub of 5lb 6oz and 6lb 3 oz. After an hour in the darkness with no more fish, I called it a day. I then headed off home, eventually arriving feeling very tired in the early hours of the morning. Despite the long drive it had been a good trip.

What I did learn from this trip was: don't take risks. We must be aware at all times when we are on the river bank, under flood conditions, that the bank can become very unstable, I had a narrow escape when talking with Will Carter on the phone, the section of bank I was standing on started to tremble, I smartly moved back. Within a minute, a chunk of river bank disappeared in the swirling water of the Kennet. On another occasion a huge limb of a tree crashed into the water, missing me and my rods by about three feet. On several occasions when the wind increased, I felt uneasy sitting close to the swaying trees, so I packed up

Around noon on the Monday I got a call from Will Carter saying the river was spot-on, with two feet of extra water and a water temperature of 50°F. "Can you get down?"

I said "Yes, on my way."

I headed off to Brimpton Mill on the Kennet, planning to fish the weir pool. Walking upstream between willows, alders and brambles, the noise of the weir pool increased, as millions of gallons of creamy, foaming spray-lashed water crashed down fifteen feet into the pool – the sound was awesome. Wagtails flitted to and fro, often settling on some piece of floating rubbish which was flowing in all directions; looking up the pool I could see camp sheathing and rotting

Martin with a double figure Barbel from Brimpton Weir Pool

piles. Two carriers flow in from the left-hand bank.

Weir pools are not for the faint-hearted or those of a nervous disposition. It can be quite a frightening experience, especially in the darkness. Sixty feet back from the water's edge, on the right-hand bank, stands an old mill-house; how I would like to have lived there and experienced all its history and character.

I used a soft action Avon rod, with a centre pin reel; these reels are not a fashion item, but a most efficient tool. I have fifty yards of 12lb line to which I attach a size 4, 6 or 8 barbless hook, depending on the bait; at no time have I felt my gear wasn't up to the job. Once hooked, I want the fish quickly in the net. My bait list today is: bread crust, flake, sausage meat and lobworms; the first two baits have accounted for a lot of chub and barbel. Without a shadow of a doubt, crust or flake is usually my number-one-choice bait. I started using bread back in the late 1940s, the days of bamboo rods, with a bored bullet stopped between four and fifteen inches from the hook by a split shot, depending on the water temperature and bait. I don't see any reason to change. Today it's LG shot on the line, between two and fifteen inches from the hook with carbon fibre rods.

Setting down my bait bag and tackle, I checked the water temperature 49°F: conditions couldn't be better. As I looked at the water-flow I decided I would need 5 LG shot pinched on the line 6in from the hook. Bait was a big chunk of crust. I made a long cast up the pool, the bait dropped into the creamy, boiling, white water. I held the rod high; within minutes I had my first fish, then it was gone. Rebaiting, I cast to the same area. I suppose it was ten minutes later when the line tightened over my index finger. Striking, I felt a dead weight for some two seconds. Suddenly the tip was savagely pulled down, the reel screeched. After a give-and-take struggle my first barbel of about six pounds was netted. In the next hour or so I had four more barbel averaging five to six pounds. Then all went quiet; I couldn't buy a bite.

After a fishless half-an-hour, I decided on a bait change. With some colour in the water I decided on sausage meat; taking off one of the LGs I moved the other LGs a foot up the line, then baited with a pigeon-egg size lump of meat which was cast into a pool to the left of a rotting wooden pile outside the white water. As the bait slowly moved around I could feel something plucking the bait, "Signal crayfish." I thought, and then had other ideas – probably a barbel. As the tension increased, I wound down then pulled back hard. A good fish was hooked which didn't hang about as it charged out of the quiet water into the foaming water of the pool; I had to take line in quickly. Cramping on the pressure I forced the fish towards me and the quieter water, where it slogged away under the rod tip, occasionally a few feet of line got taken, but was quickly recovered. Five minutes and the fish was netted.

"Could this be a double, I thought?" It was weighed-in at 10lb 10oz. By now a fine rain was falling but I didn't care. I quickly had another Kennet double at 11lb 5oz; time to head for the car for a fresh brew and some food. Lunch break over, it was back to the pool.

This time I baited with a big chunk of flake, my thinking being that the flake would rise and fall like a free offering, hopefully lasting a bit longer from the attention of the crays. Within minutes a good fish was hooked, a few anxious moments followed before I had another double-figure barbel in the net weighing 10lb 2oz. A fishless two hours followed. It was time to try other swims. Before leaving, I baited the pool with lots of mashed bread. I chose to fish the carrier in the next hour-and-a-half; I roved around taking four nice chub between three-and-half and four pounds, all on crust. As I walked back to the car, I met another member who had travelled from Hartford Cambridgeshire. Stopping for a chat, he told me he hadn't had a bite all day, I suggested he use bread. He said, "I don't have any." I gave him a loaf then showed him my tackle set-up. Ten minutes later he had his first chub, a nice fish around four pounds. I continued my way back to the car for a fresh brew, then returned to the pool.

Within minutes I had a good pull on crust, hooking into a good fish which stayed on the bottom, I had to cramp on the pressure and drag the fish slowly down the pool. Occasionally having to give line, a few seconds later I got it back, plus a bit more. I had visions of a very big fish, perhaps fifteen pounds. Some minutes later the fish was netted. The scales said 10lb 6oz – how lucky can you get – four doubles in a session. I still had four or five hours in the darkness. In the fading light I decided on another mug of tea.

Returning to the pool, I again baited with crust, catching several more barbels. What amazed me was, the average size of these fish; they were probably no more than three pounds and like peas in a pod. About seven o'clock I felt the line tighten over my finger, striking hard I connected with a heavy, powerful fish. I didn't feel it was a barbel, but was it a big chub. After a few heart-stopping moments I pulled a good fish over the net. Switching on my head lamp, I could see I had a big, out-of-season, brown trout.

Another member watching said, "I've never seen such a big brown-trout, I'd like to hook that on a fly!" It was quickly weighed at 5lb 8oz and released. Hopefully, a fly-fisher will catch it next summer. What staggered both of us was, an hour later the same fish was caught again on a chunk of crust. It had been a great session. Meanwhile the Hartford angler, fishing on in the darkness, caught two barbel and five good chub. After spending the night in my car I travelled back home, a trip of about 500 miles and well worth the effort.

One of my great pleasures in life is helping another angler catch a good fish or a few fish. One such angler was Ron Jackson, a seventy-one year old pensioner, he wanted my help in his quest to catch a barbel, Ron, a Cockney, was born in Hackney London and evacuated to Norfolk during the war. In 1945 he was back to London, playing football, cricket and boxing for his school and Eton Manor BC, in those days, one of the top clubs. In 1960 he moved to the new town of Stevenage joining the Woodsman Angling Club, where he learnt to fish. Then, for twenty years, Crown Green Bowling took over from fishing. In 2007 he returned to fishing, but not catching much, he sought help via Google, finding my website. In his letter he stated, "angling has changed so much, I need your help and advice." I replied very quickly, then I phoned him to offer a day's fishing in return for a donation to one of my charities and a date was arranged.

With a water temperature of 41°F, bright, sunny weather with an easterly wind, conditions couldn't have been worse, but I had to try and make this pensioner's dream come true: Ron was desperate for a barbel.

In the Warren car park I was joined by Ron, Will Carter and Brendan Ince. First job: on with the kettle. Waiting for it to boil, we discussed plans for the day. I said, "It will be very hard, fishing today, even a bite will be reward enough but I'll do my best. We won't be sitting in one spot but roving the river trying all the likely-looking spots." I made up a two piece rod with a flexible top joint and a fixed spool reel and 10lb Gamma line to which I tied a size 4 hook.

Baits would be bread, sausage and cheese paste, if these didn't work, I had a few lobworms. Despite the horrid conditions I felt Ron might catch a chub, if not a barbel. As Ron is a bit unsteady on his legs, I picked up his gear, my bag of tricks, landing net and rod rest, and we moved off down the frozen, frost-covered bank, with me pointing out several areas worth fishing under better conditions. Our first try was the well known 'Ivy Tree Swim', with no bites after twenty minutes we moved on.

Reaching 'The Willows' I told Ron that we were going to fish this well known chub holding-area for half an hour, where I reckoned he stood a good chance of a hook-up. Having made sure he was safely seated, I showed him how to bait with bread crust. I then dropped the bread so it would roll under an overhanging willow tree. Within twenty minutes the rod tip pulled round an inch, ten seconds later it pulled round in a determined fashion. Ron's answering strike connected with a good fish. Within seconds Will Carter picked up the landing net while I helped Ron to his feet and issued instructions on playing the first fish of the session.

A few minutes later Will had a big chub in the landing net, it weighed 6lb. Taking Ron's hand, I said, "Well done, that's a big fish!" The smile on his face said it all.

Leaving 'The Willows', we moved downstream to 'The Beeches'. Bread crust was the bait; I cast out so the bait came to rest close to an island of rubbish. Within ten minutes Ron had made a strike and was into another fish. I immediately realised he was hooked-up to that dream barbel. After a five minute struggle, I netted his first barbel: a fish weighing 4–5lb. We took a quick picture then watched it swim off strongly.

I cast another chunk of crust out into the fast, swirling water allowing the bait to settle in a nice crease. "With luck Ron you should get another fish." I suppose twenty minutes went by before the rod top whacked round in a most savage fashion. Ron was hooked-up to a big, powerful fish. For several minutes it was give-and-take. I suppose ten minutes had gone before I was able to net a barbel which I though might weigh ten pounds. On the scales it weighed 9lb 6oz. Though not quite a double, it was a great fish. Ron flopped down in his chair, completely shattered, with a big grin and two sparkling eyes. He was hardly able to speak for a few minutes. After some pictures we watched the fish swim off. Ron said, "I'm shattered, my arms ache and I am ready for home!" We called it a day. Back home in Lancashire I got a lovely letter from Ron which read:

> "Dear Martin, I am over the moon with meeting you and all the advice you imparted to me. The result of the day's fishing was beyond my wildest dreams and has only just begun to sink in. I will never forget you and the day's fishing as long as I live. Thank you once again Martin.
>
> All the best, Ron."

Reward enough for me. Ron also sent a cheque for £50 to Ribble Valley Crossroad Care, one of the charities I support.

As I was putting together the tackle and bait requirements for a week-long fishing session on the rivers Bain, Upper Ouse and Kennet, the telephone sounded its strident note. Picking up, I said, "Hello there." I heard Kevin Rolls say, "Martin, the Kennet is up a foot with a rising water temperature it should be good fishing." "Thanks mate," I said, "I'll be down early tomorrow morning." I hung up. Change of plans. It was to be the Kennet for Sunday, Monday and back home late on Tuesday evening. Wednesday I had to work on a travel feature, I would go back to the Kennet on Thursday morning, if the fishing was good. My travelling companion for the first three days was a young Martin James who works for the EA. He would also do the driving on this trip. Martin deserves the praise of every angler for spending so much time helping the beginners to this fine sport.

Arriving on the banks of the Kennet at Brimpton a Wasing fisheries syndicate water, we were surprised to find just one vehicle in the car park. Checking the water temperature we got a reading of 47°F which eventually reached 53°F by the Tuesday morning. I gave Martin the choice of swims; he immediately said, "I'll fish the weir pool." I decided to fish the Warren beat using a roving approach; if I thought a swim needed to be fished for an hour or two I would do so. Martin was equipped for anything, with a selection of good quality tackle and a wide variety of baits: pellets, boilies, bread and meat. On the previous evening, Martin, instead of going off to the pub, had stayed indoors making up small PVA bags of small pellets for attaching to his line, which would ensure the free offering would be around the hook bait.

I made up two Avon action rods with centre-pin reels and 6lb BS line, I had a sliding link on one outfit with some 15in between the leger stop and hook for fishing meat and lobworms. My crust-fishing outfit had two LG shot pinched lightly on the line about 4in from a size 6 hook. Having made up our tackle, we then sorted out some baits, and then sat enjoying some freshly made tea and sandwiches before going our separate ways.

The first swim I chose to fish was 'Bramble Bend' so named because of the huge spread of brambles. Within a couple of minutes I had a chub in the net about three pounds which had grabbed a chunk of bread, fished tight to the bank. I fished on for another fifteen minutes but, with no further interest, I moved on downstream towards the 'Salmon Hut'. As I moved downstream I dropped chunks of crust into every likely-looking spot. In the two hours, I had five good bites catching two chub about three pounds apiece and a barbel about six pounds. On my way back upstream to the car park I fished sausage meat or lobworms taking just one barbel about six pounds.

In the car park I met Phil who was sorting out his tackle in the 'Bridge Swim'. "How are you doing Phil?" I asked. "I've lost two barbel in a snag, they felt like good fish." We chatted for a while. As I was leaving I said, "Would you like a fresh brew?"

"Yes please," said Phil. While waiting for the kettle to boil, I sorted out dinner, putting a big saucepan of beef stew on the other stove to heat through slowly. Two swims upstream, another angler had caught three barbel on pellet bait. Young Martin arrived saying, "I haven't had a bite in the weir pool." As we sat enjoying our tea, we discussed the prospects for the evening. Martin was going back to the weir pool for an hour then move downstream to one of the board swims. I was going downstream and fish a swim near the 'Salmon Hut'.

Dinner finished, we moved off to our separate swims. Arriving at my chosen fishing spot, I introduced two large balls of mashed bread and a dozen pieces of sausage meat, baiting with meat, I cast downstream some ten yards, then sat holding the rod. Ten minutes later I had a savage take, connecting with a powerful fish which tried to reach some sunken branches, but my control of the well-balanced tackle stopped any chance of that happening. I quickly had the barbel in the net.

A lovely, golden-coloured fish of about seven pounds, in fact, one of the nicest barbel I have ever seen. In the next hour I had two more fish a chub about four pounds and a barbel about five pounds. Having fished on for another hour without a bite, I called it a day. Back at the car park, I met up with Martin who had one chub from one of the board swims. Stowing our tackle in the car, we made our way to the B&B where delightful Jan made us some tea and toast. I rolled into bed completely shattered and slept through until 7.30 a.m. the next morning.

After a good breakfast, we drove back to the car park to find two other vehicles had arrived. Collecting our tackle, Martin decided to fish the weir pool again, while I went off downstream. The water was well coloured and the water temperature had gone up to 50°F. It was a warm, muggy day; in fact, prospects couldn't have been better. I roved up and downstream fishing various swims with bread, lobworms and sausage meat, catching three chub and seven barbel which included a couple of eight pound-plus fish. Making my way upstream for dinner, I decided to drop a bit of crust into a spot where two opposing flows of water created a quiet spot tight to the bank. It was about the size of a dinner tray. Known in my book as the 'Point Swim' it's often produced a fish on those days when it's been a struggle to catch. Within seconds of casting out, the rod tip pulled round in a slow, determined manner.

Striking, I hooked a barbel, and after a good give-and-take tussle for about three or four minutes, I was able to net barbel number eight weighing about six pounds. From experience, I knew it was a waste of time continuing to fish on in this swim. On my way to the car park I caught a chub from Bramble Bend about four pounds. During the session I had seen a kingfisher, treecreeper, jay, several robins, wrens and blackbirds. Pheasants were about in profusion now the shooting season had ended. Over dinner Martin and I discussed our fishing. Martin had lost a good barbel, caught a smaller barbel and a chub. One member, fishing pellets, had six good barbel, while another member, fishing caster and feeding hemp, had caught four barbel and six chub. We decided to fish until about 9 p.m. Martin choosing to fish a swim just downstream of the weir pool, while I was going downstream to fish a swim which had I been baiting with mashed bread, chopped lobworms and sausage meat.

I checked the water temperature; it was now 51° F with an air temperature of 54°F. The barbel were in a feeding frenzy. I lost count after barbel number 13 or 14 – perhaps it was number fifteen, I don't know. I do know I had three, eight pound and two nine pound-plus fish. Bread, meat and lobworms were all successful baits. The weather was that warm I didn't even put on my top coat. I was quite disappointed at having to leave feeding fish and head to the B&B at about 9.30 pm.

Tuesday morning, while watching the weather forecast on breakfast television, the announcer said, "A severe weather warning is in operation for Cumbria and Lancashire." We decided we would leave for home by lunchtime and not stay until after teatime. Back on the river the water level had dropped a few inches, some of the colour had gone out of the water. But the water temperature had gone up to 53°F. Martin followed my example of roving from swim to swim,

As I arrived at the 'Point Swim' I could see Martin crouched low, fishing a classic glide on the opposite bank. Moving into position, I dropped a chunk of crust into the hot spot. Within thirty seconds I had a barbel of about five pounds. Martin couldn't believe his eyes; he had just fished the swim without success. In this swim the bait has to be dropped with pinpoint accuracy, or you don't get a take. During the short morning session I had two barbel and three chub. It had been a great fishing-session in perfect conditions.

Not only a great lady but also a very good angler, Karen Smyth with
a 25lb 6 oz river Kennet carp. Credit Paul Smyth

For several months Paul Towers has been writing to me about the problems of catching big River Hull chub – and then he hit gold! This is his story:

O n this day, 2 January 2008 the weather was cold, it felt like it could snow. The outside temperature was a chilling 4°F. I had a few hours to spare and wondered if I should go and fish the river or stay warm indoors, drinking tea. I decided to go fishing.

Soon I was tramping across rain -odden ground, ankle deep in mud, with the cold wind biting and making my eyes water. It was quite late in the day so I'd decided to travel light, taking only rod, reel, landing net and a small trout bag containing hooks, shot, bait and a few accessories. I didn't take a chair or even a rod rest. This was fishing minimalist style!

I decided to bait three swims and fish them in turn, each swim receiving two balls of mashed bread. I watched them slowly disintegrate as they fell through the muddy water, and made a mental note of each swim. I threaded 6lb line through the rings of my Avon quiver rod then tied on a size 6 hook with 3 LG shot. Crust was the bait, Martin James style – simple but effective!

I cast out into the first swim, allowing the line to form a bow in the current, and gently held the line, feeling for bites. Like a heron I stayed poised, willing a fish to take the bait. Fifteen minutes later I was still biteless. I moved on to swim number two, getting the same result and wondered if I should move on or stay a little longer. An icy blast of wind made up my mind for me and I scrambled along the bank to swim number three.

The light was fading fast and angry clouds were gathering in the cold grey sky as the bait landed with a plop in the last swim. Ten minutes later the rod top dropped back and I felt a small tug on the line. I lifted the rod sharply and felt solid resistance on the end. This was not weed I'd hooked; it was an unseen force, which bored deeply across the river. I applied pressure and the rod hooped right over as I tried to pump the fish upstream. I thought I'd hooked one of the river's barbel.

The fish began to tire but it was not over yet. It kited towards the near bank as it tried to bury itself in the reeds, looking for any opportunity to shed the hook. I reached out over the water trying to lever the fish from the reeds, my rod bent at an alarming angle but at last the fish was free and coming up in the water. It tried to turn again causing the water to mushroom and boil but then suddenly it surfaced and I nearly fell in the river with shock! I could not believe the size of this fish. It was a massive chub. I prayed for the tackle to hold as I guided the fish across the net. I let it rest in the margins for a while until I got myself together. I weighed the chub: the scales registered almost 6lb. What a fish! Suddenly, all the hard work became worthwhile. I took one last look at this wonderful fish, trying to remember all its detail, and then carefully released it back into its cold watery home.

It paused for a moment, and then silently disappeared into the murky depths.

Many thanks to Martin James for his help; his advice helped me to catch this truly magnificent fish.

After a delightful weeks fly fishing in Rossshire on the Fairburn Estates water for brown trout and a nearby loch for pike, it was time to travel south to fish the River Wye near Ross-on-Wye, I had booked 2 nights B&B. Half a mile away was the White Lion a delightful inn, which served food, the soups were extremely delightful. 2 days before my arrival the River Wye had 17 feet of water, no chance of fishing in those conditions.

Driving into Ross I was greeted by a river the colour of a thick khaki coloured soup and way over the fields. Fishing was out of the question. I spent a couple of days bird watching chatting with Kevin in Wye Angling a tackle shop in Ross situated in Crofts Court off Broad Street not too far from W H Smiths. I also spent some valuable time with my daughter Sharon her husband Greg and my granddaughter Jessica who were over from Dubai for a few days. If you are planning to fish at Ross I can recommend the best eating place in town is, without a doubt, the Hunky Dory café in Broad Street, where Sallyann Moss and her team will ensure you have a pleasant eating experience. Tel 01989 764478. Just down the street is the Golden Crust Traditional Bakery. Their wholemeal vegetable pasties and bread are excellent.

Thankfully we only had a few light showers and with the river dropping I thought I might get the chance to fish despite a few football size puddles on the riverside banks I felt I could find a couple of suitable swims. Arrangements were made for Kate to go off shopping with Sharon Greg and Jessica leaving me to fish the powerful river Wye.

Weather conditions on Wednesday morning were good with plenty of cloud cover and a warm breeze with the river between its banks. My mates Will Carter, Martin Salisbury and I joined the Ross angling club this season, it was a wise choice. I had over a dozen good swims to fish in the first hundred yards of river bank. I was spoilt for choice. I chose to fish 2 Harrison 12 foot Triptych rods matched with Shimano baitrunner reels with Gamma 12lb breaking strain line, this is an excellent abrasion resistant line, I have used this line now for about six years and I cannot fault it qualities. On one rod I chose a stonze weight on a running link stopped 18 inches from the size 4 hook, on this occasion I chose to fish a Pallatrax braided hook link. This was my luncheon and sausage meat set up. On my second rod I chose to fish an inline Stonze set up with a short braided link of 8 inches with a size 10 hook and a short hair, to which I would superglue to 2 Ellipse pellets back to back, a pva bag of micro-mix pellets attached a foot above the hook bait.

The first swim I chose was at the mouth of a feeder stream, chosen on the advice of the guys from Wye Angling, using a large bait dropper I put in a pint of hemp with some broken bits of meat. I fished the two upstream swims just over the second drop off where the water flowed over a smooth bottom which I reckoned was clay. In both swims, at the upstream end of the swims I had a very large willow bush which offered cover and shelter. Having baited both swims with hemp and mini pellets I left the baited areas alone for an hour. It was time for a brew, sandwich and catch up with the news in the Anglers Mail. I suppose I had been sitting in the stream mouth swim for some 45 minutes when a fish rolled close to the bank, an encouraging sign.

I suppose it was around 11am when I cast out a chunk of meat into the mouth of the stream, twenty minutes later the rod tip whacked over and I found myself hook up to a fast moving fish which shot out into the main flow of the river. As it did so the rod top got pulled over savagely. Barbel I thought, but I was wrong as a fish rolled on the surface some twenty yards downstream. With the stream blocking any movement downstream I had to pump the fish towards me. Not an easy task in the fast swirling water. Thankfully all the knots held and after about 10 minutes I netted a common carp estimated at about 12lbs. After removing the hook I turned the fish loose to hopefully grow into a 20lb fish.

I fished on for about an hour during which I had another fresh brew, but no more bites. I didn't see any fish movements or taps on the rod tip. It was time to move, after putting in half a pint of hemp and some more chunks of meat, I moved upstream to swim number 2. I chose to fish with 2 rods one baited with meat which I positioned at the extreme downstream range of the swim downstream of the swim. My second rod baited with Ellipse pellets with a PVA bag of small pellets clipped on the line close to the Stonze weight. This was cast and positioned upstream at the end of the trailing willow branches.

I suppose half an hour must have passed when the upstream rod tip sprung back, the line went slack, and quickly picking up the rod, I tightened the line before striking, though I reckon the fish had hooked itself. Soon my first barbel of the session was in the net a nicely coloured fish estimated at 6lbs. As I was releasing the fish my downstream rod whacked round, I was thankful I was using a bait runner otherwise I would have lost my outfit. Five minutes later fish number 2 was in the net, I estimated the fish to be about 6lbs. In fact both barbel were like peas in a pod. During the next hour I had 5 bites 2 missed and 3 fish landed, two about 6lbs the other fish would probably have gone 8lbs plus. For the next 3 hours I had just 1 bite which I missed. Though it did give me plenty of time to make several fresh brews and watch the kingfishers which seemed to be around in profusion. I packed up about 5pm then went off for some food before driving home. A journey of 190 miles which I completed in just under 3hours. For company I had the England football match where it was nice to hear Walcott get his hat trick.

My best Barbel of the day

*I*t was June 1941 when I, as a four year old, was first taken fishing by my Uncle Len; I caught seven small rudd from a clay pit, close to the Alpha cement works on Cliff Marshes in Kent. For the next few years I fished with a few boyhood friends, older anglers, home from the war, would also take me, as did uncles and grandfathers.

In 1947 I moved to senior school where I was given my first bicycle – my passport to freedom; I would often cycle to fishing venues 10–15 miles or more from home. One day, I chose to fish Windmill clay pit, close to where I caught my first fish. Arriving an hour after dawn, I float-fished with bread, catching some big rudd, in fact to me, they were giant rudd. I had never seen such big and gorgeous fish.

I reckon every one must have weighed over a pound. After a couple of hours I had caught eleven of these big fish, we counted our fish in those days and, sadly, retained them in a keep net; I was then approached by a very friendly-looking man who said, "Can I see your membership card." I told him I didn't have one and wanted to buy a day ticket, offering him half a crown. I was told, "It's private fishing." I would have to join the club to fish the water. Within a week I was the proud owner of a membership card for Kingfisher Angling and Preservation Society.

They had two clay pits on Cliff marshes. I could fish Laughing Waters near Cobham, reputed to hold monster pike, though it did contain some good perch and common carp. I could fish Paddlesworth Lake and stretches of the River Beult. I had many happy years fishing those waters.

Recently, I relived those days of my boyhood when I visited my brother Tom and his wife Lynne in East Anglia, where they have an equestrian centre and riding school with some fifty-odd horses, both in stables and grazing.

Across the track from their home was an old clay pit dug in 1880 for the blue clay; it was one of only two pits in the area where it was possible to excavate the blue clay used in brick-making in those far-off days. The pit was roughly an acre to an acre and a half; the clear water averaged around 8–10 feet deep. There was an abundance of Norfolk reed and reed mace with its brown mace-like fluffy head, often mistakenly called bulrushes.

Adding to the beauty of the water were some large areas of water lilies. In the shallows I could see water starwort and marsh pennywort, in the deeper water was an abundance of spiked water-milfoil where the tench would dive for freedom when hooked. Around the irregularly shaped pit were lots of trees: ash, oak, willow; lots of nettles – the food for butterflies, red campion, and bramble bushes loaded with fruit.

Catching Rudd such as this

This old pit contained rudd,

roach, perch, tench, carp, perch and pike – as always I was told about the mythical monster in the form of carp weighing fifty pounds, I can't say it didn't exist, though I didn't see any evidence. It's a water of unknown quality, steeped in mystery and one that makes you feel full of confidence directly you go down the long drive under the oak and beech trees. Though I didn't see any evidence of big carp, perch or pike, I did see rudd to probably two pounds.

I caught some lovely rudd to just over a pound with plenty of tench, the best weighing just less than four pounds. I also watched a tench estimated at seven pound-plus roll close to the far bank. I chose to float fish using a 13ft rod, centre-pin reel with 4lb Gamma line with a size 12 Pallatrax hook tied direct to the line. To complete my set-up I chose a 4 AA shot, waggler float, 3 shot bunched 9in from the hook, another AA shot 3in from the hook. Bait and groundbait was three loaves of bread, I would fish a cube of crust or flake fished over mashed bread. Plumbing the depth, I set the float so the bait was fished hard on the bottom.

In the first couple of hours I had dozens of roach and rudd which were quick to grab the crust or flake-baited hook on the drop, long before it reached the bottom. After a couple of hours I caught my first tench of about three pounds. Though I wasn't catching big fish I was having a lot of fun and, let's be honest, that's what fishing should be all about. Around one o'clock Kate shouted across that it was lunchtime. All I had to do was bring in my gear take the bait off the hook, and then walked the few yards back to Tom and Lynne's. After an hour's break I was back on the water where I continued to catch roach, rudd and tench. During my day-long session I had twenty odd tench the best about four pounds. There were times when I thought I had hooked a bigger fish only to find it had buried itself in the thick, spiked water-milfoil. The great thing about this aquatic weed is, it's a soft weed and you can usually pull the fish free.

Tom and Lynne, with Tom's Wedding Anniversary Present

When I was at school I fished junior matches with Wingets AC, Maidstone Victory Angling and Medway Preservation Society also Kingfisher Angling Society, occasionally we fished inter school matches. I found these very rewarding, where often experienced adults anglers would coach us, I was very fortunate to have rod builder Mr. Clarkson, Denise Trim, Harry Rowland's Len Cuckoo Mr. Roberts and Mr. Wilson who took me under their wing showing me many ways to catch to fish.

Sometime in the late 1950's or early 60's I thought there should a junior match fishing league for the present generation of young anglers. I spoke to my editor about this who immediately agreed. In about six weeks we had organised a huge Schools winter angling league with dozens of schools, public and private, in the county of Kent entering teams.

We had two sections. One for an age group of 11-13 year olds. The other for those of 14-17 years. Every other Saturday from October through to the end of January, hundreds of youngsters along with some fifteen or more teachers and many parents would turn out on the banks of the river Medway in Maidstone either fishing or helping.

It was a great success featured on TV, the radio and both the National and angling press covered the events. The newspaper would have two sometime three photographers covering the event and several pages of pictures and text. One year, following a big pollution incident at Yalding, several miles of the river Medway was badly polluted, everything died. No fishing was possible and it looked as if the schools league wouldn't continue. It did, the proprietor and editor of Parrett and Neves newspapers told me to book a fleet of coaches and all the competitors and helpers were bussed off to the River Stour.

You see my editor realised that children sell newspapers. If your child appears in the local paper, you along with, grannies and aunties dash off to the paper shop. Hence children sell newspapers. Today's angling press do very little for youngsters. Where is today's Kingfisher Guild for boys and girls? Thirty years after the schools angling league, I walked into Doughty's tackle shop in Rochester where Howard Henbest, one of those youngsters, now a family man and a technician with BT was buying some bait. Turning to the man behind the counter Howard said "Martin showed me and my friends along with hundreds of other kids how to become successful anglers and that's why we are doing it today."

Many of those boys were to become excellent big fish and top match anglers the likes of John Larraman who fished for one of the countries top match fishing teams. When John was16 years of age I had the pleasure of presenting him with the Chatham Observer newspaper Fish of the Year Award for catching a 2-4-0 roach from the River Medway, other prize winning anglers who I took fishing were Lou Page, Howard Henbest, Tony Smith, Bill Cutting, Pete Burstow and Brian Hodges to name just a few.

Another series of competitions for boys and girls was sponsored by Medway Council. Councillor Fred Hepper the leader of the council at the time and an avid angler as was his son Gary, approached me to run a series of competitions to be fished during the school summer holidays. Once again they were a success.

Several heats were run during a three week period; those in the first three places would then

1 Nigel, ready to strike

3 Fish in the net

2 Hook up

4 Unhooking the fish

get a place in the grand final. My son Nigel took part in these competitions and winning though to the final using his own initiative and angling skills. Defiantly not the milkman's kid, he certainly had all my angling genes. Lou Page gave up a lot of his time coaching Nigel which certainly helped as Lou was a very proficient angler.

The press once again showed great interest reporting on the heats and the final with lots of coverage. What impressed me were Lou Page and Howard Henbest stepping forward to help out as stewards for the heats and the final. A few years previously they had been taking part in school boy competitions themselves.

In the early 1990's I organised some fishing days for beginners in conjunction with Ribble Valley BC who supplied 2 attendants from the local swimming baths, PC Dave Fish of the Lancashire Constabulary helped out, along with some of the Dads. On one occasion I had some ninety boys and girls but I didn't have a single problem. The only problems I had were some obnoxious adults who decided they were going swimming.

PC Fish soon stopped that. What amazed me were the large number of Mums who sat on the river bank watching their children river dipping, tying knots and casting floats and legers. Sadly I had to call a halt, as I couldn't get enough anglers to give me a helping hand. When I asked for help I was asked how much are you paying? When I said "We do it for free" They didn't want to know. How selfish some people are.

How many times have you heard? "We've got nothing to do and nowhere to go" We hear it often. –, to help combat Anti-Social-Behavior (ASB) and youth nuisance during the extended school summer holidays The Pendle Fishing Buddies Angling Club (PFBAC) was set up by the local West Craven neighborhood policing team headed by PC Mark Hyde of the Lancashire Constabulary in 2006. It was an immediate success.

I got involved by promoting the scheme on my angling show on BBC Radio Lancashire, often having Mark on the programme. I was in the unique position of having 2 miles of River Ribble fishing upstream of Mitton Bridge in Lancashire, water known for its game fishing with salmon, sea trout and brown trout. It also had a good head of chub dace and grayling.

When the salmon season ended October 31st I would invite members of Pendle Fishing Buddies Angling Club (PFBAC) to come and fish, I could always rely on Brendan Ince and Mick Holgate to give a helping hand, teaching the youngsters how to catch chub.

The last thing the police wanted was to be seen to be rewarding bad behavior and so young people were referred from various agencies and different backgrounds. Some were known to the police for being involved in 'low level' crime and ASB, but just as many were referred by schools, parents and the police for doing something positive in the community or for doing well at school.

In 2008 PC Mark Hyde of the Lancashire Constabulary based in Barnoldswick joined forces with Col Sgt Tam Miller of the British Army Recruiting Office in Burnley, they pooled their

resources to get kids off the streets, away from the TV or PC and show them the delights of the countryside. It's worked and many parents have noticed the differences in their children's behaviour.

At all the events I attend the behaviour is excellent, I noticed every boy and girl would say please and thank you when it was needed. Groups of 12 boys and girls attend a Kingfisher course at Newrad Fishery Darwen where they are taught in the

A group of Pendle Buddies

classroom and at the waterside. Having passed various written tests they get presented with a Kingfisher Certificate. When I attend the prize presentation many Mums and Dads will say my John, Brian, Jean or Anne now spends more time reading and doing their homework often saying "if I get good exam result I can travel the world like Martin James. You see I explain to these youngsters how important it is to work hard at school, to be successful in life. We are roll models to these youngsters.

After attending Newrad they get an invitation to fish Tewitfield Fishery Carnforth, as the guest of Les Bratsby. Also as previously mentioned days out on the Edisford Hall fishing stretch of the River Ribble where they get experience of legering, float and fly fishing, and they also get provided with a hot lunch. Prince Albert Angling Society has helped out with this scheme by inviting a group of the youngsters to fish their junior open match. Like all the youngsters who attended, the PAAS junior open days the Pendle Buddies have a great time and go home with a good prize for their effort.

These kids might not get selected for their school tennis, soccer, rugby or cricket team, but they can catch fish. They are achievers. It's been a success story all the way, with better behaved kids. Some have joined the army cadet force, others helping the newcomers to angling, some clearing rubbish away from the canal footpaths etc. There is less street crime, less drug taking, and better citizens. I reckon one the greatest gifts we can give to a boy or girl is take them fishing. If your children, grandchildren, nephews and nieces show the slightest interest in this great sport, pastime or passion, get them some gear and take them to the waterside. It's been proved that anglers often make better citizens; they become guardians of the countryside and the environment. Most important of all, every youngster who gets interested in angling means the future of this game can prosper. Remember this, if angling is practised in fifty years time it's because we encouraged the youngsters of today.

It's been part of my life for some 68 years and hopefully for many more years to come. Give a kid a fishing rod and they won't chuck rocks through your window, or stick a hypodermic in their arm later in life. Remember, most of us fishing today do so because someone was willing to show us how to get started. It's beholding on all of us to help the beginner succeed. If you see someone struggling to catch a fish, young or old, give them a helping hand, give them some tackle or bait.

In fact why not give them your winning swim. When they catch their first fish you will see a grin a mile wide and two big sparkling eyes.

Hungry youngsters waiting to be fed by Col Sgt Tam Miller of the Scots Guards and his team preparing dinner

Recently I got an e-mail from Paul Towers asking for advice on catching coarse fish on a fly. It's interesting to note that angling books pre 1950s would have a chapter on catching coarse fish on a fly. Usually the author was writing about catching dace, chub, roach and rudd, occasionally pike and perch were mentioned. Today we know that it's possible to catch most if not all our coarse fish with an imitation fly or nymph. One of the nicest things about this great pastime of angling is the different ways we can attempt to catch fish.

For me, some of the most enjoyable times at the waterside are with fly rod with artificial dry fly or nymph seeking roach, chub, tench, carp, pike, barbel, rudd, dace, grayling and perch. In fact, all the coarse fish species can be caught on a fly. One summer when I was fishing for barbel on the River Teme I spotted a shoal of perch swimming to-and-fro beneath my rod tip. Some of these perch were good size fish, perhaps going two pounds. How I wished I had some worms or a small spinner. I was thinking that all was lost in trying to catch those perch – then I remembered a film canister in my waistcoat pocket which contained some nymphs. Taking off my weight and hook, I tied on a Richard Walker's Mayfly nymph. Fishing it sink and draw, I had a delightful afternoon catching twenty-odd perch up to about a pound and a quarter.

I suppose using imitation flies and nymphs for catching coarse fish species has taken place for the last 300 years, as already stated, many of the coarse fishing books usually had a section on fly fishing. Even the biggest-ever selling angling book – with two million sales to its credit – Mr Crabtree Goes Fishing had such a chapter. Some of our greatest writers and anglers from the past, Francis Francis, H.T. Sheringham, J.W.Martin known as Trent Otter, William Senior, John Bickerdyke, Colin Willock, Bernard Venables and Richard Walker would go in search of the coarse fish species with a fly when conditions were right.

If you're already fishing for trout, you shouldn't have any problems going after coarse fish. You will already have the tackle and skill needed for most of the fish – pike being the exception. If you're fishing the canals where fish are averaging 4–6lb, your 7/8 weight rod will be ok. But for fish over 10lb, and when your fishing bigger waters, you need a 9/10 weight rod, I recommend Thomas and Thomas, Helix or Horizon, preferably the latter which has some backbone to cast the big flies, some of which are ten inches in length on a 6/0 hook. It's surprising how quickly you can beat a pike on a quality built 10 weight rod with a 15lb leader.

The minimum wire should be 20lb breaking strain. Don't use nylon or other material when pike fishing: it has to be wire. You will need a good-size reel, I recommend Gilmore X360 model; capable of holding 200 yards of 20lb backing with a good quality fly line, buy the best. I use Wulff Triangle taper, Teeny and Scientific Anglers weight forward lines. I have a range of lines, from floating to fast sinking, to cover all situations. Between the fly line and tippet you need 7–8ft of 15–20lb tapered leader to which I attach 12–20in of 20–30lb wire with an Albright knot. I use this knot for sharks: pike pose no problems. .

For chub, rudd and dace I use dry flies and nymphs; a good chub will easily engulf a 5/0 pike fly. Chub love a big mouthful so choose a fly tied up on a size 2 or 4 hook with plenty of dressing and a leader of 6lb BS. Big sedge pattern or muddlers are my favourite, fished at dusk and into the darkness, the takes can often be very savage. Last week when trout fishing I caught a chub estimated at around six pounds on a Greenwell's nymph tied to a 3lb tippet, using a 5 weight rod and floating line with a 12ft tapered leader. Dace are the toughest fish I know to hook on a fly: if you hook two in ten takes, you're doing very well. These little guys are like greased lightning. Hook sizes 14 and 16 are about right. A well greased Black and Peacock spider is a good all-round pattern – also good for rudd, but use hook sizes 10 and 12. When in search of chub and dace I usually use a 9ft leader.

Carp will take wet and dry fly patterns on hook sizes 6, 8 and 10. One good pattern is a black or white leech, fished on or under the surface, depending on the conditions prevailing at the time. Damsel, dragon and mayfly nymphs are deadly, but you must fish them very slow for success. I reckon the best nymph is the Richard Walker pattern. You should move the nymph very slowly; they are not speedy creatures when crawling around on the bed of the river lake canal or stream. A good way to induce a take is to slowly move the nymph off the bottom in very slow lifts of about an inch. The carp cannot resist a big nymph moving slowly to the surface. Chumming with bits of crust and fishing an imitation is another good way of taking carp. You will also excite tench in wanting to grab hold of nymphs.

If there is one fish designed for the nymph fisherman it has to be the barbel. The great thing about barbel is they often live in beautiful English rivers, where the water flows over clean gravel with plenty of water weeds such as water-crowfoot with its white daisy-like flower. We also have that delightful water plant, starwort in a delightful shade of green that will often harbour a crayfish. Chub love to lay under it, popping out to grab an item of food that passes by. Other plants are mare's tail, water-milfoil and, in the slow stretches, you will find potamogeton. A river rich in plant life is rich in animal life that fish eat naturally, and a weedy river is a river that usually holds some good fish.

The banks of my favourite rivers will often have a profusion of wild flowers and plants. Adding a touch of gold to the riverside scene in the cold month of March will be the marsh-marigold, usually one of our first colourful flowers to brighten a cold day. Then we have the yellow and purple-loosestrife, red campion, the various parsleys: cow hogweed, sweet cicely and hemlock to name a few. You will often see that delicate flower, the common forget-me-not. Today you can sometimes see foxgloves at the waterside and, of course, you will see the Himalayan balsam growing in profusion. We need to wage war on this invasive plant countywide and try to wipe it out. You're now probably asking what do water weeds, plants and wild flowers have to do with barbel. It's because these are often the conditions that prevail on my barbel rivers. Barbel is a fish that has had my attention over the past few years. I, along with

Stephen Collins, carp on a size 16 buzzer

several other anglers, have said barbel is a fish that could be taken on a nymph. Is not the barbel a bottom-feeding fish for most of its life? Its main diet will consist of various nymphs and caddis crawling around on the bottom of our rivers, or under the fine sand gravel or silt. If they are daft enough to eat meatballs and luncheon meat, why not an artificial nymph? It's far more natural.

I well remember being at a Barbel Society Conference and talking to the late Mike Burdon, who told me he had caught five barbel from the River Windrush on a pheasant tail nymph when trout fishing. Had not John Bailey talked about seeing anglers in Eastern Europe catch barbel on a nymph? All this information made me even more confident. Catching a barbel on an artificial fly had become a big challenge, though I knew it wouldn't be easy. The conditions I wanted would be a low, clear river where I could see and stalk the barbel.

Casting to fish I could see would make the chances of success greater, I would also be able to see the reaction of the fish to the artificial fly. My first success happened on a Monday morning just after the season started on a low, clear River Teme in Worcestershire. Conditions were near perfect: cloudy sky, warm and close weather with a light westerly wind. A few mayflies were coming off, which was even more encouraging. Seeing the mayflies made me choose the mayfly nymph as probably the most natural offering at that time. Even the finely tied nymphs that I showed to Tony Farquharson of Southport looked like the real thing. I thought, "Today is my best chance yet of success."

In some two feet of water I spotted a group of six barbel avidly feeding on nymphs. I could see them sometimes come up to mid-water to grab another food item! I chose a 9ft 7 weight rod, floating line, 12ft fluorocarbon leader with a tippet of 6lb breaking strain, then attached a size 8 weighted mayfly nymph. Creeping back to where I had seen the feeding barbel, I noticed that the half a dozen had increased to eight. Kneeling down, I pulled off some line, made one false cast and shot some forty feet of line, dropping the nymph some twenty feet ahead of the feeding fish. I allowed the nymph to bump its way down stream, retrieving line in my left hand within three or four feet of the feeding fish. I allowed the nymph to sit on the bottom then noticed a fish move across the stream towards the artificial. I lifted the rod very slowly making the nymph rise. As I did so, the fish moved upstream towards it. Lowering the rod tip, I let the nymph sit once more. After a second or so, I moved the nymph slowly then let it come to rest again. The leading fish moved over the fly as I, very, very slowly, dragged the fly along the bottom. It disappeared from my sight – the barbel had just eaten it with confidence. I tightened: my barbel was hooked! After a brief struggle this, my first ever barbel on a fly, was netted.

It weighed in at 4lb 11oz. A couple of quick pictures were taken by Tony and the fish released. In the next hour I had another two barbel weighing about four pounds – not the biggest barbel to be caught on a fly but, to the best of my knowledge, the first caught by design. I have had many fish since that first day with fish to 8lb 4oz.

I have noticed no difference in my hooking rate when fishing up or downstream. The secret is in finding your barbel, and then presenting the nymph on the bottom about two feet ahead of the fish. As it approaches, I lift the rod tip, causing the nymph to rise slowly from the river bed. The barbel will grab hold with relish, in fact they are very aggressive when chasing and feeding on nymphs. These fish are really determined to eat your nymph.

Perch are a great fish to catch with a fly

When I was nine or so, I remember having a house constantly full of 1000s of fishing flies; wherever I turned, there they were. There wasn't a 'fly-free' room in the house — there was a good reason for this: my father, David Train, was an up-and-coming supplier of fishing flies to the trade. Having started from small beginnings, he quickly discovered that there was a huge demand for fishing flies and not enough supply. Almost single-handedly, he started the mass production of Kenyan fishing flies — not famous for quality, but certainly at a price that couldn't and still cannot be beaten. Of course, this meant that fishing was a huge part of my childhood.

This household obsession went one step further on the day my cat Purdy lost a whisker! That day changed the world of fly fishing for ever, as this whisker, although it was not realised at the time, was about to give birth to one of the most famous and successful UK fishing-flies of all time – the mighty 'Cat's Whisker'. Ever since that day, the Cat's Whisker has consistently topped the 'favourite fly' charts, making it arguably the most successful fishing-fly of all time. With all of this history behind me, it was inevitable that I too would one day enter into the business.

At this stage, Tackle Discounts is currently the largest fishing store on eBay in Europe and is striving forward to capitalise on this achievement. On Saturday 5 December 2009 at 11 a.m. our first retail store was officially opened when Martin James cut the ribbon. We will stock the entire ranges from Nash, TF Gear, Airflo, Grey's, Korda, Chub, Shimano, Pro-logic, Scierra, Gardner and many more companies. We are the sole distributors for Flextec, and Cyprinus, for whom Phil Chun is designing products including new bivvies, sleeping bags, day shelters, chairs and bed chairs. We focus on giving anglers value for money without sacrificing quality, Tackle Discounts has already become the ONLY place for some people to buy their tackle. Over the next few years, we hope to become a household name in fishing and hope to do for the fishing industry what Easyjet did for the Airline industry.

Our retail store is at: Europa Industrial Park, Parsonage Road, Stratton, Swindon SN3 4RJ Tackle Discounts, remember that name!

Andrew Train

Staff at Tackle Discount who pack and send orders all over the world
Claire, Justina and Debbie

D uring the 1950s, 60s and 70s, I did a lot of saltwater fishing from the beaches, piers and boats. What I didn't realise was, how good the saltwater fishing around the British Isles was in those days, more so in the 50s and 60s; by the 1970s the fishing was tailing off.

The main cause for the decline was the introduction of bigger and more efficient trawlers, which were often under foreign ownership; I always felt we should have had a twelve mile limit around our coastline. Another problem is The European Common Fisheries Policy which has been a disaster, not only for the sea bird population but also sport fishers and commercial fishing interests. Sport today, with rod and line, is probably the worse in living memory, and it isn't getting any better!

Let's not forget DEFRA, and the last Labour Government who sold us out to Europe. They have done nothing to improve our inshore fishing prospects. For a long time, we sport fishers, through the Bass Anglers Sportsfishing Society, have tried to get the UK Government to increase the size limit above which bass can be retained, but the Government has always fobbed off the issue with weasel words. As always, it has gone in the direction of the commercial interests.

We also have a crazy situation where foreign vessels can sweep our seas for sand eels, and other small bait-size fish, to make another bag of fertilizer which the world doesn't need. These bait-size fish are the food for the bigger species, and let's not forget the sea birds who are suffering from the loss of their food source. Puffin and numerous other sea bird numbers have dropped dramatically over the past few years. My honest opinion is that we sport fishers today are trying to catch fish from an ocean that doesn't have enough food to feed the fish stocks and sea birds.

When I started sea-fishing some sixty years ago, Kent really was the top area in the UK for its quality of sea-angling; without doubt, the number one sport fish was the cod. In those days it wasn't, will I catch a cod today? It was, how many cod would we catch – with often many in double figures. The chance of a twenty pound fish was a truly realistic proposition; that is not the case today.

I first started sea fishing in 1949 or 1950 when my family would take the Medway Queen paddle steamer on a Sunday from Strood, for a day out on the beach at Sheerness. The paddle steamer, on its way to Ramsgate, would stop off at Sheerness Pier where we would disembark. My brothers and sisters, with Mum and Dad, would go off to the beach.

Not having any interest in playing on the beach or in the water, I was allowed to stay on the pier, fishing with a hand line which comprising of about sixty feet of orange line, a three boom

Author Uptiding

paternoster with a round weight that had a hole in the middle. Bait was usually cooked shrimp, but sometimes, another angler would give me some lug or rag worm. Most of the time I caught crabs, then one day I caught a flounder. This was a great turning point in my life as an angler. From that day on I wasn't just a freshwater angler, I was also a sea-fisher.

My first serious shore-fishing experience was at Landguard Point Felixstowe. It was a Regular British Army base where I had gone for a two-week camp with the Army Cadets. Apart from various exercises, night manoeuvres, and time spent on the ranges using Bren gun and .303 rifle (and with the occasional sports event), I also went fishing most evenings while my friends were off to the local fairground chasing girls. At that time I wasn't interested in girls – but I made up for it a few years later!

The beach area I fished was pebble-strewn with patches of sand and an occasional weedy rocky area. I caught eels, flounders and the occasional school bass, probably around the pound mark, using a two or three-boom brass paternoster. Bait was king rag worm which had some fearsome, shiny black nippers. This bait was given to me by a Regular British Army instructor, Sgt Maplestone, who was as keen an angler one could wish to meet. He fished with bamboo rods and bait-casting reels (multiplier reels). He told me he picked them up when he was in the United States. Sgt Maplestone spent a lot of his time instructing me on how to use the new reels which, apart from reading about them in the Field & Stream magazines, I had never seen before. Yes, I had many backlashes but eventually I mastered the reel, getting the bait out some forty yards. The line we used in those days was Luron 2: nothing as good as today's lines. It was springy and often coiled like a spring, but far better than the linen cuttyhunk type of line that was still used by many anglers in those days.

Back home from Landguard Point, I again started fishing from Sheerness in the Thames estuary. My favourite place in summer was the pier where the paddle steamer would stop to let off or take on passengers. I also fished the beaches including Garrison Point with its fast tidal run. Flounders, dabs and eels were the main species of fish in the spring and summer months. Another venue was the River Swale where I fished for mullet with float tackle and bread flake, the mullet were great fighters, never knowing when to give in.

In 1952 I was riding my bike along Rochester High Street in thick fog, when the front wheel went into a deep pothole. Apart from cuts and bruises, which didn't bother me too much, the cycle forks holding the front wheel had sheared off. After sorting myself out, I dragged the bike off to Rochester police station. I told the very friendly and sympathetic police officer what had happened, and was then asked to show him the pothole. Off we went. When we got there he was very angry, saying the hole should have been roped off and it should have a light and a warning sign. Back at the police station he took all my details, and then said they would be in touch with the contractors, and to leave my bike at the police station. A week later the local bobby, PC Blackman, called at my house to say the contractor had agreed that I should order a new bike, and then take the bill to the police station.

Next day after school, I called into Len Chambers who had a cycle shop under a railway arch near Rochester Bridge. After telling Mr Chambers what had happened, he called the police station to confirm I could have a new bike. He then asked what model of bike I wanted, pointing out several, including a Raleigh. I pointed to a bike with drop-handle bars and lots of gears. He said, "That's a Claude Butler!" I said, "Yes, I know, that's the one I want." He then told me the police had been told by the contractors that they would pay the cost of a new bike, "So take your pick!" Two weeks later I was the proud owner of a brand-new racing bike. I didn't know if I should join the local cycling club, as Mr Chambers suggested, or stay with my fishing. There wasn't any contest – fishing won hands down!

By now I had a 12ft built-cane beach caster by Modern Arms of Bromley, Kent and a small Penn multiplier reel, sent from the USA by an uncle who was living in California. After lots of bird's nests, known as tangles, I learnt how to cast with this new-fangled piece of equipment, slowly mastering the casting, getting the weight out about thirty yards – I still got bird's nests, though not so often.

During the Easter school holidays, Brian Burstow and I cycled to Sheerness, a ride of some twenty miles, in the rain. Just a few yards from the beach was a tackle shop; we scraped together enough money between us to buy twenty lugworms wrapped in newspaper. On hearing how far we had cycled, the owner also gave us some rag worm, a few hooks to nylon and a tide table, telling us the best tides to fish and where we should try. He also told us we had arrived at the right time, with two hours of the flood tide left, suggesting we might catch some eels, perhaps a flounder or dab.

On the beach we put together our gear, Brian had a 9ft rod made from a tank aerial, with an old wooden star-back reel. Having fixed our hooks to nylon onto the paternoster, we baited them with lugworm or a bit of rag worm, and then chucked the lot out as far as we could. Not having rod rests, we leaned our rods against a big chunk of timber. We stood watching the rod tops for a bite, and still it rained – it never stopped. Brian had the first bite, catching a dab. We talked about the orange spots, saying how it looked like the plaice on the fishmonger's slab. It was clonked on the head then put away in his ex army ruck bag. Soon after that, Brian caught an eel which turned all his gear into a tangled, slimy mess. Suddenly, my rod top shook; quickly winding in, I found I had caught a flounder. This was hit on the head then put in my bag. We didn't get any more bites. In the darkness, we put away our gear, and then it was a long bike ride home. It had been worth it; we were now sea anglers.

It was probably 1954 when Brian Gunn, Billy Race, Dick Bannister, Colin Barnard, Brian Burstow and his brother Peter and I, joined the Sheerness Sea-angling club. We had been members for a few years when the club purchased some fibreglass boats, which, for a small fee, the members could use. They were a bit uncomfortable but suitable for close-in fishing off the Isle of Sheppey coastline. Usually, we fished about eight hundred yards off the shoreline between the beach tackle-shop and Garrison Point. If conditions were good we went further out into the estuary. The boats were powered by Seagull Century outboard motors which I rated highly; they were very efficient. If they stopped it was either because we had run out of petrol or the plug was oiled up. In the latter case we just unscrewed the spark plug, gave it a wipe and checked the gap. Replacing the plug, all that was then needed was to give the starter cord one pull and we would be under way once more.

In the summer time our fish were dabs; sometimes you would catch fifty or more, returning most of them. Come September, the whiting would show, followed by the cod. Some nights when it was a full moon with a heavy frost, we would fly-fish from the shoreline or use small Mepps, catching more than our share of whiting. For flounders we often used the Garrard baited-spoon method with great success, not only for flounders, but also dabs, catching many pound-plus fish.

Though much of my sea fishing during the following years took place in the Sheerness area, I also fished from the sea wall on the Isle of Grain. Sometimes at low water, we would walk out to a tower built in the 1800s. This tower was similar to the Martello Towers built as a defence structure against Napoleon. If we chose to fish during a strong blow, it could be best described as a bit scary! We fished the tower for many years but we never had any problems.

Occasionally, we had a coach trip to Dover Pier or the breakwater, with the Kingfisher Angling and Preservation Society; these were learning days, when I would spend much of my time watching and talking to the more experienced fishermen. Some of my trips to Sheerness in the summer months were spent fishing for dabs, with Jack Watson from his 16ft clinker-built dinghy. We used a couple of light, one piece 6ft fibreglass rods with bakelite reels which were made from synthetic resin and plastic, and had a tendency to crack. Our line was 12lb, bait was rag or lug, fishing a nylon paternoster rig. Even at low tide in just three feet of water we caught dabs, often switching to float tackle. I reckon dabs are the sweetest fish in the ocean. We didn't just catch a few dabs, we caught dozens of them, with some fish well over the pound mark.

In my late teens, early twenties, along with Brian Long, Stuart Robinson, Brian Smith, I started to travel to more distant destinations in Brian's big Humber Snipe. Venues with great sounding names: Dungeness, Hythe, Dover, Deal, Folkestone and Ramsgate; on the Suffolk coast it was Pakefield and Southwold. During the summer we would often be out on a boat, catching plaice with spots as big as half-crowns, thornback rays, and spur dog, black and red bream. When fishing over or near wrecks we caught the occasional conger eel and pollock. We caught dabs by the dozens and lots of mackerel – what great fun, they were on light spinning tackle.

Without doubt, the best sport was during the autumn and winter months – often the last three hours of the flood, first two hours of the ebb being the best, though this wasn't always true: fish don't really follow rules! In late September, if I was really lucky, I would catch the odd codling among the whiting. In late October, given the right tide following a good onshore blow, I would be on the beach at night, with high expectations of catching cod. They were our number one targeted species.

Fishing really could be hectic: we often had five hours of good fishing, both on the flood and ebb tide. There were occasions when we started getting bites and fish just an hour as the tide started to flood, often in six or seven feet of wave-lashed, coloured water. I certainly caught my share of codling, even whiting would put in an appearance, proving to be a nuisance fish, taking bait meant for the cod. These cod often weighed as much as ten or twelve pounds. I loved being on the beach at night along with hundreds of other anglers; the beaches were a mass of twinkling lights from the many Tilley lamps. Just one fish reigned supreme: The Cod.

Dungeness was the top beach-fishing venue, not just in Kent but probably the country. Hundreds of anglers would travel many miles to fish the place, often camping out for a few days at a time, so good was the cod fishing, especially after a good blow. I also had a good arrangement with an old trawler-fishing family, the Oilers, who would supply me with black lugworm whenever I wanted, also sprats when available. There were times when I would have a day afloat with the Oilers, catching plenty of cod – often, a brace of twenty-pounders.

Dungeness was basically a gravel spit sticking out into the English Channel, a desolate place in the 1950s, with some fishermen's cottages, a lifeboat and a few trawlers, which often doubled as angling boats. The most famous beach-fishing mark was the 'Dustbin'.

It was created by the steep beaches sloping down onto hard sand and by the strong tides that raced around the point, forming what is

A brace of Cod

best described as a giant eddy where all manner of marine life would be swept in – hence the name, 'Dustbin'. Fishing this spot required long-range casting. You needed top quality casting gear. I had a pair of Penn Squidders shipped over from the States; in those early days they were probably the top casting-reel available. I had my reels finely tuned by Bill Watson, an RAF engineer. I matched these reels with 12ft bamboo beach-casting rods from Modern Arms Rod Company of Bromley.

In those early days, before we started fishing, we would collect a big pile of driftwood for a bonfire; we always carried a can of paraffin oil to help get the fire going. There were many occasions when we fished, not just a few hours either side of high, but all of the flood and ebb tide, before Brian Rutter and I crawled into the cold interior of his car for what we hoped would be a few hours sleep. Often, it never happened, due to the intense cold; in those days we didn't have the excellent outdoor clothing we have today. It was string vests, submariners' jumpers, tank suits and any other thick clothing we could scrounge. Often, all we got was an hour or two of restless sleep, sometimes waking up to be greeted by thick ice on the inside of the car; no heaters in those days. After a couple of hours in a very cold car, it took a lot of effort to get moving again to fish the next tide. In those days, eggs, bacon and sausages, with a can of tomatoes, never tasted better. Sometimes we would have a big cast- iron saucepan of rabbit or hare stew, which would bubble away on the fire's embers.

What we all waited for was a strong southwesterly gale. After it had abated we would drop everything, including work and girl friends, and head off to Dungeness. Our first job was to collect a bucket of bait: clams, razor fish, sea mice; slug like creatures with fine hair on their bodies. If we were lucky we found black lug that had been ripped from the sea bed by the storm, often a few peeler or soft crab, all proved excellent baits for cod.

Sea mice were often the number one bait. There were occasions, after these good southwesterlies, when we would get a dozen big cod on a single tide. But as the tide flooded, you had to lengthen your casting distance to get the bait into the Dustbin. When shore fishing at Denge marsh, we caught some great flounders to just over four pounds on razorfish. We experienced fishing that we can only dream about these days. Without doubt, the beach and boat angler in the 1950s up to around the early 1970s, had the finest beach-fishing one could wish for. Towards the end of the '70s the cod fishing from the beaches was really deteriorating; as we lost the cod we could see an improvement in the bass-fishing. In fact, bass were spreading into areas of the country where they hadn't really been caught before. Today you can expect good bass-fishing from both the east and west coast. Our big problem today is the commercial fishing industry where you get a pair of trawlers sweeping up the bass as they congregate to spawn. It's nothing but a disgrace!

It was around October 1962 when I first met Les Moncrieff and Tom Hutchinson, two giants of beach fishing in those far-off days. Not only were they great anglers, but very impressive casters. They could chuck weights a tremendous distance, regularly casting well over a hundred yards. Tom was a neighbour of Frank Edmunds who I fished with on many occasions. Frank was a keen beach-angler, and he was the owner of a thirty-six foot motor cruiser, which was moored in Otterham Quay on the Medway near Rainham, Kent.

We spent many happy hours, both day and night-fishing the Thames Estuary for cod, whiting and dabs. Frank, knowing my passion for Dungeness, arranged for me to fish with Tom and Les. During the first few trips, I reckon I spent more time watching Tom and Les in action than fishing myself; it was well worth it. They both gave me lots of casting tuition; soon, with practice, I was regularly getting eighty to ninety yards. After some three months I was hitting the 120 yard mark, often further with a following wind. One Friday night Tom said, "Martin, you're casting long distances these days." I was now dropping my bait into the Dustbin, even at high water, cast-after-cast, and not just when the tide was ebbing (which of course was a shorter cast). As my casting improved; so did my catches. Occasionally I matched these two giants of beach-casting with my cod catches.

I spent many hours on the field at the back of my house perfecting my casting, getting ribald remarks from dog-walkers, but I didn't care one jot! My bamboo rods were retired, and I switched to the new fibreglass models. Two companies: Modern Arms in Bromley Kent, and Martin James Company in Redditch, were producing their own beach-casting models. Later, we had the German company, Sportex, with a good blank from which I made up a pair of 11ft one piece rods, using hose clips to hold the reel. Hand grips were similar to the handlebar grips we used on bikes. I reckon the Les Moncrieff beach-caster from Martin James Company was the most popular and best seller. I still used my Penn squidders; I also had a pair of ABU 7000 reels, again, finely-tuned by Bill Watson. These reels cost me a lot of money, but I wasn't going to compromise, I wanted the best gear for the job. Even today, a fine well-tuned ABU 7000 will hold its own against other reels in the right hands.

Apart from Dungeness, I fished the beaches of Deal, Hythe, Folkestone and Dover. There were times when I fished from the sea wall on the Isle of Grain, a short drive from home. If the tides were right, with a good onshore blow, we caught our share of codling, sometimes we had two or three fish in double figures.

One Saturday evening in November, I had taken Mavis, a girl who worked in my office, to the Ritz cinema, then on to the coffee stall at Chatham station. After coffee we went off to her home. After a glass of wine and some cuddling, it wasn't long before we were in the bedroom. Having made love, we lay there sharing a cigarette; I heard the announcer on the radio say, "Thames: gale force south-westerly winds!" I'd heard enough. I knew high water was at 3.15 a.m. at the Isle of Grain. I called my mate Brian to see if he wanted to go fishing, he was up for it. I told Mavis I was going fishing for a few hours. She said, "You can't leave me now!" I said, "I have to go, the cod will be in. I'll be back about seven, we can carry on then!" Loving could wait: the cod wouldn't. An hour later Brian and I were on the Isle of Grain sea wall with a bucket of fresh lug I had dug the day before. Half a dozen other keen anglers were already in position. Baiting up a 3/0 hook with lots of lugworm, I clipped on a 4oz weight then hurled it seawards, 80–90–plus yards. I baited the 3/0 on my other rod with a load of lugworm then clipped on another 4oz weight but lobbed this one no more than fifty yards out into the dirty, churned-up water.

It was an eventful session: we all had double-figure fish, with Pat Collins of Rochester taking the first twenty pound cod we had ever known to be caught off the sea wall, in fact we had never seen anyone take such a fish from the shore except Dover Pier and Dungeness. I caught all my cod on the close-in rod, only taking a couple of flounders on the baited hook cast well out from shore. As the tide ebbed away about six in the morning, we all went off home. I went back to Mavis and a warm bed after a shower. Through hearing the shipping forecast, knowing the state of the tide then dropping everything, me and my mates had another successful cod-fishing session.

One Friday morning in July 1966 I got a call from John MacDonald at Deal. "Can you get down? I've found a mussel bed that's covered in plaice." I had a word with my editor who agreed I could leave early, on the understanding that he received a brace of plaice. I called John back to say I would be down and would he get me ten score of yellow tails? These were the local lugworm, and highly prized by anglers and fish alike. John replied that he had already got me a bucketful of fresh lug, as he had guessed that I would come down once I heard the news about the plaice. It was going to be a neap tide so I could use light tackle, which meant leads of between four and six ounces, a line of 20lb breaking strain, a small Penn multiplier reel and Milbro Neptune boat rod.

We, Frank Edmunds, Arthur Sayers, and I, that is, arrived at Deal in plenty of time. We parked the van then went along to Jim Heard's tackle shop to pick up a few bits and pieces. (Isn't it amazing how we always end up having to buy tackle which we already have back at home?) Then it was into the cafe for tea and toast, where John joined us.

The weather was kind to us with a light wind and a warm sun: perfect! Days like that make up for the ones when either you have to hold on with one hand for fear of being blown overboard, or you can't even get afloat. Once in the boat, a clinker built job that had the engine in the centre, we slid down the shingle bank and into the sea. It was a half-hour trip to the mussel bed, and during that time we set up our tackle. Our end rig was a spreader made from stainless

Simon Brown with a nice Fleetwood Plaice

steel, with two size 2/0 fine wire, long shank, Aberdeen hooks baited with yellow tails. We were ready. Once over the mark, down went the anchor and, after a couple of minutes, John said, "Okay, it's all yours." I put the spool out of gear, lowered the baited hooks to the sea bed and flicked the reel back into gear. I must have waited all of ten seconds when I felt a fish mouth the bait, and then another one. I struck, and winched up two plaice each around two pounds. It was as easy as that. I rebaited and dropped the tackle down again and soon two more fish were being brought in. Frank and Arthur were doing just as well, and that's how the fishing was for the next three hours, with some of the plaice weighing over four pounds. We put back those under two pounds whenever they were lip-hooked. It was wonderful sport: plaice fishing at its best.

By eight o'clock we had had enough, and we headed for shore and booked the boat for the next afternoon, but that trip was to be a disaster because a trawler went over the mussel bed early in the morning and scraped it clean. Between the three of us we had just two bites from small dogfish.

My biggest cod didn't come from my favourite fishing spot of Dungeness, but from a boat-fishing trip out from Deal. It was one of those lucky fish which we catch now and then; I wasn't fishing for cod but for thornback rays. It was around four o'clock in the afternoon, the tide was flooding and conditions were good for rays. I was fishing with a 20lb line class rod, 24lb breaking strain line and a size 4/0 hook on some 30lb breaking strain nylon trace.

I don't like to use wire when fishing for rays; I think it's a mistake to do so. With an 8ft flowing trace and a fillet of mackerel as bait, bouncing well away from the boat, I lifted the rod to work the bait a bit further down the tide and the rod was pulled down savagely. There was no need to strike, for the fish had hooked itself and was trying to move downtide. Grudgingly, the reel gave line and I felt the fish shake its head in an effort to get rid of the hook. This was no ray: it was a fish that could fight a bit... cod? Everyone agreed it had to be. I began to get some line back on to the reel. This wasn't the sort of fish that could strip line off a reel like a bonefish, salmon, carp or pike, but it was a dogged fighter. Slowly I pumped the fish towards the boat. Then it surfaced about ten yards from the stern, and I gasped: it was hooked lightly in the scissors – a big fish, thirty pounds I thought. It opened its mouth, the tide flooded in and the fish went below the surface. I continued pumping and then suddenly it was there alongside the boat. It looked huge. Brian put the net under it and scooped it out. It was mine. The big cod coughed up four crabs and a partially digested flatfish. We put it on the scales and they pulled down to 28lb 7oz. I was thrilled!

I have fished for mullet since I was about sixteen; I had some excellent mullet fishing from the marshes between Strood and Upnore, the creeks on the Stoke Marshes and the River Swale. From June, I would be out targeting this fine fish, and the hotter the weather the better I often found the sport. What I liked about the mullet was they could be caught on float tackle, free lined bait or with fly-fishing gear.

Some days, these fish were easy to catch, on other days you couldn't get them to take bait – there were times when I wanted to tear out my hair; these fish could be so exasperating. You will find mullet around piers, sea walls, dock areas, marsh creeks, and harbours, around moored-up boats, in fact, I don't think there is an area where you can't find mullet. Some of the biggest mullet I have seen were in Newhaven harbour. Sadly there were 'no fishing' signs wherever you looked. It doesn't make sense to me.

A couple of years ago, my friend George Koral, a police officer, called to see if I wanted to go fishing for mullet on the Fylde coast. I immediately said yes. With a cloudy sky and light winds, I thought the chances of success were quite good. I used an 11ft light Avon action rod, centre-pin reel with 4lb breaking strain Gamma line with a size 12 hook with a red tipped waggler float taking 3 bb shot. Bait was bread flake. I started off by feeding with pigeon egg-size balls of breadcrumb. I suppose I fed a ball of bread feed every five or six minutes, and with a light scattering of floating bits of bread about the size of a five pence piece. After about an hour I spotted the odd fish starting to swirl at pieces of bread. Occasionally, one would suck down a piece of crust or floating flake. It was time to put a hook into a bit of bread. I set the float at 2ft with the shot bunched under the float.

I nicked the hook into the edge of the bait, this allowed the bait to sink very slowly in a swaying motion. For about fifteen minutes I had a few bobs on the float as one fish decided to prod it. Suddenly it bobbed, and then moved across the surface before submerging – so reminiscent of a tench bite.

The strike connected with a good fish which put up a powerful fight for several minutes. Playing the fish, I noticed another one follow its every move. Finally, my fish was ready for netting. It weighed 4lb 2oz and was quickly returned, swimming off strongly.

I probably spent about forty minutes trying to get the fish back and feeding, eventually they did. Seeing several fish swirling at bits

A fine Mullet from the Fylde Coast

of floating bread, I baited with a piece of bread flake. Within five minutes of casting out, the float bobbed twice then submerged. The strike connected with another hard-fighting fish, several times line was taken off the reel, as the fish fought for its freedom. I suppose it was a few minutes before George was able to net a very good fish.

In fact it was a super fish which, when weighed, pulled the scale needle round to 6lb. After a couple of quick pictures, it was released to fight another day. It would give another angler the chance to catch this aggressive fighter. They are truly wild fish with no names – probably never been hooked before. A good attracter is cooked rice that has been through a food processor, mixed with breadcrumb. If you're looking for a fish that offers a challenge, why not go out and target the mullet. It's certainly a great quarry for the freshwater angler.

Living in the North West of England certainly gives me some excellent fishing possibilities in both fresh and salt water. Over the past few years my interest in saltwater fly-fishing has got me spending many hundreds of hours (an advantage of being an OAP) chucking flies in the salt all over the world.

I've caught many species of fish, from sharks to flounders. The latter fish can be found all around the British Isles, in fact it's one fish still thriving in saltwater, no doubt soon the commercial fishing fleet will rape the inshore marks, then our flounder will be lost – in fact, lobster fishermen today are using them to bait their pots. What a waste. Flounders can be caught in a variety of ways: spinning, legering, float and fly-fishing. Baits are numerous: rag and lugworm, crabs, shrimps and fish strips. In fact, if it lives in the ocean, a flounder will eat it. Fish numbers of most ocean species have dropped over the years. Not so the flounders; they are still around in good quantities.

The tackle I use is a 9 weight 9ft Thomas and Thomas Helix model, with a fast sinking line. As flounders feed on or near the bottom, I use either a Teeny 350 or 400 grain shooting head depending on the tidal flow. The leader should be no more than 2ft in length; most of my fishing is done with a foot long leader of 15lb line, if you use a longer leader, the fly will ride too high in the water. I suggest you don't attempt to fish the powerful, spring tides. For flounders you will do better to fish the less powerful neap tides, ensuring you can get the fly down on or near the bottom. Fly selection is quite easy: all you need are a selection of Clouser Minnows Chartreuse/White Chartreuse/Yellow Green/White Olive/White Red/White in sizes 2 and 1. Often, the take will be very savage. Sometimes the line will get pulled from your hand as the reel gives out some line.

It's not a rarity to catch a sea trout or salmon, I have caught more than my share of these fish when I've been targeting flounders in estuaries where the game-fish run. Should you hook a salmon or sea trout you will certainly know about it as the fish strives hard to throw the hook in its attempt to go back out to the ocean. Unless you have a salmon and sea-trout licence, you must return the fish immediately. If you fish for reservoir trout, go out and try for flounders. They are good fun. If you're lucky you might even hook into a bass.

Some years ago I went to Dorset to interview one of the authors of Hooked on Bass, published by Crowood Press. The authors were Dr Mike Ladle and Alan Vaughan, sadly, Alan a teacher in Devon, couldn't escape the classroom. Mike, Kent Sherrington from Burnley and I had a couple of fly-fishing sessions in the ocean. We didn't break any records but we did have some fun. We caught some small bass and a succession of small pollock, and talked lot about fly and lure-fishing in the ocean.

During the visit, Kent and I fished with Malcolm Brindle. One evening, fishing with float tackle and live prawns, we didn't get any bites, but it was most relaxing, sitting in the darkness hearing the waves lapping the rocks and watching our chemical night-lights that were fitted in the top of the floats. It's interesting to note that Malcolm, on his return home, puts his night lights in the freezer for use on another occasion. Malcolm is a mine of information, I learnt a lot about bass from the guy. On the first evening, we fly-fished for scad (horse mackerel). I fished a small closer minnow on a Cortland 8 weight Ghost tip line with a 7 weight rod. These fish certainly pulled the string, I had great fun.

About two hours after the tide started to ebb, I was getting a hit on every chuck, often as the fly hit the water. Sadly, some bait-fishers were also catching small scad and bass, and keeping them. What made it worse was that the poor fish were dumped on the ground to die a slow death. I had a heated argument, telling them in no uncertain terms what I thought, even to questioning their parentage! I have one word for these types of people: slobs! If we are going to take fish for the table then they must be of the legal size limit, and must be dispatched quickly.

I look forward to next summer when I will have a week or two in Dorset, fly-fishing for bass and mullet. Last year, Mike Ladle had a mullet of seven-and-a-half pounds on a fly – now that's a serious fish. While on the subject of big fish, it's been reported from the New England coast of the USA that a striped bass of 48lb has been caught on a 10 weight fly-rod. Another huge striper, caught from the beach by an angler bait-fishing, weighed in at 60lb. It's a pity we don't have this excellent sporting fish.

Once the autumn and winter cod-fishing ended, usually in March, my interest in saltwater fishing turned to bass from the Kent and Sussex shoreline. I've always found the month of April virtually a waste of time for sea angling, just eels, dabs and flounders; my fishing during this month centred on trout-fishing. Once mid May arrived, I would check my tide table for the next spring-tide. This was then followed by a search of the foreshore for peeler and soft crab; in those days I also used a metal hook to drag edible crabs from their holes between rocks. More time would be spent looking for king ragworm beds, which, when found, were kept a tight secret.

The start of the bass season was as exciting to me and my mates as the start of the coarse-fishing season. I would check the tide table looking for the best tide; I wanted if possible a tide that started to flood just before dawn, with a good onshore blow for a few days. Get the right tide with some colour in the water, then find a rough beach with rocks or reefs with kelp and bladder wrack. Better still is to find a small sandy or pebbled area between the rocks, about the size of a kitchen table. Get your casting spot on, bait with peeler, or better still, velvet or edible crab, then you have a realistic chance of catching bass.

Me and my friends fished several shore venues both by day and night; whenever possible, we would try to fish a flooding tide at dawn. Our venues were: Bishopstone near Herne Bay, Reculver, Kingsgate, Broadstairs, Ramsgate, Deal and Kingsdown. Beachy Head was another one of our venues, with some great fishing on a flooding tide at dawn – again, crab was the number one bait.

When it comes to boat-fishing, the Pan Sands off Herne Bay can offer excellent bass-fishing. I would usually start off with a big king-rag on a long flowing trace, bouncing it down the tide. If I started missing bites, I would make up a Pennel tackle rig with a size 3/0 hook on the bottom with a 1/0 hook on the top spaced about three inches apart. A very successful angler in the Herne Bay area in those days was Paul Cartwright.

Most of my bass-fishing was done with a small multiplier-reel filled with 15lb breaking strain line, Some venues will demand using 30lb line – even then you can get broken off on sharp flints or rocks. If you lose bass at these times you feel completely gutted, sometimes I have felt like packing in, but after a brew, it's back once more trying to catch a bass. I always use a 40lb shock leader even when the casting is usually within fifty yards of the shore line. A weight flying through the air is a dangerous missile that can kill. The only time it differed was when I fished from Dungeness beach, a venue where I had to cast a hundred yards or more, I would then step up to 20lb breaking strain line. I've also enjoyed some fairly good bass-fishing from the Sussex coast, Seaford towards Pevensey, especially from a small dinghy on a flat calm day in summer – I almost forgot to mention Rye, also on the Sussex coast, where I often enjoyed some good bass-fishing, both on spinning gear and bait. It was a place where I often float-fished with live prawns, a good way to catch school bass.

Most anglers looked upon Dungeness as just a cod-fishing venue, but the area was also good for bass, including some double-figure fish. It wasn't a venue for the guy with a forty yard cast. Fishing from many of our bass-fishing beaches, forty yards was sufficient distance – not at Dungeness beach; it's often a hundred yards-plus cast. Apart from using whole squid and fresh mackerel as bait, I would often use live pouting, on a size 5/0 hook to 3ft of 30lb nylon with a swivel link at the opposite end to the hook. Having cast out a weight into an area where I expected to find bass, I would tighten the line, and then clip the link swivel to the main line; this then allowed the pouting to slide down towards the weight, until it was stopped a few feet from the weight by a swivel. There were times when a bass would hit the pouting in midwater. Occasionally, on a flat calm sea at night, you got a hit within a few feet of the surface. We also got our share of big cod when fishing this method.

In the 1970s I often boat-fished off Beachy Head with my mate, the late John Bodsworth of Sussex. Our first job on getting afloat was to attempt to catch a few small mackerel on feathers. These were fished as live bait on float tackle. The bait would be fished between two and eight feet deep. The depth we fished the bait depended on how far down the bait fish were from the surface. Takes were the most savage I have ever experienced. The best guy at this method was, without doubt, the late John Darling from Sussex, a great angler and photographer. These days, much of my bass fishing is done with a fly or lure-fishing outfit.

The coarse-fishing season ended on 14 March, a new trout season commenced the next day in Lancashire, while over the border in the white rose county of Yorkshire the season started on the 25 March. What did please me was that, in February there were big hatches of fly life, mostly large dark olives and chironomids – often known as midges or buzzers. I was also catching the odd, out-of-season brown trout when fishing for grayling. The trout were bright and plump and in excellent condition. I was very happy to see these over-wintered fish. Whatever the conditions are at the start of the season, I will always spend an hour or two on the River Ribble.

If I'm lucky, I might catch the odd brown trout – I just enjoy immensely the experience of being there. I often share the first day with Alan Roe, who really is a great all-round angler; sea, coarse and game-angling; his fly-casting, and fly-dressing are excellent. He teaches both of these skills professionally. Alan is also a wizard with a centre-pin reel, he demonstrates Wallis casting countrywide at county shows. It's a pleasure to watch a great exponent of this art. Many OAPs complain about being retired: I don't. I can fish five days a week – many times its seven!

The early spring weather was dry and quite chilly; the rivers were low and very clear. I felt we were sitting on an ecological time-bomb whenever these conditions existed – just a small pollution incident could cause a major fish-kill. Often, between one and two in the afternoon, in a sheltered area of the river, Alan and I would see a hatch of flies; the odd trout could be seen dimpling the surface. Though fishing was extremely hard, Alan and I usually caught a trout or two; we often fished small flies on long leaders with a fine tippet. I can remember one first day, 15 March. Alan and I arrived on the river with excellent conditions – overcast sky, light southwesterly wind and very mild conditions. Fly were hatching and trout rising.

As we sat on a riverside bench, drinking a freshly-brewed mug of tea, we watched some taking-trout as olives drifted down the stream in profusion. We had both chosen 9ft 4 weight rods and floating lines with long tapered leaders. Suddenly, this huge, ignorant person, dressed in the latest fashion, carrying a new rod with its plastic covering on the handle, announced it was a Czech-nymphing day. He then plunged into the water. Making his way upstream casting the nymph, he was waving the rod about like the sword of Zorro. I suppose he had gone a few yards upstream when I noticed the trout were still taking flies downstream of this oaf. We looked at one another then Alan picked up his rod; after tying on a size 16 olive he quietly moved into position.

Making an upstream cast, he delicately dropped the fly a few feet ahead of the rising trout. As it drifted downstream the fly got eaten. I followed Alan and soon we were both catching fish. An hour later the big oaf announced the trout didn't want to feed. What an idiot. After those first couple of weeks the season opened on various waters in the Pennines. It was time to move eastwards.

In late March, Kent Sherrington and I were repairing some stiles on the River Hodder. I said, "Are you up for a day's trout-fishing next week?" Kent said, "Yes." We decided on a small Pennine river – the word 'stream' would be more appropriate. We agreed to leave just after his daughter had gone off to school. At Kent's house we had a brew, then loaded my tackle, waders

Alan Roe fishing the upstream nymph in Spring on the River Ribble

and lunch along with the obligatory kettle and gas stove in Kent's vehicle before heading off to enjoy a day's brown-trout fishing. An hour or so later we parked up in our usual spot surrounded by some delightful countryside.

Before assembling my tackle, I put the kettle on for a fresh brew. After pulling on my waders and wading boots, I put together my tackle. When I had first fished the water I had used a 4 weight rod, today I was using a 3 weight, 7ft Thomas and Thomas LPS model, matched with a Cortland double taper floating line to which I attached a 9ft Frog Hair leader with a 2lb tippet, choosing to start off with a size 16 Grey Duster which I have found very successful on this water. After a mug of tea we picked up our rods and made our way across the field towards the water. Before you see this delightful river, you hear it bubbling and gurgling as it tumbles its way downstream. Pushing through some riverside willows and hawthorns, I got my first glimpse of the tiny river; it looked beautiful in the sunlight. Fifteen yards upstream it disappeared as it made a right turn between the riverside trees and bushes.

I could see some late primroses and marsh marigolds. Blackbirds were about in profusion, a song thrush was singing its heart out in a nearby beech tree; a dipper zipped downstream, an area of water was ruffled by a light wind. Close to the overhanging horse chestnut tree, a good fish swirled on the surface. It's a spot where we always see a fish. Kent cast a size 14 Olive, the fly drifted about six inches, there was a slight dimple, and the fly disappeared. His strike connected with a small brown trout which was quickly unhooked in the water. Seconds later another fish dimpled on the surface, the artificial olive pattern was again quickly cast upstream; as it drifted over where we had seen the fish rise it was quickly taken by another small, hungry trout.

A few yards further upstream we arrived at one of our favourite pools. Kent said, "Your turn Martin." I made a cast, up towards a moss-covered rock. The Grey Duster dropped on the water like thistledown, then drifted downstream about ten feet before disappearing. The strike connected with a nice fish, and after a brief struggle, I was able to draw a foot-long trout to hand where I could bend down and slip out the barbless hook. We moved a few yards upstream to another nice-looking stretch, where the river flowed quite fast from right-to-left, then over some rocks, before flowing slowly over silt and gravel. I made a long cast upstream, the Grey Duster settled on the water and then drifted downstream. A small dimple – I tightened into a good fish which put a nice curve in my rod. An eight inch fish was unhooked in the water. It was fin, tail and scale perfect; unlike most of the stocked fish in our still waters. As always, I felt that Walt Disney could have painted these trout.

Walking quietly upstream, we came to another good-looking pool, at the tail there was an overhanging willow. A couple of yards before the pool, on the left hand bank, was a large hawthorn which was always waiting to grab a badly-cast fly. I made a parallel cast upstream and missed a fish on the first drift. It was Kent's turn – he didn't make a mistake. As his Paythorn Olive drifted downstream, Kent retrieved the slack line. Fifteen feet into the drift a fish sucked down the olive. The strike connected with a good trout and a few minutes later a fifteen inch fish was unhooked in the shallow water.

Once more we moved several yards upstream to a spot where the river was over hung by trees and bushes. Two large beech trees, some willows, alders, and hawthorns created a tunnel-like appearance. As always, some branches of a beech tree trailed in the water creating a scum line, and, as always, good fish rolled on the surface. Two warblers, with their black caps and white necklaces, were chasing olives as they hatched off in the warm sunshine; the king cups and marsh marigolds looked beautiful. More dark olives were coming off. Life was wonderful. In fact it couldn't get better. We were having a millionaire's lifestyle without being millionaires. Kent and I both caught a nice trout apiece before they were spooked.

We moved on upstream making a left turn and came to a beautiful looking bit of water, with no bushes or trees to impede the casting. It was a fly-fisher's dream bit of water and a place which had often given us a good fish or two in the past. Fish were rising freely to olives as they floated downstream looking like miniature yachts. I cast the Grey Duster upstream; as it dropped on the water it was immediately taken, I broke on the strike. I moved back from the water's edge, it was Kent's turn; the fly drifted downstream ten feet before being eaten. A trout was hooked, the rod tip was pulled down by a good fish and Kent was forced to give some line. This one needed a landing net to make sure it wouldn't be lost. It was unhooked and released and as

Spring Trouting

we often do we discussed the beauty of the fish. In the next couple of hours we fished some delightful water with lots of character. After a couple of refusals, I changed my Grey Duster to an Iron Blue dun. In the next thirty minutes I had brace of fish then after a 15–20 minute session, without any sign of rising fish, I decided it was time for a change.

With only the odd fly drifting down the stream, and no rising fish it was time to go downstairs. After changing from a dry fly to a size 16 Pheasant Tail nymph, I carried on fishing upstream. I would cast up the stream then let the nymph free drift its way down towards me as I retrieved the slack line in my left hand.

On my second cast, I spotted a tiny movement of the fly line. I tightened into a nice fish which went off upstream forcing me to give a few feet of line. Retrieving the lost line, and a few extra feet, I let this fish work its energy off under the rod tip, then, having drawn the fish into the shallow water, I was able to bend down and slip out the barbless Pheasant tail nymph from the scissors of a beautiful brown trout of perhaps twelve inches. I watched with immense pleasure as the fish dashed off to the deep water. Give me a brace of these fish any day rather than a brace of six-pounder rainbows from stocked water. Upstream, a Dipper emerged from the river with a mouthful of what looked like caddis. It was time for a well-earned fresh brew and a sandwich. During the rest of the day we caught a few more trout, I also had three fish on a small imitation Chironomid or Midge larva. I don't feel we use Chironomid larva enough in flowing water. Everyone knows how successful they are on still waters. I have learnt a tremendous amount about fishing the Chironomid, Midge or Buzzer from the book Midge Magic which Don Holbrook and Ed Koch published by Stackpole Books – a book I thoroughly recommend. As we sat enjoying a fresh brew we agreed it had been a good day's fishing on a small Pennine stream.

Sadly all the life and beauty of this Pennine stream, and others like it, could be lost by some silent enemy escaping into a water course, such as chemicals, fertilisers, pesticides or silage;

Pennine Stream

perhaps the releasing of a deadly poison from a riverside factory, garage or farm. It doesn't of course have to be by a river. That small foot-wide stream near your home eventually flows into a river. We need to ensure all these tiny veins of the countryside are kept clean and healthy. As we build more homes, factories, schools and hospitals, we must make sure we build the sewage treatment plants to cope with all the extra sewage and chemical effluent. I recommend the following reading: The Pursuit of Wild Trout by Mike Weaver, Merlin Unwin books. ISBN 1-873674-00-7. Environmental Poisoning and The Law ISBN 0 9516073 1 6. The Silent Spring by Rachel Carson published by Hamish Hamilton 1963. Of course, we should all be members of the Angling Trust, let's be honest, we cannot trust the EA which, as we know, is a Government quango.

I *have been fortunate in being able to fish the River Kennet since 1948. As a youngster I would be taken*
to this delightful Berkshire River with my father and grandfather in an old Ford 8 car with orange
indicators that would flick out from the left or right. We had no heater or radio, but we didn't care. It was
our transport to beautiful secluded places where I could shoot or fish, depending on the season. In those days
my Kennet fishing was mainly for chub, dace and roach, though during May and June we would fish for
trout. I remember them: big, fat, wild brown trout, with bellies the colour of marsh marigolds and decorated
with spots of all shades of browns and reds. A magnificent-looking fish, but then, are not all fish magnificent?

The River Kennet starts to flow near Clatford just west of the ancient market town of
Marlborough in Wiltshire; to the best of my knowledge the first fishery is in the grounds of
Marlborough College. The river then flows in a northerly direction into the Royal County of
Berkshire; it passes through some of the most delightful of English countryside: sporting estates,
water meadows, country houses, lush green meadows, mill and weir pools with coppiced,
pollarded and weeping willows, alders, ivy-clad oak and beech trees – nesting places for wood
pigeons and roosting pheasants. Dozens of carrier streams increase the mileage of fishable water.
Sadly, with urban sprawl and the water abstraction for the town of Swindon, the Kennet isn't
the river of my youth. The water meadows are now virtually a thing of the past. Today, the last
few miles are mainly through built-up areas, ending up in the River Thames at Reading. Then
we have the problem with travellers, who ignore all the rules of civilised living.

I've been privileged to fish the Hungerford Town water with both the late Mark Williams
of East Grafton, and Bernard Venables of Up Avon. The Town water was given to the people
of Hungerford by John O'Gaunt in the 1300s as a reward for helping his army in the Battle of
the Roses. Grayling and brown trout-fishing can be excellent, but sadly, it's stocked with horrid
rainbows. Upstream fly-fishing is the normal rule of engagement, and one should never allow
the fly to drift downstream. When you fish the Town water, you quickly learn about the Wine
Cellar pool, where many of the rods leave their wine to cool off. What surprised me on my first
visit to the water was seeing the well-mown banks, with a fringe of reeds, rushes and wild flowers
at the water's edge, offering cover to the kneeling angler. I feel very fortunate to have met Rob
Star, the river keeper; what a delightful gentleman he is.

Another stretch of the Kennet, where I have been permitted to fish, is the famous Kintbury
beat, going downstream for about two miles to the Wilderness beat. This is part of Sir Richard
Sutton's, Benham Park Estate. Included in this water are a maze of carriers, giving several extra
miles of fishing. There are dozens of different stretches of water to choose from: wide open
stretches through water meadows, shallow gravel runs, deep pools with overhanging willows,
slow deep runs under pollarded willows, tiny pools and narrow carriers. It's a trout-fisher's
delight; well managed by river keeper Gary Allen, and under-keeper John Colley. Both men hail
from Yorkshire where they originally worked as motor mechanics.

I had been invited to fish today by solicitor Stephen Collins, who was being treated to a day's
fly-fishing as a birthday treat. Stephen lives in Hungerford, through which the River Kennet
flows; it's an ancient town of red-bricked houses and antique shops – certainly a place of history.

The previous evening I had been the guest speaker at the Newbury AA presentation evening and Stephen invited me to stay at his house overnight. Before going off to Thatcham Football club for the meeting, Stephen and I dined on a lamb hot-pot dinner – I can certainly recommend his cooking! The evening with Newbury AA members was certainly an interesting one; the Association must be congratulated for the way in which it encourages the ladies and children into our great sport – or is it a pastime? For me it's a lifelong passion.

It was about seven o'clock the next morning when I went down for a breakfast of porridge and toast. Overnight there had been rain and, looking through the dining-room window, I could see it was cloudy with a light wind. A blackbird was tugging a worm from the lawn. The forecast was for a light shower with bright periods. Leaving Stephen's quiet cul-de-sac we made our way through the rush-hour traffic in town, and out onto the old Bath road. Having gone through the thirty miles an hour limit, we increased our speed to a steady fifty miles an hour. While others were dashing off to work Stephen and I were off to paradise. I thought to myself, "It's great being an angler!"

We turned off the old Bath road then drove down a gravel track, hedged either side by hawthorn and blackthorn, and leaving behind a crazy world for one of bird song, green fields, woodlands, hedgerows and gin-clear flowing water where trout with creamy-yellow bellies and big, brown and red spots would hopefully eat our well-presented flies. Pulling into the riverside car park my attention was drawn to the rustic bridge where two grey wagtails were flitting to-and-fro catching flies on the wing. The River Kennet was flowing right-to-left – it looked wonderful – even more so when a nice fish swirled on the surface. As we chatted about the day's prospects, we made up our chosen tackle. For me it was a Thomas and Thomas 5 weight Helix; Stephen, a 6 weight. We were both using floating lines with 12ft leaders with a tippet of 3lb. Should we need to use very small flies, we would go down to a tippet of 2lb. We also made up a heavier outfit for chucking big streamer-flies. Stephen was wearing gum boots and waterproof

The River Kennet – the home of big Perch

trousers; I pulled on my stocking-foot, chest-high waders and Korker wading boots. Finally a fly-fishing vest holding two fly-boxes, tippet material, floatant, degreaser and all those other bits of gear we fly-fishers collect. The waders are not just for wading, I can sit on the wet grass without getting damp. In my ruck bag I had a Nikon D70 camera and a Jetboil for brewing tea, milk and tea bags. Stephen had a very important bag. It contained a big box of sandwiches and buns, although sadly I was unable to share his passion for buttered currant-buns. He also had the gallon-size water container, without which there wouldn't be any tea.

Our first chosen area was a weir pool on a nearby carrier; we decided to try some big streamer-flies, On his second cast Stephen hooked a big brown trout; I watched it roll on the surface, it had a creamy butter-coloured belly, the spots looked as big as half-a-crowns. It was a good fish. Suddenly, Stephen was left with a limp line. The fish had slipped the hook. I commiserated with him.

Having lost a couple of fish, we made our way to the main river. As we slowly walked upstream, patches of blue sky could be seen; the sun was trying to burn off the cloud cover. An occasional fish could be seen sipping down an emerger. Our hopes were high. Walking far too close to the river's edge, we spooked a big trout which disappeared across the river, creating a big bow-wave as it did so. We both cursed at our stupidity. On the far bank I could see a hare slowly moving along the hedgerow. Stephen pointed skywards saying, "look, there's a buzzard!" It was a great day to be alive.

I suppose we had gone about 600 yards, when Stephen spotted a trout alongside some water crowfoot towards the centre of the river. Dropping back downstream, he tied on a size 14 Klinkhammer, and then pulled off some line. He made two false casts, then the line was going out over the water, the fly dropped lightly fifteen feet above the rising, feeding fish. I left Stephen to his work while I made some fresh tea. As I looked through the window of the fishing hut I could see Stephen had a bent stick and a pulled string. I arrived at the water's edge just in time to net the first fish of the day. It was quickly unhooked and released without being touched by hand. We celebrated by clicking our tea mugs together and toasting his trout. After tea I made a few casts in the bridge pool with a size 14 Adams; I pricked two fish – poor angling on my part. Of course, the fish stopped rising after that. We moved on upstream.

Talk about luck in this pastime: I chose to fish the inside of a bend, casting up and across. On my fifth or sixth cast I hooked a fish which didn't fight like a trout. Suddenly in the clear water I could see I had hooked an out-of-season perch – a big one. I called out, "Can you net this big perch for me Stephen?" As the fish was netted, we could see another big perch following the hooked one. I wasn't going to complain because it wasn't a trout. After a couple of pictures we watched the fish swim off, hopefully to grow into a five-pounder. Who knows – I might net the fish at that weight for Stephen. Moving upstream some 800 yards we arrived at another fishing cabin with plenty of windows and a view of the river. It was equipped with magazines, scales, table and chairs. Another small rustic-looking bridge crossed the river. The pool looked quite 'trouty.' Meanwhile, Stephen had spotted a nice fish rising twenty yards upstream. "Go on Stephen," I said. "Have a go for that fish while I sort out lunch." Staying well back from the water's edge, he moved slowly upstream.

In the cabin I unpacked paper plates, mugs, tea, milk, water and my faithful Jetboil. This piece of kit is perfect for making tea or coffee, and it's just as easy to heat up some soup or stew. After filling it with water I turned on the gas then pressed the igniter; it was all systems go. I looked out the window and spotted a nice trout rise in the bridge pool, a few olives were coming off. While waiting for the water to boil I walked across to the water's edge. It looked as if a mini-regatta was taking place; waves of olives were floating downstream. Suddenly the water was broken by swirling, bulging, tailing fish. It looked like a hatchery.

Back in the cabin I made tea, sorted out the ham rolls and the currant buns, which sadly I couldn't eat (doctor's orders). I then arranged the seats so we could look out through the window as we enjoyed our lunch in this idyllic place. Through the window I could see Stephen heading my way. No doubt he was hungry and in need of a fresh brew, but the smile on his face told me he had caught his trout. As we sat having lunch we discussed the morning's events and the wildlife we had seen: it had been a great session. Lunch finished, I packed everything away, then picking up my rod and net I walked across to the Bridge Pool. I sat quietly, looking for a rising fish. I suppose ten minutes had gone before I heard, and then spotted, the swirl on the water. Watching the spot like a hawk, I looked for some flies drifting down the stream to see what the fish had come up for.

Suddenly, two large dark olives lifted off then dropped back on the water. A fish sipped down one of the flies. I tied on a size 14 Klinkhammer with a grey body. Creeping on all-fours, I moved into a position where I could drop a fly some ten feet above the feeding trout. One false cast and the Klinkhammer dropped like thistledown on the water and slowly drifted downstream, I retrieved the slack line making sure I didn't disturb the drifting fly. It was the perfect drift; the fish rose, and then ignored the offering. Three times this happened. I changed the tippet from 6 xs to 7 xs then lengthened my leader from 10ft to 12ft. Still this obstinate trout refused to eat my fly, while occasionally sucking down the naturals. I changed the fly patterns from Klinkhammer to Adams to Greenwell's, then a Grey Wulff and finally a Blue-winged olive. Still the fish refused to eat. It was time to move on.

Two of the most common causes of failure in fly-fishing are either using too large a fly or the wrong thickness of leader. I felt I had used the correct size of flies and a fine-enough leader, and was unable to give a reason why that fish refused my offerings. Moving upstream I crossed a small bridge over a beautiful-looking pool which really did scream 'trout'. I made my way quietly downstream so I was positioned below the pool. Sitting quietly in the long grass, I watched for rising fish. A few olives were coming off, and then a trout sipped down a fly so quietly it only left the tinniest of dimples. In the next ten minutes, twenty or more olives came off.

Suddenly there was a big hatch of them; the surface of the pool was dimpled by rising trout. I must have counted five fish. Wagtails were in on the act as they fluttered to-and-fro catching flies on the wing. I picked out a nice fish rising close to a bridge support. My cast dropped the size 16 Paythorn Olive under the bridge; just before the fly landed I gave the rod a sideways shake, this put a wiggle in the line. I would now get a longer drag-free drift. Suddenly the fly was gone, a fish swirled: I lifted the rod, and tightened into a nice fish. After a brief struggle I netted a lovely brown trout about one-and-a-half pounds. Suddenly the sun appeared from behind a bank of cloud, illuminating the butter-yellow belly, the red and brown spotted flank of the fish; it looked magnificent. At last I had defeated a Kennet trout.

I moved back to the main river, conditions were perfect: warm sunshine with a light south-westerly wind. I was hoping for a hatch of hawthorn flies but I didn't see a single insect. I walked downstream well back from the water's edge, looking for rising fish. Arriving at a junction where a carrier entered the main river, I spotted one – then another. In the space of five minutes I spotted six fish, olives were floating down in profusion; the trout were gorging themselves. These were big olives. I changed over to a size 12 Paythorn Olive; it was an easy forty feet cast straight upstream.

The line gently dropped on the water in a straight line, the leader turning to the right. There was no way a trout was going to see my fly line. The fly drifted downstream. Suddenly it was gone, as a trout quietly sucked it down. I tightened into a nice fish and was forced to give a few feet of line. Slowly I gained line, allowing the well-balanced tackle to absorb the shocks; soon I had the fish in the net and hoisted it aloft. It was a nicely-marked brown trout of about a pound. I gently released the barbless hook from the scissors of the fish and released it back in the river untouched by hand. Standing up I could see Stephen coming down a grassy track from the carrier. "Have you caught?" I asked. He answered in the affirmative and said, "two on a dry Klinkhammer and one on a nymph Gold-Ribbed Hare's Ear." I said, "well done Stephen."

We then made our way downstream to the next fishing hut; it was time for more tea. As we got near, a good fish swirled on the surface. "Go for it Stephen while I make the tea." By the time tea was made Stephen was on his way down to me having taken that swirling fish. As we sat drinking and chatting about the day I recorded a short interview with Stephen for my "At the Water's Edge" programme on BBC Radio Lancashire. Tea finished we made our way back to the car park. It was nearly seven o'clock in the evening; I had a long journey home but it had been a great day. I arrived home at eleven o'clock. The following Friday I was back with Stephen for a day on the Wasing syndicate water on the River Enborne, a tributary of the Kennet, casting dry-flies and nymphs. The day after that, I was casting dry-fly on the Upper Avon.

I suppose all of us dream of catching a special fish; in 68 years of fishing I have had many special ones: I can remember them all. I suppose the most special fish was my first on 16 June 1941, using an eel hook, a ball of red wool as line, and a worm as bait. I was fishing an old clay pit together with my uncle Len, who was to die a few weeks later in the sands of North Africa. My first big fish was a pike caught from Teston Weir pool on the river Medway I believe it was in 1948. The fish weighed just over ten pounds. I killed that fish which was shared out between my family, my grandparents and the next-door neighbours.

Today, I regret killing that pike, even though it wasn't wasted. I remember a Kennet day, just before the end of the season in 2003 when I caught my first double-figure barbel, weighing 11lb 4oz on a chunk of legered bread crust. No way will I forget my best chub of 7lb 10oz from the River Ribble on a very cold February day when conditions were so poor that I suggested to Mick Holgate, "Lets forget it, it's a waste of time." That short afternoon session accounted for five pound- plus chub and a barbel of 10lb 10oz and of course my biggest-ever chub. Again, bread was the only bait used.

In over sixty years of fishing with fly, bait and lures, fishing fresh and saltwater, including tropical waters I have enjoyed many great days catching special fish. My latest not to be forgotten fish was caught on Tuesday, 15 May 2007 from the Edisford Hall water on the River Ribble, On Monday the gauge at Grindleton bridge was reading just under five feet, now that's a lot of water, but no good for fly-fishing. On Tuesday morning the gauge was reading just less than two feet, the water had cleared.

I suppose it could be described as looking the colour of strong tea, I could see the rocks in about eighteen inches of water. Good salmon and sea-trout conditions. During the morning the water cleared a little more, making the prospects for sea-trout fishing even better. Today I was due to attend a conference to pick up an award from the Chief Constable of Lancashire Constabulary; I thought I could first get in a couple of hours on the river, then head off to the Conference Centre.

Driving into the syndicate car park, I was most surprised to see no other angler's cars. I had the river to myself. How lucky can you get! The day before, I had got a new 10ft, 7 weight Thomas and Thomas Helix. I matched this with a medium sinking line with a 6ft leader with an 8lb tippet to which I attached a Hugh Falkus size 4 Medicine fly. Pulling on my chest waders, and then slipping my fly box in the top of them, I picked up my wading staff and rod and then headed off upstream. On a big rock in mid-river, a pair of Dippers were bouncing up and down, a kingfisher flew low and fast downstream, while overhead I heard that delightful bubbling call of a curlew. It was great to be alive. My chosen area to start fishing was the Minnow Pool.

For sea-trout, I split the pool into two sections, I fish the top of the pool for about forty feet, where the water is quite deep under the far bank, with a nice crease about a third of the way across the river. The fish were either resting close to the far bank or in the crease. I made a cast straight across the pool, not downstream, at about forty-five degrees as most anglers would. As the fly swings across the water flow, I often give a few short pulls or a couple of long slow pulls, as the fly reaches the centre of the river I will often lift the rod high causing the fly to swing up towards the surface. Its then I often get a hit. As my mate David said to me the other day, "Often the fish hold tight against the wall then chase the fly, hitting it in mid-river." When I have the pool to myself I make sure I fish the water hard, often a dozen casts before moving. But I only when I have the pool to myself.

The correct etiquette of fishing a pool is, you fish the cast out, and then take a step downstream, repeating this process until you reach the bottom of the pool. If you want to fish the pool again, you must go to the head of the pool, then follow the last angler downstream. As previously stated, when I am on my own I will make several casts, fishing the fly at various depths. The Minnow Pool is not only sea-trout water – it's a holding area for salmon. After fishing the top section of the pool where I expect the sea-trout to be holding, I then move down and fish the tail of the pool. I don't bother with the mid section, it's brown-trout water. That's not to say you won't catch brown trout at the top or bottom of the pool. You will.

I suppose I had made thirty or forty casts in my move that took me several yards down the pool. As the fly reached the centre of the river I lifted the rod tip pulling the fly towards the surface. A good fish hit, there was a boil on the surface, and, setting the hook, a fish shot skywards then crashed back in a shower of spray with the ripples spreading across the pool. The rod tip arched over as the fish powered downstream, the reel grudgingly released line. I cramped on as much pressure I thought the tackle would stand.

It worked, as I fought the fish back upstream. A few minutes later I had a fish about three pounds within fifteen feet. Backing in towards the bank, I pulled the fish into a quiet bit of water and close enough to reach down and retrieve the hook which was set in the scissors of the fish. I then watched it swim off strongly upstream. I thought how lucky I was to be on a sea-trout river when conditions were good. It's been said many times by far better anglers than me, "You have to be at the water at the right time to catch sea trout." How true. Wading out towards the centre of the river, I made a roll, one false cast and dropped the fly close to the far bank, quickly making an upstream mend, I watched the line hawk-like as the fly swung across the river. I probably repeated the process a dozen times, moving downstream every third or fourth cast.

Preparing to lift off for another cast, a fish hit, the rod tip was savagely pulled downwards; the reel gave a long, low-sounding growl as line was pulled through the guides. Once again the fish headed downstream, but this time in short bursts. By cramping on pressure I was soon gaining line and I suppose I had the fish to hand within five minutes. Another good size fish about three pounds. Three or four casts later I headed off downstream to the bottom of the pool. I was now fishing one of the best bits of sea-trout water on the Ribble, though one wouldn't think so to start with. I made a dozen or more casts without a touch: time for a fly change. On the advice of James Waltham, author of The Sea Trout and The Fly published by Crowood Press, I decided to fish a Snake fly, which Dave Jones of Bury had tied up for me. First cast, the fly had travelled just a few feet when I had a hit, as before, the fish moved downstream. The well balanced tackle was perfect for subduing it. Soon, fish number three was to hand, I could see the fly was well inside the mouth. Using a small pair of forceps, I quickly removed the barbless double hook, then watched the fish move quickly across the shallow water to sanctuary.

The author deciding which fly to use

Ten minutes later I had another hit; three seconds later it was gone. The same happened on my next cast. Ten minutes later I had a firm hook-up, I reckon this fish spent more time in the air than in the water. Once subdued I quickly had the fish in the shallows where I quickly lifted the barbless hook from the top lip. This was turning out to be one of my better days of sea-trout fishing. As I watched the fish swim off strongly, I was then asked for my syndicate ticket and rod licence by the EA bailiff. Thankfully, all was in order. Unlike a friend of mine who offered last year's rod licence when asked to produce his documents. Luckily, he did have a current rod licence in another pocket. Two hours later, without another fish, I decided it was time to move on. As I was retrieving the fly, a brown trout grabbed hold, just as Malcolm, the assistant river keeper turned up to fish the pool. After a chat I said, "It's all yours Malcolm, have fun."

Back in the cabin, I was pulling off my waders thinking, I could collect my award another time, I can't catch sea trout every day, I decided to stay on the river. I made a welcome mug of coffee and some buttered toast. As I sat reading the Angler's Mail, enjoying my break, two other members turned up. John said, "Any good Martin?" I said, "Yes, four nice sea trout from the Minnow Pool." I then explained how I fished and the fly patterns used. Fifteen minutes later both anglers were heading off upstream.

After my tea break, I headed off to fish another pool. By now conditions had changed, the water had dropped a few inches and the colour had gone from dark tea to a weak tea. The clarity of the water was such I could see the bottom in about three feet of water. The air temperature had risen by a few degrees, with a light wind. Conditions were excellent for brown-trout fishing. Swifts, swallows and martins along with lots of ducklings were feasting on the many flies hatching off. Fish could be seen rising in every pool.

I headed back out to the river, to a pool that in the past has proved successful for sea trout, the river above the head of the pool flows quite fast and shallow over rocks, down quite a steep incline into the head of the pool. In times of high water temperature, it's a well-oxygenated bit of water, loved by the brown trout and grayling. It's a pool where one has to take care when wading; a wading stick is a must. With the clearing water, I decided to stick with the snakefly on an 8ft leader, fishing it close as I dare to the bottom. I made two passes through the pool, without a sign of a fish. Back at the top of the pool, I made a roll cast, dropping the fly on the crease, I then lifted the rod tip allowing the fly to swing and lift. I had made about three casts. For a few seconds it seemed as if I had caught on some weedy rock. Then it was like an underwater explosion as a fish boiled on the surface before leaping clear and crashing back.

Line went through the guides in a blur. My first thoughts were 'salmon', then it leapt clear of the water a second time shaking its head as it did so. "Sea trout" I said aloud to no one! It then went off down the pool with me stumbling behind, at the same time keeping the rod fairly high and exerting as much pressure as possible on the fish. Once again it went skywards then rolled back in the water. It continued to fight its way downstream, as if trying to get back to the ocean from where it had come. Ten minutes or more and I was just a witness in this epic struggle. My mouth was dry, adrenaline was pumping, at the same time I had this horrid feeling in the pit of my stomach at the thought of losing what could well be my best-ever sea trout. The fish looked huge: every time it leapt clear of the water, it seemed to grow bigger!

Fifteen minutes later I could feel the fish was getting tired. I cramped on all the pressure I dare, slowly, I fought the fish upstream, at the same time making my way downstream in the hope of getting below the fish. Suddenly it shot up the pool, I began to sense victory. If I didn't made a mistake the fish would be mine. Inch-by-inch, foot-by-foot I gained line. A minute or two later I could touch the leader – the fish was mine; I heaved a big sigh of relief. It measured out between twenty-seven and twenty-eight inches. For a few seconds I admired this magnificent creature that had started life in the river then gone to sea and was now back to its birthplace. No way could I kill something that had given me so much excitement. If I had wanted a table fish, a three-pounder would have been big enough. I was on the river well into the night then back again at dawn, fishing until about nine o'clock; then it was time for breakfast. I didn't get another fish.

Yes the ladies make fine anglers. Sue Parker of First Nature Publishing with a fine sea trout. Credit Pat O'Reilly, MBE

Over the years, I have just enjoyed weeks of delightful wild brown-trout fishing on Loch Eye in Ross and Cromarty, just north of Inverness. My guide, Roger Dowsett, has a boat on the loch, reputed to be one of the finest wild brown-trout fishery in the Highlands.

The loch is designated as a Site of Special Scientific Interest (SSSI). In winter it acts as an important roosting site for internationally important numbers of waterfowl. During summer, visiting ospreys are seen regularly throughout the day, together with the occasional otter and roe deer.

It has extensive subsurface and partial marginal aquatic vegetation which reaches its maximum coverage in mid-summer. In periods of prolonged sunny and hot weather, the loch can be affected by algae, hence the very best fishing is from April through to July, but this loch is well worth a visit at any time. The fishing season is from the first Monday in April until 30 September and, remember, there is no fishing on Sundays. It's a relatively large, shallow loch: just 15 metres above sea level, about 400 acres in size with an average depth of just 1m–2m. Bank-fishing is not permitted, neither is the use of petrol or electric motors. The east-west length is about one-and-a-half miles, where you can enjoy some good drifts – but expect a good workout as you row back to base at the end of the day.

The shallow, weedy conditions are ideal for insect life, with huge hatches of important aquatic insect groups throughout the season: buzzer and olives all season, and sedges from late June onwards. Brown trout are present in large numbers, and the rises that accompany the big fly-hatches can be spectacular. While there are preferred drifts, trout can be caught just about anywhere. During the day you should catch several fish between one and two pounds, occasionally, fish to four pounds are caught.

Boat hire, including up to two permits, is £32 per day. On my second visit, as I was putting together my equipment for the day's fishing at the water's edge, I heard a splash then I watched as a big brown, which I reckon would be four pounds-plus, swirled on the surface, hammering into the sticklebacks in just a foot of gin-clear water. Five minutes later I watched another big trout attacking the stickleback shoals. For fifteen minutes or more, Roger and I stood in awe at the sight of, not one but two, big trout feeding in a foot of water. To catch one of those fish would be a dream come true. These are not those stocked fish of still waters, but wild brown-trout with spots the size of half-a-crown: magnificent creatures. Despite the tough conditions during my visit, Roger and I caught some beautifully-marked trout, with the best at about three pounds which I took on a wet Greenwell's.

On our first day, Roger made up a floating outfit using a 9ft 6 weight rod, while I chose to have two rods, a 9ft 6 weight Thomas and Thomas rod with a Ghost tip line, 15ft leader with a 4lb tippet, On the advice of Roger, I fished a greased-up size 12 Loch Ordie on the top dropper, known as the bob fly. On the second dropper I tied a size 14 wet Greenwell's, my point fly was a size 14 Black Pennel which Roger said imitated the black buzzer. My other outfit was a 10ft 6 weight Thomas and Thomas with a floating line, with a 15ft leader to a 4lb tippet, My bob fly was a size 12 Loch Ordie, well greased-up with gink, on the second dropper was a size

14 wet Greenwell's with a size 14 Gold ribbed Hare's Ear on the point.

I chose the 10ft rod as I feel when there is a good wave on I can get a better presentation when I dibble the bob fly on the surface. A suggested selection of flies to have in your box are: Kate McLaren, Zulu, Greenwell's (both wet and dry), some Daddy long legs, a selection of buzzers, sedges and Damsel fly nymphs. I can highly recommend the area for a

Author with a nice Loch Eye Brown Trout

family holiday with all its outdoor attractions and, best of all, the excellent wild brown-trout fishing. During our day's fishing we caught some lovely fish, lost a few and watched some giants.

As a visitor you will find delightful countryside with virtually no litter or graffiti, where you can enjoy fishing on beautiful lochs. Those in the family that don't fish can enjoy some delightful walking. There is excellent bird-watching, red kites, osprey, peregrine falcon and merlin to name a few that you are likely to see. Around the Moray Firth area you can easily view populations of bottle-nosed dolphins, common and grey seals, and roe, red and sika deer. You may also be fortunate and see some of our other more elusive mammals including otter, red squirrel, pine marten, and wildcat.

Author's Gillie on Loch Eye, Roger Dowsett

Monday was one of those lovely, soft September days, warm with no wind, and low light conditions, what I call a 'roach-fisher's day'. I started fishing on Edisford Hall water on the River Ribble with a floating line, fishing a size 8 General Practitioner fly on a 9ft, 12lb tippet. Around ten o'clock I hooked a fish, just below the big rock at the Clay Hole; it was quickly subdued, a very coloured cock fish of about eight pounds which was quickly released. Back in the cabin I had a quick brew; as I sat watching the river, a cormorant flew low up the river; this sea-going predator then started hunting in a weir pool. Finishing my tea, I decided I didn't want to catch any more coloured salmon and packed away my gear.

As I was checking my mink traps I could see some grayling feeding on tiny flies. Instead of going off downstream I decided to fish for these delightful fish, often called, 'Lady of the Stream'. I chose to use my new 8ft 5 weight Thomas and Thomas fibreglass Heirloom model. The rod has a lovely action, very much like fishing with a cane rod. I matched it with a small Ross reel and a floating Wulff triangle taper floating line. In the clear water I chose a 15ft leader tapered down to a 2lb tippet; With a large number of very tiny midge-type flies hovering over the water, I picked a size 20 Grey Duster. It's a pattern that imitates nothing special, but grayling will often take them for something they like.

Grayling are a shoal fish which you can often spend some time searching for, often trying several spots before contacting the fish. It might be a school of ten fish; there could be fifty. Grayling can also be fished for with trotting gear and small red worms though I reckon sweet corn is better bait and you don't usually catch so many trout. Having fished the first pool without seeing any signs of fish, I moved downstream to the 'Big Rock pool' where I immediately spotted the rise of a grayling as it quietly sipped down a tiny insect.

As I pushed my way through the shoulder-high Himalayan Balsam, a fox cub took fright; across the river a pheasant shot skywards, downstream a magpie was being mobbed. Using a wading staff, I waded out into the river so I could get a better cast; I pulled off some line, made a back cast, then shot the line. Just as it was going to land on the water I put a wriggle in the rod which transferred to the line, giving me a better drag-free drift.

After three casts without a fish I rested the spot for five minutes; grayling are easily spooked by the line going over their heads. When I restarted, I hooked a nice fish on my second drift; in eight casts I caught five fish averaging about a pound and a quarter. I sat on the bank and watched for further activity, I didn't see a single rise. With my Polarised glasses, I could see every stone on the bottom on the river bed; the only fish I could see was a small trout, I didn't see any grayling, it was time to move. Having carried on for a fishless hour, I gave up for the day.

I was most impressed with the new Heirloom fibreglass rod; close your eyes when casting and you will think you have a bamboo rod in your hand. As the Thomas and Thomas brochure quotes: "Claude Monet, Auguste Renoir, Paul Cezanne, Edgar Degas – the masters of French Impressionism". Each purist attempted to record his vision of reality using transient effects of light and colour. And for today's angling purists, like pro-staff member Martin James, who delight in a fly-rod that virtually "paints" the fly on the water, T&T created the Heirloom series'. The Americans certainly have a way with words. In my book they have created a masterpiece.

On Tuesday, after some overnight rain, the River Ribble had a rise of about ten inches. I spent the morning in the Radio Lancashire studio working on some programme material until lunchtime; then it was off to the river to check my mink traps which have to be inspected every twenty four hours. Back home, I had a quick lunch and, after a few telephone calls, I caught up on my correspondence including some fifty-odd emails. In no time at all it was dinner; after an hour's break away from my desk, I got back to work until about nine o'clock. Finally, I spent an hour reading Len Arbery's book, Ripples and Reflections, published by Little Egret Press, before going off to bed.

On Wednesday I was surprised to see the River Ribble holding its level, it looked great for coarse and salmon-angling. As I moved downriver, I could see that most anglers were fly-fishing for this great game-fish, no doubt knowing that the season comes to an end this month. Today it was my pleasure to host three army officers: Major Stewart Heaton, Major Ian Parker and Sergeant Tam Miller. They were on the River Ribble for a day's angling in the peaceful Lancashire countryside; we must never forget those who get killed or badly injured protecting our safety, both at home and abroad. I reckon it would be nice to see all angling clubs, syndicates and associations offer our men and woman, home on leave from Iraq or Afghanistan a day's fishing. It's the least we can do.

Though no salmon were caught we had a great day's fishing – I suppose the highlight was the all-day breakfast in the café at Mitton! During the afternoon session the guys were served tea and biscuits at the water edge. After they left the river bank for home, I went back to the car, then realised I had left my landing net on the bank so I had to retrace my steps. Back home I had some dinner then read a bit more of Ripples and Reflections before going off to bed.

Thursday I am back on the river repairing some fencing, checking my mink traps and clearing away rubbish where it had been caught up in the riverside bushes and trees during the recent floods. Friday as the rain sheeted down, I spent the morning putting chicken wire on

several stiles; as I worked away I watched the river rise a couple of feet. Then, having finished off the stiles, I headed off to the cabin for a brew and some toast. As I sat watching the river, I was privileged to see a chrome-bright salmon, about ten pounds, rise from the dark-coloured water, then crash back. Several sea trout have been seen going over the weir, and the extra water in the river has certainly helped. Let's hope we have a wet summer to keep our rivers flowing; the last thing we need is a hot dry summer.

Mink, the biggest killer in the countryside

On the occasion of my seventieth birthday, my friend David Jones suggested a fishing trip to celebrate. What a good idea I though, and said, 'Let's visit British Columbia and fish for salmon.' It was duly put in the diary.

In May of that year I visited the Black Isle in Ross-shire to see my son Nigel his wife Tracy and my first granddaughter Morgen. As always, I travelled with a selection of fly-fishing gear to cover pike, perch, and trout and salmon, I had a great week of fishing which included catching some wild brown-trout to three pounds. On my return, David and I were chatting at the waterside about my trip when he said, "I've always wanted to have a week's salmon fishing in Scotland." I said, "Let's go north and not visit British Columbia." Within the hour we had booked our fishing on the River Conon which is controlled by the Fairburn Estate in the Muir of Ord, Ross-shire.

The River Conon is in the Highlands of Scotland, the mouth of the Conon being about two miles south of Dingwall, thirteen miles from Inverness. The Conon system is by far the largest, north of the great Gen where it is fed by four main tributaries: the Orrin, Meig, Bran and Blackwater. The Fairburn estate has two-and-a-half miles of right-bank fishing with sixteen named pools: Junction Stream, Junction, Boat, Bridge, Roberts and Teal, at the Colonel's pool you will find a cabin with table and chairs, coffee and tea making facilities.

Other pools are: Moy, Plock, Bend, Rowan 1 and 2, Wires, Tommy's, Aquarium and Kettle. Most of the pools have cabins. The cost for five rods when I visited in September was just £450 per rod for a week of salmon angling. It varies from £180 in spring to £550 in August – certainly value for money in some wonderful countryside.

As we all know: successful salmon-angling is so dependent on water levels. Over the years many anglers have booked a week's angling in Wales, England or Scotland in the spring or for a September holiday, only to arrive and find no water, and no salmon. We chose the River Conon as it gets compensation water from the hydro scheme, ensuring good water levels throughout the season. I would also say that the beat fishes best from around 1ft 9" to 2ft 2" inches. I also think its fair to say that, when generating, it can go from 1ft to 3½ft, which is 2ft above summer level, and the compensation water can cause the river height to change from a 1ft to 3½ft and back again in a few hours, depending on the demand for electricity and the water available. I did notice that an influx of fresh water encouraged the fish to snap at a passing fly.

In the net L-R David Jones and Gillie Ryan Rutherford

Bank, wade and boat-fishing were practised, but during my stay anglers fished from the bank and deep-waded when the water was suitable. The wading was some of the most comfortable I have ever experienced anywhere in the world. Fishing the pools was quite easy, you could be forgiven if you thought the bed of the pools were covered with carpet, so smooth was the wading. During my week in September I witnessed a lot of moving fish and many chrome-bright ones were caught on the fly and returned.

It's possible to fish with a single-handed 10ft 8 or 9 weight rods, but for ease of fishing in covering all the pools a 14ft Thomas and Thomas Spey rod was the choice of many anglers, matched with floating or sink tip line depending on the water height. Ryan Rutherford, the head Ghillie, along with the other rods fishing the various beats during my stay, rated the Thomas and Thomas Spey rod the best they had ever cast. Apprentice Ghillie and gamekeeper, sixteen year old Sean Buchanan, who is from Marybank (the house that he has lived in all his life is only half a mile from the river) is without doubt one of best Spey casters I have seen. It was such pleasure to sit on the bank and watch this young man put a fly tight to the far bank. David Jones during his week's fishing used only two fly patterns: a Cascade brass tube for the faster water, and a Temple Dog fly pattern at all other times. They say a Collie Dog worked quickly through the pools often wakes up the salmon and makes them more aggressive. Some other successful fly patterns are Silver Stoat, Shrimp Fly, Munroe Killer, Willie Gunn, Ally's Shrimp, Cascade, and Stoat Tail. While David chose to fish for salmon, I chased the wild brown-trout above and below the salmon pools.

Another venue I enjoyed was the River Orrin: a small, 15–20ft wide river of jumbo-sized rocks, with steep gradients and lots of fast, boiling, foaming, rushing water, flowing through a high gorge of rock and forest. Fishing this turbulent water meant some tough upstream wading; on many occasions the white, foaming water tried its best to sweep me off my feet and send me downstream. Fishing a weighted nymph was achieved with a roll cast, but occasionally, a short cast of 20ft was needed as I worked my nymph into all the likely-looking spots. Some of the quieter pools were no bigger than a dining-room table. The fish averaged four to the pound, the 8oz trout I caught was a veritable monster. But it was great fun that I wouldn't want to have missed. For further details for bookings write to Estates Office Fairburn, Ross-shire IV6 7UT Tel 01997 433273 e-mail fairburn.farm@farmline.com.

John Macaskill, Sean Buchanan and Ryan Rutherford

I suppose it was around 1990 when I first visited the United Arab Emirates. As usual on my travels, I had all the fly-fishing gear needed to cover most situations, as I had just finished a four week trip in the Caribbean, chasing bonefish and other species with a fly rod. My body was tanned a nice mahogany colour from being at the waterside in warm sunshine day after day.

On my first day in the UAE I stood waist-deep in the warm water of Dubai Creek, the white, soft fine sand making me feel I was back in the Caribbean. Some fifty feet in front of me were a big school of Queenfish averaging four to five pounds. I cast a size 8 white-coloured shrimp pattern, close to the fish as they attacked the bait fish on the surface. I gave two quick strips and felt a fish grab hold, a strip strike set the hook into my first fish of the session; my 7 weight rod hooped over. After a spirited fight, fish number one was unhooked and released. I reckon I probably had twenty fish that day.

But beware of the Queenfish, it has several spikes situated around its body and gill covers. The fish will do their best to stab you in the hand. They are also classified as venomous, and it can be quite painful when you have been hit several times during a day's fishing. The use of barbless hooks makes the problem of unhooking the fish quite easy: in most cases it can be done in the water, either with forceps or by giving the fish some slack line. Sadly, today, the powers that be, have banned all fishing in the Dubai Creek. I reckon it should be opened to the fly-fishing tourist and expats. Fly fishers don't leave bait wrappers, bits of fish and other rubbish at the water's edge.

Le Meridien Al Aqah where it is really fun in the Sun

The words 'Arabian Gulf' or 'Persian Gulf' will probably conjure up visions of: war, Saddam Hussein, US aircraft carriers with their protective cover of frigates, destroyers and aircraft; desert sands, camels and oases. There is of course another vision of the Arabian Gulf. It is one that has been created by the United Arab Emirates, with beautiful hotels, parks, shopping centres and sandy beaches; also, the azure blue, warm waters of the Gulf contain many species of fish, big and small.

The second time I visited the UAE it was late October, I left Manchester on an Emirates Airlines flight; my first stop would be Dubai. I use Emirates because it's an airline that really does put the passenger first, with excellent in-flight service. Late October is an ideal time to visit. The weather is usually perfect, the fishing good. I had come to the UAE for a few week's fishing in Dubai, Abu Dhabi and Fujairah, where the sun shines all day, the fish keep pulling the string and bending the stick. The United Arab Emirates is much westernised and pro-British. In fact the Brits are, I believe, the only nationality that doesn't need a visa to visit the country.

The UAE is a confederation of seven Emirates. Dubai is an emirate, as is Abu Dhabi; on the east coast is the Emirate of Fujairah, situated on the shores the Indian Ocean. This is also a great area for sports fishing. All three emirates are very modern in appearance, with the tall office blocks, great hotels, golf courses, restaurants, night life and shops or markets (known as souks) catering for the tourist, business man and sun seeker. With its good motorway network, you could be forgiven for thinking you were in a Western City. If you enjoy Chinese food, I suggest you visit the Le Meridien Hotel where they have a very nice Chinese restaurant. My daughter Sharon took me there one night, along with a group of her friends, to celebrate my birthday. It was excellent. Why not try the sweet and sour prawns, you won't be disappointed.

Whatever your interests, you must find time to visit the fish, gold, and material souks, the latter has the finest silks in the world. The souks are fascinating. Don't forget to visit the museum at Bur Dubai which is situated down near the waterfront. Dubai is a shopping paradise for the ladies;

Emirate staff, such as these, ensure a pleasant, relaxing flight. Credit Emirates Press Office

here you can buy the material of your choice, then get your favourite blouse or dress made up for about five pounds sterling by one of the many local tailors. For the angler, one place to visit is the fish market.

In fact, whenever I am on a fishing trip to the warmer climes I always visit the local fish market. You can learn so much with reference to the species in season and the size of fish likely to be caught. There are several tackle shops in Dubai but sadly, as I write, they do not stock any fly-fishing gear. I feel this will change in the future as more anglers take up saltwater fly-fishing. On this visit I stayed with my daughter in Dubai, but as mentioned, there are many fine hotels, without doubt the best are the Le Meridien group. They have two in Dubai and one in Fujairah which really are five stars. At the Le Miridien Al Aqah on the east coast I host a saltwater fly-fishing school; Patrick Antaki, the General Manager, must be congratulated in having the courage to open such a venture – the first of its kind in the Middle East. It gets more popular each year.

Mr. Saeed Rashid Al Shaali and son – Managing Director – Almanzel Houseboats and Marinas arrives on the fly casting court by helicopter L-R Aleks Sebastien, Patrick, Maxine, Saeed with his son Rashid and Author

There are water sports for all, including: swimming, skiing, windsurfing, diving and snorkelling. The fishing can only be described as being very good, especially for this writer, who has had many exciting trips hunting and catching: tuna, trevally, jack crevall (probably the streetfighter of the aquatic world), Kingfish, Queenfish (often known as talang by the Arabic speaking people), barracuda, dorado also known by its Hawaiian name, Mia Mia, and various snapper jacks and grunts.

Staying at the Le Meridien Al Aqah doesn't mean you have to miss the delights of the city. The hotel runs a courtesy coach into Dubai for those who wish to shop. Why not take a trip on an abra, a wooden boat which is used as water taxi. They cross the creek to-and-fro all day long. You will certainly enjoy a trip along this picturesque waterway, a natural inlet from the Gulf which divides the city into Deira and Bur Dubai. From the creek, traditional wooden dhows set out for the ports of India, the Gulf and East Africa, just as they have for generations. Along its banks, all the bustle of loading and unloading make it a fascinating sight and journey.

In the past, while your partner was going around the souks, you could fish the Dubai creek which runs through the City. It was great fun – a bit like fishing the Thames at Richmond. As you caught the fish, a dozen pair of willing hands would be there to relieve you of your catch. The immigrant workers are very poor, so they welcome any fish you catch. I would always take a selection of hooks and some bulk spools of line and weights, which I gave away to many of these poor people. I often sit down with them and watch how they successfully fish with their hand lines; I don't see them miss many bites. In fact, they hit more bites than I do with rod and reel.

It's great to watch a float in the many small harbours, catching fish from a few ounces to four or five pounds. Often, I would sit chatting with the Egyptian anglers fishing with their 30ft pole using bread paste on a size 12 hook, catching many different species, including mullet, which are great fighters. I can't tell you the names of these numerous species of fish. It seems that everyone has a different name for them – depending on the nationality of the person you talk to. One fish you will come across is the saffie. Don't touch this fish. Its sting is extremely painful. It will make you go dizzy often causing a minor blackout for a second or two. Imagine poking your hand down a wasp nest then multiply the experience a dozen times, that probably sums up what it feels like to touch a saffie. I learnt the hard way.

If you're a reservoir-trout fisherman then you can have some interesting sport in the harbours and along the shoreline between October and April. In May the fishing can be OK, but choose to fish before breakfast time. A 7 weight rod with a floating line with a 9ft tapered leader down to a 12lb point will be most suitable. Don't use the normal cold-water lines you used in the UK, they are not suitable for use in the warmer climes. You need a tropics line. I find Wulff triangle taper colour-coded lines ideal. Make sure, on your return home from fishing the creek or any other saltwater fishing venue, that you thoroughly wash down your rod, reel, line and flies. Do not neglect this job even for one day.

If you hire a boatman, treat him with respect. Try to explain the type of fishing you are doing. Remember, most people have never seen fly-fishers in the Middle East. I always take an ice chest with lots of cool drinks including water and soft drinks, some fresh fruit, sandwiches and crisps. Making sure the boatman is well fed and watered. In addition to a tip, I always make sure I give my boatman some hooks, spinners, line, etc and perhaps a tee-shirt, which they treasure as a special gift. I have noticed that gifts are often shared out among their friends, especially soft drinks, food, line and hooks. They enjoy having their picture taken. I always shoot a few pictures of these migrant workers, then, when I get back home, I send the pictures to their families back in their country of origin. Remember these guys only get to see their families once a year. Most important of all, don't forget the sunscreen. Boat, beach or wading, don't forget the sunscreen, I use Rieman P20, its suits me, you might need a stronger sunscreen. Don't neglect this essential item.

Some years ago I had a day's trolling for barracuda and kingfish. I must be honest and say it wasn't for me. I find trolling very boring. I didn't enjoy it; I feel watching paint dry or grass grow to be more exciting. In fact, after an hour I asked to be taken back to the harbour. Fishing the ocean over many years with fly and spinning gear in many parts of the world, I have had many exciting moments, catching: Kingfish, barracuda, tuna, queenfish, jack crevall, dorado, cobia, bonito, wahoo, tarpon, redfish, snook, bluefish, striped bass, albacore, bonefish, sailfish and sharks – many hundred pound-plus sharks, even on a fly rod. In fact, you can catch any fish on a fly, even the milk fish are being caught with this method; one successful angler in the UAE is Brian Hearne from Idaho. Brian tells me these fish are real tough fighters.

My first choice method of fishing is with a fly-fishing outfit. Should the wind be too strong I will use a spinning outfit rather than not fish at all – though I really do love chucking big bits of fluff in the salt, especially when the fish are big and I can fish a floating or slow sinking line. This for me is the ultimate in angling and something I could do for the rest of my life, if I was a millionaire.

Flying to warmer climes can be very risky when you have to rely on the baggage handlers at the airports to treat your rods with kindness. With new restrictions in force at airports, it's now an even more worrying time for the travelling fly-fisher. Over the past three or four years I have spent a small fortune on travel rods. In the past, fishing warmer climes, I had my travel rods on board as hand luggage: sadly, not today.

I can always buy a few clothes should my luggage get lost; I can't usually replace my rods or reels at most venues. I vividly remember flying from Canada, where I had been salmon fishing, to the west coast of Florida via Miami, to fish the Gulf of Mexico for a week. Arriving at this infamous airport, I checked my luggage then noticed my rod case was missing. After reporting the loss to the airline, I decided to have a look around. Showing my press pass to the so-called security, I was allowed to wander around with ease. I found my rod case hidden behind a small office door. That rod case wasn't meant to be going on my flight! On another trip to Canada, aboard a Northwest Airlines flight from Gatwick to Calgary, all my luggage was lost. After a week, I had the airline fly me back home. My luggage turned up two weeks later, my Nikon cameras were missing. Not once did the airline call and give me an explanation or say sorry.

Class of 2010. Rear: Ettienne Vorster, Gordon Callaghan,
Carole Vandentillaart, Margot Day, Ian Day, Keith Mckay
Front: Bill Helmers Peter Vandentillaart, Karen Mckay, Martin James

To get the best out of fly-fishing in the UAE waters you need four outfits. Fishing the harbours or from the small rocky outcrops and the shoreline for the smaller species of fish, it's a 9ft 7 weight with a floating line. Many of these fish probably average around the pound mark, but they offer some good sport – better than the average stocked rainbow trout.

My two most often used rods are a 9ft 9 weight and a 9ft 10 weight Thomas and Thomas. If I am chasing jack crevall, giant trevally and other powerful fighters, I will switch to a Thomas and Thomas 11 weight, though there are times when it's a 12 weight.

I always take a selection lines designed for the tropics. All are weight forward: both floating and slow sinking. I also have several Teeny lines from 200 to 500 grain. The new clear slow-sinking lines on the market are excellent for fishing in the clear waters of the Gulf. Flies are quite a simple choice: go with a selection of surface flies such as Poppers, Sliders and Gurglers. I always take a big selection of Seaducers, Bend backs, Clouser minnows and Lefty Kreh Deceivers in sizes from 1s through to 5/0s, in various colour combinations. Some bright reservoir-flies on hook sizes 12 through to 6 hooks will also do the trick when fishing the creek and harbours. In twenty years of fishing in this part of the world I learn something new on every trip. It's been a great learning curve for me and many other fly-fishers, young and old.

After some years of heavy construction, taking place both on and offshore along the west coast of Dubai, the fishing dropped off quite dramatically, especially from the shoreline. I looked for new areas to fish, Umm Al Quwain was one spot where I reckon it's possible to get bonefish. It's an area of flats and mangroves; the wading is rather bad due to the very soft bottom. I would love to have a couple of weeks in the area with a small boat and outboard motor, fishing these waters. I reckon you could get a surprise or two with the fish that might grab hold of a fly on the right part of the tide.

Another area I prospected was the east coast from Dibba to Fujairah; it was a lovely-looking part of the coastline, where you could get good sport from the shoreline, especially at dawn on a flooding tide. From my first visit I fell in love with the place, it was like having a new girlfriend, I couldn't get enough of this area. It's where the majestic Hajar Mountains meet the ocean, in this case the blue waters of the Indian Ocean. After several years travelling down to the area with other fly-fishers, I was surprised to see a building project taking place in the area near Snoopy rock, a diving centre. I said to my wife Kate, it looks as if one of the Sheiks is going to have a palace built in this area. No doubt it will then be off limits. Eventually it became the Le Meridien Al Aqah Beach Resort .

It's situated just fifty kilometres from Fujairah city – a popular tourist destination – and a ninety

Reed fishing boat being shown by its proud owner on the East coast of the UAE

South African Wayne de Jager with a nice Tuna

minute drive from Dubai, both of which can be accessed via the regular shuttle services running from the resort. It's also within easy reach of the area's natural attractions, including ancient fjords, spectacular dive sites, palm groves, picturesque waterfalls and hot springs, plus a host of historical landmarks. It is known throughout Europe and the Middle East as a place of high quality food and service, a vacation venue for all the family to enjoy. It's certainly fun in the sun, with its unspoilt golden beach with two freshwater swimming pools and a beachside restaurant that serves delightful fish and chips. It's perfectly placed for you to make the most of the United Arab Emirate's year-round sunshine; fly and lure-fishing are top class, you also have diving and snorkelling opportunities. There are lot of amenities that cater for all tastes, from relaxing with a treatment at the Ayurvedic Centre to beach soccer, lazing by the pool, then dancing the night away in the rooftop bar.

No doubt it's the fishing you are interested in, where you have a variety of species to be caught ranging from blue, big eye, black skipjack and yellow fin tuna, barracuda, King mackerel and Queenfish, rainbow runners and dorado, also on the odd occasions, the elusive sailfish. In the shallow areas there are groupers and red snappers, sherries and several other species which can offer some good sport on light tackle or fly-fishing. If your fly-fishing, remember, you need fly lines designed for the tropics. It's rumoured there are bonefish in the Khor Kalba area. I am planning a trip in the future to explore the area.

After a day on the water, fighting some of the toughest fish that swim, you can replace all those lost calories with a wide selection of dining options, from a beachside barbecue to an à la carte dinner. Le Meridien Al Aqah Beach Resort really has it all, offering a true getaway for its guests. Don't miss out on the Thai restaurant.

I suppose the hotel had been opened about a year when I got a telephone call from Kiran Kumar, the press and publicity officer for the Al Aqah as its often known, asking if I could meet with him and Patrick Antaki in London. As I was very busy at the time, with filming commitments, I suggested they meet me at Preston, Lancashire. We agreed to meet at four o'clock in the afternoon the following Friday. The object of the meeting was to ask me to go and sample the fishing, to make a report on the action and to take part in some promotional filming, featuring fishing offshore. After several weeks planning I flew out in October, arriving in warm sunshine.

The next day I met up with South African Wayne de Jager, a guy who could cast a fly and fish skilfully with light-spinning gear. Most important of all, he really did know how to handle a boat, a skill that is needed when you're twenty miles or more offshore. Wayne and I hit it off from the start. During the next twelve days we caught a lot of fish; I was able to help get Wayne on the guide's staff at Thomas and Thomas rods, arrange for him to get Gilmore reels, and through Dick Tallents at Masterline Walker, the scientific angler's tropic lines. Before we left, Wayne put into action a plan to commission a special offshore boat built to cater for the fly-angler: it's been a great success.

Out in the boat blood and carnage are everywhere but this is no battlefield scene, result of a U-boat attack or the aftermath of a terrorist car bomb. This scene of death is taking place on the surface of an ocean where a group of big, hungry, hard-fighting, scaly predators known as Jack Crevalle, roam the warm waters in search of food.It's the result of an ambush on a shoal of bait-size fish. The fish litter the surface. Everywhere I look I can see and smell death, Jack Crevalles I reckon are the toughest of the tough, and they are the street fighters of the aquatic world. In Mexico they are known as 'Toro' – the bull. They're half a dozen Tyson's rolled into one. They will fight to the death, never giving an inch. Unlike Tyson, they won't try to bite off your ear, but will savagely grab a Lefty Kreh Deceiver or other fish-like pattern of fly spinner or surface-fished plug.

With the scent of blood in the air, it seems as if every sea bird on the planet is homing in on the area. Cormorants, terns, skuas and gulls of every description are in there, fighting, squealing, screaming and diving for food, creating even more havoc. There is no escape for these bait-size fish as they are attacked from above and below.

They are trapped in this killing zone. All they can do is hope it will soon end. I cast a big Lefty Kreh Deceiver pattern into the swirling mass, two quick strips then the line is savagely pulled from my hand. Frantically, I grab hold of the fast disappearing line, then feeling it burn as it runs across my fingers. Somehow I strike in some mad, demented way and, on feeling the fish, I lift the rod shoulder high – though not for long as the rod tip is savagely pulled down under the water. The Tibor reel grudgingly gives line as a powerful adversary dives and powers away into the depths of the warm water that changes colour from aquamarine to a deep blue, then a light greenish blue colour that allows you to see down several fathoms. The sun burns down from a clear blue sky, the thermometer edges up to the 90°F mark.

Some three hundred yards of 20lb backing have gone from the reel before I'm able to make any impression on this, my sixth, jack crevalle in the past few hours. I was feeling shattered, not even knowing if I wanted another slugging session. Hussein shouted, "Keep at it Marteen," as he poured ice cold water over my head and my sore and battered hands. I shook my head to clear the water from my eyes then cramped on more pressure, lowering the rod tip; as I did so, I got back two feet of line. I was determined that this Jack wouldn't beat me if I could help it. The 10 weight rod bent alarmingly, I could feel the corks bend under the pressure. I was fighting this powerful leviathan for what seemed hours but was probably about thirty minutes. The fight from a jack crevalle will test man and tackle to the limit; these are wild fish with no names. I lowered the rod tip to gain a few feet of line then repeated the process and so it went on. 'Toro' would shake its head then dive again, taking most of the hard-won line which would have to be retrieved once more. I started gaining line for about the fifth time when I felt everything go slack. 'Toro' the Jack crevalle, had won this fight and its freedom.

Why should I have lost this fish I thought as I wound in the limp line: the truth was then revealed. The Albright knots, which I had practised tying all through the long winter months, had busted where backing and fly line were joined. Even on heavy tackle a thirty pound jack crevalle is not going to come in easily. Jacks will take you all over the ocean, given the chance. Sometimes you will need to follow in the boat, or lose your tackle to big jacks. They will break lines and hooks. Reels will seize up, rods will get broken and your body will sometimes cave in with fatigue and pain. Your shoulder muscles will often pop, one of the reasons why a lot of big-game anglers spend time in the gym keeping fit. This is not the sport for the wimps.

For the shore-bound angler, jacks are just as exciting, but be prepared for a mile hike along the beach when you hook 'Toro'. They will cruise close to the shoreline in shoals or schools of similar size, hunting down the bait fish then working them into a ball before driving them into the beach; they then go on a feeding frenzy, attacking and killing anything that moves; you're back to the aquatic battlefield with all the blood and carnage. It beats pike fishing. Jacks will hit surface-fished plugs and flies. Spinner plugs and flies fished a few feet down will also take this bullish fighter. The Mexicans don't call him 'Toro' for nothing – we all know how powerful a raging bull can be. "Let's have some lunch Hussein," I said. "We've been on the water since dawn." Hussein switched on the ignition. The 28ft Crayfish's 200hp Volvo motor roared into life, the bows lifted and away we went, skimming across the smooth glass-like surface towards a small island.

Lunch finished, we cruised around looking for another killing zone, I had put together an 11 weight Thomas and Thomas Horizon with an Abel reel holding 300yd of backing. I wanted more of this action with Toro. Slowly we cruised around looking for signs of diving birds which would show the location of more feeding fish. For some twenty minutes there was nothing, all was silent, we scanned the ocean in all directions. Off the port bow at three o'clock, a few hundred yards away, I could see diving birds. I pointed this out to Hussein and said, "Let's go and get another jack!" As Hussein pushed the throttle forward, so the bows lifted, we quickly moved off in the direction of the diving birds and, hopefully, feeding fish.

Coming in close, he throttled back the motor, moving upwind as he did so, to give me the best possible chance of shooting line. I made a cast some sixty feet at twelve o'clock. Three quick pulls, then a shudder went through my arm as a good fish savaged the fly hard, then dived for the ocean bottom. The flyline seemed to disappear in a blur, I noticed I was down to the yellow backing realising then 150 yards of red backing had already gone. At one time I had perhaps no more than a dozen turns of line left on the reel.

Thankfully, the fish slowed down. I cramped on as much pressure I thought the tackle could take. I gained some line. This fish gave no quarter and asked none. I thought about my knots; would they hold this time? Had I tied them right? Would the 15lb leader be strong enough? Was the fish rubbing its body on the line as it twisted and turned in its bid for freedom? All was quiet on the ocean. The seabirds and feeding fish had disappeared. It was a battle between man and fish separated by a few ounces of carbon fibre rod and some line. A helicopter carrier, with United States marines lining the ship's side, sailed slowly past off our starboard bow. Some stretched their arms, as if to say, "How big?"

For perhaps twenty minutes, but what seemed an hour, it was give-and-take but slowly I was gaining the upper hand. First, all the yellow, followed by the red backing, was on the reel. At last I was taking in the first few turns of fly line. I knew then, barring knots letting me down or the hook pulling out, I was going to win this fight. Hussein shouted, "There it is! It's a big jack." He pointed downwards. I lowered the rod, taking in line then lifted again, there was a huge swirl on the surface. I caught a first glimpse of my adversary.

With his last burst of energy he dived, but only for a few feet, then I had him back on the surface. Hussein didn't need a second chance – he got hold of the fish and it was mine. I slumped back on the padded chair, punched the air with joy, grabbing a can of cold drink from the freezer box. It was time to rest before the next round. That's saltwater fishing with a fly rod for Toro. You have perhaps an hour of sitting around then it's all action. "Give me much more of this" I say.

American anglers, Bryan Hearne of Idaho and Chris Myer of Oregon, two of my pupils at the Le Meridien Al Aqah Fly-fishing School in Fujairah, got a double hook up with big, hard-fighting dorado on their first day afloat during their learning experience of blue water fly-fishing. It all started the previous day in the classroom, where they were taught how to tie various knots, which included the use of the Tie-Fast tool. Discussions covered: line configuration, rod and reel, and line maintenance;

Chef Manivelan Natarajan prepares breakfast for the Author before he goes off chasing Dorado

types of rods, reels and lines to use and when to use them; where to find fish inshore and out deep in the ocean, and the effect of tide and weather on feeding fish. A lot of time was spent on the casting court perfecting their casting, working away until six o'clock in the evening. We all then retired to our rooms for an hour before going down to dinner.

As both pupils showed a lot of aptitude on the first day, I felt they should put into practice what they had learnt, on the ocean. Our second day started with alarm call at 4.30 in the morning, meeting up in the lobby at 5.30 for the drive to the Fujairah marina. After I introduced everyone to Wayne de Jager, we all climbed aboard his sports-fishing boat for a fast ride out into the Indian Ocean, probably twenty miles offshore. The plan was to target dorado, a fine sporting fish for the fly-rodder. Wayne, an experien-ced South African blue water fly-fisher, expected to find them around some of the ships that were moored up in the area, which is also the second largest bunkering area in the world after Singapore.

Bryan was equipped with a 10 weight Thomas and Thomas Helix, Gilmore reel with intermediate line to which was attached a small tube fly but not like those used in salmon fishing. Chris had a Thomas and Thomas Horizon II rod, Gilmore reel with a floating line. On the advice of Wayne, Chris tied on a popper tied up by Mark Bachman's who has the fly shop in Welch's Oregon. Some ten miles offshore in the half light of day, we spotted diving birds, changing course we went to investigate; I reckon we arrived ten minutes too late: the fish had gone. With increased engine revs, we were once again skimming across the ocean to a bulk carrier. As we got closer, Wayne slowed the engine down so we could creep in without disturbing any fish that might be in the area. We sat around for about fifteen minutes just seeing one small Dorado and a few small bait-fish. We then moved further offshore to a large gas tanker where we hit the jackpot. Within minutes I spotted two big bulls. Pointing to one fish I said, "Chris big fish at one o'clock, sixty feet." Then: "Brian there's a big fish off your port stern."

The popper on Chris's rod was quickly cast fifty feet, dropping about twenty feet from the fish which heard the plop, it quickly turned. In the blink of an eye the fish savaged the popper. Setting the hook, the fight was on as the fish cartwheeled across the ocean, taking about eighty yards of line as it gave five big jumps. After stopping for about a minute the fish changed direction, heading off towards the large gas tanker.

Again it jumped twice more before setting off on a screaming run this time towards the anchor chain, I held my breath saying to Chris, "If that fish goes between the anchor and the ship all will be lost." Thankfully, it stayed outside. Changing direction once more, I then had Chris move down towards the stern of the boat; this was one hot Dorado that wasn't going to give in easily. I reckon Chris would have a long fight; it was one mean, powerful fish. Meanwhile Brian was having the fight of his life. This pair of hot dorado were not going to give any quarter.

We were soon joined by a coastguard launch, which had come close in to watch the action. It was a furious give-and-take; Chris would get five feet of line back then the fish had other ideas, it would take fifty feet. As the sun climbed high the temperature increased, I started pouring cold water down Chris's throat and the back of his neck. Forty minutes must have gone by and still no end in sight to what can only be described as an epic battle between man and fish, well out in the Indian Ocean. The perspiration was rolling off Chris as if he was in a shower. Inch by inch he got backing line onto the reel. Deep down in the clear water I could see where the fly line was joined to the backing. I reckon Chris must have felt like the 'Old Man and the Sea', one of Hemingway's classics.

Slowly, with a lot of grunting and lifting, more line was gained, suddenly the fly line appeared. I had hopes then the fish would be landed. It all changed as fifty yards of line was quickly taken, at first I thought perhaps a big shark had grabbed hold of the fish. But no, it was the dorado. Chris had to start all over again with more pumping, sweating, heaving, arm-aching and a back-breaking fight to come. Once more I spotted the fly line where it joined the backing, I poured more water into Chris with encouraging words, "You're slowly winning mate, every inch of line gained is hard won so keep at it!" Soon, the fly line is coming through the guides, deep down I could see a big expanse of blue, our quarry was coming closer, suddenly, in the blink of an eye, Chris is down into the backing once more. I could see despair on his sweat-stained face, "Keep at it Chris." I said. Eventually, more line was being gained than lost, the fight was going our way; once again fly line was coming through the guides. Down in the water I could see this bull Dorado who had given so much in its bid for freedom, shaking its head as it continued the battle, there were more words of encouragement to Chris from Wayne, Bryan and I. Brian could only watch, having lost his big bull.

Wayne handed control of the boat over to the Sri Lankan deckhand, Dixon, and then picked up the big landing net. Inch by inch the fish was being pulled closer to the boat, soon we could see the leader; if it could be touched then victory would be with Chris, better still if we got this beast into the landing net for a picture.

Ten minutes later it was all over as Wayne got the big net over the fish's head, then the body followed, just the

Chris Meyer with his big Dorado

last third of the fish including its powerful tail were outside the net; Wayne smartly swung it aboard, laying it on the soft seating.

I quickly took out the popper. A few quick pictures of the fish were taken, then both Wayne and I nursed that fish back into the water where it struggled to escape Wayne's grip before diving deep into the cool ocean. There were smiles all round, even the coastguards congratulated us on returning such a magnificent fish which had fought so bravely. We should never kill big fish: I get rather angry with trolling anglers who kill everything and often dump them on the boat dock. These people are not sports fishers, they are fish killers.

The following year, I arrived at the Le Meridien Al Aqah beach resort at Fujairah in the United Arab Emirates having booked a week of offshore, blue water fly-fishing. I chose the Le Meridien as it offered a superb service, where you are treated as a very welcome guest and friend – not just a number, as I have experienced at some hotels.

I planned to fish for various members of the tuna family, trevally, queenfish. Often known as five fingered jack or talang, I believe the latter name is the Arabic word for this fish. I also hoped to target dolphin fish, not to be confused with our friend 'Flipper' the bottle-nosed dolphin, a mammal and not a fish. The Spanish call the dolphin fish, Dorado, the golden one; in Hawaii it's known as the Mahi mahi. It's a pelagic schooling migratory fish of deep water. Though it inhabits the surface of the ocean, it's an extremely fast swimmer. It's favourite food is the flying fish and squid. Of course, it will eat all the bait fish species when they are in abundance.

This great game fish has a liking for cover: buoys, seaweed, logs, and planks of timber, in fact any floating object could hold the dolphin fish. I well remember seeing a three foot square piece of cardboard in the Pacific Ocean off Mexico with a dozen good size fish underneath it. In the 1970s and 80s the Sea of Cortez in Mexico was the place to hunt these fish. Today, I feel the Indian Ocean off Fujairah could rival Mexico. Sadly, this fish is rated highly as a table fish, but not in these waters of the UAE. In other parts of the world it's being slaughtered by the commercial fisherman. I say now: 'It's worth far more to the tourism dollar when it's swimming in the ocean, than in the fish market'. Many of these commercial fishermen could be trained as guides for sports fishing where they could probably make a better living. Most of the commercial fishing boats, with their centre console, only need a few slight modifications to be ideal for the fly-fisher or light-tackle angler. It's believed a hooked dolphin fish can reach speeds of fifty miles an hour in short bursts. Having hooked into some very fast swimmers, I can believe this figure.

My day started around 3.30 in the morning when the alarm sounded its strident note. Throwing back the bed cloths, I staggered off to the shower room, switching on the kettle as I did so. Unless I start my day with porridge, toast and tea, it's not going to be a good one. Having had my shower, I dressed in shorts and tropical shirt. I light knock on the door heralded breakfast. I left the Meridien hotel around 4.30 for the drive to the Fujairah marina where my friend, Wayne de Jegger of East Coast Sports Fishing was waiting on the slip. As I made up a Thomas and Thomas Helix 11 weight rod with an Aaron reel, we discussed the day's prospects. I decided to use a Teeny .350 grain line, to which I attached a Gamma Bluewater leader with a 20lb tippet using an Albright knot. This knot was designed by the late Jimmy Albright of Florida. It's perfect for joining leader to a fly line or leader to wire. I then attached a size 3/0 white Clouser with some red super hair tied in at the throat.

My other outfit was a Thomas and Thomas 12 weight Horizon with a Tibor Gulf stream and a Teeny T500 line. Again I used some Gamma Deep Blue leader material to make an 8ft long tapered leader with a 20lb tippet. I then attached a size 4/0 Sea Habit buck tail. This second outfit was for the big dolphin fish or tuna should I get the chance of chucking a fly in their direction. With rods made up and tackle stowed, the bow and stern lines were released, the ignition switched on.

The hum of the twin outboards was music to my ears, as we moved slowly across the harbour for the open ocean. Once clear of the harbour, Wayne opened up the twin outboards. The bow lifted; soon we were skimming across the smooth glass-like surface of the Pacific Ocean heading in a southerly direction. I stayed up in the bows keeping a lookout for fishing nets and pots. As we cruised the ocean I could see a few flying fish and the odd small group of queenfish attacking bait fish. Today the queenfish were left in peace. I was on a mission to seek the 'Golden Ones' unless we spotted some yellowfin tuna – then I would change my mind. Off the port bow I could see a big ball of orange emerging over the horizon, though it looked as if it was coming out of the ocean. Through the haze on my starboard side I could just make out the Hajar Mountains. The twin motors throbbed and purred, not missing a beat. I suppose it was half an hour, perhaps forty minutes from leaving the harbour when we changed direction, heading for the horizon. Hopefully not too far, I didn't want to end up in Iranian waters. Thirty minutes later and some fourteen miles offshore Wayne pointed then shouted, "Feeding fish, two hundred yards off the starboard bow at about three o'clock." Wayne made a big swing to port to put us upwind of the feeding fish. I felt the bow dip as the engines slowed down to a steady tick over, slowly we moved within casting distance.

Up in the bows I picked up my 11 weight outfit. Stripping off some line, I let it fall on the deck. As we got within casting range of my quarry, I made a couple of false casts and shot the 3/0 white and red Clouser minnow out some fifty feet. It dropped six feet in front of my target fish. As I made a fast strip, the bull dolphin nailed the fly before I had moved it twelve inches. A firm strip strike set the hook; he shot away like a missile. The reels screamed, the line cut through the water leaving a rooster tail eighty yards away he leapt clear of the water then dived.

A few minutes later he leapt clear of the ocean again, then again. By now he had taken one hundred and fifty yards of line. I was well into my backing; then he went deep, very deep, then swam slowly but powerfully away from me. The reel drag was tightened down as much as I dare. The rod was hooped over; occasionally I felt a big hit on the line either caused by the tail of the fish or another fish bumping the line. I have seen dolphin fish do this on other occasions.

Wayne said, "That's a hot fish Martin!" I had to agree. I just wished I had hooked this fish on my 12 weight rod and not my 11. I would gain a bit of line then the fish would take it back. Several minutes later the pressure started to tell then slowly, by winding in as I lowered the rod, then smoothly lifting, I started to gain a few feet of line. I was winning. Suddenly it dived, the reel grudgingly giving line. As I fought this 'Big Bull' I could see a dozen more fish. This is the time when another angler can often get a hook up. After a long, slogging scrap lasting some twenty-plus minutes, I had the fish ready for netting. Yes, my arms ached – but it felt great! A quick picture and the fish was released. As it swam away all the other dolphin fish went deep with it. During the fight the fish gave sixteen big jumps. It was awesome fishing.

During that day I caught fourteen fish between ten and thirty pounds, some near the surface others down about ten to fifteen feet. I used a selection of flies from size 1s up to 4/0s. I found I had to change the rate of retrieve, the size and colour of fly throughout the day. I was certainly happy to have a big selection of flies so I could make the changes. When I couldn't see the fish, I used the countdown method. Not all takes were aggressive; some fish gave a tentative pluck, more like a trout – this from one of the quickest and most aggressive fish swimming in the ocean.

Changing to a size 3/0 white Clouser with red tinsel tied in at the throat, I made a long cast, letting the line sink twenty-five to thirty feet. On my second strip I felt a hit. Strip striking, I set the hook, a powerful fish dived for the bottom. The reel screeched like a scolded cat, line peeled off the spool. I was well into my backing before the fish stopped on its first run. Every now and again the rod tip stabbed below the surface. I could feel a lot of head shaking. All I could do was hold on and increase the pressure, hoping all the knots would hold. This wasn't a dorado: it was a tuna – the power was awesome. It was

These guys can cook what ever you want L-R Abhishek Kumar - Sumith Dileepa Rodrigo - Avaz Fayziev - K. Ismail Kureshi - Bahtiyor Islombekov

going to be a long work out. Ten minutes into the fight, I started getting some line back on the reel. Only inches though, but I was winning, then fish would take it all back.

With the temperature in the 90s Fahrenheit, it was hot, tough work, perspiration poured off my brow. I gulped down ice-cold water at every opportunity. Slowly I got more line back on the reel, and then the fish took some back. I could feel the action of the fish, a distinct throbbing through the line. I got my first glimpse of it and cramped on the pressure, then lowering the rod tip I gained some line, then lifted in a smooth movement, lowering the rod tip once more, gaining more line back on the reel. Never, ever, jerk the line, make sure all your movements are smooth. Soon the fish was on the surface, it was quickly netted. I punched the air with delight. It probably weighed some fifteen to sixteen pounds. It was quickly returned to grow into a thirty-pounder. I hope I am around when it reaches that weight.

Back at the hotel I was welcomed with a cup of tea. After a shower, I had the opportunity to chat with some of the guests. Dinner was in the world famous Thai restaurant where the chef performed miracles in providing me with an excellent meal, designed for someone who is diabetic and cannot have any fats or creams.

On another occasion, I had planned a few days stay at my favourite hotel in the UAE. The Le Meridien Al Aqah beach resort at Fujairah. It's a place where you immediately feel at home. The staff are the most pleasant I have ever met in my travels worldwide.

Once again, I joined up with my friends Wayne and Roger of East Coast Sports Fishers. I had a thirty minute drive in the pre-dawn darkness along deserted roads to the marina. I was quickly out of the car with my tackle bag and two rod cases. Thanking the driver, I said, "Please pick me up at 6.30 tonight," then I headed for the ramp down to the boat dock. Roger and Wayne were

waiting ready to go. Stowing the gear, the ignition key was turned; immediately the two engines purred into life. The sound of outboard motors in the light of a false dawn is music to the ears of a fly-fisher going out on the ocean. I removed the bowline and stored it safely in the centre console.

The boat moved slowly away from the dock heading towards the marina entrance

Roger and Wayne

and the ocean, a heron stood motionless as it peered intently into the water, no doubt looking for an early breakfast. Once clear of the marina, Wayne opened up the twin motors which roared and throbbed as we accelerated; the bow lifted. Soon we were skimming across the glass-like surface of the ocean leaving a rooster tail in our wake.

Three miles out an escort of dolphins joined us; these big beautiful and powerful creatures looked magnificent in the early morning light. In the east a huge red ball had slowly emerged from the ocean, to the west I could just make out the Hajar Mountains through the haze. All too quickly we were within a mile of our first location where we hoped to find some bonito, or albacore, as they call them in the United States. I could see flying fish skipping across the ocean.

I had with me 4 Thomas & Thomas rods, 2 Helix models in 9 and 10 weights, and 2 Horizon II models in 11 and 12 weights I had the latter two rods in case we found some big tuna, perhaps big dorado. I stowed them away until needed. On the 9 weight Helix I had a Tibor Riptide reel

Patrick Antaki, GM of Le Meridien, with son Sebastian who caught this Dorado

with a 350 grain Teeny line, My 10 weight carried a Tibor Gulf stream; this time I chose a 450-grain shooting head. Our target fish were going to be the bonito where I would use the nine weight, should I find some extra big bonito I could easily switch to the 10 weight.

I would suggest, if you are going to fish these waters, and you only have one rod, make it a 10 weight, but make sure your fly lines are designed for tropical waters. Forty-five minutes after leaving port we found a group of diving, screaming gulls; bait fish were on the surface trying to escape from what can only be described as a killing zone. The bonito were tearing the baitfish apart; bits of dead fish littered the surface. You could smell death in the air. Wayne throttled back the twin motors; we slowly moved within casting range, the engines were cut. We had just the sound of ocean birds and flapping bait fish. On my fifth or sixth cast I had a hit, line was quickly taken off the reel, and the fish dived deep. Having fished for these tuna for several years, I knew I had a scrap on my hands. This one lasted for several minutes. Albacore, or bonito, certainly give you a work out. It was tug-of-war, first the fish would take some line then I would get it back, if the fish took ten feet I would win back fifteen. Eventually the fish was netted. Slipping out the barbless hook, we shot a quick picture then plunged the fish head first into the ocean from about five or six feet. Do not hold these fish by the tail then wait for them to swim off. They will die.

In the next two hours we had a dozen or more fish, this was then followed by a quiet spell, though we did have the pleasure of seeing a rather large green turtle close up. After a sandwich and cold drink, we cruised the ocean looking for diving birds, occasionally spotting small groups of tuna on the surface, but we couldn't get close enough to get in a cast. I do find it difficult at times to approach these small groups of tuna, I reckon it's because they are feeding on a small school of bait fish, by the time we are within casting distance, the bait fish have split up leaving the tuna to go off hunting.

I suppose it was around twelve noon; I was up in the bows of the boat on lookout, when I spotted a solitary dorado of about ten pounds heading off the port bow at about ten o'clock. I

Author's daughter Sharon playing a dorado off Fujaira

called, "Single dorado heading towards the small tanker anchored fifty yards away." Twenty yards from the tanker I could see several more dorado. They were not big fish, but well worth chucking flies at, hopefully they would want to eat. I chose to use a 9 weight, replacing the size 2/0 Clouser with a size 3/0 red and white Deceiver. While I sorted out the business end of the tackle, Wayne lined me up for a drift, and then switched off the ignition. It was that quiet you could have heard a pin drop. I stood poised up in the bow, line coiled neatly on the deck, the rod in my right hand, the fly between thumb and finger of my left hand ready to shoot, should I see a fish.

I peered intently into the clear water, with beads of perspiration on my brow; I was like a coiled spring. We drifted some thirty feet, and then, as we were coming out of the shadows into the sunlight I spotted a cruising fish. With one false cast I shot the line. Twelve feet in front of the cruising fish the fly landed with a quiet plop. I watched it sink down three feet then made two, one foot long, fast strips; the fish moved towards the fly, its pectoral fins changing to an electric blue colour. In the next instant the fish grabbed the fly. With a firm strip strike, I set the hook. The fish dashed off at a fast rate of knots; fifty yards away, it leapt clear of the water. These fish are certainly the greyhounds of the ocean. It then dived; I cramped on the pressure and two or three minutes later it jumped three times in quick succession then cartwheeled across the ocean. This was blue water fly-fishing at its best. It couldn't really get any better. Five more jumps and ten minutes later, the fish was ready for netting.

What a great fighting fish these are. If you should be lucky to hook up to one of these fish, please return them to the water. They are too beautiful to kill for the table and the fighting quality is second to none. In the next three hours I reckon I had a dozen follows, eight or nine hook ups and landed six fish the best at about twenty-five pounds. It had certainly been a great day. In fact, this dorado fishing is as good as anywhere in the world and better than most locations.

On my second day of blue water fly-fishing in the Indian Ocean, I had as my companion AJ, an air-traffic controller who lives in Dubai with his delightful wife Janine and two children. AJ is an avid and knowledgeable fly-fisher in both salt and freshwater. We left the marina at dawn heading in a northeasterly direction towards a small coaster, which had been anchored up for a few days, where Wayne had seen dorado.

Both AJ and I tackled up with 10 weight outfits and fast sink lines. I suggested using these lines after my experience of the previous day when I had seen some good fish down deep. Should the fish be near the surface we would start to retrieve a bit quicker. As we got within casting range of the coaster, Wayne set us up for a nice drift then cut the motors, AJ, on his first cast, hooked up to a fast-moving fish, it jumped twice then threw the hook. We both agreed the power of these fish was awesome. Ten minutes later AJ was down to his backing, a good fish had moved off fast. Seven times it leapt clear of the ocean. A super aerial display; this was 'Fun In The Sun'. After a fifteen minute tussle with one of the great sports fish of the ocean. Wayne was able to net AJ's first dorado. The fish was returned to fight another day, grow bigger and offer another sports fisher the delight AJ had just experienced. We certainly had an exciting couple of hours. If you are trolling for dorado you don't get the excitement of sight-casting to a fish. In fact when you're trolling it's the skipper who does the work. The fish hook themselves, you just wind them in, usually on equipment designed to bring in a two hundred pound shark. Change your life. Take up fly-fishing or light spinning-gear.

I flew from Manchester to Dubai by Emirate airlines, they have two flights a day. My fishing with East Coast Sports fishing was booked through the hotel. Apart from blue water fly-fishing, you can do light-tackle fishing. In the past I have fished many beach venues on the East coast, enjoying good sport, though the fish are not as big and powerful as you can catch offshore.

I usually take some 400 flies, rods from 8 to 14 weights, a selection of lines floating to extra fast sinking. Deep blue leaders from 10lb through to 30lb, spools of deep blue leader material, fly line cleaner, a bag of bits and pieces, polarising glasses and a plentiful supply of sun protection. I also make sure I wear clothing designed for the tropics.

Returning to port after a day on the Indian Ocean L-R
Author's Son-in-Law Greg, Daughter Sharon Author and Kate, Author's Wife

For some years I have searched the UAE waters for bonefish, without success, though I am pretty certain I spotted one at Umm al-Quwain, on the west coast. A fish that certainly is in UAE waters is the milkfish. You reckon bonefish move fast? – wait until you hook up to a milk fish; these critters are turbo charged, and yes, despite many people saying you can't catch them on a fly, you can.

As I have said dozens of time, you can catch most fish on the fly, though parrot fish are different, they eat corral. An area to hunt the milkfish is the flats around Abu Dhabi. The following is an account of a day's fishing by American angler, Brian Hearne and English angler, Adam Harvey, published with Adam's permission.

Adam writes: If you have never caught a milkfish, then make sure you put it on your list of things to do during your lifetime, you will not regret it. These fish are difficult to catch and very easily spooked. Many fly-fishers have tried to catch these mysterious fish only to fail either due to lack of research on what they eat (algae not squid, shrimp, etc) or by casting every possible fly in their box to the fish, eventually scaring them away.

I shared a wonderful experience with Bryan Hearne from Idaho with whom I have been fly-fishing for a few weeks. We had set off rather later than was usual on a Thursday morning. During the previous week I had sourced the fly-tying materials needed to make a milky dream fly, from a contact in Dubai. As I set up the rods, reels, lines, etc for myself and Bryan, my fishing partner tied up some milky dream flies. Now this was the first time either Bryan or I had tied one of these flies, not difficult when you know how, but when you have your fly-tying vice clamped to the arm of a deck chair and the wind is blowing, you need a certain degree of patience and skill.

Twenty five minutes later, we were ready to walk out to the flats and fish the outside channel where the fish could often be seen cruising.

With the tide ebbing away, we crept quietly along the side of the channel, staying well back so we didn't spook the fish. After we had been walking and creeping for ten minutes, Bryan

AJ with a big milkfish

spotted something about 100 yards ahead. He asked me what I thought it was in the water. After staring into the distance, I confirmed it was our target. Now, without wanting to exaggerate, you could say my heart was pounding like it was trying to break out from my body, could this be our lucky day...? There must have been a school of about twenty milkfish swimming around with their abnormal size tails and fins sticking out of the water, no more than twenty-five feet from the water's edge. We moved back a little further to double check that our lines and flies were set up correctly;

everything was fine with the tackle, now down to business.

Creeping down to the water's edge like two school kids about to play a joke on some unsuspecting individual, we reached our spots without spooking the fish. I was quick off the mark, casting the recently tied fly to the school of fish. As my milky dream landed between three fish, the water erupted. Suddenly, my reel was screaming as line was pulled off at a fast rate of knots. I kid you not when I say, 170 yards of line was stripped in less than five seconds – and it was still going! I had to do something otherwise the fish would have headed towards Dubai with me water skiing behind it (now that would be a sight...!). I managed to put some pressure on the reel, then start to slow the fish down, it turned and headed right towards me so I reeled in like there was no tomorrow to get slack line back onto the reel. Within two seconds, he was off again, this time taking a similar amount of line. This process went on for about 20-25 minutes, and I'm not joking when I say I was relieved to get this fish landed. I'm also not ashamed to say that, at thirty years old, I was exhausted after he was finally on the flat and... Could have my picture taken with him? AWESOME...!

Bryan, hooked into a milk fish, and landed it, after going through the same tiring process. After that we thought we had lost the school due to the commotion of the last two being caught. No, they were still around! Bryan hooked another one after he'd sat down to take a rest; suddenly his reel started screaming as line was pulled off again...! Luckily, he had hold of his rod otherwise he would have kissed goodbye to his outfit.

The Author has always enjoyed travelling with Emirates. Credit Emirates Press Office

*I*n 1999 I, along with Swedish fly-fisher Gregor Johnson, visited St Lawrence County in New York where we planned to fly-fish the Grass and St Lawrence Rivers, for smallmouth bass, pike and muskies. Joe Babbitt, who had a carp-fishing camp on the St Lawrence River near Ogdensburg, also invited us to fish for carp. The carp-fishing was easy, in fact Gregor and I fished an afternoon session where Gregor not only caught his first carp but it weighed over twenty pounds, I had several fish the best a common at thirty-five pounds. What caused a lot of excitement was when I caught a rare mirror carp of twenty-six pounds which even tried to go tail walking. It was the first fully-scaled mirror that anyone had seen.

Gregor and I decided it would be fly-fishing for the rest of the trip. Two rivers I can certainly recommend are the delightful St Regis and Grass Rivers; all you need is a rod licence. Don't attempt to fish without one, your likely to get arrested. The Grass River fish are willing to feed under most conditions, wading is good and you can often spot your quarry in the clear water. Grasshopper patterns work extremely well. I suggest a 5 weight rod for smallmouths, and a 9 weight for pike and muskies.

Our next day's fishing was on the Grass River near Madrid in St Lawrence County. Pushing my way through the long grass, I arrived at the water's edge. The early morning sun in the clear blue sky was slowly climbing high over the riverside trees. A kingfisher flew low over the water. Suddenly, a dozen minnow-size fish jumped skywards to escape the feeding bass. Wisps of mist drifted across the river as big fish rolled on the surface. 'Was it a pike or muskie?' I asked myself. I cast a medium size popper some sixty feet across and slightly downstream. Retrieving line in a series of six inch pulls, the lure popped and gurgled across the mirror-like surface. Suddenly, there was what seemed like an underwater explosion, the water erupted as the popper disappeared in a boil of water. The strip strike connected with a good fish which leap skywards then crashed back in a shower of spray, sending out ever-increasing circles, the reel grudgingly giving line. For several minutes it was give-and-take, several good jumps and a couple of runs from the fish. Pulling it towards the bank, could see I had a good bass of some three pounds. Bending down, I lipped the bass, extracted the popper then released it back to its watery kingdom. It felt great to be alive in a delightful part of the world catching good size fish.

Fishing with big streamer-flies and small popping plugs on a 6 weight outfit and floating line, I caught a succession of good size smallmouth bass, also losing a couple of good size pike when they bit through the nylon line. I tried to overcome the problem by using a small length of wire but the bass – numbers dropped quite dramatically. Other days were spent on the St Lawrence River fly-fishing for bass and pike, also trying for the muskies, but sadly they eluded me on this trip.

Joe Babbitt said, 'Let's go and fish The Ausable.' This water is one of those 'must fish' waters. It is one of the Blue Ribbon Rivers in Upstate New York. While you're on the river, the family, if they don't fish, can spend a very pleasant day at Lake Placid. Take a look at the ski jump and ask yourself if you would want to emulate Eddy the Eagle! I had been told that this was a river one had to fish. It was low and very clear, you could see the smallest stones on the bottom. I was disappointed at the number of rods on the water, and I didn't feel they were in tune with the river or its fishing and history. I got the impression these anglers wanted to move down the pool as quickly as possible – probably to the next can of beer, judging by the large number of empties on the bank side. I reckon drinking was the priority.

The tackle being used was a bit crude. I asked one guy what weight rod he was using. He answered, "A seven weight man." I felt I could cover all the fishable water with my 4 weight. Another guy asked why I was creeping up stream and casting a dry-fly, suggesting I would be better off working downstream, roll-casting a bead head nymph. I caught a few stocked fish, using a dry-fly pattern such as Ray Bergman would have done back in the 1950s. My choice was a size 14 White Wulff on a 12ft tapered leader to a 2lb tippet. These stocked fish could be quite tricky at times. Though the scenery was delightful, I couldn't say the fishing was that challenging, some beats were that crowded, I passed them by.

I would often fish early mornings and evenings, then during the day visit some of the many places of interest. Driving around and sight-seeing in St Lawrence County is like going back in time to the 1950s. It's a delightfully slow pace of life; the local people are extremely pleasant, friendly and helpful. For those who like to catch lots of big carp my advice is, go and fish the St Lawrence River Experience with Joe Babbitt. You're guaranteed a lot of string-pullers, and from my experience it's excellent value for money. I have witnessed many anglers catch a lot of big fish through the expertise of Joe.

Later in the year I was back in St Lawrence County, this time to check out locations for a proposed television programme. Apart from locations, I wanted to sample more of the fishing available, before committing to an hour-long show. Karen St Hilaire of St Lawrence County Chamber of Commerce was the perfect host. I don't think the project would have got off the ground without her immense knowledge of the area, its people and places of interest. After three weeks researching the project I felt confident enough to tell the film company to book a flight to New York State.

No doubt many of you are now thinking it would be another fishing programme. Not this time. This was to be a different type of entertainment. You, the viewer, got to see me taking part in several activities. One day I joined John Scarlet, the local blacksmith, swapping rods for reins when I teamed up him to try my hand at oxen driving. We had to drag some felled trees from the nearby forest. We were introduced to oxen, which were a pair of castrated bulls trained as draught animals for pulling loads with. My oxen team didn't understand this Brit's accent when I shouted, "Wow wow and wow," slang for stop or slow down. They just galloped on towing a large tree trunk in a cloud of dust. I just fell about laughing. John regained control and finishing the job; then it was off to his blacksmith shop for a day where I was given the offer of two types of hammer for my work. One was a cross pane hammer in the French style the other an English model. I chose the latter. After making a poker we went off to John's house for dinner.

The next day I was allowed to go fishing with Tim Damian who was a guide with a local tackle-shop. We chose the St Regis River, catching some nice brown trout. All too quickly my fun-time was over. I was back at work, this time to learn something about boat building with Everett Smith in an old barn built back in 1854, that's an old property in the States. Everett was also a skilful musician who could play various instruments, and a member of a local band. During the day I planed then pinned a new plank to one of the boats being built.

The next day was booked for filming, on the St Regis River. I made arrangements to meet Tim Damon at the Riverside diner where Clary, a good-looking blond waitress made sure our order was taken quickly. Breakfast was scrambled eggs, sausage, crispy bacon with toast, and a mug of tea. Just as we were finishing breakfast, John, our driver for the day arrived. Glancing out the window, I could see a gleaming Model T Ford parked waiting to take us off to the St Regis River. Half-an-hour later Tim and I were on the river, it looked resplendent in the morning sunshine after the previous night's rain; I must say, going fishing in a Model T Ford was certainly not an everyday experience.

After tackling up with a 5 weight rod and floating line, I tied on a 12ft leader with a 2lb

Martin and Everett in the workshop

tippet. Looking upstream, I could see a stream flowing in from the opposite bank. Fish were rising just downstream of the stream, prospects looked good. Tim suggested tying on a size 18 Grey Duster. Moving out from the bank, I made a cast upstream, the fly drifted fifteen feet, no more, then disappeared in a swirl of water. By lunchtime I had taken several brown and rainbow trout. Sitting on the bank, we enjoyed some fresh beef sandwiches, I had a mug of tea made with water boiled over a riverside fire. Tim chose a can of beer. The afternoon session wasn't so good. After taking a couple of fish on dry flies, we had to switch over to nymphs for catching our fish. Mid-afternoon I spotted another angler further upstream, so decided to walk up and have a chat. I was surprised to see a good-looking woman. Erin Clanson was her name and she did know how to fish; she was casting a beautiful line and catching fish. It turned out that this lady fished and guided in the Catskills. At the end of the day

Erin, Tim and I enjoyed a dinner in the local restaurant.

The following morning I was back at work, this time as a cook for a day; I even got to cook a meal for a group of bikers – getting a ten dollar tip in the process! That evening, a group of ladies and I were filmed having a night out at the local bowling alley, something I hadn't done since the 1950s, it a good evening of fun, knocking over skittles, the girls having a few beers, while I stayed with orange juice. The next day was a rather special one for me: we were visiting the world famous Frederic Remington Art Museum. With the camera running, I explained the finer points of his sculpture and art work. He was without doubt the person who best captured the Cowboy and Indian wars out West, in the 1800s. For me it was truly a special occasion. Coming out of the museum, a young lady grabbed my arm saying, "I have just watched you discussing Remington's work in front of the camera. Are you a famous artist or sculptor?"

Next day I went carp-fishing with Joe Babbitt, where the film director caught a couple of twenty-pounders. After a couple of days rest, the film crew packed up and then flew home, while I had a few day's fishing left.

The following year Kate and I left our home in August for a ten-day visit to St Lawrence County in New York, on the banks of the St Lawrence River, to stay at Joe Babbitt's carp-fishing camp. It's a place where you can expect some of the greatest carp-fishing in the world. These are not stocked fish, but truly wild ones, with no names – growing to perhaps ninety pounds. One afternoon, as Kate and I peered deep into the clear water searching for smallmouth bass in a weedy bay off the St Lawrence River, a big carp appeared. No . . . it was a huge carp! We could clearly see this leviathan in four feet of water, it passed within three feet of the boat. The fish was at least sixty pounds; it could have gone ninety pounds. We stood spellbound as we watched this awesome fish dip its head in to the silty bottom. A minute later it moved off slowly. All I could do was watch the giant disappear and curse under my breath that I didn't have any tackle or bait in the boat. We caught a few bass and pike, but that carp stayed in my vision for days afterward. As the light faded, we made our way back to our riverside log cabin for dinner. There was only one topic of conversation. That huge carp which was so tantalizing close.

Next day, Kate and I attended a special luncheon with various celebrities from St Lawrence County and the City of New York. During the course of the luncheon several celebrities made speeches thanking me for my work in helping to get the World Junior Carp Fishing tournament off the ground. Also my involvement in promoting the area in my magazine and newspaper features. I was presented with the Key to St Lawrence County and a framed certificate. It reads:

Certificate of Recognition
This certifies that
Martin James
has been issued with the Key to St Lawrence County
for his outstanding promotion of travel and tourism to the same.
And that, this the 12th Day of June 2002,
has been proclaimed as
Martin James Day.

Key to St Lawrence County

The key is certainly a work of art by one of New York State's leading Blacksmiths. Following several radio and press interviews I went off to the Grass River to fish for bass. After a few days more days fishing we then took a flight to Massachusetts to spend a few days at The Thomas and Thomas rod-building plant.

August the next year we were back in St Lawrence County, for the Junior World Carp Fishing Championships. I, along with actor Tom Felton who played Draco Malfoy in the Harry Potter films, were the joint judges for the Championships. During the week we visited a school in Massena, where both of us entertained some 500 young kids – young Tom being the big attraction with lots of girls who had turned out to meet their hero. Young Tom from Essex impressed me with his carp-fishing knowledge and the treatment of his fans. One afternoon, he was down to sign autographs for thirty minutes, actually spending over ninety minutes, talking and signing. He is a nice likeable lad who isn't a spoilt prima donna like so many actors. Tom, along with his older brother Chris, was a class act. I admire them greatly for giving up so much of their time to help all these young prospective carp-fishers.

Tom, his brother Chris and I, spent a lot of time teaching the youngsters how to fish for carp. Starting off with a full day in the classroom at the Donald Martin Civic Centre, Waddington NY. In the winter, this classroom was an ice rink. During the summer months it's used for various activities, it was perfect for a carp-instructor's class room. The entrance had been designed so every one had to walk through the mouth of a huge model carp made by Waddington artist Patty Vanpatten. What pleased me, was the number of local anglers who helped with instructions. Joe Babbitt of the St Lawrence Experience contributed free of charge several sets of carp-fishing gear for these youngsters to use.

Day two was spent on the casting field, where youngsters from all over the United States, Italy, Canada and the UK, were taught to cast accurately, they were encouraged to ask questions, and we got many. At the end of the session, they were then given plenty of baits, hooks and weights so they were well prepared for the next day.

On day three. hundreds of boys and girls lined several miles of the St Lawrence waterway, some local, others from as far away as Illinois, Florida and California. Television film crews, radio reporters and an army of press men and woman were in attendance to capture the action: they were not disappointed. During the tournament many of the youngsters caught their first carp, with many twenty pound fish being taken. The best weighed in at over forty pounds. On both days, I would visit every competitor, giving them encouragement; advising them where to put the bait, help them to tie hair rigs, bait with boilies and sort out many tangles.

What really impressed me was how quickly these boys and girls mastered the various skills needed to catch carp. The enthusiasm of the girls was incredible, many having travelled several hundred miles. I asked a lot of the girls if they were just there to see actor Tom Felton, Draco Malfoy, or to catch carp. They all answered,

Martin receiving his Certificate of Recognition

"To catch carp, then meet Tom!" On the second day of the competition, I gave some advice to Ovid Reichelt who was from Hyde Park NY. He was fishing the Ogdensburg length. He followed up my advice by catching three fish, the best weighing 31 lb 4oz ending with a total of 73 lb 4oz. Another youngster to catch a big carp was eleven year old Connor Loomis from Waddington NY who had a 25lb 9oz fish which, with another carp, gave him a total of 41 lb5 oz.

Without doubt the greatest achievement by the competitors must be that of young Milly Mason from New Jersey. Fishing on the first day, she caught her first carp of about 16lb, I was present when this girl caught her first fish, and it's true that the first one gives you a grin a mile wide and two sparkling eyes. That's how I would describe Milly that day. The gear she was using wasn't the top-of-the-range tackle used by some competitors. It was a 6ft white fibre-glass rod with a fixed-spool reel. The story didn't end there: later on, our young Milly, fishing with the same tackle with a boily bait caught a 44lb common carp – a huge fish by anyone's standards, a fish that anyone would be proud to catch. Again the 6ft white fibre-glass rod and fixed-spool reel was up to the job.

Without doubt the girls were equally as good as the boys, catching many excellent fish, and with several girls winning much of the prize money on offer. These youngsters from all over the United States, Canada and England were a credit, not only to their parents, but also themselves and their countries. Their behaviour was excellent.

After the second day's fishing, a party atmosphere descended on the ice rink as competitors, Mums, Dads, instructors, helpers and sponsors gathered for the prize presentation, food, drink and disco. Karen St Hillair of St Lawrence County was the perfect MC. When Joe Babbitt stepped up to receive a plaque every youngster in the place gave him a well deserved standing ovation. Praise was due to: Kathleen Kelly of Stellar Marketing Solutions, Massena and her team, all the staff of the St Lawrence County Chamber of Commerce and the wonderful people of Waddington New York who had all worked so hard to make the tournament a great success. The wonderful hospitality, provided by Patty Vanpatten, Nancy Oaks, David and Kathy Duprey,

Nancy Putney and all the other volunteers from Waddington, wasn't forgotten. Without these dedicated and hard-working people, the boys and girls wouldn't have enjoyed so much fun and enjoyment. They now possessed a skill that will now give them a lifetime of enjoyment. Young Angela Peterson from Crystal Lake IL was certainly one of the girls who had a lot of fun. Seeing this young lady full of enthusiasm, vitality and joy, rush up on stage to receive her prize, put a smile on everyone's face.

After I had presented many of the prizes, I had to leave and go back to our accommodation. I felt lousy: I was having dizzy spells, sweating one minute ,shivering the next. Trying to pass water was virtually impossible, the pain was excruciating. The next day Joe Babbitt took me off to the local doctor, I was diagnosed as having a kidney infection, from past experience I knew then I was in for a rough time. Having just one kidney is always a worry. I was glad my health insurance was in good order. The doctors were extremely efficient making sure I was as comfortable as possible. I lost seventeen pounds in a week. There was no fishing for trout, bass, carp or pike, all I could do was sit around, feeling lousy and at times just wanting to die. I could have done without this illness.

Ten days later we flew out of Ogdensburg NY for Pittsburgh then Chicago and on to Portland Oregon. A few weeks before our trip to Upstate New York, Cheryl and George Burgermeister invited us to tag on an extra few weeks so we could spend time with them in the city of Portland, Oregon, and at their beach house on the Pacific coast at Netarts near Tilamook. We got to know George and Cheryl, when they came and stopped with us in Lancashire a few years ago. We had offered Oregon Trout, a conservation body, a two-week stay in our home as a fund-raising auction prize. The Burgermeister's made the highest bid. We all had a great time fishing the rivers Hodder and Ribble.

Big Al on the Umpqua River

Oregon is well known for its beautiful coast line stretching from Washington State in the north to California in the south. The State was also proving extremely popular for the Californians. Some years ago the two terms State Governor Tom McCall, said in the Portland Civic Auditorium on a June morning in 1972 "We want you to visit our State of Excitement, often." Then said, "Come again and again. But, for heaven's sake, don't move here to live!" McCall was a great conservationist who introduced the Oregon Bottle Bill (the very first recycling scheme of its type, years ahead of the rest of the USA) which nine Oregonians out of ten think is a great law. It's a pity we do not have a similar bill in the United Kingdom.

Our stay with the Burgermeisters at their beach home in Netarts was perfect; I could rest up, and get my strength back. George was a surgeon. Sitting out on the deck some fifty feet up on a hillside just reading and drinking tea, was the perfect convalescence. I could look out over the ocean, and witness an ever changing scene. The dawns and sunsets were often magnificent. I can recommend it to everyone. I had just purchased a new Nikon Digital SLR camera, and I spent much of my time reading the instruction book and getting used to this new bit of equipment. My time wasn't wasted.

We enjoyed some great food cooked by Cheryl, visited many shops including Camera World, Kaufmann Streamborn, and Powell's bookshop in Portland. During my visit I also gave a talk and slide show at Mark Bachman's Fly shop at Welchs near Mount Hood. After some four weeks, I was feeling a lot better.

During my stay in Oregon, two other friends, Scott and Barbara Richmond, collected Kate and me for a visit to Frank and Jeannie Moor at their log-cabin home on the Umpqua River near the famous Steamboat Inn, which they had run for many years, looking after the many steelhead anglers who visited, not just from the United States but from many European countries. Both Frank and Jeannie are great conservationists. Through their efforts, the Umpqua River today is a fine steelhead river, being just as famous today, as in the Zane Grey and Major Mott era of the 1930s. On the wall, next to my desk is a picture of a young Frank as an eighteen year old D-day soldier in France. Jeanie was housebound recovering from a fall, in which she had broken her ankle in three places. After lunch, we made our way to the banks of the Umpqua river where I could see a chrome-bright steelhead about ten pounds,alongside a rock. If that fish could speak, then no doubt it would be saying, "Catch me if you can!"

A week later I got the chance to go fishing. The Kesterson family warmly invited Kate, George, Cheryl and me to visit the Big K Ranch set in 2,500 acres of private land on the banks of the Umpqua River, in the quiet, serene, and natural beauty of southern Oregon. It has an incredible ten miles of fishing for smallmouth Bass, American shad, chinook and silver salmon. You will see wild turkeys and deer, if you're lucky you might get a glimpse of elk, bear and cougar.

Over the years I have seen most of the wildlife and caught my share of salmon, big smallmouth bass and shad – the poor man's tarpon, fishing with a fly-rod. It's not only a great place for the angler but also the artist and photographer. The lodge is some ten thousand square foot where you will enjoy great home-style cooking; there are twenty spacious cabins, where many families take a vacation. Companies big

Often, my four legged friend was the best form of transport

and small often treat their employees to a weekend getaway at the Big K. You can plan your wedding or reunite your family at the Ranch. It's a great experience. I have often been a lunchtime speaker there and I always get a very warm welcome from the guests, and lots of friendly hugs from the girls who run the Big K Ranch.

Though there were many chrome-bright coho and king salmon in the river, George, Cheryl, Kate and I chose to float the river in search of smallmouth bass, with our guides. Richard, looked after George and Cheryl, while young Quinton guided me and Kate. I had a 6 weight outfit with floating line for Kate, I chose a 5 weight, as always we used Thomas and Thomas fly rods. I've known Quinton for some years; he is a fine angler, hunter and guide. A big influence on Quinton, his brother, and cousin Gary, is Big Al, their grandfather who has truly made them into even better hunters and anglers than those twice their age. I well remember Gary as a fourteen year old, catching a big salmon on an English 10ft spinning rod.

Kate, Smallmouth Bass Fishing on the Umpqua River at the Big K Ranch, Oregon

Richard is one of the resident guides, along with his twin brother. Despite the heavy rain showers we all caught a lot of bass while enjoying a wilderness experience. There were many occasions when we would see a dozen or more salmon pass by the McKenzie drift boat After a couple of days at the Big K ranch it was time to move on.

Over the years I've had dozens of trips to Oregon, fishing all the rivers in the State for most fish species, from carp to salmon, the carp-fishing can certainly be spectacular with plenty of fish, I well recall catching a carp when a passing boat stopped to watch the action. As I landed the fish I heard someone say, "It's only a carp." As I weighed the fish I heard someone say, "It's being weighed now – it's gone back in the water!" In the early days, most Americans just killed carp, usually by dumping them on the bank. I was at another angler's house one evening when he pointed out his roses saying, "They grow on carp." I remember taking Dave Hughes, one of the leading fly-fishers in the States and author of many fly-fishing books, out for a day's fishing. After he had caught a carp, I said, "Take your glasses off Dave, so I can take a picture."

"No way!" he said.

Scott Richmond is another Oregonian author and all-round angler with whom I have fished on many occasions. Kate and I have stopped at Scott and Barbara's home on several occasions, when we have been made very welcome.

Scott fishes for carp with the keenness of an English carp-fisher, catching his share of fish. One day, as I walked up a boat dock to get some gear from the car, an angler said to Scott, "Is that guy up there really fishing for them damn carp?" They couldn't understand what this interest was in great fish. Some time later a bass- fishing magazine carried a five page feature entitled The toughest sports fish, it was all about carp. Enough said. After a few days of fishing with other anglers and some valuable time in Kaufmann's tackle shop it was time to leave for my next stop in Denver.

Two days later I was in Denver for the Fly-tackle Dealer's Show, on the Thomas and Thomas stand, meeting many other dealers and friends. The show is certainly a great meeting place for the trade to show-off their new products to the many hundreds of dealers from all over the world. During the show I was able to get some interviews with authors: John Gierach, Stephen Grace, Chico Fernandez, and Simon Gawsworth who is with Rio Lines. Tom Dorsey of Thomas and Thomas explained how he designed the new Horizon II rods, while company chief Lon Decker told my listeners how he got into the fishing-tackle business. All in all it was an interesting show. I reckon it's one that everyone in the trade should attend.

*O*ne of the most exciting places in the world to visit must be the Bahamas, and I was desperate to catch a bonefish on the fly. In fact, it had been an ambition since the 1950s when, according to Joe Brooks in his book Saltwater Game Fishing, published by Harper and Row, the first recorded bonefish taken on the fly was caught accidentally in 1926 by Colonel Thompson while he was fishing with veteran bone-fishing guide J. T. Harrod at Long Key, Florida. I also read the various articles that appeared in Field and Stream, and other American magazines.

The hunt which would satisfy my forty year dream to catch a bonefish happened in May 1998 when my wife Kate and I visited several of the Family Islands, as they are known, where we experienced incredible hospitality from the local people wherever we went. In Abaco we would go off fishing to a delightful beach known as Tahiti Beach – straight out of the Bounty Bar advertisement! Each morning after breakfast we would jump on our bicycles; with rods and tackle bags on our backs, it was just a two or three mile cycle ride to the beach.

I find that the families who visit the Bahamas do so for several reasons: to get some badly needed sunshine during the winter months, take part in scuba diving, or go sailing or fishing. Very few want to visit Nassau, Paradise Island, or Freeport with their huge glass and chrome-plated hotels, noisy music, gambling and drinking. Most of the English visitors, I meet in the Bahamas, visit the group of islands, known as the Family Islands. It's the real Bahamas, where families enjoy extremely good weather, first class beaches, good diving, sailing and fishing. When you arrive at the island of your choice, collect up all your watches and clocks, and then stuff the lot inside a suitcase! You're now on Bahamas' time. Don't get tensed up if your flight is an hour late, the taxi hasn't arrived or the waiter hasn't taken your order right away – have another beer, relax and unwind. If you rent a car it will probably be owned by one of the fishermen. The Bahamian people are incredibly honest, friendly and most helpful.

I have visited many of the Family Islands: Abaco, Long Island, Green Turtle Cay, Crooked Island, Exuma Cays, Eleuthera and Andros. This latter island is the fifth largest land mass in the Caribbean/tropical Atlantic and is about 100 miles long by 40 miles wide, with three big land areas: North, Middle and South – most of it unexplored – and home to the third longest reef system in the world. Its complex ecology is relatively pristine even though it sits in the back yard of one of the most developed nations on earth. The variety of eco-systems is astonishing: to the north, soft tropical sands sweep back into surprising sweet-smelling pine forests; in the centre of the island, thick, low-lying bush opens to inland waterways and tidal flats; along the eastern shore, coral rock splits open to underground rivers, while the western shoreline eases out into the Great Bahama Bank. Everywhere, mangrove marshlands feed a pristine reef.

Andros is very old but not volcanic in origin; it is made from coral limestone, layer upon layer. Most of the island lies underwater. Dive deep enough along Andros' walls and you will find ancient beaches, ghostly white remnants of the last ice age (or perhaps the one before that). Underwater caves are filled with stalactites and stalagmites, attesting to the time when water barely dripped from ceilings. Taino Indians (The Lukka-Kairi or Lucayans), who were here long before Columbus, and buried their dead in some of these caves. If it's diving, fishing, birding, or just lazing around, then Small Hope Bay is for you and your family. The food is excellent and plentiful, even your drinks come free.

You can fly-fish, spin or use bait for a large variety of fish; please note, I don't mention trolling; I wouldn't wish that on my worst enemy – watching the grass grow would be more exciting! On the reefs you can catch jacks, snappers, barracuda, schoolmasters, hogfish, dorado, etc. Offshore there are kingfish, yellow-fin tuna, wahoo, dorado and barracuda. On the flats your number one fish is without doubt the bonefish. Early summer will get you the chance of catching various shark species: snappers, tarpon, jacks, and the elusive permit; this last fish is probably the toughest that swims the flats. Most anglers though, seek to catch the bonefish on a fly-rod. This fish is very important to the Bahamian economy. The bonefish are without doubt the spookiest fish or animal I have ever hunted; they have a fantastic burst of speed often reaching thirty to thirty-five miles an hour. They have incredible eyesight and hearing, making them a very difficult target to approach – especially by boat. All their lives they live in fear of the lean-mean-eating-machine: the barracuda, plus the sharks and the species Homo Sapiens that hunts them with rod and line.

The bonefish can be found in many tropical and subtropical areas spanning thirty degrees north and south of the equator. Some of the best areas are: the Bahamas, Florida Keys, Belize, Venezuela, Christmas Island, Bermuda, Cuba, Yucatan and Honduras to name a few. I have been told there are bonefish in the UAE at Khor Kalba among the Mangroves, where they like to hunt around for crabs and shrimp. I will be doing exploratory trips to the UAE in search of the spooky bones.

The bonefish has a reputation for being difficult to catch: it's not really true. Providing you don't spook them, you have an excellent chance of getting them to eat. In fact, bones can be very aggressive in their feeding, especially when there are three or more fish pursuing your fly. Your two big problems are, spotting your quarry, and the wind. Some days, it will be blowing 20–25 knots, then it's a 9 weight rod, or a day of cabin fever – though you can spend your time doing other things: swimming, biking, snorkelling, or lazing in a hammock and reading. Without doubt, if it's your first visit, book a guide, then listen and learn. You will find the guides at Small Hope Bay are helpful and friendly.

Andros is my favourite island. If you're visiting the Bahamas as an all-male group for the fishing, I can recommend Moxey Town at Mangrove Cay on Andros but it's not really suitable for families. Mangrove Cay also has a small airstrip; it's a 15–20 minute flight from Nassau. If it's fishing, diving and a family holiday you're looking for, then Small Hope Bay on Andros is your best camp, with Andros Town your nearest airstrip. It's a great place to stay; they even have a baby-sitting service.

If you stay at Moxey's bonefish lodge you need only walk about fifty yards to

Joel Moxey – A Great Guiide and Fly Fisher

reach a good bonefish flat, where it possible to catch half a dozen bones before breakfast. The food is plentiful at Moxey's, and you will find the rooms are clean and tidy; in addition to this, there is an excellent fly-dressing room. It has all the materials and tools you might want, for tying any fly.

The fish most anglers want to catch are bonefish; it's the perfect quarry for the fly-fisher. The question I'm most often asked is, "What is the best time of the year to visit?" I can best answer this by saying I have visited the Bahamas in March, May, June, August, October and November; I have caught fish on every visit. During the height of the summer it can be hot, but it doesn't bother me. I make sure I keep covered up and drink lots of water. Often you will have a cooling breeze on the flats. During the winter you will sometimes get a strong wind blowing from a northerly direction. It doesn't stop me fishing unless it's a 20–25 knot wind. Most days you can find sheltered creeks, mangrove-protected flats and bays, although the wind can often be to your advantage when stalking bones on the flats.

In my lifetime I have been privileged to read many fine books; travel, natural history and fishing being my favourites, in fact in my study at home, I have over 2,000 angling titles from the 1700s to the present day covering all aspects of salt and freshwater angling. Some have become classics in their own right and have stood the test of time. Since the days of sailing ships, British anglers have been great travellers. During the 1800s they were fishing all corners of the world. Then, on their return home, some of these adventurers would put pen to paper, and write about their travels, catches, and exploits. This in turn made others follow in their footsteps.

I suppose it was in the 1980s when the bonefish became a cult fish. Salmon anglers no longer wanted to spend a couple of thousand pounds sterling on a fishless river in Scotland with rain

Bonefishing

and mosquitoes as company. Why should they when, for the same amount of cash, they could travel to exotic locations such as the Florida Keys or the Bahamas to fish for bonefish, tarpon and permit, perhaps even achieve the grand slam. What wife or girl friend wouldn't swap rainy Britain for the sunny Bahamas? No longer would she look upon fishing as, "that old boring game". You, the angler, were encouraged to go in search of the bonefish.

During the past thirty-odd years, several books have been published about catching this great sporting fish of the flats, and hundreds of articles have been printed. Two books changed the face of bone-fishing: Del Brown's, 'Fly-fishing for bonefish', published by Lyons and Burford and, 'Bonefishing with a Fly', by Randall Kaufmann, published by Western Fisherman's Press. Before my first bone-fishing trip, the latter book became my bedtime reading for several months. Even today, two or three weeks before a trip to chase bones, Kaufmann's book once again becomes important reading.

I have been very fortunate in meeting some excellent bonefish anglers who have helped me in my quest for this glamour fish of the twenty-first century. To them all, I will always be grateful. It really started back in 1991 on a visit to Oregon in my hunt for the steelhead. I met up with those great anglers, Gordon Nash, Randall Kaufmann, and Jerry Swanson, who worked in Kaufmann's Streamborn fly-shop at Tigard near Portland, Oregon. There I would sit for hours at a time, as they regaled me with tales of bonefish trips. The book you must read is Randall's latest publication titled 'Bonefishing!' this is not just any bone-fishing book. This is truly the bible for all bone-fishers. Don't go after those silver bullets of the flats before you have read it. This volume has 414 pages measuring 9" x 11" and weighs in at around four pounds. That's the size of bonefish which will pull your string and bend your stick like no salmon ever could.

In this book, Randall Kaufmann, Brian O'Keefe, and Mike Stidham have captured the magic and mystique of bone-fishing. I can do no better than quote the following:

> "You sense the freedom of the wind and feel the surf and tide tugging at your psyche, you experience the adrenaline rush of a speeding bonefish and savour the tranquil ambience as the sun transforms into a fireball and sizzles into the ocean".

Fly-fishing for bonefish does not require mythical prowess or exceptional angling skills. It is much less complicated and technical than fly-fishing for trout. Neophyte anglers often hook bonefish on their first adventure. This book, Bonefishing! tells you where, when, and how to do it. It is the definitive work on the subject. If you are a bonefish aficionado, you must have this book. If you are not yet a bonefish angler, you soon will be. It's without

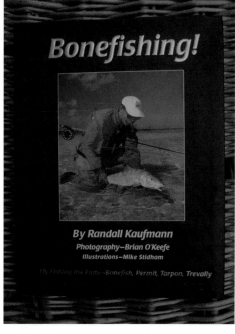

Bonefishing!

By Randall Kaufmann
Photography–Brian O'Keefe
Illustrations–Mike Stidham

Fly Fishing the Flats—Bonefish, Permit, Tarpon, Trevally

doubt the best book on this great sport of angling it has been my pleasure to read. In fifty years time bonefish anglers will say, "Have your read that book by Randall Kaufmann?"

I feel it's most important that you have the best equipment you can buy, don't skimp on rods, reels and lines – you will regret it. I know it's possible to get a rod, reel, and a line for about £150; my advice is, don't buy these cheap outfits. Without doubt the most important item of gear is the line. Never use the lines you use for trout-fishing in the UK; they won't work in the tropics. You need a line designed for use in the warmer climes. There are four line-manufacturers to choose from: Corland, Scientific Anglers, Rio, and Wulff Triangle Taper.

I suggest a weight forward floating line for an 8 weight rod. At the present time I am using the Wulff two tone, Bermuda triangle taper floating line with a 30ft tropics blue head which is connected to a yellow running-line. Another line I like to have is an intermediate one for fishing in deeper water; I find these lines cast well in windy conditions. Depending on the prevailing conditions I use leaders of 9–12ft to Froghair deep blue, with Froghair tippet material. This is my choice: I cannot fault Gamma products.

The rods I use for all my fly-fishing are the Thomas and Thomas models made in Greenfield, Massachusetts. Their rods are the best on the market – that's why I use them. If a Thomas and Thomas rod is rated for an 8 weight then that's the line to use – unlike some rods on the market, where you often have to go one or two line weights heavier. I reckon some of the so called fly-rods would be better for growing beans. For most of my bone-fishing I use the T&T Helix model, but should the wind be aggressive, I then switch to a Horizon II model. When the wind is a hooligan, then it's a 9 weight Horizon.

Once hooked, a bonefish immediately wants to get as much distance from you as possible, and at thirty miles per hour it certainly does not pay to use a cheap reel; it will burn out very quickly. Hopefully there will be occasions when you hook a big bone which will take 100 yards of line off the reel. I have several reels. One is a handmade Richard Carter model made by Richard for me on the occasion of my sixtieth birthday. I can do no better than recommend The Gilmore X400 model reel, I also have reels by Tibor and Abel for bone-fishing – in fact I use them for all my saltwater fly-fishing.

There are a few items you certainly need when bone-fishing, the most important one is sun block. I use Riemann P20, a once-a-day sun filter, high protection SPF 20 which I have used for several years, both in the Caribbean and the Middle East. I reckon it's the best. To see the fish on the flats, you will need some Polarized glasses, with both amber and grey lenses. You will never see the bones without them, and you will damage your eyes without having good Polaroid lenses. As I wear spectacles, I have prescription Polaroid's manufactured by Optilabs www.optilabs.com which are excellent. You will need a good hat with a long peak, one which is dark underneath. Make sure the hat has a covering at the back to protect your neck – the Foreign Legion kepi is perfect. Footwear is most important, don't use those soft, neoprene boots, they are useless on coral. I suggest you get Patagonia, Simms or Bite footwear. I have used all three with confidence.

You will need fly-boxes with a selection of flies; make sure you have some crab patterns. I purchase all my flies from Kaufmann's in Oregon: Jerry Swanson is your man. I always carry a spare, floating fly-line. Other useful items are nippers, insect repellent, drinking water, spare hat, some leaders and spools of tippet – and don't forget a waterproof jacket. I have only touched briefly on the subject of bone-fishing. It's a fascinating sport which is becoming more popular each year.

One of the biggest problems facing the bonefish angler on the flats is wind, calm days are very rare; usually the wind will be blowing at 5 –10 miles an hour, and often winds of 20–25 miles an hour will be encountered. Several weeks before my trip I visited the local cycle shop where I collected a couple of old tyres. These would be my casting targets. Every day, whatever the weather, I would lay out the tyres on a local field and practice, practice and practice again – including the double-haul casting.

Bonefish rarely move slowly in a straight line but take a zigzag course, often moving quite fast. Trout-fishing on rivers is very easy compared with the bonefish. On a river the trout usually stays on station: not so the bonefish. Fishing from a flats boat with a guide, the bow is at twelve o'clock. The guide will use the clock face to guide you to the fish. One moment he will whisper, "bonefish at ten o'clock, forty feet." The next second he will perhaps say, "two o'clock, twenty five feet." Then it might be another instruction, "twelve o'clock, fifty feet." This is very intense fishing and you have to be spot-on with your casting. Make sure you get plenty of casting practice, especially the double-haul, before you go. If necessary, visit a fly-fishing school.

Spotting bonefish on your first trip is the most difficult thing you will have done in your angling life; you should hire the services of a guide for at least the first couple of days, they are worth their weight in gold, and you will learn a great deal: muddying or milky water, nervous water, tailing bones, are terms you will often hear spoken on the flats. Muddying or milky water is when the fish are, "head-to-hell, tail-to-heaven!" In fact it's the same as when carp are 'smoke-screening' on the shallows.

Nervous water is hard to spot until the guide explains it and shows you an example. I quote from Randall Kaufmann's book, Bone fishing with a Fly, page sixty six:

"Nervous water is the tip-off to underwater movement".

As bonefish move, they push water, and their movement causes surface water to move. The surface is not broken, only disturbed.

Look for slightly rippled water or a surface pattern that is at odds with, or moving against, the surrounding water. Single moving bonefish causing nervous water are difficult to spot, but a large school can be spotted from 100 yards or more, especially if the water's surface is calm. A patch of nervous water will move around, reflect light, and sometimes take on a shade of gray, brown or green. "High frequency" nervous water is not created by bonefish, but by erratically-swimming smaller fish'.

Tailing bones are usually in shallow water and quite easy to spot. The first time you see them your heart rate switches into overdrive, adrenaline pumps through your veins. Your mouth will become dry, perspiration appears on the brow, and your hands will start to shake as you nervously try to aerialise some line. There in front of you is a bunch of feeding bones, perhaps only twenty feet away. The fish have their heads in the sand, mud-feeding on clams, shrimps or crabs, with their tails often poking out of the water. The first tailing bonefish I spotted were at

Freshwater Creek on Andros Island. In fact I pointed them out to my guide who gave me a pat on the back for being observant. I shot thirty feet of line and had a bone from that group, about three pounds, all very exciting.

When wading the flats, you don't walk but shuffle your feet. This way you will create vibrations and the sting rays will move away. Try not to scratch yourself on the coral as it can be very painful. Most important is the sun screen and sun block. If you're of dark complexion go for a factor 25 and make sure you use it liberally. My advice to fair skinned people is, go for a factor of 35–40. Don't think it's macho not to use sun screens – only the fools go on the flats without protection. The sun block should be used on the nose, lips, ears and any other sensitive parts of the body exposed to the sun. I protect my hands and wrists with a pair of fingerless flats gloves called 'sun checkers'. I purchased mine from Kaufmann's. Make sure you drink plenty of liquids; there are waist packs available which contain two drinking bottles. This piece of equipment is also perfect for the roving angler, even on the lakes and rivers at home during the summer months.

Reaching the age of sixty, I realised I had so much more to do with perhaps little time left to do it. Every two or three months I hear about another friend who has gone from this world. There are true sayings: "You can't take it with you" or, "Shrouds have no pockets". It was time to go off fishing, in my case to catch many of the exotic species on a fly-rod. Fish such as tarpon, permit, bonefish, mutton snapper, sailfish, tuna, wahoo, redfish, dorado, snook and many more. It was time to trade in my investments such as: my two thousand angling books, paintings, cane rods, centre-pin reels – then go off fishing. The trips that I've booked include:, bone-fishing at

Miss Bahamas

Moxey Town on Andros Island in the Bahamas, striped-bass fishing in Connecticut and Massachusetts, muskies in upstate New York, sailfish, tuna, jack crevales, sharks, kingfish and wahoo in the Arabian and Persian Gulf, and hopefully there would be time to tackle the tarpon again in the Gulf of Mexico. I am desperate to make a trip to North Carolina to chase the blue fish, false albacore and stripers during the fall season.

One of my many trips to the Bahamas included taking part in the Bahamas World Bonefish Invitational Tournament, A three-day event where I finished in third spot. On my desk is the trophy. A bonefish carved from a conch shell, mounted on another conch shell. It reminds me of the delightful, friendly people of these islands in the Bahamas. I even got to fish with Miss

Bahamas and other beautiful woman; what more could a guy want?

For my latest trip I flew from Manchester by American Airlines to Nassau via Chicago and Miami. After a three hour wait in Miami, I caught another flight, arriving in Nassau around nine o'clock that evening. Collecting my case containing a few clothes, I hefted my rucksack containing cameras, fly boxes and reels on my back, before picking up my rod tube, then making my way to customs.

There I was received with a, "Good evening sir, we hope you have a pleasant stay." Once they see you're an angler, it's smooth going all the way with the officials. As I came out of the airport, another official pointed to a taxi. I asked the driver to take me to a hotel for the night, explaining I wanted the cheapest, clean room available. Let's be honest, why pay hundred dollars when you can get one for fifty – after all I was only going to put my head on a bed for a few hours. Within fifteen minutes I had checked in, perhaps twenty minutes later I was asleep. 6.30 next morning, I was waiting for a taxi to the airport, seven o'clock I'm being greeted by a very friendly girl on the Bahamasair check-in desk. "Good morning young lady can I have a return ticket to Mangrove Cay please?" "That will be 110 dollars sir." I passed over my plastic card. The flight was due to depart at 8.30; but remember, I was on Bahamas time. I left at 10.35, but it wasn't a problem. I arrived in Mangrove Cay about ten minutes later. At eleven o'clock I was at Moxey's bonefish lodge. Having been shown my room, I was left to do as I pleased. After a shower, I covered myself with P20 sun protection, then got dressed in shorts, shirt and wading boots. After assembling an 8 weight outfit, I picked up a box of flies then headed off to the beach.

Author with boneshaker

From my room it was 16 steps and 120 paces to the beach. On my second cast with a Gotcha fly pattern, I caught my first bone of the trip. A light onshore breeze ruffled the surface of the bay, a few feet away I watched a turkey buzzard, or vulture, fly by. Under some palm trees that offered shade, a couple of old guys and two younger ones were sitting on a bit of timber that rested on a couple of oil drums, drinking beer. One of them said, "After the bonefish man?" I said "Yes," stopping for a chat. They made room for me on the makeshift seat; I sat down among a group of friendly guys, two of them, Ezra and Oscar were bonefish guides for Moxey. We discussed the attractions in the area, one of which I reckon was the off-licence for these guys, by the amount of discarded cans and bottles I could see. I soon formed a friendship with Ezra, a very knowledgeable bonefish guide, they don't come better. We also chatted about the forthcoming General Election – they had about as much trust in their politicians as we do in the UK! An hour later on the advice of Ezra, I went off along the beach to Small Cove in search of bonefish.

Stopping on the way, I cast a fly to a snapper which quickly grabbed hold, this was followed by a blue runner then a small barracuda, after one jump it threw the hook. What a fun way to enjoy yourself in the sun I thought to myself. Getting as far as a blue hole, I was joined by Ezra. "Hello man," he said. In his hand was a fly-rod; we walked side-by-side chatting like lifelong friends. We reached a small cove and quickly spotted a small school of resident bonefish. I

Poling the flats

watched Ezra slowly wade out on the flat for some yards, then make a long cast, dropping a Gotcha some three feet in front of a bone. In the blink of an eye he hooked the fish. I got great pleasure from watching him play the fish close to hand, where he bent down, slipping out the barbless hook. The fish quickly moved away to join the others in the school. It was certainly a great exhibition of angling; I told him so. We ended up the short session with two fish each. It was time for a beer and some dinner. Ezra was an excellent fly-fisher. Over dinner that night I discussed bone-fishing tactics with a group of American anglers who were staying at Moxey's lodge. Dinner finished, I went off to join the local guys in the bar. It had been a good day.

On day two I fished with Joel Moxey. Dressed in shorts, shirt and wading boots with a liberal covering of sun protection I went down for breakfast. Joel said, "We are going up Moxey's Creek today, a boat trip of several miles. We'll be wading some very big flats, hunting big bones in very shallow water." Breakfast over I grabbed my kit, Joel grabbed the ice chest; it was just a short walk to the skiff with its fifty horse power motor. Putting everything in place, Joel turned the ignition key, the motor purred into life. Gradually, we gathered speed, then, as we reached the deeper water, Joel pushed the throttle forward. The bows lifted and we skimmed across the lightly rippled

Another Bone

surface of the ocean. Fifteen minutes later Joel was bringing the skiff into Moxey creek. To the left was Little Moxey, to the right, Big Moxey – we turned right.

Joel cut the motor: the only sound was the water lapping the side of the skiff. He said, "Martin make yourself ready on the bows, I'm going to pole us alongside those mangroves." My tackle was an 8 weight rod, Tibor reel, Cortland Ghost Tip Lazerline with a 10ft tapered leader. I pulled fifty feet of line off the reel then coiled it carefully on the decking making sure the first of the line was at the top of the coils. On Joel's advice I had tied on a red-eyed Clouser. For the next hour Joel poled us along the edge of the mangroves, seeing the odd bonefish, barracuda and shark.

We arrived off a shallow sandy point where I spotted an osprey sitting on a mangrove branch. Joel said, "We'll leave the skiff on the point, then wade." I nodded in agreement then lowered my body over the side, feeling the warm water against my legs, it felt wonderful. For as far as the eye could see there was nothing to remind us of the twenty-first century, nothing had changed in the past five hundred years, except the mangroves had grown a lot more. Joel pointed then whispered, "Martin, good bone at twelve o'clock, sixty feet." To keep a low profile we knelt down in the soft white sand; a good bone was slowly making its way up tide looking for food: it was a good fish. It stuffed its snout into the soft white sand to grab some item of food, the water turned milky-white. The fish moved on in its quest, seconds later it was some fifteen feet away. I roll cast a size 8 Crazy Charlie; it dropped with a slight plop some five feet ahead of the fish. Hearing the gentle sound, it moved forward, I gave a tiny strip, the fish pounced. Setting the hook, I struggled to my feet sticking the rod high. The reel revolved in a blur, line disappeared at a good rate of knots, the fish moved off fast through the shallow water. As the line cut through the water it left an emerald green scar – something I had never seen before in all my many bone-fishing trips.

The fish had probably taken some 80–90 yards of line in its first rush, and then kited to my left. I managed to get some line back on the reel, the rod tip was pulled down savagely, the reel screamed in protest as more line was taken; once more the emerald green scar appeared around the line as it sliced through the water. For some minutes it was give-and-take but slowly I was getting line back on the reel; we waded through the water towards the fish gaining even more line. Soon I was able to get a good look at my first bonefish of the day. It was a nice fish perhaps five pounds, slowly it was bought to hand. I bent down and lifted it a few inches above the water. Joel shot a quick picture and I slipped the barbless hook from the fish, and watched it swim strongly away. That would be the only fish I would touch by hand, any other would be unhooked in the water – unless I had a ten-pounder, then I would want a picture. Why keep taking pictures of fish after fish. I have dozens of bonefish pictures at home. After catching a few more bones we moved off to another big flat near Mangrove Cay Island, a journey of some twenty minutes; time to have a sandwich and a drink. A mile off shore Joel cut the motor and poled us towards the shore line. I spotted the odd, good size bone in the distance; there was no chance of catching those fish.

After anchoring the boat in some shallows, we slid over the side into the warm water where the bottom was so different from Big Moxey Creek. Here, it was very firm sand with patches of turtle grass, making fish-spotting quite difficult; to make matters worse, a big cloud obscured the sun. Joel said, "At low tide you can walk out from the shoreline to Mangrove Cay Island but if you leave it too long on the flooding tide you have to spend a few hours on the island." The island was well known in the old days as a stopping-off point for the mail boats.

I grabbed my rod and followed Joel. We had gone some hundred yards or more when he whispered, "Bone at nine o'clock, point your rod Martin, a bit more left." I spotted the fish; it was some eighty feet away. We stood still, barely breathing, my mouth was dry, I strained my eyes to keep in contact with the moving fish. It moved closer. At around sixty feet Joel said, "Tie on a small green crab then shoot for it Martin." I made a roll cast, two false casts then shot the line, hearing it hiss through the guides. The small green crab landed like thistledown, as a dry-fly would on a chalk stream, four or five feet in front and slightly to the left of the fish. Joel said, "Good shot, leave it Martin," he then whispered, "It's moving to the crab now, give a short strip, it will see the puff of sand, strip – strip!" I watched the fish track the crab – then grab hold savagely.

Pointing at a Bonefish

Setting the hook, I stuffed the rod high. The fish moved off fast across the flat towards the deep water: the fight was on. Seven or eight minutes later I bent down and slipped the hook free from a fish we estimated at seven pound-plus. Releasing it, we watched it swim off towards the deeper water. It was now Joel's turn to catch a bone. We slowly moved across the flat, shuffling our feet so as to spook any sting rays. At sixty yards I pointed, before saying, "Joel, tailing bone fifty feet, two o'clock." Joel spotted the fish immediately, made a roll cast, one false cast before dropping the size 4 red-eyed Clouser minnow in white and chartreuse, four feet ahead of the fish, which quickly dived for this morsel of food. In the blink of an eye, Joel's rod tip was being pulled down towards the water; a good fish moved off fast. I switched on my Nikon to sports action and proceeded to shoot film.

The light conditions were perfect for 100 ASA film. Joel would gain some line, the fish would take it back, but the bone's runs were becoming shorter. Joel was winning the fight, when a small lemon shark appeared sixty feet down tide. I warned Joel, and moved between fish and shark. Joel cramped down hard quickly gaining line, and in another minute he had the fish to hand. Moving in close, I shot a couple of pictures. We released the fish close to some mangroves, where the shark couldn't grab hold. We continued on in search of more bonefish catching several on the flooding tide until it was too deep to wade, then moved off to another flat, catching some jacks and a couple of bones. Joel Moxey had proved what a good guide he is.

Breakfast on my third day was bacon and eggs, with lots of tea and toast. I was going fishing with Ezra on some flats and we would also go up Miller Creek, the home of very big tarpon, barracuda, sawfish, bones and permit. It was a boat ride of some fifty minutes. At eight o'clock I met Ezra at the skiff as he loaded the ice chest. "Good morning Ezra, another great day in paradise." Answering, he said, "Yes man, its perfect weather for hunting bones." Sitting on the stern of the skiff, I kicked the mud off my feet and swung my legs into the boat, making myself

comfortable in one of the padded seats. Ezra pushed us out over the shallow water until we had enough depth to start the motor. He climbed aboard and turned the ignition key, the motor burst into life. Minutes later we were skimming across the glass-like surface of the ocean, bows high, leaving a creamy-white trail in our wake.

We passed a small palm-tree lined island with beautiful sandy bays, occasionally an osprey would appear overhead. On-and-on we motored, twisting this-way-and-that to miss coral reefs, which, if hit, would rip the bottom out of the skiff. I marvelled at the wilderness, it was great to be alive. I heard the engine noise change as Ezra throttled back. Up front I could see a big flat; slowly we came to a stop. "Are you ready for those bones Martin?" Ezra said. I turned, smiled and whispered, "Yes," then moved up in the bows, as Ezra climbed up on his platform. This was set about five feet above the stern. The water

Ronnie Sawyer poling Martin on the flats

was flat calm, about a foot deep, with a very soft bottom; it was so soft that you would immediately sink to your waist. There wouldn't be any walking on this flat today. With no wind to keep the horse-flies away, I slipped on a long-sleeved shirt, and long, lightweight pants, plus a hat with a big peak, side and back flap to keep the sun off my ears and the back of my neck. These clothes would help protect me from the stinging, biting flies which were out in large swarms; as I had taken these sensible precautions, they shouldn't cause me a problem.

As Ezra slowly poled along the edge of the flat, I squinted into the water seeking one of those grey ghosts, I call them silver bullets. Ten minutes later he said, "bone at nine o'clock, fifty feet". I spotted it immediately; making a roll cast with one false cast, I shot the line. A size 6 Gotcha landed three feet to the right and six feet in front of the fish, it only heard a slight sound, such as a shrimp would make as it moved through the water. The fish went around in circles looking for the food item. Giving a tiny half inch strip, the fly kicked up a puff of milky-grey silt; I watched the fish turn. I gave another short strip, and the fish pounced like a cat on a mouse. I set the hook, and the fish moved fast across the shallow water for the deep channel, the reel giving line. As the line cut through the water it left an emerald green scar. On-and-on went the fish until eighty yards of line had gone; suddenly it turned, coming back towards me fast. It was a case of winding like mad, as I tried to keep in touch. I quickly got line back on the reel. Tibor reels might cost around £500, but, at a time like this, they are worth every penny. Slowly I was winning the battle; soon the fish was mine, and bending over the side of the skiff, I released fish number one.

Once more Ezra poled us along the flat, five minutes later he said, "bone at three o'clock, twenty feet." I made a quick cast, dropping the Gotcha within two feet of the fish. It moved across then inhaled the fly, fish number two was on. The fight was similar to the first fish, soon this one was released. This fish wasn't bothered by the boat or the fly dropping close by, it was very aggressive. Fifteen minutes later we heard a splash, then spotted a big pool of milky-grey water where a big bone was hunting. Ezra whispered, "Martin, I want you to shoot for the spot." I picked out the distant mark and looked at Ezra, thinking, "this man reckons I can shoot eighty feet of fly line." I would give it my best shot. Turning to Ezra, I said, "Should I change to a Crazy Charlie?" "Yes Man," he answered. Tying on a size 2 Crazy Charlie, I pulled more line off the reel. Making a roll cast then three false casts, I shot the fly to the target, watching with satisfaction as it landed in the middle of the coloured water, "Well done man," said Ezra. I let it sit, then thirty seconds later I gave a two inch strip.

A fish aggressively hit the fly; I made a strip strike and missed the fish. I let the fly sit in the clear water. I could see the fish – it was a good one – six feet from the fly; I gave a quick strip of three inches, the fish spotted the fly then turned savagely, grabbing the Crazy Charlie. Setting the hook, I made no mistake this time; a big powerful fish went off across the flats. "Well done, Martin." shouted Ezra. "That was good casting." I watched the line disappearing fast from the reel – first the fly-line then a hundred yards of green backing followed by some of the red backing-line before the fish stopped. I managed to gain a few yards before the fish went off in another direction. I could feel the power. "Take it easy man, that's a good fish," said Ezra. For some ten minutes it was a give-and-take tussle between angler and fish, but slowly I was wearing it down, gradually getting it close to the boat. The runs from the fish were becoming shorter; soon it was close enough for me to lean over the side of the skiff, bend down and slide the Crazy Charlie from the its mouth. Ezra said, "that's about seven pounds, the best of the trip so far." I held the fish in the water for a couple of minutes until I felt it kick free, watching with satisfaction as it made its way over the shallow water flat to find a better, safer, feeding spot. We fished on, catching five more bones; it was great, fishing in this tropical paradise – things just don't get much better than this.

Around twelve noon Ezra said, "Martin, let's go and find a nice spot for lunch." He climbed down from his poling platform and turned the ignition key. The motor purred and then, as the throttle was opened up, the sound turned to a roar and the bows lifted. We skimmed across the smooth clear water heading for Miller Creek. Fifteen minutes later Ezra cut the motor. He climbed up on his platform and poled us to the edge of a flat. "Martin," he said urgently. "Twelve o'clock, fifteen feet, big sawfish." I gasped. It must have been ten feet long with an awesome set of saws in front of its head. It was asleep in two feet of water. Boy! Was I glad I wasn't wading close to this fearsome creature! Suddenly the water erupted, a huge, silver-scaled body rose from the water; it was a tarpon of perhaps a hundred pounds. What sort of fishery was this I thought? I peered into the dark, deep water on the edge of the flat. A big, no, a huge barracuda drifted by. Why didn't I have my 12 weight rod? My eyes were once again drawn to the deep-water channel as the water erupted – this time two big tarpon rolling on the surface, the sun glinting on their silver scales.

Close into the mangroves, a big hawksbill turtle surfaced, then lay motionless in the sunshine, no doubt sunbathing. During this fascinating lunch break I was amazed at the amount of aquatic life and fish we saw. Jacks, various snappers, grunts, schoolmasters, more big barracuda, and another huge sawfish I estimated at fifteen feet which drifted from the deep water up on the flat to seek food. Just looking at these big fish sent a shiver down one's spine – they were awesome but fascinating; a couple of big rays drifted by the boat. I could hear lots of splashing coming from the mangroves as fish hunted crabs, shrimps and other items of food. Ezra drew my attention to a big manta ray; what magnificent creatures they are.

With lunch over, Ezra started the motor and we slowly cruised further up Miller Creek until we reached a big flat on the right. Switching off the motor, Ezra climbed up onto his poling platform and we then commenced the hunt for bones. In quick succession I hooked and landed three, all taken within twenty feet of the boat in some eighteen inches of water. The bones were hungry and savagely grabbed any item of food. Ezra poled me into a backwater pool; I spotted a tailing bonefish at forty feet. I dropped a Crazy Charlie three feet in front of the feeding fish, it moved forward; I gave a three inch strip, the fish pounced. I set the hook, but sadly after the first run, the fish shed the hook. We moved on and five minutes later I hooked another bone, this also shed the hook. Strange, I thought, losing two fish in succession. I checked the hook, it seemed sharp enough, but I decided to change. During the afternoon session I hooked up to several more good bones all landed without trouble. Around five o'clock Ezra said, "It's time to leave, Martin." I wound in all my line, clipped off the fly, stowed the rod away, and then sat down in my padded seat. It had been a great day, one of my best ever on the flats.

I didn't spook a single fish, hooked up to every fish I cast for and lost just two fish. Now that's what I call a good day's fishing.

It was without doubt my best trip chasing bonefish. I have had more fish in a session and bigger fish, including a nine pound bone; Millers Creek made it a better day. At Moxey's bone-fishing lodge you'll find good food, nice rooms, and very friendly and helpful staff. Most important of all, it's close enough to a bonefish flat for you to fish before breakfast, and after dinner – which I did on many occasions. The people of Moxey Town are nice and friendly, it's very safe and you're only a short distance from the airport to Moxey's Bone fishing Lodge, Moxey Town, Mangrove Cay and Andros Island. I suggest you take an 8 weight rod with floating line, a 10 weight rod and floating line for the big barracuda, permit and medium size tarpon. Why not pack a spinning rod. Masterline International has a nice telescopic rod which I have found to be ideal for bones, snappers, jacks and medium size barracuda. I always take some wire crimps and crimping pliers and a few swivels. Don't forget the sun protection lotion and lip balm. I drink bottled water but use tap water for cleaning teeth and making tea.

I was booked to go fishing on Green Turtle Cay for a few days; staying at Bluff House where the manager, Martin Havill, had booked me with Ronnie Sawyer, who is rated the number

one guide in the area. I met up with Ronnie the following morning about eleven, after a friend's wedding on the beach which was followed by a champagne breakfast. My tackle was an 8 weight rod, my Richard Carter hand-made reel, and a floating line. I attached a 12ft fluorocarbon leader with a 12lb tippet to which I tied a Gotcha.

Martin's personal best Bone, 9lb

I was now ready to hunt the bones of Cocoa Plum Creek. As Ronnie quietly poled me away from the shoreline, we passed mangroves and a couple of small flats. We moved on. Ronnie spotted a mutton snapper, and told me to make a cast. I dropped the fly ahead of the snapper then made a retrieve as the fish followed. Near the boat it turned away. Some two hours into the trip Ronnie spotted a big bone, sixty feet at twelve o'clock, I cast as directed, the fly dropping perfectly. I made a couple of six inch strips; the fish spotted the Gotcha, and we then watched as it pounced. I felt the fish take, and tightened. It seemed as if the bone had been inhaling rocket fuel and then switched on the after-burners as it set off across the flats. I stuck the rod high in the air and watched the line go and go!

Far in the distance I could faintly see the fish swirl as it tried to get in among some mangroves. Then it turned and came straight back towards me while I wound in the line like mad, wishing that I had my big Loop reel – it would have been very useful at a time like this! As I started to gain line, the fish shot off again, taking most of my hard-won footage. For some minutes I had the feeling that the fish was the winner. Ronnie said, "I think it's off," but I carried on winding, then I felt its head shake. "It's still on Ronnie," I shouted. Slowly I started to gain line, the fish was tiring. Ronnie said, "Be careful, Martin, it's a big fish." My knees trembled, my hands shook; then I had my first good look at the fish. Taking it easy, I gained valuable line back on the reel until the bone was within reach of Ronnie. He made a grab for it and then it was mine. I punched the air with delight, Ronnie weighed the fish at exactly 9lb, my best bonefish. I sat down shaking, I was on a high. A couple of quick pictures then we watched the fish swim off hopefully to grow into a ten-pounder. I've had lots of bones but that's still my best. In the dining room that evening a guy called across saying, "Well done on your big bonefish, what was it like?" I called, "Better than sex – and it lasts longer!" We all laughed.

During a day's trout fishing on the River Ribble, David Jones of Bury, Lancashire, asked if he could join me on one of my bone-fishing trips. I said, "Yes, no problem." I arranged for us to visit Moxey's bonefish lodge on Andros Island in the Bahamas for a week in late March. Weeks prior to our departure David spent many hours reading that delightful book, Bonefishing! by Randall Kaufmann, covering everything about fly-fishing for these fish. Of course, you don't have to fly-fish for bone; you can fish with an Avon-action rod, fixed-spool reel and 10lb line using either shrimp, bits of conch or crab, or even small lures if that's your favourite way of angling.

David wanted to fly-fish and so had equipped himself with Thomas and Thomas Helix 4 piece travel rods, large size Loop reels carrying 200 yards of 30lb backing with an 8 weight Cortland bonefish line designed for use in the warm-water climes. Wading boots and tropical shirts were on the shopping list. Dozens of flies were purchased: Gotchas, Crazy Charlies, Clouser Minnows, Slider Borskis, Mini-Puff. Gold Gotchas were tied up on various sizes of hooks. Other flies were purchased from American fly-tiers.

I have visited Moxey's on many occasions, often stopping for two weeks at a time; it's situated on the southern half of Andros Island close to the Middle Bight on the east coast. It's a poor settlement, which was hit by big hurricane Andrew back in the 1990s, causing major damage to homes, boats and the environment. Most of the people earn their living diving for lobsters or sponges; others use hand-lines to catch fish for local restaurants. We, the tourists hunting bones, give these friendly people the chance to earn a slightly better living. I have found they are good at the job which demands a lot of knowledge – not only about the tidal movements, but the aquatic food supply the bonefish feed on, and boat-handling; this includes standing on an elevated platform some four feet above the stern of the flats boat with a fibre-glass pole around fifteen feet in length. The pole is used to push the boat along the edge of the mangroves or across the flats. You, the angler, will be up front in the bows ready to cast whenever bonefish is spotted. There will be times when the flats boat is anchored, the guide then takes you wading the flats in search of the bonefish. I feel this is the best way to go when possible. You're the true hunter after the hunted.

Andy with a big crawfish from a blue hole

Just a short boat-ride across the water from Moxey's you will find Gibson Island – these days often known as Martin James' Island, due to the amount of time I spend fishing the area. In the centre it has a dark, secretive, blue hole. Fishing around the island I've caught many species of jacks, including: crevales, averaging ten pounds – the street fighter of the aquatic world; numerous species of snappers, including the hard-fighting mutton snapper, yellow tails, schoolmasters, grunts, shad, blue runners and more.

On the east of the island you will find a huge flat where it's possible to fish through the flood and ebb tide for bonefish. It's a place where I often target the sharks with a 12 weight rod; this can be great fun. One day, Kate chummed up the sharks with chunks of barracuda, three fish were swirling and fighting over the 6/0 fly-size chunks of bait, one a black- tipped shark about four feet in length, and two lemon shark. I cast a big size 6/0 fly.

I let it sink about three feet, and then started a fast strip. Suddenly, from nowhere, a big bull-shark pushed aside the lemon shark and grabbed my fly before I could lift it off the water. The fish tore off across the flats to the deep water channel. All we could do was watch in amazement. After the fly- line, with two hundred yards of backing was gone, all I could do was point the rod down the line then wait for a break. The next day we were fishing a blue hole for jacks with Ezra, who pointed and said, "That's a big bull, Martin." I said, "yes, it's like the one that grabbed my fly yesterday." He laughed, saying, "not that big, Martin." Ten minutes later Ezra said, "it's got something alongside its mouth," then we could see my fly! Ezra was amazed.

Another interesting day was when both Kate and I caught some boxfish, Kate on a piece of conch, mine on a small clouser minnow that represented a lime-coloured glass minnow. These bluish-green milk carton-shaped boxfish have a solid base, unlike the softly curved belly of most fish. When hooked, they go off very fast, fighting as hard as any bonefish. Like the bones, they are bottom feeders, but are rarely caught.

Before leaving home for my latest visit to Moxey Town with David, I collected a large holdall of clothing from friends, which would be given to Ezra and distributed to the local children; Kate and I, on a trip to Dubai, purchased pens, pencils and writing pads for the local school. Goals for Life, a Rossendale company gave me a cricket bat, and two footballs for use by the school. After breakfast, David, Joel and I visited the school, to be greeted by friendly, smiling children and staff. The boys quickly got to know the right way to hold a cricket bat. The girls were more interested in the football – which could be used as a net ball! Having handed over the badly-needed equipment, we said our goodbyes, then headed off for the shoreline to meet our guide Ezra.

On the beach, I introduced David to Ezra. I call Ezra, the Godfather of bone-fishing guides.

He shows the newcomers the art of spotting the bones, how to pole the boat along the edge of the mangroves and over the flats. He shows them how to put the flats boat into the position that will give the best chance of casting the fly. He also keeps the more inexperienced ones in order, making sure all the guests get plenty of shots at fish. Ezra is a gentle, six foot guy with powerful shoulders, big hands, a lovely smile and a quiet,

One of many shark caught on the fly

gravelly voice. Ezra knows everyone, and is highly respected by other bonefish guides and clients.

After the rods were stowed away Ezra said, "Get aboard." Before doing so, we washed off our boots. The last thing you want in the boat is sand and mud; it doesn't do your fly line any good, or make the guide happy. We were soon skimming across the wind-rippled turquoise water towards Little Moxey Creek. Some distance from the creek, the motor was cut.

Picking up his long fibre-glass pole, Ezra climbed up onto his poling platform. Slowly we moved along the creek some thirty feet out from the mangroves. We spotted two sharks and several rays including a huge manta ray. Sitting in the mangroves were several egrets, occasionally a heron could be seen hunting. Several bones were spotted, two were targeted but they didn't want to eat or were not happy with the presentation. Two hours later it was time for a break. We sat chatting and drinking cool water, or a soft drink. Ezra told us about some of the big bones he had seen on other flats over the years. A loggerhead turtle surfaced a few feet off the boat; it spotted us and quickly dived. With our rest period over, we moved off once more in search of a feeding bonefish.

The sun was high in the vivid blue sky; a light wind rippled the turquoise water of the Caribbean which shimmered and glittered like a million diamonds. Ezra, David's guide for the day, was high up on his poling platform, his eagle-like eyes peering into the clear depths, trying to see the grey ghost of the flats. In the bow, David was bent forward in a typical pose of those hunting bonefish: rod at the ready, fifty feet of line neatly coiled, the fly lightly held in his fingers. Ezra quietly whispered to David, "Bonefish at twelve o'clock, forty feet." Making two false casts, David dropped the gold, crystal flash Charlie, three feet in front of the fish. All was silent as we quietly waited not daring to breath, Ezra whispered, "Small strip," and then, "Another small strip." The next second, David's rod was stuck up high as a bonefish dashed across the shallow sandy flat heading for the deeper water.

The fight was on as David tackled his first ever bone. His first task was to land the fish,

David Jones with a nice Bonefish

which had quickly gone off at a fast rate of knots towards the horizon. Some 140 yards of line and backing were gone. For some minutes it was a give-and-take contest with David slowly winning back some of the line. Then, as in most cases of fighting a fish, he quickly got the upper hand. Checking the water was safe, we went over the side of the boat where the fish was quickly bought to hand. As David lifted his first bonefish he had a grin a mile wide. After shooting some photographs we released the fish safely. Congratulations were toasted all round with a cool drink. We moved on in the hunt for more bonefish.

During our trip we both caught a lot of bones. While David hunted the bones exclusively, I went off to Gibson Island to target the bones, snappers, barracuda and sharks. I was equipped with a heavy spinning outfit with 15lb line, a light spinning outfit with 6lb line. I also had 8 and 10 weight rods. In my bag were big and small popping plugs, a selection of lures and three boxes of flies, including big flies for jack crevals and sharks. I also carried some wire leaders for the sharks and barracudas. I targeted the lemon sharks, hooking two and landing one, a good fish, nearly six feet in length. No way do I try to bring these beasts in close. I bring the fish in just close enough to touch, and then cut the leader. The barbless hook would be quickly gone and no harm done. Light-line fishing with a small plug, I caught several jacks which were great fun. Why not take time out from catching bonefish and hook-up to a few other species on your next visit.

With a good dollar exchange rate, there was never a better time to visit the Caribbean, and recently I chose to return to Belize. My destination was Turneffe Flats in Central America, not for bonefish but for snappers. This area of the Caribbean has some of the world's most pristine marine habitat. Belize is a leader in environmental protection with nearly one third of the country under a National Park or some other protected status. It is home to three of the four coral atolls in the Western Hemisphere, Turneffe being the largest and most diverse. The atolls provide a unique and remarkably diverse marine eco-system with an extensive coral system. In fact, during my stay at Turneffe, a barge delivered all the building materials and equipment to build a recycling centre. These people really care about the environment.

David and I are both retired, travelling together to exotic locations, enjoying our passion for saltwater fishing. David has been to several locations in the Caribbean in search of bone fish while I enjoy fishing for all the species, in fact David targets the bones with great success. These days I spend my time fly-fishing over the reefs while David will be off wading the flats. At seventy-plus years of age I aim to get in as many trips as possible, I don't know when it will all come to an end.

Belize is very British: many of the people have a picture of the Queen in their home. It is a sovereign democratic state which enjoys a rich and diverse social heritage. The country was called Belize long before the British took over and renamed it British Honduras. In 1973, the locals changed it back to Belize as a first step to independence. In 1981, it gained independence but remains part of the commonwealth, something which the locals give you the impression they are very proud of. The British Army also have a jungle training-camp in the country.

David and I booked our flights with Nigel Pratt of Clitheroe Travel, flying Manchester to Orlando then Miami, where we stopped overnight, before taking a flight to Belize the following day. Arriving in Belize City airport, we quickly cleared immigration and customs, I must say the staff were most friendly. It was a lot quicker than clearing an American airport and far more pleasant. As we cleared customs, a representative from Turneffe Flats was on hand to take our bags then lead us to a large station-wagon for the trip to the docks. As we walked along the dock, I stopped to watch a bunch of snappers swimming around, thinking, I could spend the rest of my days in this place. Some fifteen minutes later we were aboard a forty-five foot jet boat for an hour-long boat trip to Turneffe Island, some thirty miles offshore

The social centre for Turneffe Flats is the air-conditioned 'Lodge'. A pre-dinner gathering for hors d'oeuvres and refreshments is customary; the screened veranda is a wonderful place to enjoy the tropical evening with new and old friends, where a breathtaking view from the upper and lower decks makes the 'Lodge' a favourite spot with everyone. Meals are a tasty combination of Belizean and American dishes served family-style. Fresh seafood, local produce and home-baked pastries are standard fare. Three delicious meals a day are part of your package.

Every person at Turneffe Flats: from the owners, Craig and Karen Hayes; the cooks who ensured we were well fed, the maids who looked after our rooms, gardeners, guides and fishing manager Jeff Pfaender, were committed to make my stay one of enjoyment and fun. I couldn't have wished for a better crew – they were wonderful.

Depending upon your plans and your preference, you will have the option to take a packed lunch or return to the lodge to eat. Following hors d'oeuvres and refreshments, dinner is the big meal of the day comprising soup or salad, entree and homemade dessert. Entrees vary between seafood, chicken, pork and beef. If you have special dietary needs, they will do their best to accommodate you. Being diabetic wasn't a problem, on every trip the ladies looked after me.

The bar is well stocked with scotch, bourbon, gin, rum, vodka, tequila and several liqueurs. In addition, they offer a variety of wines as well as local Belikin beer. Cuban and Dominican cigars are also available. The bar is located in the 'Lodge' just off of the dining area with plenty of open space to gather around after a day of adventure.

You will stay in one of eight spacious, air-conditioned cabanas located on the beach with panoramic views of Turneffe's coral reef. All rooms are furnished with a queen-size bed and an extra-long single bed, ample closet space, chest of drawers and a sitting area. Each room has a large private bathroom with two sinks and a shower.

Imagine awakening in your air-conditioned beachfront cabin with an incredible tropical seascape of white sand beach, tranquil bonefish flats, lush mangroves and the surf breaking over

the reef for miles in either direction. Many mornings I would stand on the veranda watching a few tailing bones and hear the great-tailed grackles. Get up early and watch a spectacular sunrise from your veranda then, when night falls, the stars look close enough to touch.

The island has been popular with British anglers for many years; it's a place where all the guides are experienced and know the waters extremely well. Bonefish, permit and tarpon are what most anglers target – not for me on this trip. I let all the bone fishers disappear about eight in the morning for distant flats while I went for breakfast. This area offers some excellent fishing for jacks and snappers, with an excellent chance of a big mutton-snapper – in my book it's one of the prize fish in tropical water. This fish grows big and they can often be difficult to catch at times. The world record is 28lbs 5oz. A good fish is one of five pounds-plus. They are a tough fighter and will savage a surface-fished popper either on fly-tackle or

The right tool for the job

spinning gear. Let's not forget the schoolmaster fish, another member of the snapper family; I've had these pushing four pounds. You have the lane snapper, yellowtail snapper, red snapper, rainbow runner, trigger fish, skip-jack, big-eye jack, and if you're lucky, a jack crevale – the street fighter of the aquatic world. Last but not least, the barracuda with its mouthful of razor sharp teeth. It can weigh sixty pounds but the average is probably twelve pounds.

For all my fly-fishing I use the best available, including Wulff Bermuda Triangle taper fly-lines, which are built for use in the tropics. These days I have been using Gilmore X400 reels, taking a Tibor as a back-up reel. Being on the pro-staff of Thomas and Thomas, I get to use what are the best fly-rods for fresh and saltwater fishing. They are an all-American built rod, even down to the reel fittings. I carried Helix and Horizon in 8 and 9 weights. Choosing the right leader is most important, I put my trust in Deep Blue leaders from Gamma, and they haven't let me down. I see no reason to change. I had a large selection of Deceivers, clousers and other streamer patterns, I also included some poppers.

Often when I hunt the mutton snapper I would stand on chunk of coral to give me a better view of the underwater scene. In the gullies between corals of various colours I would often see a parrot fish, a fascinating species of the reef which could often be seen feeding on the coral. Without doubt, what can only be described as an exciting experience, is watching a snapper or jack savage a popper that you're working across the clear, emerald green water. Suddenly the water boils as the lure is savaged aggressively by your quarry.

You're instantly on a high, adrenaline courses through the veins. Your strip strike sets the hook into a fish that's doesn't know about submitting to well-balanced tackle. The rod tip is pulled down to the water surface as the reel grudgingly gives line. If you're lucky you will get the fish to hand but often you will get broken off. One day while hunting snappers I spotted two trigger fish, in slightly deeper water over clear sand One was huge and must have gone fifteen pounds-plus.

I well remember fishing an area of deep emerald green coloured water two hundred yards from the boat dock. As I caught a succession of nice sized mutton snappers on a shrimp pattern, my attention was drawn to fifteen frigate birds within fifty feet of where I was fishing. These magnificent birds, which could work the thermals for hours without moving, were hovering twenty feet above the ocean. Who said fishing was boring? No way, there is always something interesting happening around us.

My week at Turneffe flats was all about relaxing, I would fish for an hour or two, and then take a nap perhaps have a mug of tea and read a novel. There were a couple of days when I didn't even bother to fish, though I would perhaps walk the reef or lay on the boat dock watching a variety of fish, observing their movements, occasionally watching them feed. I found it all fascinating. I would have lunch in the lodge with some of the divers who I found to be charming company. The only downside was the occasional guests who were loud and boorish. At times the dining room sounded like the House of Commons at Question time. My mate David on one occasion said, "If you were to make all this noise in an English restaurant you would be asked to leave!" Their behaviour improved. There were times when I couldn't escape quickly enough from their rather loud chatter for the peace of the tropical wilderness.

Taking the advice of Pocco, one of the locals, I fished a spot some two hundred yards to the left of the boat dock and twenty yards offshore, where I had some great fishing for mutton snappers. After catching a succession of fish between a pound and two pounds I hooked the fish I had been seeking for several years; it was not only aggressive but ripped lines off the reel at a fast rate of knots for a snapper, soon the fish had me down into the backing.

It's not often a snapper will do this. For some ten minutes or more it was give-and-take, slowly I backed closer to the shore winning a few feet of line then letting the fish slog away, hoping it would tire. Suddenly the fish swirled on the surface its prickly dorsal fin erect. It was my dream fish, a far bigger prize than a double figure bonefish. It was twenty yards away; I reckon it might go six pounds. Slowly I worked line inch by inch back on the reel, occasionally a foot or more. Then disaster: the fish dived and I tried to stop it. The result was a broken leader where I had joined three feet of fluorocarbon tippet to my leader. How did I make such a silly mistake? I am always practising the tying of knots so I get it right on the water, but not this time. If you're looking for a new adventure why not visit Turneffe Flats.

Due to the pristine waters and the healthy marine environment, Turneffe is home to a large variety of game fish. On the reef you can target cubera snapper, perhaps weighing thirty pounds, several grouper species, including the jewfish which may weigh two hundred pounds – a tough fish for any angler, I rate the mutton snapper a top fish of the flats or reefs, it's an incredible fighter, often making long runs with lots of head shaking. Many times I have had these fish take me well into my backing. In my book they are as prized as the bones or permit.

Fishing one morning on the inside of the reef, I spotted two big fish. Now and again they stuck their heads in the soft sand, tails out of the water waving provocatively. I cast clousers, deceivers and poppers, but nothing interested them. Just as I was giving up, Mark Hyde our guide appeared. I pointed out the fish and said "They don't want to eat flies or poppers." He said "They are big trigger fish, try a crab pattern." Quickly tying one on, I looked for the fish. They had gone over the reef: a chance missed. One afternoon Mark suggested an area of the reef I should fish, then he and David went off hunting the bones. I fished on the edge of the reef on a flooding tide; I reckon I must have had fifty or more snappers. Jacks, skipjack, big-eyed jacks, rainbow runners, blue runners, red snappers, lane snappers, yellow tail snapper, small groupers and schoolmasters on poppers, clousers and deceivers.

I can remember a few years ago, fishing at night off Andros Island in the Bahamas, catching five schoolmasters averaging four pounds. After lunch the next day, I was once again fishing the flooding tide on another part of the reef where Mark suggested I should fish. I chose a big popper with a 9 weight rod and floating line. An hour later, after catching a mixture of grunts, jacks and snappers, and with perfect conditions for making long casts, I chucked the popper some sixty feet. On my third cast I got it right as the popper landed in an area of deep water between some big rocks. As I stripped the popper it came twisting, gurgling and popping across the swirling, boiling water over coral and weed-covered rocks, suddenly something caught my eye, I watched in amazement as a big mutton snapper swept upwards from behind a chunk of coral, savaging my popper like a terrier with a rat! It was just two rod lengths away from where I stood chest-deep in swirling water. It was an awesome sight. This mutton snapper was a big one. With a firm strip strike I set the hook, a big angry fish dived slamming the rod tip downwards into the water. The reel screeched; line flew through the guides in a blur. This fish was quickly off the shallows into the deep water on the ocean side of the reef. For fifteen minutes – it could have been more, I battled with this angry powerful head shaking twisting snapper, worrying about the line fraying and getting cut off on the rocks or coral.

Some years ago while fishing Cocoa Plum Creek at Green Turtle Cay in the Bahamas, I was told by Ronny Sawyer that mutton snappers were a prize quarry. How right he was. These fish are awesome; this one was certainly giving me a tough work out. Several times the fish took me down into my backing, I could feel the head shaking. After sometime I started thinking I might win this one. Finally I was able to start walking back towards the shallow water of the flats. I managed to put on enough pressure to drag the fish through a big gap in the coral and rocks. My prize was starting to feel the exertions of trying to gain its freedom.

At last I was slowly winning the fight. Suddenly, I got my first clear view as the big mutton snapper swirled on the surface, a beaten fish. Pulling it across the calm water on the inside the reef, I got the fish close enough to scoop it up. Slipping out the barbless hook of the popper, I held my prize fish in the water, where I admired this supreme specimen that had given me such

Mark Hyde poles David Jones as they hunt the bonefish

an adrenalin-packed work-out, with lots of action. I released the fish in the gin clear water; it looked magnificent with its erect dorsal fin, the silvery to reddish tinge of its deep body with blue stripes below the eye, and a black spot near its lateral line.

I didn't have the guide alongside me but Mark had done his job in suggesting the area to fish. Meanwhile David had enjoyed a successful session with Mark in their hunt for bones. Mark had been an outstanding guide.

Bone fishing at Turneffe offers something for anglers of all levels of experience. Novice saltwater anglers can expect to see hundreds of bonefish, providing a great opportunity to learn the basics of flats fishing. Experienced saltwater anglers will find plenty of challenging fish, particularly when targeting smaller schools and larger singles. Tarpon inhabit the creeks, channels and lagoons of the atoll. Most tarpon are 60–90 pounds, with some fish in the 100–150 pound range and occasional monsters approaching 200 pounds. You also have the chance of hooking up to a big snook. As more saltwater anglers have come to enjoy the challenge of permit-fishing, Turneffe flats are recognized as one of a few locations to experience the excitement of casting to tailing permit. The area has an exceptional population of permit and increasing numbers of anglers are visiting to sight-fish for them. Often these fish will weight forty pounds. A great predator is the barracuda, a worthy target, often overlooked by many anglers, the 'cuda is a challenge on popping plugs or big streamers. Sometimes they attain sixty pounds, the average fish is twelve. On my last day I watched an immense fish just off the boat dock. It would have gone fifty pounds-plus. It was huge.

If you're not a fly-fisher I suggest you take two spinning rods, one for lines of 12lb the other

for 20lb lines, carry a selection of swivels, wire traces, poppers, various floating and diving plugs along with some big, bright-coloured spoons. You can of course rent a spinning rod at the lodge, though I reckon its much nicer using your own gear. Remember to wash down all your gear after a day's fishing. It only takes ten to fifteen minutes but it's worth that little effort. Remember saltwater is very corrosive.

A Fishing Companion

I approached the pool on all fours; in the three feet of gin-clear water I could count the pebbles on the bottom of the river. Forty feet out from my position, and within twenty feet of the tree-lined far bank, a good-size trout sucked down a free-drifting Hendrickson. It left just a small ring of the rise which spread across the glass-smooth surface in ever-increasing circles. It would be difficult and tricky to cast over two varying flows of water, and I would only get one chance. If I messed up, the fish would be gone. I extended my leader from 10ft to 12ft with the addition of 2ft of 3lb fluorocarbon tippet. I then tied on a size 16 Dark Hendrickson. According to my old friend and top fly-fisher and tier, Dave Hughes of Portland Oregon, this fly fishes for the darker phase of the same Hendrickson hatch (Ephemerella subvaria) and it can be used to represent many other species of mayfly.

Pulling off enough line to reach my target, I made two false casts then shot the line. Just before the line dropped on the water, I gave the rod a sideways shake ensuring the line landed with several wiggles, helping me to get a drag-free drift. The leader unfurled, with the imitation Hendrickson landing like thistledown several feet upstream of the feeding trout. Under my breath I said, "Bloody good cast, James." I got a drag-free drift of about three feet, the water rocked slightly under the fly, suddenly it was gone. I set the hook into a very angry fish which shot off down the pool. A few minutes later I was unhooking a lovely brown trout.

I hadn't chosen the best time to visit Trevor and Christine Bross in Greenfield, Massachusetts in New England, where the third coldest month of May had just been recorded. During my two week stay, the weather was a mixture of strong winds and heavy rain showers, sometimes with several hours of non-stop rain. Even so, I did get three delightful afternoons of warm sunshine with blue skies and fluffy clouds, with temperatures in the region of 60°F.

Massachusetts is blessed with some delightful trout streams, and none are better than the Deerfield River which is probably this state's second longest river after the Connecticut. The Deerfield is a tail water river, not freestone water. As with many rivers in the United States, there are several dams along the length of the Deerfield which have to release water to generate electricity. This can increase the height and flow rates considerably, making fishing impossible in many areas.

By going to www.h2oline.com you can access water-flows, though they can be unpredictable and change hourly. The message will often tell you what time of the day the dams will stop releasing water, and the experienced angler quickly works out the times he or she can be on the river. Browns, rainbow and brook trout are your quarry, though the latter are not as plentiful as the other two species. Other fish to be found are tiger trout, dace, carp, sucker salmon and shad. The latter are great fighters – they never know when they are beaten; they are often called the poor man's tarpon. In some areas there are smallmouth bass to be caught. But from my limited experience, I rate the Millers River a better smallmouth bass water.

For the small fee of $38–$50 you get to fish all the Massachusetts State's water for a season. Certainly, it represents excellent value for money, but I must say I wouldn't want this system in place in England. We just don't have the miles of rivers and stream that are available to the citizens of Massachusetts. I also feel many of our waters would be badly abused and ruined within twelve months if it was a free-for-all. Let's keep our system of angling clubs, societies, syndicates and commercial fisheries. Some of us, me included, like the exclusivity we get from joining certain clubs and syndicates. I personally am not a fan of commercial fisheries for my fishing, much preferring a more wilderness experience – the fisheries still have their place in the angling world, especially for the beginner and the youngsters.

All you need to fish this beautiful river is a State Fishing Permit

I suppose it's a forty minute drive from Greenfield to the catch-and-release stretch of the river near Charlemont, a quaint town of nice, timbered homes set either side of the highway and along the river. It would make a delightful place to live for an artist, photographer or writer, and property prices are good by UK standards. If I was twenty years younger I might well want to move out West. The countryside is magnificent, with mountains, hills, fields, woods and forests, interspersed with rivers, lakes, ponds and streams; and we must not forget the beautiful coastline which offers some the finest saltwater fly-fishing you could wish for.

It was about two-thirty in the afternoon when Trevor and I arrived at Hopper Field Pool to find we had the water to ourselves. A light wind blew upstream, the sky was blue, flecked with clumps of white fluffy clouds. A few Hendricksons were coming off as we pulled on our chest-waders and Korker's wading boots. We both wear these excellent boots with their changeable soles which make them perfect for the travelling angler.

We both chose to use the Thomas and Thomas 9ft Helix rods rated for a 5 weight line. With flies coming off in good numbers, the only line we would need today was a floater with a 12ft tapered leader to a 6 X tippet. As I was putting together my gear, Trevor was making his first cast; the fly had travelled about six feet when it was taken in a swirl. Trevor was either rather shocked or very excited at getting a take so quickly only three feet from the bank. He got well and truly broken. It's been said many times by many anglers, "Don't go wading until you have fished the inside seam." Trevor had proved the wisdom of that advice.

Trevor, being the perfect host and guide, saw that I was ready to fish and suggested I should try the same run. My size 18 Klinkhammer had drifted ten feet when it was taken in an aggressive manner. Within minutes of starting to fish this delightful river, I was playing a good rainbow in the fast-flowing water. Two – no three times, the fish jumped clear of the water. Slowly, I worked it into the quiet backwater where it was soon netted – the Deerfield had once again given up its rewards. It's a friendly river, with good fly-hatches when conditions are suitable. It has a good head of stocked and wild fish; it's a water I have fished on many occasions – only ever blanking once. I well remember that day: it was very cold and windy with no fly-hatches. I had to fish nymphs: not the most exciting of methods. Trevor's Dad, John, had a fish on his first cast, but nothing more.

An hour after we started fishing, there was a big hatch of Hendricksons, the duns floating on the surface gave the impression of a huge yachting-gala; it was like mayfly time on the Kennet. Fish were rising, swirling and slashing at flies all over the river, but I couldn't raise a single one despite getting some good drifts over feeding fish. Trevor pointed out a nice specimen feeding within inches of the bank where a bush overhung the water. I tried various patterns without success. He then gave me one of his Hendrickson patterns resembling the dun of the species. Three times I cast the fly, making good drifts, but the trout ignored my offering. I extended my tippet with a couple of feet of 7X then retied the fly.

On my left side, the river, flecked with white foam, flowed fast over some rocks; 35–40ft below me it split into two sections. As most of the flow continued downstream, part of the river swept away to my right creating a large back-eddy with a big area of scum – virtually a still water. I made a long cast upstream into the fast water. As the fly reached the spot where the water flow swept back into the eddy, I lifted the rod high and made a big mend to my right, guiding the fly into the run close to the bank. Lowering the rod tip, I had the fly on a perfect drift, retrieving line when needed. As the fly reached the end of the drift without a take I lifted off then made another cast. Three times I had the fly drifting perfectly. And still the fish wouldn't eat it. After drying off the fly so it would float high, I made another cast. Trevor said, "That's a good drift Martin." I murmured, "Yes, let's hope the fish thinks so!" In the blink of an eye, the fish sucked down my imitation. I tightened and the fight was on. A good brown trout went ballistic, taking line off the reel.

For several minutes it was a good old tug-of-war between man and trout. The well-balanced tackle, and light hand holding the rod were in charge, and after a few minutes a good-size brown trout was landed. I gently eased out the barbless hook with a Ketchum disgorger. As the fish was released a kingfisher flew low across the river. American kingfishers are rather drab compared with the colourful birds we see on English rivers. Meanwhile Trevor was also catching; I took time out to shoot some pictures as he played and netted a good fish. Trevor had been given strict instructions to be home for six o'clock as we were going out to dinner. We had about fifteen minutes of fishing time left. I decided to take some more pictures, while Trevor caught two more good fish. I left the river thinking how exciting the fishing would be during the evening hatch.

As I was finishing lunch around one o'clock Trevor said, "Let's go fishing; I've got a gas stove so bring your tea bags!" Wow! It was going to be one of those good days that I enjoy: sitting at the waterside with a fresh brew. On the way to the river we picked up Trevor's Dad, who is an excellent nymph-fisher. It was Memorial weekend and there was a lot of traffic on the road; the journey of normally forty minutes probably took fifty-five. We reached Hopper Field Pool, and I left John and Trevor to get kitted-out in the car park while I walked through the trees to the river, where I spied a fisherman standing well-out in the river. In the very place where he should have been fishing his fly, I was shocked to see he was using a float (bobber) with a nymph underneath it. I find it hard to understand why people should fish in such a crass way when there is so much good angling literature available. Still, we see idiots who think they know it all – in every country.

I sat on the bank and looked up and downstream. Apart from our 'bobber', I could see my friend John Carpenter and two other anglers; they had all been on the river for some time. I pulled on my waders, put together a rod and reel and was ready to go off fishing. I collected my wading staff and tackle, and headed across the river, picking my way carefully in the fast-flowing water. Once on the far bank I made my way downstream to Rainbow Run, which meant another crossing of the river at the top end of Bear Island. I passed two good-looking riffles. At the second one, behind a car-size boulder, a good fish rose to take a struggling crane-fly. I made a mental note to try the spot on my way back upstream. I continued my walk slowly and quietly downstream. As I rounded a bend in the river, I could see a slower-moving stretch of water. Fifty yards further on it flowed into Maple Pool: it looked magnificent.

I sat speechless at the beautiful scene before me. In the late spring sunshine, the thickly-wooded banks along the river looked resplendent in their new cloaks of green – all shades of green. Half the pool was overhung by trees, giving the water a wonderful pale green colour. The other half of the pool was a vivid blue, reflecting from the sky. A raven, the biggest perching bird in the world croaked from a nearby tree. It's interesting to note that the feathers on their crowns and shaggy throats are raised when they croak. A beaver slid down the far bank dragging a good-size branch. No doubt it was tea-time for beavers. I said to myself, "It can't get better than this."

But it did, as four more Hendricksons were sucked down by a good fish. I extended my leader by adding another 3ft of 7X Frog hair tippet giving me a leader around 15ft. The fly I tied on my tippet was a Hendrickson dun, tied up by Trevor Bross, my fishing buddy and guide. I pulled off some line and made two false casts then shot the line; a light upstream-breeze lightly ruffled the water surface and laid out my leader, the fly dropping like thistledown. It was on a perfect drift; I made several small mends, easing the fly down the stream. As it entered the taking

zone, my concentration was intense, my mouth was dry, with no saliva – I couldn't swallow; I was like a coiled spring. Would the fish be fooled into taking this creation of silk and flosses with an added bit of steel, believing it to be the real thing? I soon got my answer. The fly disappeared in the tiniest of dimples; I raised the rod tip then felt the resistance of a good fish.

Suddenly the rod tip was pulled down savagely as the fish realised it was hooked, but I had no fear of breakage. The T&T Light

Beavers are a common sight on the Deerfield

Presentation Series rod was made for such occasions. The fish took a few feet of line as I let the combination of a well balanced rod; reel, line and leader take the strain. I was the driver and in command of the situation. Three times I gave the fish some line, which was quickly retrieved. Five minutes later I had an eighteen inch brown at the water's edge. I bent down and quickly slipped out the barbless hook without touching the fish. Realising it was free, it shot off across the pool for sanctuary under the far-bank trees, creating a bow wave as it escaped.

Author brings a fish to the net on the Deerfield River

In the next couple of hours I had five more fish on size 16 Klinkhammers and size 10 Stimulators. When fishing the Stimulators I increased my tippet to 6X and only targeted single rising fish. It meant sitting quietly at the water's edge watching for rising fish; when a fish had shown itself three or four times I would then attempt to catch it. Lady Luck was on my side: the river and wildlife belonged to me; it was sheer bliss. I caught a few fish, fluffed a few casts and lost some fish. It was just great being there. Suddenly the glass-smooth surface of the pool was rocked as small waves spread out in all directions. Looking about me for the cause of the disturbance, I was shocked to see an idiot who had walked up to the pool from downstream. With this behaviour, and with etiquette not being in his vocabulary, I decided that, with the pool being ruined for the time being, I would move off upstream to the riffle. There, I caught my last fish of the session, a sixteen inch rainbow. As I went off upstream looking forward to my tea, I got the chance to take some cracking pictures of the beaver. Sadly I didn't get my fresh brew, though I was offered some lukewarm coffee from a Thermos flask; I declined.

Tackle: I had three rods with me, all Thomas & Thomas models. LPS 9ft 5 weight for small dry-flies, which I used with the finest of leaders. For the bigger dry-flies I used a Helix 9 ft 5 weight for dry-fly work. I wouldn't want to be without my Helix 10ft 6 weight for fishing both dry-flies and nymphs. If you're good at Czech-nymphing you can expect some great sport. The 10ft rod is just the weapon. You will find floating lines will cover 85% of your fishing, but I would also advise a 6 weight nymphing line.

Many of my friends reckon I take too many flies, but you don't have to use them all. Occasionally, I might just need that fly I rarely use. I suggest you take a good selection. All attractor patterns work – hare's ear, copper john, prince nymph, adams. BWO in sizes 18 and 20; March Brown; Hendrickson; Green Drake both dry and nymph; olive woolly buggers. Caddis nymph and hoppers.

Rule of thumb is to fish one size smaller than hatch on still to moderate moving water (fly colour important). 6–7X tippets for dries, these fish have seen a lot of flies.

Dinosaurs, mammoths and dodo have all disappeared from the planet, but there are still some great creatures from the past who continue to survive. This, despite the destruction and changes to the environment, pollution of the oceans and over-fishing, which has seen a massive decrease in fish stocks to the extent that many species are now in danger of disappearing. All this has been caused by the species, Homo sapiens.

We are now seeing the cruel, barbaric practice by evil, wicked men of using nets for taking sharks: then cut off the fins and chuck the fish back into the ocean to die a slow, cruel death. I am told the Orientals are prepared to pay a high price for these shark fins. Not only do the Oriental's encourage the killing of sharks, they also target bears' bladders, rhino horn, herring roe, etc. All these animals are being killed, we are told, in the name of aphrodisiacs. All I can say is, if they need this rubbish there must be something wrong with their mental state. My aphrodisiac is a good-looking woman. I would suggest you stop buying goods from China and Japan, two of the nations who encourage these practices.

We have massive amounts of rubbish being dumped into the oceans of the world, from ammunitions, acid-rain, PCBs to atomic waste. Out of sight, out of mind, seems to be the motto. Then, there are ocean-going ships, illegally washing-out their tanks, causing even more pollution, the list is endless, the destruction of the world's habitat continues. Despite all the horrific treatment of sharks, their food source being depleted through over-fishing and pollution, the planet's perfect predator is still around.

Twenty to thirty years ago most people who hunted the sharks did so with heavy, broom-handle type rods, hundred pound lines, and hooks that would have done justice to a butcher's shop. When landed, the fish was killed, taken to port and hung up with the proud captor standing alongside sporting a big grin as if to say, what a clever person I am. Then the corpse was dumped to rot away. How barbaric. Thankfully, today it's a different story, as we have become more educated, and angling has progressed. Today we fish with more sporting tackle, practice catch-and-release, and respect the shark for what it is, a fine sporting-fish. I don't know of any angler today who kills sharks. I have had many sharks using bait-fishing techniques, but my first day's fly-fishing for sharks was a day I won't forget in a hurry. I had come out to San Diego in California to do some radio shows, speaking engagements and to go fishing. The trip had been on the cards since I met up with Jon Wurtmann of Wurtmann Advertising who gave probably the best seminar during the Denver fly-tackle dealers show in September. El Nino decided otherwise as regards the fishing was concerned – the most important part of the trip.

The week-long storms had left the San Diego beaches closed, rubbish was dumped everywhere. Power lines were down, sewer pipes had burst, roads closed. On the coast, some houses were dumped into the ocean. Inland, other homes had slipped into flood-swollen rivers. You couldn't help but feel sorrow for these unfortunate people. There was even more disaster over the border in Tijuana Mexico, a few miles south from San Diego: 13 people were drowned in one night. El Nino had lived up to its advanced publicity. For thirteen days I was shore-bound. A heavy bang on the bedroom door awakened me from a disturbed sleep. I had one of those nights when the body wouldn't rest. I tossed and turned drifting in and out of sleep. "Time to get up and go fishing," shouted Jon. It was Friday the 13th – what a day to be out on the ocean, I thought to myself. After a shower and a mug of tea, I was ready to go.

The early morning sky was a leadened grey colour and seemed to touch the roof tops; rain was falling: a heavy drizzle. This was more like Manchester than sunny California. "What a day to go after the shark, one of the most powerful predatory fish in the ocean," I thought. I zipped up my jacket, for extra warmth and protection from the elements, then hurried to the car. Thirty minutes later, Jon and I arrived at Mission Bay boat park where we met up with thirty-one year old Conway Bowman who was captain of the 'La Mosco' a Parker 18 footer with a 130 hp Yamaha engine. Conway was an experienced blue-water angler and skipper. I looked out through the harbour entrance to the Pacific Ocean; I could see the waves crashing on shore.

It was going to be a rough trip out to the fishing ground some 12–15 miles off-shore over the 'Nine Mile Bank' which runs north to south for nine miles and is some ninety fathoms deep. It's a natural up-welling of the ocean floor, possibly volcanic, or perhaps a geological fault. The surrounding water is 600 fathoms. This bank creates a lot of water movement, and bait consolidates in the area, which draws the sharks. After stowing tackle bags and cameras in a Montana Guides waterproof bag, it was on with waterproof clothing and life jackets. The trip was going to be rough, tough and wet; my old body was in for a painful session. Who cared, I was going sharking! It's interesting to note that up until two days previous all boats were confined to port. I was told by Conway that any boat leaving Mission Bay harbour for the ocean until authorized was liable to a $30,000 fine. Conway had a last check around the boat then turned the ignition key, the powerful engine came to life, Jon removed and stowed the mooring rope, as we moved off to the bait barge to pick up fresh sardines for chunks, frozen chum for the rubby dubby bag. Pelicans, sea lions, cormorants and herons competed for fish that spilled from the net as the bait boxes were filled with live sardines.

A few days earlier on a trip to the bait barge, I had grabbed a pelican which had line wrapped around its wing. After a tough struggle, I removed several feet of 40 -50lb nylon line and a size 4/0 hook embedded in the pelican's wing. After being released he drifted away; every now and

again he tried exercising his wing. Thirty minutes later he made a couple of short flights. Then, realizing he was able to fly, flew off to join his friends. One lucky pelican, thanks to a caring Brit.

A five mile speed limit is enforced in the harbour, but as we hit the ocean waves, Conway opened up the throttle, the motor roared into life. As we hit the first big swell we became airborne then crashed down. Time and time again this happened, salt spray stung the eyes, and water trickled down my neck. I clung on to the safety bar

Author fighting a blue shark on the Pacific Ocean

as if my life depended on it. I was cold, my hands and legs were painful there were times when I thought, "What am I doing out in these inhospitable conditions?" Encouragement from Conway and Jon kept me going. Some ten miles out we passed the Los Coronados Islands off Mexico, Conway throttled back the motor, "This is better," I thought, as we rolled about on the ocean. Around the Islands we could see American Marines exercising. Helicopter gun-ships flew overhead, flares could be seen arcing down from the helicopters, and gunfire was heard. We even had a submarine for company for a while. Meanwhile Conway and Jon were busy getting the rubby dubby boxes sorted, Conway put the motor in gear and we slowly made our way to the Nine Mile Bank where we expected to find mako and blue sharks. As we cruised we created a nice slick for the sharks but it was the sea lions who first picked up the scent and homed in. Meanwhile, I tackled up with two rods, both 4 piece saltwater fly-rods for 12 weight lines.

A few days before this trip I had purchased an Aaron saltwater fly-reel, which I attached to the 12 weight. It had 250yd of 30lb backing and a weight forward, 12 weight floating line. My other 12 weight was fitted with a Stratos reel, 250yd of 30lb backing and a weight forward, slow sinking line. With the use of a Bimini twist and the Albright knots, Jon attached the leader material to the fly lines. This was 3ft of 50lb Mason hard nylon and a wire trace of 50lb single strand on the 12 weight. The other 12 weight was fitted with a 40lb nylon-coated multi-strand stainless trace. Jon tied on a chunk fly which was a lot of red, white and blue hair with a small amount of black, tied on to a 5/0 to represent the chunks of sardines that Conway was feeding, it's called 'matching the hatch.' I was ready to go.

On the Nine Mile Bank the water had changed from big swells to short waves with the occasional white horse. I could see the current breaks and the odd sea lion. Conway cut the motor then attached a drogue to slow our drift. I sat waiting for the sharks to show and Jon told me about other sharking trips, while Conway worked the chum slick and looked for the perfect predator. Perhaps fifty minutes later I heard Conway shout, 'Blue shark about sixty pounds get ready Martin.' It was a nervous James who stood in the bows ready to shoot a 12 weight line to his first shark on a fly rod. I peered intently into the water looking for a sign of life then, some twenty feet from the boat, I spotted a blue shark. As directed, I cast the fly some three feet in front of the fish and let it drift slowly down. The shark engulfed what it thought was an easy food item.

I let the fish turn and struck hard, with three or four powerful strip strikes I set the hook. All hell was let loose as the fish dived. Loose line somehow had wrapped itself around the rod tip. Jon was quick off the mark grabbing the line as it angled down into the ocean. He quickly freed the twisted line from the rod tip. I thought the four piece rod was going to be a ten piece! The reel screamed as yards of line and backing disappeared. This is what I had come for, to get my string pulled and stick bent. Some ten minutes later the line went slack: I was gutted. The fifty pound leader had been chaffed away by the shark as it twisted and turned its body.

A new trace and fly was fitted, I was ready to chuck that fly to the next shark. Ten minutes later I cast to another fish. The fly was grabbed, I struck and the fish dived and kept going, taking the backing line at a fast rate of knots. I kept a steady pressure on the fish waiting to see what would happen next. After a few minutes I decided to cramp on the pressure. Jon grabbed the back of my jacket to help steady me in the rolling boat as I shouted, "I've got ya, you old bugger, your mine!" Then, I piled on the pressure.

Fifteen minutes later I started to get line back on the reel, then the fly-line appeared, I was winning the fight. Suddenly there was a huge boil on the surface as a big fish thrashed the water to foam. Then it dived, but it was his last, I stopped him in his tracks. It's surprising what a 12 weight fly rod will do. I pumped him back to the boat. Jon released the hold on me to shoot some pictures. Conway leaned over the port side, grabbed the trace, then, with some long nosed pliers, unhooked a blue shark that was estimated at 70–75lbs. I watched it swim away. I wanted more of this adrenaline-pumping and string-pulling action but now it was time for lunch.

As we sat eating, drinking and chatting a big mako shark appeared, Eagle-eyed Conway had spotted it finning some fifty yards away. Lunch was forgotten as Conway started to feed chunks of fresh sardines. It was a big fish with a ragged dorsal fin. I was ready to shoot line and did when requested by Conway, A blue of about eighty pounds wanted my fly. Conway screamed, "Don't let that blue take your fly Martin!" It was hard to pull one's fly away from an eighty pound-plus fish, but did as I was told. They said, if I hooked the blue it might spook the mako. Minutes later the mako was alongside the boat but it wouldn't take any chunks, not even a live sardine that was thrown its way. Conway said, "That mako's only interested in driving the blue sharks away." A blue then appeared, "Get ready Martin." Jon shouted from the stern. "It's a big one." I aerolised some line then cast the fly some three feet from the blue, it turned and engulfed the fly. I struck hard, setting a 5/0 hook into a very angry fish which powered away fast. After some forty yards of staying near the surface, the fish dived and dived deep, very deep. I could feel at once this was a special fish.

It was going to be a long, tough scrap. Halfway through the fight the fish seemed to double its weight. I relayed the information to Conway who said, "Perhaps it's a sea lion or the mako that has grabbed your blue!" It was a battle of give-and-take but slowly I started to win. Down in the depths of the Pacific Ocean Jon spotted the fish, and as I pumped it closer to the surface, I too was able to see some nine or ten feet of swirling, twisting, heaving, angry shark. Then the fish spotted daylight and dived, yards of the hard-fought-for line disappeared from the reel as this powerful predator dived once more in its bid for freedom. I had to start all over again. Probably some thirty minutes later, but what seemed like an hour, I had the fish coming to the boat. Soon Conway was able to grab the leader. The fish was mine; A few pictures were taken by Jon. Then the fish estimated at over 100 pounds was released from the barbless hook. I fell back into the bows of the boat shattered. But it was a wonderful feeling.

That day was one I shall not forget in a hurry. It was full of incidents and action. I had seven hook-ups, landed five of them, all blue sharks over sixty pounds. The12 weight rods performed for what they were designed and built for – that's playing and landing tough, hard-fighting, blue water fish. If you're in San Diego on holiday and want some excitement give Conway Bowman a call on 001-619-697-4997 or write 8863 Lemon Avenue, La Mesa, California 91941. Don't worry about tackle, Conway can supply it and you're pretty certain to get your string pulled and stick bent in a serious way.

For many years I have made an annual pilgrimage across the Atlantic Ocean to fish the saltwater environment off the New England coastline. During those many visits, I fished from Rhode Island down to Chesapeake Bay in Maryland. Even as a youngster I knew about Chesapeake Bay, as I was given a six-month-old Chesapeake Bay Retriever dog in 1949. In the late 1800s, early 1900s, Chesapeake, off the Maryland coast, was known for its world famous duck-hunting and bass-fishing.

In 1950 Joe Brooks, one of the legends of American sports-fishing had his book Salt Water Fly-Fishing published by Putnam. I was immediately captured by the article on the striped bass. In 1968 Harper Row published Joe Brooks' book Salt Water Game-Fishing. Again the bass gripped my attention.

On page 206, Brooks writes:

"Frank Woolner, Editor of the Salt water Sportsman took fourteen stripers over forty pounds in weight, in one day".

My interest in striped-bass fishing increased dramatically. My mind was made up in 1973 when I walked into a second-hand book shop and picked up a copy of Modern Saltwater Sports-Fishing by Frank Woolner. Having read the book from cover-to-cover about three times in a week, I realised I had to go and fish for these stripers off the New England coastline. I was truly captivated by the stories and romance of this saltwater sports fish.

My first few trips to Chesapeake Bay, Maryland were stress-free. In the early days I could take my travel rods, reels and fly-boxes on board as cabin luggage: sadly that's all changed. Today I get told I could strangle someone with the fly line, or my rods could be used as a weapon. No one stops us from taking a bottle of whisky aboard a flight. A broken bottle would make a far more deadly weapon than would a fishing reel – and is not whisky inflammable? I feel a lot of the hold-ups are down to "Elf and Safety issues!" How did I become a pensioner in my seventies without the dreaded H&S? Today I hardly fly the Atlantic, so bad are the hold ups – often caused by delayed flights and the long wait to check-in and clear security, then to be told to be at check-in three hours before our flight. No doubt, like me, you have been held sitting on your flight waiting for a passenger who decides to turn up only half-an-hour before take-off. It's time they were refused boarding. Why not have a system of profile check-in. I am sure security personnel have ideas of those who could be trouble makers: rant over!

Let's return to the delights of striped-bass fishing. My flights usually went from Manchester to Baltimore where I would collect my bags and rod case from the carousel before exiting the airport. On the first few trips I would be met by my old friend Brandon White. Having checked into a hotel, Brandon and I would go off for dinner where the conversation was all about stripers.

During those first few sessions we caught fish on flies and lures, I much preferred the fly-gear. It was certainly a great experience, with Brandon acting as the perfect teacher – or was he a guide? I reckon both. His knowledge about the bass was extensive; not only about how to catch them, but more importantly their movements in Chesapeake Bay. To protect the stocks of bass, it's important to note that Chesapeake Bay striper-fishing is only open during the month of April.

On my next trip we fished flies and plastic worms, catching our share of bass, including some big ones. I well remember Brandon's friend, Tom McMurrey catching a thirty pound-plus carp on a vivid green plastic worm. There was a time especially just after dawn when we worked the shoreline, casting flies into two feet of water. At other times we fished well out in the bay or around bridge supports; we also fished close to old wrecks – in fact, something was happening on the water at all times. If we were not catching, there were plenty of sea birds and ducks to look at.

During the first few trips I would always take time out from fishing to visit the many museums in the area which featured the duck-hunting history in the late 1900s and early twentieth century. With other enthusiasts, I took a step back in time; we looked at and discussed the exhibits of hand-carved duck decoys, various shotguns, including black-powder muzzle loaders, duck-hunting punts, with their large single-bore guns and the many pictures painted by some of the world's greatest painters of wildfowling scenes, with wildfowl and duck-hunting scenes adorning the walls.

I made the decision to spend at least two or three weeks a year fishing for stripers, a great sporting fish. Brandon White was my guide for the first few trips; if he was busy he would put me together with one of his many friends. Just before another trip was about to start, Brandon had acquired a new flats-boat, equipped with all the latest technology, including a virtually silent engine. It was the perfect boat for Chesapeake but it didn't come cheap costing many thousands of dollars: we had some great fun.

I met a new bunch of striper fans including one guy who was a member of the security team on Air force One, the Presidential jet. Above all, we caught some fine fish, both on flies and plastic worms, often in Day-Glo colours – it's surprising what a predatory fish will eat! With a short season in Chesapeake Bay, I needed other venues. Making enquiries from other anglers and writers, I was told to try Rhode Island, Massachusetts and Connecticut further up the east coast. I wasn't to be disappointed.

The following year my travel agent called to say American Airlines were starting a daily service from Manchester to Boston between May and October, a schedule which covers the best times of the year for striper fishing. Previously I would have to take two flights, unless I travelled to Heathrow or Gatwick. This of course entailed a long drive south. With the new Manchester–Boston service I was able to leave Manchester at noon, arriving in Boston just after 2 pm. Clearing immigration and customs, I then picked up a hire car and within an hour I could be at a striper-fishing location.

Rhode Island was the first venue for stripers. You had a choice of fishing offshore or inside the various bays. When you have travelled thousands of miles, the last thing you wanted was to be sitting around in a hotel if it was too rough to go afloat offshore. No problem in Rhode Island; you had Narragansett Bay offering excellent fishing for stripers and bluefish. One day as David Jones and I were chucking flies for stripers, we watched five big blitzing schools of bluefish hitting menhaden. From my experience if your looking for a guide in this area there is only one to consider, that is Captain Jim White www.whiteghostcharters.com

Massachusetts has a lot to offer the saltwater fly-fisher, three locations spring to mind: Cape

Cod, the offshore islands of Nantucket, and Martha's Vineyard, home to the wealthy. I well
remember fishing the flats at Cape Cod, with Capt. Andrew Cummings, and being surrounded
by dozens of big stripers and bluefish, in the gin-clear water where I had a great view watching
a striper or blue savage a fly – its something special.

Along the Connecticut coastline, fishing in Eastern Long Island Sound could be excellent.
In 1992 an angler caught a striped bass of seventy-five pounds from New Haven harbour, the
third largest striper on record. I got to know this area when Ed Mitchell's first book Fly-Rodding
the Coast was published by Stackpole books in 1995. I arranged to record an interview with Ed
while I was across at the Thomas and Thomas rod-building plant in Greenfield, Massachusetts.
Ed suggested I stay at his beachside home for a few days. We fished, chatted and recorded an
interview for my "At the Water's Edge" series on BBC Radio Lancashire. It was during this trip
that I met Dixon Merkt, when Ed and I joined him on his boat for a few hours. I enjoyed the
experience and we caught quite a few stripers.

Having met Dixon the previous year, I booked him for a week's fly-fishing in the Eastern
Long Island Sound of Connecticut. Captain Dixon Merkt is an author and writer, also a very
enthusiastic duck and goose hunter with a great knowledge on the history of duck and goose
decoys. His book on the subject is a must-have book for many people. I couldn't have wished
for a better guide. I won't forget my first day's fishing. Dixon had told Ed that I was across and
invited him to join us. On the boat dock, Ed, Dixon and I discussed the weather, it was touch-
and-go if we would go afloat. The wind was blowing twenty knots, white caps were rolling
down the Eastern Long Island Sound. Dixon said, "Do you want to fish Martin?" I thought if
Dixon is willing to go afloat it must be OK. I answered in the affirmative.

The first few miles were pleasant enough as Ed, Dixon and I fished our way down the

sheltered coastline catching stripers. We
then crossed the Sound to fish a rocky
shoreline, the boat bounced around, the
occasional white cap crashed over the bows.
Looking around I could see huge boulders
being lashed by an angry sea. One minute
they were visible, the next they had
disappeared in the spewing, foaming, wind-
lashed green water. It was planned that we
would target the albies.

Dixon shouted above the howling
wind, "Albies off the port bow at fifty feet."
One minute I could see the horizon, the
next just a wall of green-coloured water
before it hit the boat. The boat shuddered
from bows to stern. As I pulled off enough
line for the long cast, I dropped it on the
boat deck, I made three false casts then shot

the line. Counting down to five I started a fast retrieve. After retrieving some twenty feet of line I felt a hit. Setting the hook, I felt a powerful surge as the rod tip was savagely pulled down, line was stripped off the reel in a blur. It felt as if I was hooked up to one of the submarines stationed in the town of London further up the coast. My Tibor reel hummed nicely (so it should at around £500!). Line was being steadily taken; Dixon shouted "Put on more pressure." This slowed the fish down; I started to pump the fish back to the boat while Ed was hanging onto my coat to stop me going over board in the bucking and rolling boat. I also decided to kneel down so I could lean against the boat. Ten minutes later I had the fish close enough for netting.

Dixon, despite handling the boat, was there to help and the fish was soon netted. It was a good fish of about twelve pounds and a team effort. We did high fives all round. I punched the air with joy and relief. We then departed for the calmer water, I wasn't sorry. We spent the rest of the day fishing for stripers. I won't forget that first albie, which was all down to Ed and Dixon and a big chunk of luck. I had many more great trips with Dixon.

During a trout-fishing session on the River Ribble I was telling my friend David Jones about my next striper-fishing trip, he expressed an interest. Having had some trips to the Caribbean with David, I knew that I would enjoy his company, and if my multiple sclerosis played up, I would be in good hands. The following year David and I arrived in Old Lyme, Connecticut, ten hours after leaving Manchester airport. Having picked up the hire car in Boston, we headed south on I 95, a pleasant drive of less than two hours to Dixon Merkt's house in Lyme where we were greeted by Carol, Dixon, children: David, James and Lisa, plus three dogs: a black labrador, a King Charles spaniel and a beagle.

After the usual welcome and a mug of tea, the conversation turned to fishing. Dixon said "The False Albacore known as albies arrived two days ago and there are also plenty of bass and bluefish, the forecast is good for the next few days." It was the news we had wanted to hear. David is now a great fan of the albies while my first choice fish is the striper. Having said that, I enjoy catching any fish. We all then went off for a relaxing dinner in an Italian restaurant a few miles down the road.

For our first day afloat conditions were perfect, light winds from the south-southeast, high water at midday, a blue sky and warm sunshine. Just after ten o'clock we boarded Dixon's Surf Scoter, a twenty-four foot centre console Mako, designed with safety in mind and to cope with the rough waters of Long Island Sound. It's equipped with all the safety features you would expect on a charter boat, including ship-to-shore radio, telephone, echo-sounder and fish-finder; though I haven't seen the latter used in all my trips – Dixon's experience, great eyesight or spotting diving-birds, often a combination of all three, usually puts you on the feeding fish. Captain Dixon Merkt comes highly recommended, with over fifty years of ocean sailing, including many years as a member of the prestigious New York Yacht Club. Once on board Merkt's Mako, you certainly feel you're in safe hands. We slipped our mooring at Old Lyme on the mouth of the Connecticut River. A few hundred yards further downstream we passed under the railway bridge into the sound. On my port side was a large salt-marsh where I could see several groups of ducks, also a couple of egrets, Suddenly an osprey dived; it didn't miss its target and it lifted off the water with a fish about two pounds in its talons. Further down the marsh a skein of geese was flying across the Sound. Various gulls and other wading birds worked the tide line.

A light wind ruffled the surface; David and I had each made up two Thomas and Thomas rods. Mine were, a Helix 9 foot 9 weight with a Cortland ghost tip line to which I had attached, with an Albright knot, a 9ft Gamma Blue-Water leader with a tippet of 12lbs. The other rod was an Horizon 9 foot 9 weight matched with a Teeny 300 grain shooting head. This latter rod had a faster action than the Helix. I would use this model should the wind get above twenty knots. David used the same model of rods, choosing a slow sink tip on one; the other rod was matched with a floating line. He had also tied on a 9ft leader with a 12lb tippet. Dixon gave David a Deceiver fly to use.

On Dixon's advice I tied on a size 2 white and chartreuse Clouser minnow to complete the Helix outfit. Fifteen minutes after leaving the mooring slip, Dixon throttled back the engine as we moved within casting distance of the shoreline of the marsh. I made a cast, dropping the fly on the edge of the marsh. Two short strips, a fish hit, and strip striking, I connected with my first bass of the trip; within seconds David hooked his first fish. As Dixon poled us along the marsh, we caught several more bass, we also missed some.

Dixon said, "Wind in, we're moving." He turned the ignition key and the motor hummed into life, then increased in sound as the throttle was opened up. Our guide soon had us skimming across the sound towards the Teapot Lighthouse. As we neared the lighthouse I could see lots of diving birds; several small boats were moving into position. Dixon throttled back, the bows dipped, I could see bait fish crashing from the water, albies, blues and stripers were hitting the bait fish. Dixon said, "It's not often you see all these fish together. If we hook blues they will bite us off". Blues are part of the piranha family with a mouthful of razor-sharp teeth.

Dixon shouted, "There are some big stripers." I decided to use my Horizon rod with the sink tip and a size 3/0 Deceiver. Pulling off some 50–60 feet of line, I made a long cast, then I quickly retrieved the line back in the boat. With the fly in my left hand, I watched the water, looking for one of those bass. "Three o'clock, fifty feet." said Dixon, Making one false cast I shot the line, then made several nine to twelve inch strips; suddenly I felt a savage hit. A firm strip

strike connected me with a very angry fish that went off like a greyhound. The reel whirred as all my fly line disappeared, and then I was into the backing.

Down deep in the water I could feel the head shaking from a heavy fish. I would then get some line back on the reel, before the fish took some back. Thankfully I was getting few inches each time. I could sense the fish was slowing up in its effort to break me off or get rid

Martin with his 22lb Striper

of the size 3/0 barbless hook. More

pumping and I had the fish coming towards the surface; fifteen feet below the fish dived and I was forced to give line.

Twenty feet of line was gone then slowly inch-by-inch I retrieved it all back. As the leader appeared I could see the fish, it was a good one, perhaps a twenty-pounder, I hoped. Slowly I retrieved the leader until I had the fish on the surface, it had a mouth like a bucket. Dixon leaned over the gunwale and grabbed the leader then my fish by the bottom lip and lifted it clear of the water. Reaching for his Bogo grip he weighed the fish saying, "twenty-two pounds!". I punched the air saying, "Yes, that will do me." Dixon then took a couple of pictures before we watched the fish swim off hopefully to grow into a forty-pounder.

David was fighting a good albie. I checked my leader then my hook point and made another cast. I counted to three and started to retrieve. On my second strip I felt a hit, then set the hook; I was into another good bass. Several minutes later Dixon lipped another fish for me. It weighed eighteen pounds – it was one of those good days. Meanwhile David had landed his albie. All then went quiet as the bait fish moved away. We moved off looking for more bait fish shoals.

During the day we fished several shore marks catching more bass averaging some five pounds, I then caught a bluefish; I now needed an albie for my Grand Slam. Suddenly Dixon shouted, "Albies!" Offshore looking towards the horizon we could see diving birds. As we got in closer, albies were often coming out of the water in their pursuit of the bait fish. Five minutes later we were within casting range. David and I quickly had a double hook up on our first casts. These

Author with his best Albie caught during his grand slam

fish quickly had us well into our backing, and then it was a real tug-of-war. You never know when an albie is tired; it's a fish that never wants to give up. It might have been ten minutes before Dixon had a chance to tail David's fish, estimated about eight pounds. Meanwhile my fish was getting near the surface; suddenly the leader appeared I could see the fish.

Dixon said, "That's a good albie, Martin." He grabbed the fish by its tail, swinging it aboard. I took out the barbless hook as Dixon picked up the Bogo grip weighing the fish at just over ten pounds, a good fish for this part of the ocean. As the albies get further south to Harkers Island, North Carolina, they would probably weigh fifteen pounds or more. Several more albies were caught before the action was over. The bait fish had gone, and with them the albies. It was back to the shoreline, hunting for bass. All too soon the fishing was over for the day. Three happy anglers cruised back to the mooring site in the setting sun.

Our next destination was Rhode Island, with Captain Jim White: photographer, author and writer, From Old Lyme it was an hour's drive up I 95 then taking exit 7 turning left at the traffic lights and your at the Hampton Inn, where a double room cost just $90 a night. In those days we had an excellent exchange rate of $1.76 to the pound. Good value – and we got breakfast. Having checked in, we went across the road to a diner for supper. Then it was back to our room for an early night, Jim was picking us up at five in the morning. He was spot on time; on

David Jones and Dixon Merkt admire David's Albie

the way to East Greenwich boat dock we stopped off for coffee and a bacon sandwich at Dunkin' Donuts. We were robbed! My piece of bacon was the size of a fifty pence piece and it tasted horrid. Fifteen minutes after leaving our hotel we were pulling into the car park on East Greenwich dock.

As I stood on the quayside looking east, I could see the first glimmer of the false dawn, a few gulls drifted to-and-fro looking for tit-bits, and it was so quiet you could have heard a pin drop. Jim quickly had the boat ready to go. Rods had been stowed in racks, all the other gear including cameras and tape recorders were stowed in waterproof lockers.

Having flipped the bow-rope free, Jim slowly backed the 2004 Triton Centre Console with its 225 Honda outboard, out of the berth. The start of another day on the water, as we moved out of the East Greenwich dock with its hundreds of moored yachts; it reminded David and me of the River Dart in Devon. Jim's boat is equipped with Lowrance LX-104c fish-finder, GPS, radar, VHF, and cell phone with bathroom on board. Jim is USCG Licensed, Insured and Drug Tested. He is on the Pro-Staff for Triton/Honda Marine, Thomas & Thomas Fly Rods, Quantum Pro-Staff, and Lunker City Lures. You can rest assured the tackle Jim has on board for your use is top class.

The plan of action was to move into the lower end of the Providence River to fish in the area of Snake Fly Cove for bass and bluefish. In my book, Captain Jim White is the only guide to fish with. He's a full time guide, not just a weekend-fishing boatman. One guide fishes from a flats boats; these are not suited to offshore waters, even when you're guaranteed light winds. From my experience of over sixty years on tidal waters, you can't ever say when the wind will pick up – one more reason for a life jacket. If the wind should kick up around fifteen knots and above, then you could be in trouble, at the very least, you will have a very bumpy and wet trip. When booking a guide, go with the professionals.

Fifteen minutes after leaving the dock, we are moving into in a beautiful cove. In the distance I could see the birds wheeling and diving into the calm clear water, I said to Jim, "Birds diving at two o'clock." Jim had already seen them and was changing course. As we headed in the direction of the feeding fish, I started to pull line off the reel, ready to shoot a size 2/0 blue and white Lefty Kreh Deceiver. At fifty yards, the water was boiling, fish swirled and slashed into the baitfish, hundreds of birds were diving and screaming.

The bass were in a savage feeding mode. It must have been a killing zone below the calm surface of the cove. From below bass were programmed in on the bait, while from above the diving birds were in on the kill. There was no escape for the bait: all they could do was get into a big ball and hope. The fish were certainly in feeding frenzy, tearing into anything that moved. Dead and dying baby peanut bunker or small menhaden were scattered everywhere. Half a dozen cormorants appeared to join in the feast. There was no escape for the tiny bait fish from this deadly situation. I cast some sixty feet of line, as the fly hit the water I started to strip it back. Suddenly, the line stopped and I set the hook into my first fish of the day. Looking towards the stern, I could see David was into a fish. For the next thirty or forty minutes minutes we followed those bass around the bay. It was good sport with fish hitting Deceivers Poppers and Clousers. Then, all of a sudden, it was over.

An old friend, seventy-four year old Gene Matteson, who fishes over 200 days a year, pulled alongside to say good morning. We chatted for some twenty minutes-or-so about the fishing. As we chatted, I was keeping on eye on the water, looking for feeding fish. Jim then said, "Diving birds, two hundred yards, at three o'clock. Let's go." We said good bye to Gene, and moved off towards the birds. Moving in close, Jim said, "Look at that big ball of flat-sided menhaden." (Often called bunker or pogy.)

These bait fish were averaging some two pounds apiece. The bluefish were savaging them, chunks of menhaden floated on the surface. Picking up my 9 weight Thomas and Thomas Horizon with a Teeny 350 line, I attached a wire trace. With a haywire twist, I tied on a size 4/0 red and white Clouse minnow. Pulling off some fifty foot of line, I made a long cast to the outside of the balling baitfish. After taking three foot long strips, I felt the fish hit. I set the hook with a firm strip strike, the line was savagely pulled from my hand as it shot through the guides, more line followed from the reel. A good fish crashed out of the water in a shower of spray, then dived. I was down to my backing in seconds, this was a powerful fish. Again the rod tip was pulled forcibly down towards the water and stayed there.

I piled on the pressure, gaining a few yards of line; the fish would shake its head then take it all back. My mind went to the trace: would the Haywire twist hold; were the nail knots tied properly, were they going to hold? These were questions going through my mind. I looked around, all the birds had gone, all was silent – other than the reel giving or taking line, or the sound of waves slapping against the hull. Slowly, I was beating this powerful fish. A few minutes later I had a good bluefish in the boat. I let Jim handle this critter with its razor sharp teeth. It was then released.

The flat-sided menhaden were balled up so tight it was a job trying to get a fly down to the bluefish. I often foul-hooked these bait fish, which were quickly bitten in half by the bluefish.

As we moved away, Jim pointed out a group of diving, squealing sea birds several hundred yards away. In an area about an acre in size were a mass of bait fish being attacked by slashing bluefish and fish-eating birds. As Jim eased the boat within casting position, David and I cast our flies. Minutes later I had a hook-up; glancing to the stern, I saw David was also in action. Despite an increase in the wind strength often gusting at twenty-five knots, we had a hook-up on every cast, though we did lose some. This was fishing at its best. In the next two hours David and I hooked and boated forty-four good-size bluefish; of course, we lost a few. You couldn't wish for better fishing – but that's what you get when you're out with Captain Jim White. Some of the great fly-fishers and writers on the east coast, Lefty Kreh, Nick Curcion, Bob Popovics and others, have fished with Captain Jim; even notable anglers, such as Don Blanton from California, have come across and fished with this guy. We can't all be wrong: in Rhode Island he is the best in the business.

*O*nce American Airlines had started a new schedule from Manchester to Boston for the cost of £300 return. I could leave Manchester around noon, arriving in Boston about 2 p.m. At that time there was an excellent exchange rate of the US dollar against the pound sterling: there wasn't a better opportunity to fly the Atlantic. It was a good time to visit and fish the Catskills area of New York with its history of fly-fishing in America – an ambition I had held since the 1950s.

Most people, when they hear mention of New York, immediately think of Central Park, theatres, shopping malls, museums and the Statue of Liberty. But there is much more to New York: it's a state with an area of 40,108 square miles, roughly the size of England, and it's not all concrete, glass and chrome. A huge area of the state is covered by forest, lakes, rivers and streams, with an exciting coastline offering some magnificent fishing in both fresh and saltwater. The two major areas of freshwater fishing are the Adirondacks in the north of the state, where I had fished on many occasions, and the Catskill Mountains, north of New York City and west of the Hudson River, where I was now to visit. It offers some of the toughest fly-fishing anywhere in the world; in fact the world's best anglers have probably cast a fly on the waters of the Catskills.

Many anglers recognize the Catskills as the historic home of dry-fly fishing in America – as the place where it all started, but from my research I get the impression that dry-fly fishing really got started in Long Island and Pennsylvania, with much of it taking place on the Brodheads and its sister rivers of Pennsylvania. A magnet for fly-fishers visiting the area in those early days of 1835 and onwards was Henryville House, though it was just one of the numerous places hosting fly-fishers; many inns, boarding houses and hotels prospered in the latter years of the nineteenth century. Fly-fishing celebrities who visit the area included such personalities as John Sullivan, Lily Langtry and Jake Kilrain, who added the glamour of music hall and prize fighting to the area.

In 1895, fifteen well-known anglers, who were bankers and brewers, formed The Fly-Fishers Club of Brooklyn. In 1897, after a poor season of brook-trout fishing, they moved north from the Brodheads into the Catskills and to a log cabin at Hardenburgh farm on the Little Beaver Kill. No doubt they would have known that Theodore Gordon was already fishing the area and perhaps this prompted their move, but their shift north could have been a bit premature, as the fishing on the Brodheads greatly improved the following year.

Among the great anglers, legends and fly-dressers who lived or fished the Catskills was Thaddeus Norris (1811–1877). His book The American Angler's Book (1864) is of great interest and Thaddeus, when writing about chub-fishing states: The best season of the year is September; a grasshopper or grub-worm, or a small cube of cheese, is good bait. Later in the chapter he writes about Bologna sausage as bait – there is nothing new in fishing! Thaddeus was also one of the great, bamboo rod-builders in the 1800s. Probably the greatest legend of the past was Theodore Gordon: his dry-fly, the Quill Gordon is still in use today. Rod Steenrod, the inventor of The Hendrickson was a Gordon disciple and was also resident in the Catskills. So great was the friendship between Steenrod and Gordon that in 1890 Gordon willed his famous collections of flies to Steenrod. These had been sent to him from Hampshire, England by Frederick Halford.

In 1929, the great Lee Wulff, whilst fishing the Ausable River in the Adirondacks, developed the Gray Wulff, one of the most popular dry-flies of all time He was yet another Catskills resident. It must have been a wonderful sight to see Lee and wife Joan fishing these historic waters. Today the lady, who is in her eighties, can still cast a fly as good as any male angler. She is without doubt a great ambassador for this magnificent and wonderful sport. Fly-dresser Harry Darbee, known as the Dean of the Willowemoc, lived in a farmhouse above the river not far from the Covered Bridge Pool that John Atherton used in his exquisite pencil drawings of the river. Writer Art Flick, author of the best selling classic, Streamside Guide to Naturals and Their Imitations (1947) lived in The West Kill Tavern which sadly has gone. George M L La Branche's, Dry Fly and Fast Water (1914), is a book I recommend to all fly-fishers (even though it was published in 1914). Ed Zern, who was at one time the fishing editor of Field and Stream, fished and lived in the area. Another great Catskills fly-fisher was Leonard M Wright Jr, author of Fishing the Dry-Fly (1988). Other great names from the past who fished the Catskills were Lew Beach, Reuben Cross and Ray Bergman (author of several books including Just Fishing, 1932), John Alden Knight, Preston Jennings and Sparse Grey Hackle who once said, "Livingstone Manor, Hearthstone and the Ward's DeBruce hotels in the Catskills are our Mecca."

Having arrived at Boston airport after a seven hour flight, Kate and I were soon clear of immigration and customs. As we came out of the airport I noticed a guy holding up a sign on which was my name. We introducing ourselves and he grabbed our bags and then headed off to a large van parked nearby. Two hours later we were in Greenfield, Western Massachusetts at the home of John Carpenter and his daughter Ellie. Also waiting for us were Trevor Bross, his wife Christine and their baby daughter Autumn.

John, Kate and Trevor in the Catskills

For the next two hours John, Trevor and I gossiped about the weather, fishing and the prospects for our coming trip to the world-famous Catskills where we would be joined by New Jersey tackle-shop owner Harry Huff and his son John. I had met Harry – a larger-than-life character, at many of the fly-fishing shows I attend as a pro-staff member of Thomas and Thomas; the company who make the fine fly-fishing rods that many of America's anglers ardently wish to own. From my many conversations with Harry I realized that he was an extremely experienced and knowledgeable fly-fisher. Watching this man-mountain, I had no doubt that he could cast with the best, either with single or double-handed rods. His son John is following in Dad's footsteps.

Our journey to the Catskills started on the third day of our trip, it was some four hours from John's home to the town of Hancock close to the east branch of the Delaware in the Catskills. We drove through clean, green and pristine countryside with no signs of litter. After driving south to Springfield, we travelled west across the Berkshire mountains, crossing the Appalachian Trail (which crosses the highway via a footbridge) and route 90's highest point of elevation in the east, and to the Taconic Parkway. We then drove south along the eastern border of New York State, also the eastern edge of the Hudson Valley. Looking west across the valley to the Catskills you realized how verdant and lovely this part of the world looked in the afternoon sunshine.

Crossing the Hudson River on the Tappen Zee Bridge, we continued south to Harry Huff's tackle shop in New Jersey. Harry, I suppose, could be best described as a modern-day legend who stands tall alongside other great Catskill legends from the past. After some time with Harry in his shop we left, following him northwest back to the Catskills on route 17. We drove on, crossing over the historic Willowemoc and Beaver Kill rivers before arriving in the town of Hancock.

The Catskill Mountains were green and magnificent. A huge forest of hardwoods, hemlocks, maple, pines and oaks covered the mountains between the Hudson and the Delaware. When first seen, one is reminded of the Smoky Mountains of Tennessee. In one area near the town of Hancock, I could see where a tornado had torn through the riverside trees scattering them like matchsticks. Amazingly, three houses were left untouched, all the rest had gone. Along the riverside were rhododendrons and dogwood. At dawn there is the chance of seeing wild turkeys, black bears, grouse and a dozen of bird species, including red and yellow-winged blackbirds. If you are extremely lucky you might even hear the pileated woodpecker in a hemlock thicket. At dusk or during the darkness, if you're on the river you might hear the very rare horned owl.

In the town, our first stop was the local tackle and gun store to purchase our fishing licences. Never ever attempt to fish in the United States without a fishing licence, you could end up in jail. Then it was into the grocery store to pick up food and drink for a few days. Back in the vehicles, we drove over the east branch of the Delaware River into Pennsylvania where our recently-purchased New York licences were legal. Fifteen minutes after leaving Hancock we arrived at Harry Huff's fishing camp on the banks of the west branch of the Delaware to witness fish sipping down 'mayflies' as the Americans called them; but these were olives not the three-tailed mayflies that we know as Ephemera danica.

We jumped down from the truck and were introduced to Harry's son John and another couple of fly-fishers. It was warm handshakes and hugs all round. After dumping our bags in the riverside cabin, Harry fired up the BBQ and we all enjoyed steaks. While the rest of the gang washed their food down with cold beer, Kate and I had big mugs of Yorkshire Gold tea. Within an hour, the Huffs, Kate, Trevor, and John and me were getting ready for an evening session in conditions which could only be described as perfect. Across the river I watched an angler strike, a few minutes later he bent down and released a fish. Overhead two buzzards worked the thermals. Lots of bugs hovered over the water making it look as if someone had emptied a huge box of confetti!

I made up two outfits: for Kate I chose a 9ft 5 weight Thomas and Thomas Helix with a Joan Wulff Signature floating line and a 10ft leader tapered down to a 5 X point. I chose to fish an identical make of rod and line in a 4 weight with a 12ft leader tapered down to a 6 X tippet. I have been using the Joan Wulff Signature fly-lines for several months for my grayling and trout-fishing. I find they shoot smoothly, pick up quickly and have no memory. In my book they are an excellent line for dry-fly fishing. Having made up the tackle I checked my vest, making sure I had fly floatant, tippet material, Polaroid glasses, fly-boxes and digital camera. It was time to change the soles of our wading boots from a hiking sole to a felt one. The new Korker wading boots with their five different soles have certainly taken wading boots into the twenty-first century; no longer do I have to carry two pairs of wading boots when I go abroad on a fishing trip. We pulled on our chest-waders and quickly laced up our boots; we were ready for an evening on the river.

From our camp, just a few yards from the water's edge of the Delaware, it was a ten minute drive on a tarmac road before turning off and driving several hundred yards alongside a railway line then parking under some trees. Pushing our way through the bushes, shrubs and long grass, we were soon at the water's edge – it was the perfect evening: warm with a light breeze. Bugs were coming off the water in profusion but I couldn't see any rising fish.

Kate and I went off upstream, John and Trevor downstream while Harry chose to fish at our point of arrival. Sadly, within thirty minutes of arriving, the temperature dropped and the bugs were gone. In the two hours before dark we didn't see any rising fish, but it did give Kate the chance to practise her casting. As we met up in the darkness we were pleased to hear that Trevor had caught a nice fish on a size 10 March Brown. Harry and John had also caught fish leaving John, Kate and me fishless, but it was great just being there. With no bugs and a dropping air temperature we all headed off to camp where Harry cooked more steaks, burgers and sausages.

It was about eight in the morning when Kate and I climbed from our sleeping bags. After a shower and a mug of tea we were ready to face the day. I spent some time recording material for my programme "At the Waters Edge" on BBC Radio Lancashire, while Trevor and John fished the river in front of the camp. John Huff tied flies and Harry cooked himself more food: that guy could eat! We left him at camp while the rest of us went off to Hancock for breakfast. Even though I have visited the United States for many years, I continue to be surprised at the excellent service one gets in American diners and cafés, also the good-quality food and low prices. When it comes to service we can learn a lot from the United States. What does always amaze me is the amount of food my friends put away, and yet none of them are out-of-shape – except Harry, who could lose a few pounds. My mate Trevor even plays a high standard of tennis two or three times a week.

After breakfast it was back to camp to get ready to fish. Kate and I were to join Harry Huff in his drift boat for a drift from Shehawken, which is the lower part of the west branch, down to Buckingham – a trip of about ten miles, while John Carpenter, Trevor Bross and Mark Kondak would drift the river in pontoon boats. John Huff was away, rowing and guiding a client on the river for a full day.

At about twelve noon the wind increased and by mid-afternoon it was gusting at 25–30 miles an hour; I shivered then pulled a sweater from my bag. It had turned icy cold; the wind lashed the water creating small white caps in the more exposed areas. I was gutted. My first full day in the Catskills and it felt like being on an English river in January. If I was to see a fish rise, I would be well tested to reach it with my 4 weight outfit in these condition.

As we rounded a bend, Harry noticed a fish rise under the near bank where the water was sheltered by some riverside trees. Harry held the boat in position for some 10–15 minutes; twice the fish showed on the surface. Five minutes later two more fish showed within two feet of each other. Harry said, "Go for it Martin!" I made a side-cast then watched the March Brown land some six feet upstream of the first fish. It was a perfect drift. As the fly reached the spot where the first of the two fish had shown, a small dimple appeared – the March Brown was gone. The answering strike connected with a fish, sadly not a trout but a dace of about twelve inches. This American dace had the head of a chub, the body of a dace and the anal fin of a dace. On the Grass River in St Lawrence County NY it's known as a chub.

As you get older, the body doesn't always work as it should, I was getting colder and more sluggish by the minute. Some three miles further downstream I clambered from the boat and started to wade ashore to stretch my legs, the cold from the water gripped them, causing me to have problems with wading; cramp was taking hold. I turned back towards the boat. I was feeling lousy as I pulled on my SST jacket and mittens, hypothermia was setting in, I couldn't focus my eyes, my coordination was lost – I felt terrible. Suffering from multiple sclerosis and being diabetic with one kidney, does have its problems.

I let Harry fish his way downstream to the take-out point. All I wanted was a mug of tea and a hot shower. I think Harry realized I was having problems even though I was putting on a brave face. Half an hour later Harry was hooked into a good fish on a Sulphur Spinner. The fight had taken him well into the backing. I switched on the tape recorder and taped the action. It was a brown trout of about twenty-five inches. We covered the last couple of miles in the darkness; as we did so we could hear good fish crash or swirl on the surface. Why did the weather turn so rough I thought to myself? Still that's fishing. Fifteen minutes later Trevor, John, Mark, and John Huff arrived; they had all caught fish. We said our goodbyes to Harry, John and Mark, climbed into John's truck and headed for home, arriving about 3.30 in the morning. I had slept most of the way.

The size 12 Stimulator drifted ten yards before disappearing in a swirl of water. The answering strike connected with a Bow River brown trout – a second or so later it made a long, powerful run downstream, and after several minutes of intense excitement which only an angler can understand, I netted a good fish. Leaning down I slipped out the barbless hook, and lowering the net deeper into the water, I watched my first Bow River trout, weighing some two pounds, swim free. I'm told it's an average size by Bow River standards. In six drifts I had three more nice browns all on the size 12 Stimulator. Overhead, skeins of geese, along with small flights of duck, were moving south for the winter. This was fly-fishing: as good as it gets anywhere in the world.

My mate, (the now late) John Bodsworth of Sussex, and I had come to Alberta to sample the fishing and watch the wildlife. We had booked our flight from Manchester to Calgary. Apart from fishing on the Bow River, we would visit Jasper National Park and Edmonton. After a few days in the capital, the plan was that we would travel to Fort McMurray: a bustling oil town. After a couple of days there it would be a trip by float plane to a wilderness area in the north-east of Alberta close to the Saskatchewan border. We were to fish a huge lake with a reputation for lake trout and big pike – I've heard that one before and I was looking forward to seeing just how big these pike were. Our accommodation would be a trapper's cabin built in the late 1800s. Our company for much of the adventure would be just the bears, perhaps some Indians and hopefully a couple of good-looking squaws as company: at least we could dream!

Arriving in Calgary, Alberta, I was feeling rather tired after the long flight from the UK – thankfully wheelchair assistance was available. My multiple sclerosis really does cause me problems when flying. Having collected the hire car, and with John doing the driving, we navigated our way out of town. From there, it was a very pleasant drive to the town of Canmore, about an hour from Calgary airport.

Canmore is a delightful place. Set in the Bow Valley amid the rugged majesty of the Front Ranges of the Canadian Rockies, yet astride a major transportation corridor, it's a community with a vision based on the conviction that environmental sensitivity and economic sustainability can be reconciled. Following its founding in 1883, Canmore served both as a railway division point and mining town. When the last coal mine closed in 1979 it was clear that the community's economic viability would turn to relying on the developing tourism industry. In 1965, the town was formally incorporated, with an elected mayor and council. Today, it is the administrative centre for government services in the Bow Corridor and has a present population of 9900 and growing! No way could you imagine this was a coal-mining town – it's a beautiful place. We certainly enjoyed our visit and fishing the world-famous Bow River.

The Bow River – featuring some fifty-odd miles of excellent fly-fishing water, starts in the Banff area. It resembles a giant-size chalk stream, but with faster water and lush vegetation, and a tremendous head of aquatic life which allows the Bow River trout to grow big, giving the opportunity to catch large wild browns of perhaps eight pounds, and of course big, rainbow trout. Heavy caddis and mayfly hatches allow for spectacular dry-fly fishing. Fishing can take place from drift boats, but wading is 'the norm'. July is an excellent month for the green drake hatch, according to Jamaica-born John Samms of The Green Drake fly shop in Canmore. What a delightful, friendly and knowledgeable guy John is. He certainly knows the river and its fishing. If it's a guide you want, then choose John. One animal you will see on the river will be the beaver.

Another good time to visit is September, It's also the hopper season, so grasshoppers and caddis patterns are the usual fare. A San Juan Worm can often be a productive pattern along with Black and Brown Woolly buggers. Fishing streamers after dusk will often produce some big fish. Your guide will probably have all the flies you need but it's always nice to have some patterns in your fly box. I would certainly have had some size 14–16 Elk Hair Caddis, size 12–18 Parachute Adams, Parachute Hopper, size 16–18 Pheasant Tail nymphs and Stimulators 10–14, but as stated the guide should have it all.

The Bow is a shallow but wide river making it a great dry-fly river – at the same time it can offer some tricky casting when the wind blows – which it often does. I would advise a 9ft, 6 weight Thomas and Thomas Helix model, even a 7 weight rod would be my choice on those days

Taxi for James!

when the wind blows – in fact, if you are drifting the river, take both 6 and 7 weight rods.

A hooded merganser scuttled away as the Mackenzie type drift boat floated downstream. Dead pines washed away by the spring floods were piled up and wedged into grotesque shapes like a petrified forest. Green pines lay at various angles over the water like the tentacles of an octopus, ready to catch any badly-cast fly; they certainly caught their share of mine! The Bow River in September flowed between snow-capped mountains. In places, the river narrowed to barely a boat's width. Ravens squawked in the pines and the odd osprey passed overhead. The Alberta Bow River is a beautiful place to visit.

In the Province of Alberta there are great tracts of wilderness where human beings still play second fiddle to the wildlife. The five national and sixty-six provincial parks contain a healthy population of bighorn sheep, mountain goats, elk, bears, wolves, bison and woodland caribou. Alberta is a mixture of prairie, boreal forest and mountains. It contains some 300 bird species, 90 mammals, 50 species of fish – big and small, with 1,700 different flowering plants. Alberta is also a wealthy oil province: with the high price of oil these days, the economy of Canada is in a very healthy state.

Not to be missed is the drive through the Jasper National Park to the town of Jasper. The view I had was the very same that struck awe into the railway workers, miners, explorers and Swiss guides who criss-crossed these valleys in the late 1800s. Today, you can follow in their footsteps or blaze a new trail. Because they left lots of the park alone, only the Town of Jasper has changed. It's a place where any fly-fishers can enjoy this great playground, but it's not just for anglers, it's for all the family to enjoy. It's where I met Krista Roger of Jasper Tourism and Commerce. What a kind, knowledgeable, efficient and helpful lady she was.

Jasper gets its name from two small trading-posts. One of these was under the charge of Jasper Haws, a Northwest Trading Company clerk in 1817. He gave his name to this post, which became 'Jasper's House'. This name was also given to the community around the post and eventually to the National Park. Many people told me Jasper National Park is how national parks were meant to be, before traffic jams and tour buses took over. It's situated three and a half hours west of Edmonton or three hours north of Banff. You won't need to wonder what it must have been like 100 years ago because, apart from the tarmac road and the other tourists, it's still exactly as it was then.

Revered as the largest tract of wilderness in the Canadian Rockies, Jasper National Park has earned its reputation by claiming the most extensive back-country trail system in any Canadian park – and it's less developed: an absolute haven for wildlife. Elk, moose, mountain goats, woodland caribou, lynx, cougars, bears, coyotes and some 248 species of birds have been recorded in Jasper at various times of the year.

After spending a day and night in the town we had an interesting four hour drive to Edmonton, passing numerous oil wells on the way. Edmonton is a bustling city of hotels, skyscrapers, night clubs and a huge shopping mall. The latter I was told is the world's biggest, from where you can take a submarine trip and see dolphins. After a good night's sleep and breakfast we spent the next day with Wayne Miller of Birds and Back-country, this included seeing several big bison from a distance of just a few feet. Dinner was cooked to perfection in the wilderness back-country.

Fort McMurray in northern Alberta is a bustling, booming oil town. They say there is as much oil in the sands of Alberta as in the Middle East. Huge, powerful, steam-pumps are used to force the oil from the sand, sand and soil are then replaced, and the whole area is planted with trees. Insects and wildlife follow, in some areas the moose are back. Our final destination was Colin Lake, 300 miles further north. Allan Proulx and Tim Gillies of Air Mikisew / Mikisew Sports Fishing were our hosts, what great company these two guys were. They had a tremendous work rate; it seemed as if they didn't stop for more than five minutes in any day. Allan and Tim worked hard to ensure that John and myself, along with the four Canadian anglers: father and son, Roy and Dan Bamber, Rick Wright and Glen Shaw, would have a good time. We were the last group of anglers to fish Colin Lake before it closed down for the winter months. John and I booked ourselves a room for the night in the Quality Hotel in Gregoire Drive just a short distance from the airport where the price was right and the staff were extremely friendly and helpful, even storing our equipment ready for our next destination.

Mikisew Sport Fishing has three other lakes: Charles, Cornwall and Ryan, all in this northern wilderness area of the Canadian Shield. Here, the only sounds you are likely to hear are the cry of the bald eagle and the call of the loon. You may catch sight of the osprey and ravens, and at night you might hear the wolves. Moose and bear also inhabit this environment. Colin Lake is situated in the north-east corner of Alberta some sixty miles south of the 60th parallel, close to the Saskatchewan border. The lake covers an area of 10,510 acres. Fish species include: northern pike, lake trout, perch and whitefish. There are two cabins, one sleeping four, the other a small, trapper's cabin, measuring 12ft x 16ft, sleeping two people. A generator pumps water from the lake to the two cabins and shower room. You will find plenty of wood for a fire should you need one. The camp site is located on the north-western shoreline in a small cove with a sandy beach and boat jetty; boats are 14ft aluminium with 9HP Mariner engines.

Our pilot, Paul Hagopian of Air Mikisew, is well experienced in flying the amphibious Caravan 1. Having done all his checks, and making sure we passengers were aware of the safety arrangements, we taxied down the runway. Sitting up front, I could hear Paul talking to the control tower, receiving the all-clear. He turned up the revs and we roared off down the runway, quickly getting airborne. Reaching cruising speed

Inside the plane

and altitude, Paul switched to auto-pilot. After bringing his log book up-to-date, he told my listeners to 'At the Water's Edge' programme on BBC Radio Lancashire all about the aircraft, our flying time, route and other bits of interesting information. He was constantly keeping a close watch on the various gauges, not just relying on the auto-pilot. As we passed over Lake Athabasca, Paul discussed the local history, pointing out various places of interest. A few miles from Colin Lake, he returned to manually flying the plane. After coming out of some thick cloud I got a glimpse of Colin Lake. As we dropped down to 300ft I spotted a group of moose.

Up ahead the lake looked magnificent in the autumn sunshine. We flew over it and made a right turn along the western shoreline. A group of guys who were leaving, stood close to the jetty. Paul made a pass, then circled back round for his landing. As the revs dropped, we lost height then glided in for a smooth touchdown. I didn't even feel a bump – this pilot was good. The next minute we were alongside the jetty and tied up.

Before Paul left he gave us the satellite phone, and then pointed out some 12ft x 6ft wooden boards covered with protruding six inch nails standing against the cabin wall, saying, "You put those boards on the ground in front of the cabin door and window before locking the door with a wooden bar between those two U-shaped pieces of steel, that will keep the bears away." I laughed quietly to myself knowing how easy it is for a bear to rip the side out of a cabin if it really wanted to – I had seen bear-damage on several occasions in Northern Saskatchewan. Half-an-hour later, John, having stored away all the food, made some sandwiches and the longed-for mugs of tea.

I didn't plan to unpack my bag as we didn't have anywhere to hang up shirts, etc – I just grabbed things as I wanted them. Each day I washed my pants and socks, drying them off the best I could, usually in front of the fire at night. Some items didn't make the trip as they got badly scorched! My other dirty clothes were dumped in a spare bag. I had come with three Thomas

Our home was a trappers cabin built in the late 1800's

and Thomas rods, two 9 weights and a 10 weight, each one carrying a different line. One, a Cortland Ghost tip; the second, a fast sink, while the third rod was matched with a Teeny 500 grain shooting line, which really does get down fast and deep. These three set-ups would hopefully cover all depths of water and fishing conditions. Within three hours of landing, everything was ship-shape, and we were ready to tackle the 'toothy critters'. I put on some warm clothes including chest-high waders, and we slipped the life jackets over our heads. Having checked each other to make sure all the straps were in place, we headed for the boat jetty. We loaded all our gear into the bows of the boat and I made sure the fuel tank was topped up, and that we were carrying an extra, spare can of gas: you should never go afloat without extra fuel.

With one pull of the starting-cord the engine was purring nicely, John untied the mooring ropes, and then pushed us away from the jetty. I put the motor into gear and slowly moved away onto the lake. As we reached the deep water I opened the throttle, and pointed the bows for the eastern shoreline. I had been told by the group who had just left, that the wind had been blowing in this direction for three days; hopefully the pike would have followed the bait fish.

We spotted a small bay with lots of rocks, sunken branches and weed. We edged close then dropped both anchors – don't try fishing with a single anchor; you can't present the fly correctly as you will be swinging one way, then the other. Within twenty seconds of casting – no probably only ten, I hooked up to my first fish of six or seven pounds on a Polar fly fished on a Ghost tip line. What a start! As I was playing my fish, John got to hook-up a nice fish of about twelve pounds. In the next four casts, I had four more pike averaging some six to seven pounds, John had two more fish both scraper doubles. After ten minutes with no more takes, we moved off along the shoreline for another spot. I was quickly into a fish of about fifteen pounds, another about ten pounds followed within minutes.

Fishing was good, with several around the eight pound mark. It seemed as if John and I were matching each other, fish-for-fish. If the rest of the adventure was as good as this we wouldn't complain. No doubt if we had got up well before dawn, we might have stood a chance in the half-light of connecting with one of those big ones we had been told about. After two hours of fishing, the wind freshened up considerably from a westerly direction. I could see white caps in the channel; it was time to seek shelter of the lee shore. The first part of the journey was quite bumpy; a few of the bigger waves crashed over the bows, but closer to the lee shore the water was quite calm. Conditions looked good and we fished several spots, but apart from two hits we didn't have a single fish. I wouldn't be surprised if the two hits were from perch, it seemed like something was nipping the end of the fly, which perch will often do. Having had a very early start, we were both feeling quite tired; it was time to call it a day.

We moved off for the jetty and our warm cabin. As we rounded a small island, I said to John, "Let's have a few chucks." We caught three pike. Unhooking the last fish John said, "That will do for supper." It was retained.

On the jetty John cleaned and filleted the pike, while I carried all the gear back to the cabin. I then topped up the gas tank, making sure the oars and rowlocks were safely stowed away. Back in the cabin we had fried pike, potatoes and a couple of mugs of tea. The wood-burning stove glowed red; it was all fuggy in the cabin. Outside the temperature was way below zero and later it snowed. After cleaning and polishing our fly lines, I had a mug of chocolate. Before crawling inside my sleeping bag I made sure the wooden beam was across the door. I was tired out and within seconds I was asleep.

The following morning, I opened the cabin door and looked up the lake; I could see big, white caps. The tree tops were swaying in the fierce wind, and the snow was replaced by icy-cold rain. It was going to be a tough day afloat, but we were ready for the day's fishing. No chance today of reaching Eagle Bay at the southern end of the lake, it would be suicidal to try. I chose instead to fish the lee shore, hoping for a picture-fish. Breakfast over, we got kitted-out in wet-weather gear, I then loaded all our tackle in the boat, having checked the gas tank and the extra gas tank in the boat, I was happy there hadn't been any leakage of fuel overnight.

Meanwhile, John cut some extra logs for tonight's fire. The other crew decided to stay in their cabin, but then, they hadn't travelled the several thousand miles that we had – we couldn't miss this opportunity. Remember, you can't catch if you don't have a fly or lure in the water. After telling the other guys where we were heading for, we motored down the western shoreline seeking the shelter of the islands as we did so. We arrived at our planned destination and for three hours, cast, retrieved, changed flies and tackle set-ups without a hit. It was tough going: the only excitement was watching a bear grab a decent, lake trout from a fast-flowing side stream. Rounding a rocky point, we came into a shallow, weedy bay, it looked an attractive spot. Another bear appeared on the shoreline and still the rain sheeted down. After a lot of casting and retrieving, I had two small pike, with several strikes from small, lake trout, while John, who was fishing with Mepp's spinners, caught lake trout averaging about four pounds, and a jack pike. I could see several trout hitting my fly; some got pricked, none were cleanly hooked. The wind

I didn't feel threatened by this black bear. I reckon he wanted to know who the new neighbours were

increased in strength; it was time to move. We motored across some rough, windswept water into another small bay. After an hour or so of being battered by wind and rain, with only one small fish each, we decided to call it a day.

We kept close to the lee shore, with John in the bows watching out for rocks – which could be the size of a small car; we slowly made our way back to base, shipping a lot of water as we did so. When we reached the jetty I said to John, "That was a cold, wet and tough day." We learnt that the Canadian lads went afloat and were back in less than an hour. They chose to play cards rather than troll lures. That night we were invited to join them for dinner. The one thing John and I would have liked was a hot shower, we had to make do with cold water – but we did have a good covering of goose pimples! It was a good evening with the other lads, as the whisky flowed and we told each other fishing stories (or were they lies?). Dinner was steaks, chips, beans and fried onions, followed by some good cheese and biscuits. A great evening was had by all; it was around ten o'clock when we went off to our cabin. I reckon within sixty seconds of crawling into my sleeping bag I was fast asleep.

Overnight several inches of snow had fallen; it was a cold morning with the temperature several degrees below 0°F. Thankfully the wind had decreased, with no white caps on the lake; we decided to hit Eagle Bay where the water varied in depth from three to twenty feet. A creek flowed in, which attracted lake trout; not far away from these fish, we should find the pike. We were well wrapped-up in warm clothing, wearing life jackets as we did every time we went afloat.

We left the jetty about 9 a.m. The only thing missing on this trip was my gas stove and kettle; but today I had a saucepan as I planned to boil some water and enjoy a mug of tea. I was fed up drinking icy-cold water. I headed straight down the lake, and after about twenty five minutes we passed through the narrow neck of water with huge boulders everywhere, that would take us into Eagle Bay. I must point out that we would only visit this place on a calm day: any waves above two feet would make it extremely dangerous. Once inside the bay we moved close to a creek mouth, then John dropped the anchors.

Ten minutes later we were ready to fish. I chose to try with the Cortland Ghost tip line and a Sally Rand fly pattern. It's a big fly with lots of orange marabou tied up on a size 5/0 hook, looking fan-like until it's in the water, when it takes on a fish shape. It got its name from a fan dancer at the 1938 Chicago Fair by the name of Sally Rand. Now, she would have made a good companion in our cabin! Five chucks, five hook-ups all hard-fighting fish around the seven to eight pound mark. John was catching lake trout on his Mepp's. On my sixth retrieve, a very big, lake trout in the twenty pound bracket, tried to grab the fly as I was lifting off for another cast. It came as quite a shock. I didn't expect anything to grab hold – neither did I expect to see such a big, lake trout in five feet of water. I tried to catch the beast but without success.

We then moved the boat a dozen yards or so to the mouth of a weedy bay. I chucked a big, popping-frog pattern deep into a weedbed. It was hit by a good pike, first cast; weighing perhaps sixteen pounds. A dozen casts later with no more bites I said to John, "Let's try the narrows." He agreed. We motored across the bay and dropped anchors so we could fish both the shallow and deep water. I picked up my Thomas and Thomas 10 weight matched with a Teeny 450 grain line with a Ballydoolagh bomber tied up by Kent Sherrington on a size 8/0 hook. It's a fly with a very buoyant head of plastazote. As you retrieve, the fly goes downwards, when you stop retrieving, it rises a couple of feet off the bottom. Looking up the bay I could see some huge rocks plunging down to the water's edge, giving the appearance of very deep water. I made a long cast, probably seventy feet, then fished the 'bomber' along this drop-off, it was tough, casting these bombers, they are not the most aerodynamically designed fly pattern especially when they are tied up on a big hook.

A bald eagle sat sentinel-like at the top of a dead tree. The sun was shining down from a gap in the clouds, piercing deep into the clear water. A strong breeze ruffled the surface of the lake. Bait-size fish sought sanctuary in a dense, weed bed. Nothing moved, except the boat as it glided slowly through the water; the only shade was from my long-peaked cap. Optilabs polarised sunglasses helped my eyes to seek and search deep into the dazzling, shimmering water.

I blink, and then squint – can it be, or is it a shadow? I squint again: Yes, there it is! I spot a fin movement, and then a tail moves slightly. My squinting, blinking eyes move slowly up the length of a fish – it must be forty five inches long. I gasp! My heart beats a little faster. It's a big one. Perspiration rolls off my forehead into my eyes, stinging as it does so, despite the cold wind. My hands shake a little, I start to feel nervous. My brain (yes I have one!) goes into overdrive, it's like a computer as I work out the angle of the cast, the distance to target. I aereolise ten yards of line, I need another five. I pull this off the reel quickly, all the time keeping my eyes on the big one. I'm the hunter: the hunted is a fish that goes back a few million years. It weighs twenty pounds-plus, it's there for the catching, if I don't make a mistake.

The fish is moving ever-so-slowly away, I only have one chance. I shoot line to land the fly at the interception point which is two feet to the left and a foot in front of the quarry. My cast is spot-on. The fly lands with a plop hardly breaking the surface of the water. The fish moves its head slightly then slowly turns. This is the moment I have been waiting for as I twitch the line to impart life into the fly – a fly that was created in Northern Canada. It's tied-up on a 3/0 Partridge hook using polar bear hair and a few strands of crystal flash. It's some six inches long and comes alive in the water when retrieved. Slowly I take in six inches of line, the pike's off the starting blocks moving fast towards the fly, creating a bow wave as it does so. I give a quick, three-inches pull, the fly has really come alive – the big one can't resist it and hurls herself at it! You see a huge head appear, the fly has gone – there's a rocking of water, a big swirl. I feel the fish and strip-strike then strike sideways as hard as I dare. Her speed and momentum carry her skywards like a Polaris missile, head shaking, gills flared.

For several seconds, I stand spellbound watching twenty pounds-plus of fighting fury crash back into the water, it's like an explosion as the water erupts. The ever-increasing circles spread out over the bay. A water bird screams in disgust at having been interrupted from its peaceful slumbers. The tip of my 10 weight Thomas and Thomas rod is savagely pulled down to the water, the reel screams likes a scolded cat or demented demon. Fly-line disappears in a blur – this is fishing as goods it gets; just one of the great joys of wilderness Canada.

I shouted to John, "It's a big one!" Suddenly the rod tip was pulled downward by a powerful force; line was dragged from the reel. I could feel the awesome power of a good fish as it slowly moved up the bay. Was this was my picture-fish I thought! It could be if I was lucky enough to be the winner of this titanic scrap with a big, powerful, angry pike. If I got this fish in the landing net, I would be a happy angler. Some anglers would probably think, "It's a big lake trout." I knew differently. This was a pike, a big pike – one I had travelled for thousands of miles to catch. For several minutes the fish was boss, as it slowly and powerfully took line from the reel.

I cramped on as much pressure as possible, lowering the rod tip to make use of the extra power in the butt section. A few minutes later I gained some line. Suddenly the fish changed

Author with another good Pike on the fly

direction. Winding like a demented demon, I managed to get the slack line back on the reel. Occasionally my heart missed a beat, when the fish moved faster than I could gain line. Occasionally it shook its head in a bid to remove the big fly on its barbless hook. This pike tried every trick in the book as it fought for its freedom. The fight then turned into a give-and-take scrap and some minutes later the pressure started to tell – I was winning the contest. We discussed how big the fish might be, agreeing it was a big twenty-pounder – possible a thirty; we had seen such an awesome fish in the mouth of a stream early in the morning. Big pike gather in this area to ambush the lake trout moving into the streams. Meanwhile John retrieved both anchors, we didn't want this fish to get snagged up on something of our own making.

Ten yards from the boat, the water erupted: then boiled. A big fish swirled then tried to lift itself from the water; only the head and shoulders appeared. With flared gills it shook its head, the mouth looked huge, its large, dark eyes seemed to be directed at me as if saying, "Give me one chance to bite you and I will!" I could see the 'bomber' in the corner of its mouth. This was one, big, angry fish at the end of my line. Suddenly it dived, I gave line quickly. Within minutes I was getting line back on the reel as the fish tired. John stood holding the big landing net, the Masterline mat/weight sling was on the hard bottom of the boat to protect the fish. With the net sunk deep, I tried guiding and pulling the fish close to the net but it had other ideas, it twisted and swirled as slowly inch-by-inch it came towards the landing net. As I pulled it over the net, I shouted, "John, lift the net!" The handle bent under the weight of the fish. Laying down the rod, I grabbed the net with both hands and we lifted and swung the fish inboard onto the padded mat. What a super fish: it taped out at forty five inches. Punching the air I said, "Yes, Yes, Yes!" The scales gave a reading of around twenty six pounds.

We shook hands. After some quick pictures, the fish was held in the water until it fought clear of my grip and swiftly moved off. We went ashore where I soon had a fire going; I was going to celebrate in the best way I know these days and that was with a mug of tea, even though I didn't have any milk. After a thirty minute break we started fishing again, I wanted another one of those 'toothy critters'. We caught several more good pike including an eighteen-pounder to John, I also had some nice lake trout with one fish weighing ten pounds.

With the wind starting to blow strongly from the north east, John changed back to spinning. I was watching the white caps growing bigger and more awesome as they swept down the channel, a stretch of water we had to cross before we reached the lee shore; I hoped the wind would abate before we had to move. We fished on catching more fish. Flies certainly out-fished the spinner or the plug 20–1.

An hour before dusk, I hooked a big fish that wouldn't move off the bottom. Twice I felt its tail hit the line, the fish went where it wanted for some ten minutes, until the fly was thrown back at me with contempt. We called it a day. With John in the bows looking for rocks, I guided us back to camp, arriving well after dark; I didn't feel we had been in any danger, having had lots of experience in small boats.

I couldn't wait for a welcome mug of tea. Roy, Dan, Rick and Glenn were waiting on the dock looking rather worried. A few minutes later, when they heard about our fishing, they were all smiles and congratulations. Once again we were invited to join them for dinner – this time we ate lake trout, rice and vegetables; they all had something strong to drink, and I enjoyed my Yorkshire Gold tea!

The next morning, stepping out of our cabin, I was greeted with several more inches of snow covering the ground. I made a quick dash across the open wind-swept ground to the loo which consisted of a hole in the ground next to a squatting pole. With bears in the area one didn't hang about – in fact the previous day I had come within twenty yards of a bear when I got out of the boat at lunchtime to stretch my legs.

It was another windy day, but we decided to go afloat and fish Eagle Bay. Thankfully we were dressed in Patagonia waterproofs with good life-jackets. Only a fool would go afloat on these big waters without a life jacket, even on a flat-calm day. Motoring straight down the lake to Eagle bay we went through some very rough water and white caps. Waves and spray were forced into our faces by the powerful wind; my hands were cold and numb. After thirty minutes I was able to use the islands and lee shore for shelter, and as we went through the narrows into Eagle Bay I gave a sigh of relief. We started fishing along the deep drop-off, twenty yards further on from where I had the big one the day before. On the second cast I was into a good fish on a Sally Rand fly using a Cortland Ghost tip line. It stayed deep, taking line under pressure, slowly moving up the bay – you can't hurry these big fish. Minutes later the pressure started to tell; as I gained line I could feel the fish shaking its head in its bid for freedom. John was ready with the net. The padded mat was on the bottom of the boat. The wind was blowing from all points of the compass.

Yesterday it was gusty, today it blew all the time. Slowly I pumped the fish to surface, and before it could dive John had it netted. The pike came alive turning the water into white foam as it thrashed and twisted in the net. Laying the rod aside I bent down grabbed the net with both hands and we lifted the fish over the side of the boat onto the padded mat. It was a good fish which taped out at thirty nine inches. After a couple of pictures it was released. I suggested to John he should occasionally use a mouse pattern. An hour later he had a good fish grab the mouse close to the boat. A surprised John said, "I didn't think a fish would eat that mouse!" I said, "They make them for pike to eat!" John used a Masterline telescopic spinning rod which proved ideal for the job. We were both impressed with the rod's action. I picked up the net pushing it deep in the water, and as John pulled the fish over the net I lifted. A good fish was engulfed in the deep netting. It taped out at thirty eight inches. We took some pictures and released it back into the lake. During the day I caught lots more pike on flies. John had one nice lake trout on a spoon and I caught a couple on flies fished deep. Before we realised it, it was beginning to getting dark so I decided to run straight up the lake to our camp site; a very bumpy and spray-swept trip.

This old stove was a welcome sight when we got back from a long cold wet day on the lake

I didn't fancy being on the water after dark again. An hour after leaving Eagle Bay we were back in our cabin having a mug of tea. The only food and drink we had each day whilst on the water were a couple of crunchy bars and a mouthful of water. While I built up the fire in the wood-burning stove until it glowed red, making it all fuggy in the cabin, John sorted out our dinner of lake trout fillets, beans and chips. The other guys had gone home, we were the only inhabitants of this island except for the bears – and we had no squaws for company!

After a good nights sleep, I slipped out of my sleeping bag and peered through the cabin window; snow lay thick on the ground. Our only way of communication, and then only in an emergency, was the satellite phone. If the weather really turned bad the float plane couldn't get in to us. We could be stuck in for the winter. We had been warned by the pilot that this could happen, but were quite happy to take the chance.

Providing we could catch fish or perhaps trap some animals for food, we would survive. We were surrounded by trees so warmth wasn't a problem – we could stoke-up the fire as much as we wanted. I reckon I was quite capable of surviving – as was John. In just my pants and boots I dashed to the lakeside for a bucket of water, and to have a quick wash. I just kicked off my boots and pants then submerged in the icy-cold water. I came out freezing but invigorated. I slipped on my boots, grabbed the bucket and my pants and ran back to the warmth of the cabin. John was beginning to stir. After chucking two more logs on the fire, my skin slowly changed from dark blue to a pink colour as I dried myself off and got dressed in warm cloths, using the layering system.

Breakfast today was eggs and bacon with chipped potatoes, a real treat. We were lucky as the other guys left us a lot of canned food and potatoes, plus a full bottle of scotch for John. We could now feast like kings. I planned a big fillet of pike for tonight's dinner; John was having a chunk of steak. With breakfast over, John chopped logs, while I went down to top-up the fuel tank and the extra gas container, making sure we had a plug spanner and other tools. After putting all the tackle on board, I made sure the oars were safely roped in.

Back at the cabin John and I put on our top-coats and life jackets. At the boat dock we checked we had everything. As we were both satisfied with our preparations, we stepped aboard. One pull of the starter cord had the motor bursting into life. I said to John, "Let's try the narrows." He agreed. I kept close to the shoreline, while John in the bows was on the lookout for boulders – these were house-size rocks! If we hit one of them, all would be lost, no way could we survive even if we did get to the shoreline; I reckon hypothermia would quickly set in. We dropped anchors as close as possible to the drop-off where I had the big fish a couple of days before. John was going to spin the shallow water; I planned to fish the Ballydoolagh bomber in the deep water.

I had a couple of good fish in as many casts, then nothing for half an hour or more. John had several pike with one good fish about fifteen pounds. I was on the point of suggesting a move when the line stopped dead. For a few seconds I thought I was hooked on a snag. Then it moved slowly forcing the rod tip down under the water before I gave it some line. I said to John, "This is a big one, can you clear the decks." Again the rod tip was pulled down by a powerful, unseen, underwater force; line was dragged from the reel. I asked John to bring up the anchors, and then take over the motor; I felt we might be following this fish as it slowly surged up the narrows. More line was dragged from the reel. I could feel the awesome power of a big fish. I cramped on as much pressure as the 10 weight would allow, I had handled big dorado on a 10 weight, and so felt quite confident in my tackle. I made sure I used the extra power in the butt section – that's what it's for. John started the motor, then slowly moved the boat forward so I was able to gain some line.

The unseen leviathan shook its head and made a surge up the channel taking a few yards of line, occasionally shaking its head in a bid to remove the Ballydoolagh bomber tied on a barbless hook. This fish wasn't ready to give up the fight as it struggled for its freedom. Probably fifteen minutes later the pressure started to tell; I was beginning to gain some line. John was giving me words of encouragement as we talked about this fish, agreeing it could be a thirty-pounder. We had seen big fish in the area, no doubt there to hit the lake trout which congregate for spawning in the streams. Suddenly I was gaining line. The water erupted as a big fish rolled on the surface then tried to lift itself from the water, no way could I see a fish this size go tail-walking after such a long fight. With gills flared it shook its head, the mouth was huge. I couldn't see the 'bomber'. Just the wire trace disappearing into this cavernous hole. This was one big angry fish at the end of my line. I was forced to give line as it dived but I was soon getting some back on the reel. I reckon I had the fish beaten as I slowly pumped it to the surface; John stood ready with the landing net submerged in the water, and slowly, foot-by-foot, my prize was getting closer.

In the gin-clear water I could see a huge fish twisting and head-shaking in its bid for freedom. I moved as far back in the boat as possible, drawing the fish close to the surface, then within reach of John. Suddenly the fish was over the big net John lifted and the fish folded inside mesh. The prize was mine. I dropped the rod, and with both hands gave John some help to get the fish inboard and onto the padded mat. What a super fish: it taped out at fifty one inches. Punching the air, I shouted, "Yes!" The scales gave a reading of around thirty two pounds, we shook hands. John started the engine and we motored across to the shallows where I could rest the fish. Fifteen minutes later it had its freedom, and it moved off strongly for a deeper part of the lake.

John and I celebrated with a crunchy bar and some water. I would have given anything at that moment for a cheese-and-pickle wholemeal roll with a mug of tea! We fished on for another couple of hours then, with the wind gaining strength, we decided to head back to base. It was a wise choice as the wind increased to gale force. The trip was long and exhausting, lasting at least an hour more than normal. That night, with the wind howling outside and snow falling, we were snug-as-bugs in the cabin as the stove glowed red giving off plenty of warmth. John enjoyed a mug of whisky – we didn't have any glasses. It was two happy, exhausted anglers who climbed into their sleeping bags.

We had another two day's fishing left before our trip was over but next morning, looking at the big white caps, we stayed at the cabin – only a fool would have gone afloat. On our final

day we were confined to fish the sheltered water close to the cabin catching a few, jack-size pike and a couple of lake trout. It had been a great adventure, one we thoroughly enjoyed, nothing in our book beats the wilderness experience. We'd had a scare or two on the lake in rough weather, made some new friends, watched bald eagles, bears and caught some good fish.

John Bodsworth and Martin enjoy dinner after a day on the lake

As a writer and broadcaster I wanted to bring my readers and listeners tales from interesting places around the world: one such was South America. I had been intrigued by this huge continent since I was a youngster reading the Boys Own magazine; my history books about the Spanish Conquest of this part of the world had me enthralled. Above all, I had been inspired by stories of the Amazon Jungle and the famed Amazonian woman in one of the Tarzan films.

These woman do exist: you see them in Bogotá riding Harley motorbikes, dressed in tight pants, knee length boots and looking most attractive, they are police officers. I didn't see a single one that I would have kicked out of my bed!

Colombia, the country, can be a lovely place to visit, with its history scenery and wildlife, it can also be extremely dangerous, especially the capital, Bogotá. It's all down to drugs: gunfights and bomb blasts are the norm in this crime-ridden city. Though it's a place of enormous wealth, it also has enormous poverty. We were once given a guided tour of the gold museum. Walking along the road after our visit, I said to Ginger Roberts, "What we looked at in that place could have covered our national debt!" Though if Gordon Brown, the then Chancellor, hadn't sold off our gold reserves at rock bottom prices, we would be a lot better off today.

Bogotá certainly has squalor equal to any place in the world. It's so bad that kids are on the streets trying to sell you their sister – in some cases their mothers! Bogotá is a scary town. I was in the bathroom one morning when a huge car bomb went off, blowing-in all the windows of our hotel. Thankfully, my bathroom had no windows: that saved me from being cut to ribbons. One day I saw a guy lying on a stretcher holding out a begging bowl, I asked the interpreter to ask what had happened to him. It turned out that he had been in the army and had taken a bullet in the spine. What a shameful way to treat those who are looking after your safety. We gave him thirty dollars.

I have been very fortunate in spending a considerable amount of time in Peru, Colombia, Brazil, Ecuador and Venezuela as a writer, photographer, traveller and angler. It was a most fascinating experience, especially when I left the towns and villages and moved onto the rivers or into the jungle. This was a different world, and at times a very inhospitable one. In the jungle I came across snakes of all sizes, including the giant anaconda. There were also dangerous spiders and ants; however, most of the animals and birds were quite harmless. In fact, and contrary to what we had been told, they usually moved away from us as we hacked our way through the thick undergrowth. We had been led to expect attacks by ferocious animals such as the jaguar or the cayman, a South American alligator. We never even saw a jaguar. The biggest and most savage species we had to contend with was homosapiens. He was a savage, a killer, a thief: you could never trust him.We saw macaws, parakeets, herons, egrets, toucans and many other birds of quite magnificent colours – numerous species that I couldn't identify. Whenever I saw a toucan I thought of a cooling glass of Guinness and imagined that I was sitting in an Irish bar, far away from the stinking villages that we often use to visit in our South American travels.

Most of the jungle towns were groups of hovels smelling of excrement, dead dogs, rotten fruit and fish. Don't ever talk to me about poverty in the United Kingdom: we don't know what

Martin unhooks another big fish from an Amazon jungle lake

it is. You have to go to Third World countries to see real poverty. In Bogotá young children live in sewers and old ladies in concrete storm pipes. On the outskirts of big towns like Leticia the filth was ever present, as was the problem of exhaust fumes.

Howler monkeys were everywhere. I had many a meal of monkey and rice, but I found this meat rather stringy. We often had snake meat, which was quite good, even if a bit tough. Another good meal was pineapple, papayas, bananas and rice with snake or catfish; it was quite excellent. Alligator was one of my favourite meats – far better than the more generally available cow or donkey.

I enjoyed my time with the Ticuna Indians, who live in villages often deep in the Brazilian Amazon rainforest, intersecting the borders of Brazil, Columbia, Peru. They are also one of the last largest indigenous population groups left in this area. Most Ticuna live in Brazil; the population is thought to have increased dramatically in the last fifty years. The tonal Ticuna language is said to be a language of its own, not clearly related to any other tribe. Of all the tribes in the Amazon, the Ticuna were the first to be contacted by the 'civilised' world way back in the early times; however, they still live a traditional lifestyle. We would sleep in the long hut as they did, share their food and drink, even go hunting with them. They were deadly with a blow pipe; however hard I tried I didn't get a single kill, in fact I couldn't get the dart to move more than a few inches.

Crossing the many rivers was a major problem, especially when you had to wade the shallow stretches. We also rafted some areas, often jumping off the raft just before it went over a waterfall. The most dangerous creature of all, in my opinion and that of many other experienced travellers in this region, is a tiny parasitic minnow-like fish known as the candiru. It is far more deadly than a piranha or a water snake. If a candiru gets inside you, it can eat your guts out, and, according to local Indians, it can even swim up a stream of urine. Another nasty of the rivers is the stingray, which lies under the sand ready to strike at the unsuspecting traveller. A lot is spoken about the cayman or alligator, yet these were no problem to us: when we approached them they invariably slid off the bank and moved away. The animals that really grabbed my attention were the pink dolphins. They are big, about the size of a beluga whale, and when they rose up alongside our dugout canoes and crashed back, they rocked us about dangerously. The pink dolphin is now in danger of being wiped out in the Amazon.

Another hazard that we and all other river users faced was bandits. They would appear from nowhere, heavily armed. It could be a bit scary, especially when guns were actually being used. Our main weapon was a cut-down 12 gauge pump-action shotgun, along with a Beretta sidearm.

The three main problems out in the field were: the mosquitoes which attacked every bit of exposed flesh; the bushmaster, the largest poisonous snake in the world and one which captured its prey by ambush tactics; the last was being robbed and killed by cocaine smugglers and terrorists, though usually we were in control. In Peru, the Shining Path terrorists or guerillas were a particularly vicious group of people. They were a guerrilla group just beginning to come to prominence. They could butcher you alive and smile at the same time.

I had a very narrow escape one morning: it was just after dawn when I stepped out of a the jungle onto a track no more than eighteen inches wide and staring me in the face was the dreaded bushmaster, coiled and ready to strike. I froze. I was bloody frightened – and that is an understatement! I felt the blood drain from my body. Was I going to die in this steamy, stinking, hellhole of a country? Would it all end here? Without a sound, my friend Ted, a giant of a man from Utah, appeared beside me and blasted the bushmaster to pieces with his sawn-off pump-action shot gun. You can keep all your automatic weapons and pistols: in the jungle one weapon reigns supreme. It is the 12 gauge pump-action shotgun, cut down for ease of use.

Colombia, Peru and Ecuador were the countries where cocaine smuggling seemed to be at its worst, but they also had some wonderful fishing in the Amazon: the Cayaru River which flowed inky black through Peru, the Yavary River, and many huge jungle lakes. The European rivers hold around 150 species of fish, but I'm told that the Amazon system has 1,800. Just think: some of the tiny fishes we keep in aquariums at home can grow to a foot long or more in the Amazon River.

Colombia has one and only one tiny port on the Amazon. Leticia is two thousand miles from the Atlantic coast and 312 feet above sea level. There, the river is over two miles wide, and when it floods the water can rise forty feet. It seemed that its only claim to fame was as a smuggling centre for all kinds of goods, from cocaine to rare animals. It boasted several brothels, all staffed by girls flown in from Bogatá.

One afternoon I flew in from Bogotá in an old Dakota. I was with Ted (the bushmaster killer); Rick, a short blond-haired lad from Texas, Warren, a New Yorker, and Jordon, a bear of a man who continuously smoked cigars, and who came from Iowa. After clearing customs and paying the usual bribe, we collected our truck from alongside the grass airstrip and headed into town. As we did so, we passed several banners announcing the opening of a new brothel! That's the sort of town Leticia was. The town was surrounded on three sides by jungle and on the fourth by the mighty Amazon. The place was full of people, and shops selling everything the human race desired: dresses from France, silks from China, shoes from Italy, cameras from Japan. Whisky could be had, providing you had American dollars. The only ways in and out were by air and by boat.

The locals had nowhere to go, and so they used to spend their time driving round and round the square blowing their horns. As a Letician, it seemed that as soon as you made your first few bucks you bought yourself a Japanese motorbike. Later, when you had made lots more dollars, you bought a car. But there was still nowhere to go until you had made enough to buy a home in Bogotá, preferably in the colonial district.

Down on the waterfront, Indian dugouts were tied up beside modern fibreglass boats fitted with the latest Johnson, Evinrude and Mercury outboard motors; there were even outboards fitted on the sterns of dugouts used by the Indians. We often travelled by float plane. It was perfect for our needs, and both Ted and Jordon were top-class fliers. I sometimes took the controls and even brought the plane down on the lakes when the conditions were good. The float plane was ideal for us, because we often visited as many as three countries in a day. A couple of miles away from Leticia, over the border, was the Brazilian town of Tabatinga. The town was run by the military. It's a highly militarized region, almost uninhabited, approximately five million square kilometers in size, and the government considers it a national priority; a beautiful treasure that Brazil is determined to defend. We would often have drinks with the commandant who was in the Air Force. Tabatinga was just a small Amazonian jungle town, quite different from Leticia, but you still had to pay the usual bribes in American dollars.

On my trips it was often possible to fish. One such day started around dawn, when my Indian boatman, Ramon, picked me up at the dock. We were to fish the Cayaru River in Peru, and there I hoped to meet some of my Ticuna Indian friends who acted as guides. We moved off. I sat in the bows, tackling up with a 7 foot spinning rod, a multiplier reel and 12 lb line. I fixed on a wire trace and a small spinner. Some thirty minutes after leaving the dock we stopped the boat and I began spinning. Soon the piranhas were coming quick and fast, but I soon tired of this and we moved off to the mouth of the Cayaru River to fish for the Pirahyba catfish which grow very big. The mosquitoes were trying to eat me alive, but the fishing was more important and so I had to let the mosquitoes feed undisturbed.

For these big fish I used my 9ft glass rod, a Penn multiplier reel, a 40lb line and a thick wire trace with two size 5/0 hooks. Bait, supplied by my Indian guide, was a one pound hunk of fish. The whole lot was thrown over the side and line paid out. We sat back sharing a coke and watching the odd cayman moving around. To my left a tree overhung the water, and there I spotted an Indian lad no more than five years of age. He was armed with a spear, and I asked Ramon what the boy was doing.

"Fishing," Ramon replied. "He will have to learn to hunt if he is to survive."

In the next four hours the boy struck twice with the spear, catching a fish each time. He would grow into a good warrior and provider for his family.

Line began to trickle from the reel. Click, click, and click. Then the line began gathering pace, spilling rapidly from the reel. Time for action! Ramon looked at me and said, "Big fish for Mr. Marteen?" I nodded. Down in the dark, deep water something had taken my bait. I picked up the rod and snapped the reel into gear. The rod slammed down hard and banged on the side of the boat. Was it a fish or a cayman that had picked up the bait? Line was still streaming from the reel; the check screamed in protest, and the fight was on. For about half an hour the fish moved up and down the river with Ramon following; a huge freshwater dolphin leapt out of the water. I crammed on the pressure but still the battle raged up and down the Cayaru River. It was another thirty minutes before I began to get some control over this powerful underwater force and I started to pump the fish towards me. As I fought the fish, Ramon moved the canoe slowly towards the bank. Twenty yards downstream the fish rolled on the surface, thrashing the water to foam. I had never experienced anything like this; but slowly I was winning the battle. Even the little Indian boy had stopped his fishing to watch.

We bumped the bank and the dugout was made firm so that I could get ashore. I planned to finish the fight from a solid platform. Ramon was at my side with an evil-looking gaff attached to a five foot bamboo pole; not only was it well pointed but it had barbs up each side. I continued to pump. The fish was tiring fast, and soon it was within reach of Ramon, who didn't waste a second. The fish was dragged up the bank, flipping, twisting and turning in its bid for freedom. It had no chance once Ramon had set the gaff. The fish was mine. What a fight these Dorado catfish give – quite different from catching trout or carp.

We returned to the young lad's village, presenting the fish to the villagers, who made us most welcome. As the sun burned down with a vengeance, we sat swinging in hammocks, drinking foul-tasting coffee laced with Jack Daniels. Later, after dining on catfish, I was offered the usual reward of a woman for the night; I declined the offer as we had to be ready for a job in the morning. In the inky black darkness on the Amazon River, Ramon gunned the motor and we headed away from the Ticuna Indians to our own camp and some decent coffee. It was the usual hair-raising trip in the pitch black of night, there was always the risk of running into bandits or, even worse, drifting tree trunks that could so easily wreck our boat. Thankfully, we arrived without mishap.

The jungle, the rivers and lakes were a great source of fun. Although I've had a lot of scary moments there, given the chance I would certainly pay a return visit. I also travelled and fished other waterways, not only the mighty Amazon River. There were two tributaries of the Amazon we travelled and sometimes fished: the Yaguacaca River and the Loreto Yacu River. On one occasion we moved around in three countries: Brazil, Colombia and Peru. Border checks only exist in a few areas; this was a vast country where you could disappear for months, in fact years. You didn't need a passport.

Another big fish from the mighty Amazon River

Why do I use Pallatrax terminal tackle, well firstly, I can assure you that in no way do I get paid to use and extol the virtues of the company and their products. Simply put, I use them as they are of a high quality, innovative and, most importantly they help me put a few extra fish on the banks.

I first got to see the Stonze® weights when I visited Pallatrax to fish the River Frome and record a programme with Simon Pomaroy. I was impressed with the man; his thoughts on fish culture the environment and his care for his fishery. The Stonze® are a real stand alone angling tool that truly make common sense to use as they are actually made from natural stone and not of toxic lead. A real bonus for the environment, and when did you see a fish spook off a stone? I must say now the use of a stone as a weight isn't new, back in the 1950's and 60's my mates and I would scour the beaches looking for pebbles with a hole, when fishing for bass on the clean patches of sand between the bladder wrack-covered rocks, the stones were not only camouflaged but cheaper than lead should we get hooked up.

We don't realise how lucky we are with the great choice of hooks available today, when I started angling the only good hook was the Alcock Model Perfect, that's if you could find a stock of them. On many occasions I would visit six or more tackle shops in London before getting what I wanted. Today you can visit most tackle shops and find a decent hook.

For some forty years I have used barbless hooks, yes I have lost fish, not because it's barbless, because I made a mistake. I use them for ease of unhooking fish in the water. I don't want to struggle to take the hook from a fish. I've seen many people squeezing fish, which of course damages the internal organs. Others just tear out the hook often with bottom or top lip attached.

On many occasions apart from rod, reel and bait these are all the items of tackle I need to catch fish

I require a hook that is strong and sharp with the right shape, having lost the choice of Model Perfect hooks I tried the B James Richard Walker range, and then they disappeared. A hook that met my requirements was the Au Lion d'or model. Visiting Peter Drennan's factory I was taken to a room with a designated temperature control where all the hooks were kept. I was impressed at this quality control. Sadly these after some time disappeared.

Without a shadow of a doubt Partridge hooks were the best, they were hand made by a team of dedicated workers, many were females that had followed there mothers and grandmothers into the trade which started off making needles in the town of Redditch. When visiting the factory it was like stepping back into Dickensian Times. Today Pallatrax hooks are what I use with confidence.

A new name in the bait sales is the name of Pallatrax; I find their Jungle Paste baits ideal for many of my coarse fishing needs, having said that, I would like to see a soft paste in the Jungle formula, especially for chub fishing. I don't like to use a hair rig for chub; I feel I miss too many bites. Lets be honest one missed bite is one too many. That missed bite could be your best ever fish. If you want to know more about the company have a look at their website at www.pallatrax.co.uk or alternatively you can always give them a call where a member of the team will always take the time to assist you.

On the left Tony Miles with author at the 2010 Barbel
Society Conference where the author was one of the speakers. Credit Patrick Leigh

During my lifetime, I have had the privilege of meeting many of the top people from the world of politics, show business, sport and the military. Without a shadow of a doubt my vote for the two nicest goes to: the late Richard Stuart Walker 1918-1985, Britain's top angling writer and photographer; he was also angling's best known personality in his day. The other is Bernard Kreh, born in 1925, who is acknowledged as America's top angler, outdoor writer and a top class photographer.

Today, Kreh is probably the world's best. Both men made a major impact on the sport of angling with new ideas covering various aspects of the sport, including rod building, fly-tying and the catching of big fish. (Remember Walker's record carp of 44lbs from Redmire Pool on 13 September 1952?) Both personalities have written several excellent books about our sport. How I would love to have got Walker and Kreh together and then recorded the conversation between these two great men as they talked about all things piscatorial.

During the spring of the year 2000 I was invited by Brandon White to be his guest for a couple of week's fishing. Brandon is one of the new breed of young anglers fly-fishing, or using light tackle techniques, for the striped bass in Chesapeake Bay. The idea was to fish the Susquehanna flats at the north end of Chesapeake Bay, these being opened up to sports-fishing for just twenty-eight days during April. I would start my latest American trip with a visit to Florida, fishing the Indian River and Mosquito Lagoon for redfish and sea trout with a group of lady fly-fishers, who were not only great fly-fishers and excellent at boat handling – to put the icing on the cake, they were also good-looking! What more could a guy wish for? After two weeks I would then fly north to Maryland.

Arriving in Florida, I called Brandon who told me, "No fishing, the rivers are flooded; the Susquehanna flats are all shot out. The guides have cancelled all their trips. Give me a call in two or three day's time." My next call received the same message as before. On the advice of Brandon, we postponed the trip until the autumn, I stopped over in Florida another week, then headed north to Oregon

In September I flew out of Manchester, bound for Newark, New Jersey; then a flight to up-State New York where I spent a couple of weeks fishing for carp, pike, muskie, trout and smallmouth bass. In early October I booked a flight to Baltimore, Maryland. Brandon was waiting at the airport gate. We made the usual introductions, then he collected my bags and we headed off to Kent Island on Chesapeake Bay. This would be home for the next couple of weeks to fish for stripers, and visit with angling writers Bernard Kreh and Boyd Pfeiffer. After a few days spent sightseeing, partying and fishing, which included catching stripers and blue-fish on fly and light-tackle jigs, I was ready to visit Bernard Kreh, America's master angler, known to millions worldwide simply as, 'Lefty'.

It was a cool, grey day when I knocked on the door of his house in Hunt Valley. Lefty appeared, zipping up his pants. "Martin, come in, you caught me on the loo, you're early! I certainly enjoyed reading your book, "Up Against It". He laughed warmly as we shook hands and I looked into his sparkling bright eyes. For a seventy-five year old he was certainly a live wire, full of chat, jokes and laughter. As we sat talking we discussed all things piscatorial. I was in seventh heaven. At the many shows in the states that we both attend, Lefty often tells people, "That Martin is about as lively as a bumble bee in a jam jar – he never stops!" I reckon the same could be said of Lefty.

Occasionally, one gets the chance to be in the company of a great person: it was certainly true of this particular day. During my memorable visit, Lefty showed and demonstrated for me his line-testing machine. We discussed various aspects of photography, he even took time to show me the fishing rods he had painted white, so they could be photographed better against a dark background for his fly-casting book published in the 1970s.

Fly-casting was discussed in great detail. The great man even corrected my casting faults on a nearby pond. Every cast Lefty made was ninety-footer. He certainly is the master of his trade; they don't come any better. I was amazed at how easy he made casting look. Back in his house, we talked in great detail about photography and travel. He also found time to demonstrate tying a winning fly for the bonefish in the Bahamas.

Visiting Lefty's basement, I was staggered with how neat and tidy everything was. Boxes were all labelled with their contents, and filed in a much-organised fashion. Fly lines were neatly stacked on shelves in order of line weight, etc. Bulk spools of nylon were displayed on wooden pegs in order of the breaking strains. Neatly laid out on one wall were all types of fly and spinning reels, clearly labelled with line size or breaking strain, including his first ever reel, a Pflueger Medallist, with part of the casing cutaway so Lefty could apply pressure to the spool when playing a big fish. In a nearby rack was an armoury of rods covering every type of fishing.

Along another wall stood several cabinets full of tackle, all laid out neat and tidy. At one end of the basement were displayed dozens of tools, jigs and bits of equipment designed for testing all the types of tackle that have a job to perform in angling. In another part of the basement were

housed his studio lights and backdrops. We moved on to his darkroom which was very professional. It was immaculate, everything neatly stowed: slides, negatives, printing paper, etc. were all labelled and filed. Lefty wasn't only a great angler but also a master photographer; but life wasn't always good for this nice guy, as you will read.

Lefty started life in Frederick, Maryland in 1925. When he was aged six, his father passed away, leaving his Mum, Helen, to

The Master Lefty Kreh with his first ever fly fishing reel

bring up four young children. Lefty was the eldest of two other brothers, Richard and Ted, and a sister Eileen. This was in the days before social security and all the benefits available today. Life was very hard in the early 1930s.

One of Lefty's jobs was to collect food from the welfare. He hated this so much he would seek out all the back alleys on his way home so his friends didn't know where he had been. In those days this youngster spent all his spare-time hunting and fishing, which no doubt put food on the table. He would set trap lines for catfish then sell them at ten cents a pound. Those extra funds went towards Lefty's clothing, school lunches, and no doubt, a few more fish hooks, line and bullets. One certainly has to admire this youngster, who wasn't born with a silver spoon in his mouth. He was a worker and hunter who, after graduating from high school, joined the army. Then, some months before D-day, 6 June, Lefty was posted to England for further training in the art of warfare.

Then he, along with thousands of other Allied troops, went across to France for D-day. From there, on to the Battle of the Bulge at the Ardennes in Belgium, where a major World War II battle took place that lasted for several weeks during December 1944 and the following January. Despite some havoc caused by atrocious weather conditions, with snow drifts up to four feet and the Germans infiltrating the American lines dressed as GIs, the Americans soon broke this last desperate offensive by the Nazis, who failed in their attempt to push the Americans back. Lefty collected five battle stars and a purple heart. Following on from this major battle, Lefty and his platoon fought their way through Europe to Germany's River Elbe at Torgau where his platoon met up with some Russians arriving from the east. Finally, with the war in Europe over, he was returned to the States for some well-earned leave.

Then, a posting to the Pacific for the battle against the Japanese! Thankfully, the Manhattan project created, for better or for worse, the Atom Bomb. This was dropped on the cities of Hiroshima and Nagasaki in August 1945 ending the war against the Japanese – no doubt saving many thousands of Allied lives.

Lefty was now back in civilian life, it was time to look for work. Near his home town of Frederick was the Army's Biological Warfare Laboratory at Fort Dietrick. During the war it was staffed by hundreds of servicemen and women. With the war over, most of them were discharged. Hundreds of jobs became available. Lefty applied and was accepted. He started off working shift patterns, then after some months, he asked for the evening or night shift. As he was a senior supervisor, this was granted. Now he could hunt and fish during the daylight hours. At this period in his life, Lefty was guiding on the Potomac River and one of his clients was six foot two inch Joe Brooks, fly-fisher and writer. As Lefty carried his thirteen foot canoe down the bank to the river he noticed Joe fixing up a fly rod.

"Sir," said Lefty, "I have a light spinning-rod for you to use."

Joe answered, "Do you mind if I fly-fish? Then, if I don't catch, I will switch over to your tackle." Naturally Joe, being Lefty's guest was told to carry on.

As Lefty told me, "Joe was a quietly spoken gentleman who courted respect". He also caught many more fish than I did, which didn't really happen to a guide on his own river! I remember quite clearly, Joe fished a red ant pattern, taking fish after fish by casting to the rings of rising fish.

I was amazed! I said to Joe, "I've got to have some of this fly-fishing!"

The next day, Joe Brooks took Lefty off to Baltimore where he purchased a fly-rod kit which included a Pflueger reel; he still has that reel. It was the start of a long friendship with one of America's greats, in fact it was Joe Brooks, through his writings in the 1950s that got this English angler into fly-fishing for bonefish!

It was about this time that Lefty met his future wife Evelyn. Unlike most guys, this wasn't a planned meeting with a pretty girl. Our Lefty didn't ask for a date or plan the meeting with the young movie theatre usher. It was, as he told me, a meeting arranged by the lady. Occasionally I would leave the fields, rivers, streams and fly-tying bench for a night out with my friends. Sometimes we would go off to the movie theatre for an evening out. During one of these theatre visits I was refused permission to enter the theatre, I had been given the wrong ticket. In those days girls didn't ask for dates, so theatre usher Evelyn had to find another way to get me to notice her so she gave me a child's ticket. It worked! You see Evelyn was a good-looking blond girl. That night I walked her home. In 1947 we were married and we are still happily married to this day.

Having got married, Lefty took on more guiding work, trapped mink, started exhibition-shooting for the Remington Arms company and tied flies for Orvis. One of his clients was the editor of the Frederick News-Post who offered him a job of writing an outdoors column, which he quickly accepted. Very soon the local sportsmen started to rely on his column for their information: Kreh the writer was born.

In those days, the outdoor writer would have his work illustrated by an artist. Many of Lefty's clients were photographers with National Geographic. They often gave him lessons in photography. Now Lefty, being Lefty, and a quick learner, soon picked up many photographic skills. He then needed a camera. He didn't purchase the usual Rolleiflex type with its twelve shots on a roll of film, he decided on a 35mm camera, with its thirty-six shots. It was very unusual in those days for photographers to choose 35mm cameras. This made him very popular with newspaper and magazine editors as they didn't have to get an artist to accompany him on his outdoor trips.

Come the 1950s, Lefty was teaching photography, writing regular columns and shooting photographs for twelve newspapers including the top magazines of the day, Field and Stream and Outdoor Life. He was given the contract to write LL Bean's, Guide to Outdoor Photography. Life was certainly moving at a fast pace for this very likeable guy.

Joe Brooks and Lefty spent some time sorting out the fishing in Chesapeake Bay, the world's largest estuary, containing some huge fish. Lefty designed the Deceiver, a fly pattern that has been used with great success in both fresh and saltwater. Today the Deceiver and Clouser minnow are probably the two best known saltwater fly patterns ever devised. In fact, Lefty's fly, the Deceiver was chosen to be displayed on a United States postage stamp in 1991.

In 1961 Lefty and Evelyn moved home to Florida. No more winters with snow, frost and cold foggy weather. Joe Brooks, director of the Miami Metropolitan Fishing Tournament – known as the MET – with over two hundred and fifty thousand competitors, had tempted Lefty to join his show. Upon Joe's retirement, Lefty became the director. During his stay in Florida he was invited to write for The Miami Herald. As he told me, "During one of the demonstrations there were one or two older guys who wanted to know if this guy from up north, trout country, could cast far enough for the ocean fish. As you know Martin, in those days the hotel key was fixed to a chunk of wood. I tied the key to the end of the fly line, and then cast the lot across the casting pool! On another occasion I cast a fly line without the rod and I was then accepted as one of them!" It was also a time of tremendous change and development in saltwater fly-fishing. Such gems as the Albright Knot, Duncan Loop and the Stu Apte tarpon flies, to name three. At the same time, Miami was the centre where all the fast movers in ocean fly-fishing were getting together: Mark Sosin, Stu Apte, Jimmy Albright, Flip Pallot and others.

Listening to Lefty talk about those days, made me think of a similar situation that happened over on the West coast of America in 1898 where a group of anglers gathered to form the Tuna Club at Avalon on Catalina Island off San Diego under the leadership of Dr. Charles Holder. In 1998 The Tuna Club celebrated its Centennial. This English broadcaster considered it a special honour to be invited as one of the guests.

Back in Florida, Lefty was proving a very popular speaker and demonstrator at clubs, fishing shows and seminars. After ten great years in the sunshine state, Lefty and Evelyn packed their bags and headed back to Maryland. The Baltimore Sun had 'head-hunted' Lefty, (not a word used in those days): they had made an offer he couldn't refuse. He started off writing three columns a week for the paper; he was also in great demand as a speaker at shows and seminars all over the United States.

Apart from fishing, he was writing books and features for several magazines, shooting lots of photographs and organising many casting and fishing clinics. Life was certainly hectic for this most loveable of guys who had come a long way from the days of catching catfish at ten cents a pound. He told me, "One of the good things about being booked for speaking engagements is I get to fish all over the world and not just the United States. I have fished South America, Canada, Australia, Africa, England and many other exotic locations."

During the past fifty years Lefty has given us several books. His latest published work is Presenting the Fly published by The Lyons Press. I feel it's his best book ever – in fact, it was my choice for top fishing book title in 1999 on BBC Radio Lancashire. Another excellent book is Fly-fishing in Saltwater – I have all the editions. The third and fully revised edition should be on the bookshelf of all saltwater fly-fishers. Another great set of books are Lefty's Little Library of Fly-fishing, sadly not available in the United Kingdom. I have eight of the titles; hopefully, I will be able to collect them all during my coming visits to the United States. When not fishing, I spend a lot of time in second-hand book shops. Lefty with Mark Sosin gave us Fishing the Flats and Practical Fishing Knots. Other books by Lefty have covered casting and fly-tying. You can even catch up with Lefty on his web page entitled Lefty's World – www.lefty.net

During my visit, we went off to a local restaurant for lunch. Brandon, Lefty and I all asked for the bill. As our friendly and very attractive waitress handed Lefty the bill, no doubt because he was the best looking guy, my hand shot out and grabbed that account. No way was I going to let the master pay for lunch. The time spent in the company of Bernard 'Lefty' Kreh was a privilege. I will treasure the memory for the rest of my days.

Lefty has given us all so much and is still going out most days helping others. Thank you, Lefty for your time, knowledge and expertise, and for helping to make me a better fly-fisher.

Before leaving Lefty's home he gave me the following Casting Principals to share with you, the reader. Regardless of your fly-casting techniques, all casters are governed by the following four principles:

1. *You must first move the line end before you make a back cast or forward cast. This causes the rod to bend or load. It is also advisable to lift all line from the surface before making a back cast.*

2. *Once the line end is moving, the only way to load the rod is to move your casting hand at an ever-increasing speed and then bring it to a sudden stop. This sudden stop is often called the power stroke. Applying power often spoils a cast – It should be called a 'speed up and stop' stroke. The faster you speed up and stop the rod tip, the faster the line will travel. The size of the loop is solely determined by the distance the rod moves in the final moment of the cast during speed up and stop.*

3. *The line will go in the direction the rod speeds up and stops. If on the back cast, the rod tip stops at any angle the line will go straight at that angle. If the rod tip stops going down and back, a sag is produced in the line which must be removed before you can make a forward cast. With almost all forward casts, the rod should be stopped so that the line travels to or slightly climbing above the surface.*

4. *The longer the distance the rod travels on the back and forward casting strokes, the less effort is required to make the cast. The shorter the rod moves during the casting stroke, the harder you must work to put the same load in the rod. When you need to cast further, throw heavier flies, defeat the wind, or make a number of special casts, the rod must travel farther back and forward. Taking the rod well behind you on the back cast will allow you to make many more fishing casts that will produce more fish.*

Lefty's other aids to better casting are:

5. *If you're right-handed, the right foot should be positioned to the rear and the left foot slightly forward. Left-handers should do the reverse.*

6. *When the rod stops at the end of the back cast and again at the end of the forward cast, the thumb should be positioned behind the rod handle from the target. This accomplishes two things: a. Energy in the cast is better transmitted back and forward. b. Accuracy improves.*

7. *The elbow should never be elevated on the cast. If you walk up to a shelf and place your elbow on it without lifting it. That is the correct elevation of the elbow. Think that, during the entire cast, the elbow is determined by the angle that the rod hand stops. But the elbow should not be elevated.*

For angling, the birth of the internet in the mid1990s was like a snowball rolling down a hill: a few email mailing lists quickly developed into websites and then became fully fledged on-line angling magazines. These early websites had little competition and huge memberships. One of these was www.fishing.co.uk.

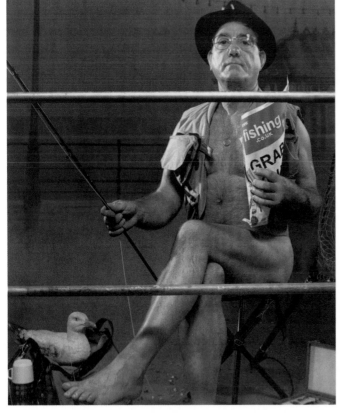

Geoff Maynard writes . . .

It was a great magazine but well ahead of its time. I was the managing editor. It closed after a few years due to a combination of ownership changes and mistrust of the medium from the angling industry. Fortunately, before its demise, we all had a lot of fun with it. One of the yuppy-brained ideas pulled out to promote the website was an attempt to emulate the recent success of the Women's Institute naked members' calendar – a venture which led to the highly successful movie, Calendar Girls.

"We can do that too" said the pony-tailed, red-rimmed specs wearers from the PR department. So followed a public relations exercise that took a full year's advertising budget; it had little to do with angling, nor the prostate cancer charity it claimed to promote, but was a bundle of fun nevertheless.

We ran a competition on the website for members who wanted to participate, then scoured our contributors for volunteers unafraid to strip off. We had no shortage of members . . . hmmm, perhaps I should rephrase that – we had no shortage of readers wanting to participate in the calendar, but there were very few of our big-name contributors wanting to strip off for charity. The notable exception was . . . Martin James!

What a great sport he was! In the photographic studios, his driving cockney wit kept us amused and entertained for the days of hours and hours of boring drudgery entailed in sitting around photographic studios with beautiful, naked, young females with firm, young, healthy, fit, voluptuous…Harrumph! Never mind – I think you get the point!

The end result was, in fact, a very tasteful set of photographs: nothing smutty at all. And after spending all that money on it! I'm ruddy sure I could have got at least one or two . . . Oh well.

T*he following is my contribution to the debate that took place at Oxford Brookes University entitled "Who Is Britain's Greatest Freshwater Angler?" After consideration, I was declared the winner.*

Good afternoon honoured guests, ladies and gentlemen. Fellow speakers let's not forget every generation has its great freshwater angler. It's not possible in the next twelve minutes to tell you all the things I would like to say about the greatest freshwater angler of all time who, in my opinion, was not just the most charismatic angler of the 20th Century but of any century. That man is Richard Stuart Walker, affectionately known as Dick, who was born on Oak Apple day, May 29, 1918 in Hitchin, Hertfordshire.

Walker brought a new dimension to freshwater angling. He created change and added to the Art of Angling. It was his depth of thought that made catching fish not just an exciting challenge but also a successful one. Much of today's angling stems from those roots planted by this man.

It's impossible to understate the achievements in the angling world of Walker and his impact on today's angling scene. When he caught his record 44lb Carp in the early hours of 13th September 1952, it was of immense interest to the angling world, which sat up and took notice. You must remember that most anglers thought that you had to spend a lifetime trying to catch a big Carp, in those days a 10lb fish was considered big, and then only if you were very lucky.

In those far-off days of black and white televisions, Walker's 44lb Carp was featured on BBC TV, being seen by viewers on a Saturday evening and thousands flocked to London Zoo to see the huge fish, the largest in England. Some years later he hit the headlines again, landing a record Rainbow Trout of 18lb 4oz.

Bernard Venable's, angling writer and artist, described Richard as: "The stormy petrel of angling", no doubt justifiable since his pronounced views on a wide variety of freshwater angling subjects aroused either strong partisanship or bitter opposition; though when his opponents met the great man they were captivated.

Walker's great success as a freshwater angler wasn't difficult to understand, as you could not fail to learn from watching the master fish or from reading the many hundreds of thousands of words which have been published. His first paid article on Trout fishing was published in the Fishing Gazette and as he later said: "That was enough money to keep me in food for a couple of weeks, and far better than washing dishes or taxis".

Inspired by this, Walker sent in another article that didn't get accepted. Instead he received a two-page letter, part of which read: "You have written about what you thought would happen rather than what you knew from experience did happen." The great man once told me: "I have never forgotten that piece of advice."

His series on Carp fishing in the Fishing Gazette, under the nom-de-plume of Water Rail, opened the eyes of thousands of anglers. His weekly column, Walker's Pitch, in Angling Times was, I believe, the reason for that paper's great success. Walker's Pitch was the first page that my friends and I turned to on a Thursday morning. He was also a great photographer, and he had attended some meetings of the London Camera Club. He was able to send in top quality photographs, which made his column even more interesting and exciting. Walker became our messiah; the teenagers and twenty-year-olds at the time all became his disciples - we all had a floppy trilby hat, which was Dick's trademark in those days.

He showed us that it was possible to catch all species of fish from rivers, streams, canals, ponds, lakes and reservoirs. He disliked the artificial barrier between game and coarse fisherman, correctly arguing that we were all anglers.

Two of the reasons why Walker was so successful were his analytical mind and wide knowledge of natural history. He was educated at The Friends' School in Saffron Walden, then St. Christopher in Letchworth. He then read Engineering at Caius College, Cambridge. During World War 2 he was a boffin at the Royal Aircraft Establishment at Farnborough, helping to defeat Nazi Germany.

Not only was he a brilliant freshwater angler, he was also acknowledged as the leading authority on the Flemish Giant Rabbit. His book on the subject is still widely acknowledged by today's Rabbit breeders. His top prize- winning Rabbit was called Laura. His first published angling book was Rod Building for Amateurs in 1952. But the book that changed the face of freshwater angling was Still-Water Angling, published in 1953 by MacGibbon & Kee, in which he showed us we could catch big fish by design and not by luck. In the same year, Drop me a line by Walker and Maurice Ingham was published, a book full of knowledge of all species of fish in freshwater.

Through the writings of Walker, no longer did we need to talk about a glass case specimen as if it only happened once in a lifetime. Through his teachings catching big fish could happen several times a day if you followed his five principles:

1. *Locate your quarry:*   2. *Don't frighten the quarry:*
3. *Use the right tackle:*   4. *Choose the right time to fish:*
5. *Use the right bait.*

The man designed and built the rods we needed to catch those big fish. He showed us how to use the fixed spool reel having hooked our big fish. How would we get the big fish onto the bank? Walker had the answer with his landing net design, which consisted of laminated cane arms with a spreader block and a six-foot handle. Another problem solved by Walker was casting long distances when fishing a big stillwater. He gave us the Arlesey bomb, a streamlined lead weight used for distance casting, named after Arlesey Lake where he caught several huge perch over 4lb in the early 1950s.

Today, I use a thermometer, which helps me catch lots of good fish. Walker gave me that knowledge. When I started Carp fishing we used silver paper or a penny on the spool of the reel, which dropped onto a plate when a fish picked up our bait. All that changed when Walker gave us the electronic bite alarm. The first commercial alarm was called the Heron bite indicator, produced by Jack Opie of Faversham in Kent; but it was Walker's idea.

He was extremely skilful at passing his knowledge on to you and me, to his viewers, listeners and readers. He was recognised by millions of non-anglers as a great freshwater angler through his many appearances on television and radio, including Desert Island Discs with Roy Plomley.

In the early 1950s he was commissioned by BBC television to catch a Carp on the opening day of the season at 5.30am. On that glorious June morning, Walker caught a 16lb 8oz Common Carp.

Another high point in angling during the 1950s was the three matches with Tom Sails, the Lincoln Angling Club captain. Tom's choice of venue was the Witham and he was the winner. Walker then chose the Bain, where he won but was still behind Tom on aggregate weight. The third match was on a neutral venue, the Royalty Fishery on the Hampshire Avon, which Walker won. He caught a 10lb 2oz Barbel, his first double. The final weights were Walker: 27lbs 4oz 4drms, Sails: 21lb 11oz 8drms. Many thousands of anglers waited with bated breath for the result after each contest. Tragically, Tom died from an accident in 1956, and it was Walker who wrote a fine obituary to him in Angling Times.

The river Beane in Hertfordshire was a gin-clear chalk stream containing big Roach and Dace; everyone said they were uncatchable as they fed only on snails and silkweed. For several days Walker fed gentles into the swim, until he had the fish feeding with confidence. On his first fishing outing he caught a 2lb Roach and a 1lb Dace. On another occasion he caught more than a dozen 2lb Roach in a session. Angling by design, in practice.

With the opening of Grafham, Rutland and other Trout waters, he was there showing us how to catch those Trout. Working with Hardy Brothers, he designed some superb reservoir rods and also perfected many flies, including the Polystickle and the Mayfly Nymph. The latter was my first choice of fly when seeking Barbel. He encouraged his army of coarse-fishing fans to try Trout fishing; we did in fine style by following the master's example and were very successful.

In the early 1960s he joined the Moncrieff Rod Company, which had a tie up with Hardy Bros. In the 1950s, when we needed a carp rod, Walker gave us the MKIV and B James & Son supplied it.

In 1964, Minister for Sport Denis Howell was given the task of improving British Sport. In 1965, under the chairmanship of the Earl of Antrim, the then Prime Warden of the Fishmongers' Company appointed a deputation to meet the Minister. During a meeting at the House of Commons, Mr. Howell and the Director of the Sports Council, Walter Winterbottom, urged the deputation to formulate a structure for a National Anglers' Council. Walker served on that council in its first year, representing the voice of Mr. and Mrs. Angling, in other words you and me, the ordinary anglers. He had many true sayings like: *"A fish will eat anything unless it's taught not to."* Or: *"Never say never"* and: *"Never say always"*.

Finally, I believe we all owe a debt of gratitude to Richard Stuart Walker, Britain's greatest freshwater angler.

In the audience was Richard's widow, Pat, who collected the award. After thanking Pat, Fred Buller and others for their congratulations, I left for the long drive north. I had achieved my aim.

Richard Walker (radio ham) while at Cambridge
University. Credit Tony Meers

I've said it before, I will say it again. Fish don't feel pain. How many times have you caught a fish that has been badly bitten by a seal, otter, pike cormorant or mink; often that fish will have chunk of its body missing – but still that fish continues to feed. If you were attacked by a lion or tiger or some other animal, ending up with a bit of your body missing would you want to eat a big steak? I don't think so.

How many times have you caught a fish, or a number of fish with one, two or sometimes three hooks in the mouth, often with some line attached to the hook? That fish carries on to feeding.

On several occasions over the years, I have caught a good fish, then, as that fish tries to reach a danger zone, I have slackened off the pressure, the fish often just acts, as if it isn't hooked. It just relaxes on the river bed, as if it was a free swimming fish with no hook and line attached to its mouth.

I well remember fishing the River Teme, hooking a good barbel. As it tried to reach the sanctuary of some willow branches I slackened off the pressure. The fish just stopped in its tracks and settled on the bottom. Within minutes other barbel were back in the swim and feeding. My hooked fish then moved forward and sucked in a bit of mashed bread. Do fish feel pain? I don't believe so otherwise, that hooked fish would not have continued feeding. I have seen and caught lots of brown trout with lacerated and bleeding mouths where they have been feeding on perch. They still continue to eat my flies.

In an article by Rajeev Syal, in The Sunday Telegraph, 9th February 2003, titled 'Anglers are finally off the hook: fish feel no pain'. He states:

> Anglers, rest easy. Fish cannot feel pain. Or so the largest study into piscine neurology has concluded.
>
> An academic study comparing the nervous systems and responses of fish and mammals has found that their brains are not sufficiently developed to allow them to sense pain or fear. The findings represent a significant victory for anglers, whose sport has been under attack from animal rights activists buoyed by their success in securing a partial ban on fox hunting.
>
> The study is the work of James D. Rose, a professor of zoology and physiology at the University of Wyoming, who has examined data on animals' responses to pain. His report, published in the American academic journal Reviews of Fisheries Science, concludes that awareness of pain depends on functions of regions of the cerebral cortex which fish do not possess.
>
> Professor Rose, 60, said that previous studies which had indicated that fish can feel pain had confused 'nociception' – responding to a threatening stimulus – with feeling pain.
>
> "Pain is predicated on awareness. The key issue is the distinction between nociception and pain. A person who is anaesthetised in an operating theatre will still respond physically to an external stimulus, but he or she will not feel pain. Anyone who has seen a chicken with its head cut off will know that, while its body can respond to stimuli, it cannot be feeling pain."
>
> Professor Rose added: "There are people who aren't comfortable with my findings, but even those who don't accept them have yet to raise any scientific challenge."
>
> More than two million Britons are anglers, making it the nation's most popular pastime.

Rodney Coldron, from the National Federation of Anglers, said that he hoped the new findings would vindicate the sport. "I am glad this report has come out and killed off that silly argument. Fish can obviously become distressed, but anyone who actually goes fishing knows that they don't feel pain in the same way as mammals," he said.

As expected, the study has failed to persuade the animal rights group, People for the Ethical Treatment of Animals (PETA). A spokesman said, "We believe that fishing is barbaric. Of course animals can feel pain. They have sensitivity, if only to avoid predators." This statement is from an organisation, who believe we shouldn't have any type of pet. According to PETA We shouldn't drink milk, eat beef, lamb, pork or other types of meat. In fact, we should all live very boring lives. I feel PETA are burying their heads in the sand, they don't want to know the truth. It might stop them receiving donations in cash and cheques from many of the liberal left-wing Hollywood actors and actresses. Remember, when you next purchase a video, a percentage of the royalties might end up going to the very people who want to stop you fishing.

At the Royal Lancashire Show, the author presents the Prince Albert Angling Society with the Kingfisher Award for Conservation and their contribution to Angling. Dennis Meredith, the Chairman received the Award.

*A*ngling was given the Royal seal of approval, at the Royal Lancashire Show, with the presence of the *Countess of Wessex Princess Sophie. I spent some thirty minutes showing Sophie around the Piscatorial Centre, where she showed considerable interest in everything that was being demonstrated, from fly-tying to Spey and Wallis Casting.*

The Prince Albert Angling Society organised a tombola with prizes donated by Thomas and Thomas, rod builders of Massachusetts, Stephen Turner www.Bensen.co.uk of Preston and Pendle Fly-Dressers Guild. During the two-day show Prince Albert AS raised £214.50 for Ribble Valley Crossroad Carers Charity.

Where many shows only feature game-fishing, the Piscatorial Centre featured beach and boat-fishing demonstrations. There were talks on chub, pike and bass-angling. A team of fly-tiers were on hand to instruct the visitors. Among the many other interests for the visitors, was the riverside walk with Dr. Malcolm Greenhalgh, which proved very popular.

Richard Walker signing one of his books for Martin   Lefty Kreh

Richard Walker (seated), Maurice Ingham and Pete Thomas at Redmire. Credit Fred J Taylor Estate

Son Nigel and granddaughter Morgen   The author's much abused best friend

The author, Tom Dorsey and the late Ernest Schwiebert at the Denver Fly Fishing Show

Bernard Percival Venables MBE, angler, artist, naturalist, writer, broadcaster and environmentalist, was born London 14 February 1907 passed away in Salisbury, Wiltshire 22 April 2001. Bernard, who was Mr. Crabtree to millions of us, has gone from this life. No oak coffin for our Crabtree, he was laid out in a creel; there was no church service.

His family and friends gathered in a village hall. Some wore the dandelion flower in their lapels. They wore country clothes. After a few talks by his beloved friends he was buried in the Hampshire countryside. Some dropped mayflies in the creel, one dropped a Crabtree type float. They then all went off to a local pub to quaff some ale.

Throughout my life I have been very fortunate to have fished and met some great men. Two of my angling heroes are Dick Walker, and Bernard Venables, who created Mr. Crabtree. The Crabtree influence came to me through a comic strip in the Daily Mirror. Every time I got hold of the paper I used to read about Garth, Karen, Dawn and the professor; then it was Jane; and finally Mr. Crabtree, the angler who was always catching big fish.

I was enthralled by his writing and drawings on perch-fishing. In my last year at Temple School I decided that I would have to work hard if I was to get a good report; in doing so I won the school Book Prize. The school secretary told me to choose a book to the value of one guinea, and I opted for Mr. Crabtree Goes Fishing by Bernard Venables. It sold two million copies.

The secretary came to me a few days later and said, "The book you have chosen is only five shillings, and you can have one for one guinea."

"I know Miss, but that's the one I want. Could I have some floats with the rest of the money?"

"You can't do that, it's one book only," she replied.

"Then it's got to be Mr. Crabtree." I said.

Mr. Crabtree showed us how to enjoy being by the waterside, and in a wonderful way, he showed us what fishing was all about. When I read about the Royalty Fishery on the River Avon, I thought it was where King George VI fished! I was an avid reader of Bernard Venables and collected all his books. It was Bernard who made Creel such a wonderful magazine but when he left the editor's chair it immediately went downhill and became just an ordinary magazine.

On my fifty-second birthday I had the best present I could wish for when I travelled down to Bernard's home to record a series of programmes for BBC Radio 5 and Radio Lancashire. He was ever so kind, and his wife Eileen made me a wonderful lunch. I took all my copies of his books and Bernard signed every one for me. We chatted about angling and about all the nice things from the past. Since that first visit Bernard, Eileen, my wife Kate and I often got together over a meal and a bottle of wine. The conversation was always sparkling and full of interest, and it was a real treat to be with them.

At one of these get-togethers, the subject turned (as it usually does) to the old days when we both lived in Kent. But on this occasion we went further back in time, back to the days before I was born, when Bernard lived on Romney Marsh. He told us a story about the Romney Marsh sheep fairs when he was just six years old and his mother dressed him up as a bluebell fairy; I can just imagine him! Bernard was first and foremost an artist, and I know no one who can capture the countryside, its wildlife and fish quite the way he did. His paintings, in oils or in watercolours, are to my mind the best. For me, he captured the true spirit of angling.

In 1949 Bernard had a wonderful book 'A Fisherman's Testament' published by A & C Black. There is a chapter simply entitled 'Pike', and in it Bernard writes about his good friend St John Cooper catching a pike of thirty-and-a-quarter pounds from a Berkshire lake. One summer Bernard and I visited that same water to fish for tench, in true Crabtree style, with bamboo rods and centre-pin reels. Bernard enjoyed being at the waterside as much that day as he did all those years ago when he was fishing on Romney Marsh as a boy. Thank you, Bernard, for Mr. Crabtree and for all the other books which have flowed from your pen and for the pictures from your brush.

Rest in Peace, Dear Friend.

Mr. Crabtree

When I first held rod and line,

Mr. Crabtree was my guide,

His teaching and his sense of fun,

The knowledge that I drew upon.

The pages seemed to come alive,

His love that was the countryside.

A hero to so many boys,

He painted wisdom, offered joy.

And now I've realised a dream

And met the man who gave to me

This firm foundation in my life.

To shake his hand filled me with pride;

Bernard has become a friend,

To share the love and to defend

The beauty that is God's alone,

The beauty that is Nature's home.

Lorraine Davies

Fred J Taylor MBE 1919-2008

W*riter, author, angler, keen shot and naturalist Fred J Taylor MBE sadly passed away on 7 May 2008. Our Fred, and for many of us it was our Fred, was born in 1919 in the County of Bedfordshire. As a toddler he was taken fishing; so he couldn't fall into the water a length of rope was attached to young Fred and then to a nearby tree.*

During the Second World War Fred served in North Africa as a member of the famed Desert Rats, part of the Eighth Army. In 1941–42, the Desert Rats defeated Rommel's Afrika Korps in the Battle of El Alamein. Fred served during the siege of Tobruk.

After the war he returned home and back to his trade as a baker and pastry cook, in his spare time he returned to his sporting passions in life: fishing, ferreting and shooting. When Richard Walker's book Still-Water Angling was published Fred didn't agree with everything Walker had written, and sent Richard a letter saying so and outlining his thoughts. From that day until the passing of Walker they remained very firm friends.

I first met Fred J as he was affectionately known to his friends and followers in the late 1950s. It was about this time he started working for Efgeeco, and began a successful career as a writer with published articles in the Midland Angler, Creel, Anglers Annual, Fishing, Angling Times and other magazines. I well remember his article on Fishing for Pike with herrings as the bait.

I believe he was the first man who taught us all that we could catch big pike on dead baits. Fred gave me many valuable lessons on fishing, ferreting and outdoor cooking. It was through his skills of the latter that I was able to teach others how to live comfortably in the outdoors.

His books have certainly been an inspiration to me and without doubt they have helped me put more and bigger fish in my landing net. The classic I believe was Angling in Earnest published in 1958. Other titles are Favourite Swims, Fishing for Tench, One for the Pot, (highly recommended), Game and Fish Cookery, Guide to Ferreting, My Fishing Years Reflections on the Water and more. Fred J was a long-time member of NASA and supporter of SACG and then the SAA, as well as many other angling associations.

Without a shadow of a doubt Fred will be remembered for his writings on fishing and countryside matters, his kindness and generosity as an individual and a very good friend to many. The world is a poorer place for his passing, but a wealthier place for his having been here.

Fred you were a great friend. Rest in Peace.

Ivan Scott Duxbury 1940-2006

Throughout my life I have been very fortunate to have met and fished with some great men and women. An equal was Ivan Scott Duxbury the river keeper on the Edisford Hall Fisheries who sadly passed away on Tuesday, 10 January 2006. Ivan was a countryman with immense knowledge of the aquatic and land-based wildlife. He taught me and many others a lot about the rivers Ribble and Hodder.

Ivan stood alongside some of the great river keepers including those of the famous southern chalk streams such as the Test, Itchen and Kennet. You never heard Ivan say a bad word about anyone. Whenever I wanted him as guest on BBC Radio Five or BBC Radio Lancashire he would oblige with many sound words of advice for the listener. He was a true gentleman.

Ivan was born Brockholes, Lancashire on 12 July 1940, where, from an early age he roamed the countryside, and like so many of us, he started off fishing with a small net and jam jar, progressing to rod and line. Then followed ferreting, shooting and a dozen things country boys did. Ivan was certainly a very knowledgeable countryman, fly-dresser and stick-maker. In his roll of river keeper for the Edisford Hall Estate Fishery, he encouraged many people to take up the sport of fly-fishing, including local children. Many of those youngsters are now adult members of the syndicate. His cremation in Preston and the wake in the Aspinal Arms was packed with family and friends from the world of angling. Everyone had a story to tell about this very popular country man and character who will be sadly missed, not just by those of Lancashire but countrywide, and the United States where Ivan had many admirers.

There have been many days when I have been trying to catch a wily old trout that, every time the fly passed over its head, ignored it. Ivan would turn up, "Any luck lad?" "No Ivan, I've got this trout and it won't take anything." He would then give me a nondescript fly. Often on the first cast the fish would eat it. Yes, Ivan was one of the great river keepers and certainly a great character.

Rest in Peace, dear friend.

Andy Robbins 1964-2009

Game and coarse angler Andy Robbins sadly passed away on Saturday 28 February 2009. He was recently featured in Angler's Mail with a River Ribble pike weighing 34lb.

Just days before his passing he was featured on At The Water's Edge programme on BBC Radio Lancashire discussing his life as an angler. Forty-six year old Andy was unmarried and lived in Blackburn, Lancashire with his parents, His mother once said to Fred Higham that Andy wasn't interested in girls 'he only lived to fish'.

A great all-round angler, he was very popular member of both Ribblesdale, and Ribchester and District AC. Last season he was presented with the shield for the best salmon caught on fly at twenty pounds-plus by Ribblesdale AA member. He was fishing at Calder Foot, and in true sporting fashion he returned the fish to continue its way up river, hopefully to spawn successfully.

Andy will be greatly missed not only by his family and close friends but by all who came in touch with him either through work or fishing.

R.I.P.

Terry Mansbridge 1943-2006

erry has without doubt been a great servant to angling, and he will be greatly missed. I doubt if he can ever be replaced. During his time in the Metropolitan Police, where he was a Detective Chief Superintendent, he still worked tirelessly for angling.

During his last murder inquiry before he retired from the police force, Terry found time to give me an interview in Hyde Park on a cold winter's day, where he discussed his work with the River Lea consultative. Terry has given a huge amount to angling in recent years. It was through his leadership and his hard work that NAFAC (now The Angling Trust) has grown to being the biggest single membership body within angling.

To honour Terry, let everyone join The Angling Trust.

He will be sorely missed by his friends and colleagues in angling. I am sure all anglers will join me in offering our condolences to his family and friends.

Terry, Rest in Peace.

James Holgate 1957-2009

ngling has lost one of its nice guys who was also an excellent angler and a great worker who promoted the sport of angling. On Friday 12 June 2009, fifty-one year old James Holgate, a journalist and editor of Pike and Predators magazine, who was also joint Editor of Coarse Angling Today sadly passed away. Many experienced anglers rated Coarse Angling Today the best published magazine in the shops today.

I first met James along with his friends when I attended Lonsdale AC headquarters for the annual prize presentation. It was the first time I met James and his friends who were probably in their early twenties. I was amazed at their keenness and energy. Not only did they serve on the committee , they also created their own lake, at the time I was using a wheelchair, due to having MS. I spent many happy hours fishing the water.

David Mason Secretary of Lonsdale AC said, "James is a great loss to us, he will be greatly missed at our meetings, having been a member of the club and committee in the region of 30 years-plus."

Jon Neafcy secretary of Region 31 of the Pike Angling Club of Great Britain said, "I considered James a mate, I will miss our correspondence. He was a great ambassador for the sport. We will be implementing a James Holgate memorial trophy, for the member who contributes the most to pike fishing." (as James did).

Rest in Peace my friend.